College Writing Skills

Annotated Instructor's Edition

College Writing Skills

Fifth Edition

Annotated Instructor's Edition

John Langan

Atlantic Community College

McGraw-Hill

Boston   Burr Ridge, IL   Dubuque, IA   Madison, WI   New York   San Francisco   St. Louis
Bangkok   Bogotá   Caracas   Lisbon   London   Madrid
Mexico City   Milan   New Dehli   Seoul   Singapore   Sydney   Taipei   Toronto

McGraw-Hill Higher Education

A Division of The **McGraw-Hill** *Companies*

This book is printed on acid-free paper.

1 2 3 4 5 6 7 8 9 0 DOC/DOC 9 0 9 8 7 6 5 4 3 2 1 0 9

ISBN 0-07-228322-X (student ed.)
ISBN 0-07-228328-9 (annotated instructor's ed.)

Editorial director: *Phillip A. Butcher*
Sponsoring editor: *Sarah Touborg Moyers*
Developmental editor: *Alexis Walker*
Editorial assistant: *Bennett Morrison*
Director of marketing: *Margaret Metz*
Project manager: *Pat Frederickson*
Production supervisor: *Rose Hepburn*
Designer: *Kiera Cunningham*
Cover illustration: *Paul Turnbaugh*
Supplement coordinator: *Carol A. Bielski*
Compositor: *Electronic Publishing Services, Inc., TN*
Typeface: *11/13 Times Roman*
Printer: *R. R. Donnelley & Sons Company*

http://www.mhhe.com

Credits and Acknowledgments

Donna Barron, "American Family Life: The Changing Picture," pp. 274–276, reprinted by permission.

Tom Bodett, "Wait Divisions," pp. 309–311, from *Small Comforts* by Tom Bodett, pp. 53–56. Copyright © 1987 by Tom Bodett. Reprinted by permission of Perseus Books Publishers, a member of Perseus Books, L.L.C.

Glenda Davis, "How to Do Well on a Job Interview," pp. 238–240, reprinted by permission.

Pete Hamill, "The Yellow Ribbon," pp. 202–203, reprinted by permission of International Creative Management. Copyright © Pete Hamill.

Molly Ivins, "Ban the Things, Ban Them All," pp. 329–331, from *Washington Post,* March 16, 1993, p. A17. © 1993, Washington Post Writers Group. Reprinted with permission.

Beth Johnson, "Lou's Place," pp. 183–186, reprinted by permission.

Andrew H. Malcolm, "Dad," pp. 219–221, from Andrew H. Malcolm, "About Men: Dad," *New York Times Magazine,* January 8, 1984, p. 58. Copyright © 1984 by The New York Times Company. Reprinted by permission.

Desmond Morris, "Why Do Most Mothers Cradle Their Babies in Their Left Arms?" pp. 256–257, from *Babywatching* by Desmond Morris, pp. 175–177. Copyright © 1991, 1992 by Desmond Morris. Reprinted by permission of Crown Publishers, Inc.

Marie Winn, "Television Addiction," pp. 293–295, from *The Plug-In Drug,* rev. ed., pp. 23–25. Copyright © 1977, 1985 by Marie Winn Miller. Published by Viking Penguin.

About the Author

John Langan has taught reading and writing at Atlantic Community College near Atlantic City, New Jersey, for over twenty years. The author of a popular series of college textbooks on both subjects, he enjoys the challenge of developing materials that teach skills in an especially clear and lively way. Before teaching, he earned advanced degrees in writing at Rutgers University and in reading at Glassboro State College. He also spent a year writing fiction that, he says, "is now at the back of a drawer waiting to be discovered and acclaimed posthumously." While in school, he supported himself by working as a truck driver, machinist, battery assembler, hospital attendant, and apple packer. He now lives with his wife, Judith Nadell, near Philadelphia. Among his everyday pleasures are running, working on his Macintosh computer, and watching Philadelphia sports teams on TV. He also loves to read: newspapers at breakfast, magazines at lunch, and a chapter or two of a recent book ("preferably an autobiography") at night.

Contents

Part Four: Handbook of Sentence Skills

Part Four: Handbook of Sentence Skills page: 407

To the Instructor

College Writing Skills will help students master the traditional five-paragraph essay and variations of this essay. It is a very practical book with a number of special features to aid instructors and their students.

- *Four principles are presented as keys to effective writing.* These four principles—unity, support, coherence, and sentence skills—are highlighted on the inside front cover and reinforced throughout the book. Part One focuses on the first three principles and to some extent on sentence skills; Part Four serves as a concise handbook of sentence skills. Parts Two and Three show, respectively, how the four principles apply in the different patterns of essay development and in specialized types of writing. The ongoing success of *College Writing Skills* is evidence that the four principles are easily grasped, remembered, and followed by students.

- *Writing is treated as a process.* The first chapter introduces writing as both a skill and a process of discovery. The second chapter, "The Writing Process," explains and illustrates the sequence of steps in writing an effective essay. In particular, this chapter focuses on prewriting and revision as strategies to use with any writing assignment. Detailed suggestions for prewriting and revision then accompany many of the writing assignments in Part Two.

- *Activities and assignments are numerous and varied.* For example, in Part One there are more than ninety activities to help students apply and master the four principles or bases of effective writing. There are over two hundred activities and tests in the entire book. A variety of writing assignments follow each pattern of essay development in Part Two. Some topics are highly structured, for students who are still learning the steps in the writing process; others are open-ended. Instructors thus have the option of selecting those assignments most suited to the individual needs of their students.

- *Clear thinking is stressed throughout.* This emphasis on logic starts with the opening pages of the book. Students are introduced to the two principles that are the bedrock of clear thinking: *making a point* and *providing support to back up that point*. The focus on these principles then continues throughout the book, helping students learn that clear writing is inseparable from clear thinking.

- *The traditional essay is emphasized.* Students are asked to write formal essays with an introduction, three supporting paragraphs, and a conclusion. Anyone who has tried to write a solidly reasoned essay knows how much work is involved. A logical essay requires a great deal of mental discipline and close attention to a set of logical rules. Writing an essay in which there is an overall thesis statement and in which each of three supporting paragraphs begins with a topic sentence is more challenging for many students than writing a free-form or expressive essay. The demands are significant, but the rewards are great.

    At the same time that students learn and practice the rules of the five-paragraph essay, professional essays representing the nine patterns of development show them variations possible within the essay form. These essays provide models if instructors decide that their students will benefit from moving beyond the traditional essay form.

- *Lively teaching models are provided.* The book provides two high-interest student essays and one engaging professional essay with each assignment. Students then read and evaluate these essays in terms of the four bases: unity, support, coherence, and sentence skills. After reading vigorous papers by other students as well as papers by professional authors and experiencing the power that good writing can have, students will be encouraged to aim for a similar honesty, realism, and detail in their own work.

- *The book is versatile.* Since no two people use an English text in exactly the same way, the material has been organized in a highly accessible manner. Each of the four parts of the book deals with a distinct area of writing. Instructors can therefore turn quickly and easily to the skills they want to present.

- *Helpful learning aids accompany the book.* The *Instructor's Edition* (ISBN 0-07-228328-9) consists of the student text complete with answers to all activities and tests, followed by an Instructor's Guide featuring teaching suggestions and a model syllabus. The *Instructor's Manual and Test Bank* (0-07-228326-2) includes the Instructor's Guide along with thirty supplementary activities and tests. Also available are an Online Learning Center at **www.mhhe.com/langan**, which offers a host of instructional aids and additional resources for students; a computerized test bank for both Windows (0-07-237126-9) and Macintosh (0-07-237127-7); a PowerPoint grammar tutorial available on disk (0-07-237128-5) and online; and *AllWrite!,* an interactive grammar tutorial program on CD-ROM. Please contact your McGraw-Hill sales representative or consult McGraw-Hill's web site at **www.mhhe.com/socscience/english** for more information.

Changes In the Fifth Edition

There are major changes and additions in this new edition of *College Writing Skills:*

- The most substantial change in the book is its far greater emphasis on prewriting and revision. A new chapter titled "The Writing Process" uses a model student essay to demonstrate how prewriting and revision are essential parts of the act of writing. And while Part One of the book continues to focus on four bases of effective writing—unity, support, coherence, and sentence skills—students also learn how prewriting and revision will help them achieve the four bases. Finally, detailed strategies for prewriting and revision are now part of many writing assignments that accompany the nine rhetorical patterns of essay development in Part Two.

- A major addition to the text is the professional essays that illustrate each of the nine rhetorical patterns. While the book continues to teach the traditional essay model, the professional essays show students other uses and treatments of the essay form. Students still learn the rigors and rewards of the strict five-paragraph essay, but they also see the rich variations that are possible once the rules, having been learned, can be broken. Questions on unity, support, coherence, and sentence skills follow each of the professional essays, just as they do the model student essays, further reinforcing the four bases of effective writing.

- The book includes a new model research paper that examines a contemporary topic and follows the latest MLA guidelines, including citation of sources found on the Internet.

- A revised and updated chapter—Chapter 21—provides a highly practical guide to the library and the Internet. This chapter illustrates how the author of the model research paper was able to draw on the resources the traditional library and the Internet.

- Another addition to the book is Chapter 45, which presents pointers and brief activities for ESL students.

- Here are some of the other changes in this revision. As part of the book's new design, chapters are now numbered, making the text even easier to use. Chapter 1 helps students see writing, from the start, as both a skill and a process of discovery. Some of the skills that deal with writing effective sentences (parallelism, consistent point of view, the use of specific and concise language, and sentence variety) have been moved from Part Four to a major new section on revising sentences in Part One, Chapter 5. A section on word processing has been added to Chapter 1. And throughout the book, student models and practice materials have been updated and revised.

Acknowledgments

Reviewers who have contributed to this edition through their helpful comments include Pamela Arlov, Macon State College; Sabri Bebawi, Long Beach City College; Jeannie Dobson, Greenville Technical College; Beverly B. Holmes, Okaloosa-Walton Community College; Michael Hricik, Westmoreland County Community College; Debbie Nordstrom, Northern Michigan University; Abraham Oseroff, Miami Dade Community College—Kendall Campus; Rachel Ritter, Miami-Dade Community College—Wolfson Campus; Joe Szabo, Mercer County Community College; and Sandra M. Trammell, Kentucky State University.

I am also grateful for help provided by Janet M. Goldstein, Beth Johnson, Paul Langan, Carole Mohr, and Judith Nadell, as well as for the talented support of past and present McGraw-Hill editors: Susan Gamer, Tim Julet, Sarah Moyers, and Alexis Walker.

John Langan

College Writing Skills

Annotated Instructor's Edition

Part One

Essay Writing

1 An Introduction to Writing

This chapter will explain

- the importance of supporting a point in writing
- the structure of the traditional essay
- the benefits of writing the traditional essay

The chapter will also

- present writing as both a skill and a process of discovery
- suggest keeping a journal
- recommend word processing

The experience I had writing my first college essay has helped shape this book. I received a C– for the essay. Scrawled beside the grade was the comment, "Not badly written, but ill-conceived." I remember going to the instructor after class, asking about his comment as well as the word *Log* that he had added in the margin at various spots. "What are all these logs you put in my paper?" I asked, trying to make a joke of it. He looked at me a little wonderingly. "Logic, Mr. Langan," he answered, "logic." He went on to explain that I had not thought out my paper clearly. There were actually two ideas rather than one in my thesis, one supporting paragraph had nothing to do with either idea, another paragraph lacked a topic sentence, and so on. I've never forgotten his last words: "If you don't think clearly," he said, "you won't write clearly."

I was speechless, and I felt confused and angry. I didn't like being told that I didn't know how to think. I went back to my room and read over my paper several times. Eventually, I decided that my instructor was right. "No more logs," I said to myself. "I'm going to get these logs out of my papers."

My instructor's advice was invaluable. I learned that clear, disciplined thinking is the key to effective writing. *College Writing Skills* develops this idea by breaking down the writing process into a series of logical, easily-followed steps. The four steps, combined with practical advice about prewriting and revision, will help you write strong papers.

Here are the four steps in a nutshell:

1 Discover a clearly stated point or thesis.

2 Provide logical, detailed support for your thesis.

3 Organize and connect your supporting material.

4 Revise and edit so that your sentences are effective and error-free.

Part One of the book explains each of these steps in detail and provides many practice materials to help you master them.

Point and Support

An Important Difference Between Writing and Talking

In everyday conversation, you make all kinds of points or assertions. You say, for example, "My boss is a hard person to work for"; "It's not safe to walk in our neighborhood after dark"; or "Poor study habits keep getting me into trouble." The points that you make concern personal matters as well as, at times, outside issues: "That trade will be a disaster for the team"; "Lots of TV commercials are degrading to women"; "Students are better off working for a year before attending college."

The people you are talking with do not always challenge you to give reasons for your statements. They may know why you feel as you do, or they may already agree with you, or they simply may not want to put you on the spot; and so they do not always ask, "Why?" But the people who read what you write may not know you, agree with you, or feel in any way obliged to you. If you want to communicate effectively with readers, you must provide solid evidence for any point you make. An important difference, then, between writing and talking is this: *In writing, any idea that you advance must be supported with specific reasons or details.*

Think of your readers as reasonable people. They will not take your views on faith, but they are willing to accept what you say as long as you support it. Therefore, remember to support with specific evidence any point that you make.

Point and Support in a Paragraph

In conversation, you might say to a friend who has suggested a movie, "No, thanks. Going to the movies is just too much of a hassle. Parking, people, everything." From shared past experiences, your friend may know what you are talking about, so that you will not have to explain your statement. But in writing, your point would have to be backed up with specific reasons and details.

Below is a paragraph, written by a student named Diane Woods, on why moviegoing is a nuisance. A *paragraph* is a short paper of around 150 to 200 words. It usually consists of an opening point called a *topic sentence* followed by a series of sentences which support that point.

The Hazards of Moviegoing

Although I love movies, I've found that there are drawbacks to moviegoing. One problem is just the inconvenience of it all. To get to the theater, I have to drive for at least fifteen minutes, or more if traffic is bad. It can take forever to find a parking spot, and then I have to walk across a huge parking lot to the theater. There I encounter long lines, sold-out shows, and ever-increasing prices. And I hate sitting with my feet sticking to the floor because of other people's spilled snacks. Another problem is my lack of self-control at the theater. I often stuff myself with unhealthy calorie-laden snacks. My choices might include a bucket of popcorn, a box of Milk Duds, a giant soda, or all three. The worst problem is some of the other moviegoers. Kids run up and down the aisle. Teenagers laugh and shout at the screen. People of all ages drop soda cups and popcorn tubs, cough and burp, and talk to one another. All in all, I would rather stay home and wait to see the latest movie hits on cable TV in the comfort of my own living room.

Notice what the supporting evidence has done here. It has provided you, the reader, with a basis for understanding *why* the writer makes the point that is made. Through this specific evidence, the writer has explained and successfully communicated the idea that moviegoing can be a nuisance.

The evidence that supports the point in a paper often consists of a series of reasons followed by examples and details that support the reasons. That is true of the paragraph above: three reasons are provided, with examples and details that back up those reasons. Supporting evidence in a paper can also consist of anecdotes, personal experiences, facts, studies, statistics, and the opinions of experts.

Activity

The paragraph on moviegoing, like almost any piece of effective writing, has two essential parts: (1) a point is advanced, and (2) that point is then supported. Taking a minute to outline the paragraph will help you understand these basic parts clearly. Write in the following space the point that has been advanced in the paragraph. Then add the words needed to complete the outline of the paragraph.

Point   *There are drawbacks to moviegoing.*

Support   1.   *Inconvenience.*

       a.   Fifteen-minute drive to theater

       b.   *Long time to find parking spot and long walk to theater.*

       c.   Long lines, sold-out shows, and increasing prices.

       d.   *Sticky floor.*

   2.   Lack of self-control

       a.   Often stuff myself with unhealthy snacks.

       b.   Might have popcorn, candy, soda, or all three.

   3.   *Other moviegoers*

       a.   *Running kids*

       b.   *Laughing, shouting teenagers*

       c.   People of all ages make noise.

Point and Support in an Essay

An excellent way to learn how to write clearly and logically is to practice the traditional college *essay*—a paper of about five hundred words that typically consists of an introductory paragraph, two to four supporting paragraphs (the norm in this book will be three), and a concluding paragraph. The central idea, or point, developed in any essay is called a *thesis statement* (rather than, as in a paragraph, a topic sentence). The thesis appears in the introductory paragraph, and the specific support for the thesis appears in the paragraphs that follow. The supporting paragraphs allow for a fuller treatment of the evidence that backs up the central point than would be possible in a single-paragraph paper.

Structure of the Traditional Essay

A Model Essay

The following model will help you understand the form of an essay. Diane Woods, the writer of the paragraph on moviegoing, later decided to develop her subject more fully. Here is the essay that resulted.

The Hazards of Moviegoing

Introductory
paragraph

I am a movie fanatic. My friends count on me to know movie trivia (who was the pigtailed little girl in <u>E.T.: The Extra-Terrestrial</u>? Drew Barrymore) and to remember every big Oscar awarded since I was in grade school (best picture 1994? <u>Forrest Gump</u>). My friends, though, have stopped asking me if I want to go out to the movies. While I love movies as much as ever, the inconvenience of going out, the temptations of the theater, and the behavior of some patrons are reasons for me to wait and rent the video.

First
supporting
paragraph

To begin with, I just don't enjoy the general hassle of the evening. Since small local movie theaters are a thing of the past, I have to drive for fifteen minutes to get to the nearest multiplex. The parking lot is shared with several restaurants and a supermarket, so it's always jammed. I have to drive around at a snail's pace until I spot another driver backing out. Then it's time to stand in an endless line, with the constant threat that tickets for the show I want will sell out. If we do get tickets, the theater will be so crowded that I won't be able to sit with my friends, or we'll have to sit in a front row gaping up at a giant screen. I have to shell out a ridiculous amount of money—up to $8—for a ticket. That entitles me to sit while my shoes seal themselves to a sticky floor coated with spilled soda, bubble gum, and crushed Raisinets.

Second
supporting
paragraph

Second, the theater offers tempting snacks that I really don't need. Like most of us, I have to battle an expanding waistline. At home I do pretty well by simply not buying stuff that is bad for me. I can make do with snacks like celery and carrot sticks because there is no ice cream in the freezer. Going to the theater, however, is like spending my evening in a Seven-Eleven that's been equipped with a movie screen and comfortable seats. As I try to persuade myself to just have a diet Coke, the smell of fresh popcorn dripping with butter soon overcomes me. Chocolate bars the size of small automobiles seem to jump into my hands. I risk pulling out my fillings as I chew enormous mouthfuls of Milk Duds. By the time I leave the theater, I feel disgusted with myself.

Third
supporting
paragraph

Many of the other patrons are even more of a problem than the concession stand. Little kids race up and down the aisles, usually in giggling packs. Teenagers try to impress their friends by talking back to the screen, whistling, and making what they consider to be hilarious noises. Adults act as if they were at home in their own living room. They comment loudly on the ages of the stars and reveal plot twists that are supposed to be a secret until the film's end. And people of all ages create distractions. They crinkle candy wrappers, stick gum on their seats, and drop popcorn tubs or cups of crushed ice and soda on the floor. They also cough and burp, squirm endlessly in their seats, file out for repeated trips to the rest rooms or concession stands, and elbow me out of the armrest on either side of my seat.

Concluding
paragraph

After arriving home from the movies one night, I decided that I was not going to be a moviegoer anymore. I was tired of the problems involved in getting to the theater, resisting unhealthy snacks, and dealing with the patrons. The next day, I arranged to have premium movie channels installed as part of my cable TV service, and I also got a membership in my local video store. I may now see movies a bit later than other people, but I'll be more relaxed watching box office hits in the comfort of my own living room.

Parts of an Essay

"The Hazards of Moviegoing" is a good example of the standard short essay you will write in college English. It is a composition of over five hundred words that consists of a one-paragraph introduction, a three-paragraph body, and a one-paragraph conclusion. The roles of these paragraphs are described and illustrated below.

Introductory Paragraph

The introductory paragraph of an essay should start with several sentences that attract the reader's interest. It should then advance the central idea, or *thesis,* that will be developed in the essay. The thesis often includes a *plan of development*— a "preview" of the major points that will support the thesis. These supporting points should be listed in the order in which they will appear in the essay. In some cases, the plan of development is presented in a sentence separate from the thesis; in other cases, it is omitted.

Activity

1. In "The Hazards of Moviegoing," which sentence or sentences are used to attract the reader's interest?

    a. First sentence

    b. First two sentences

    (c.) First three sentences

2. In which sentence is the thesis of the essay presented?

    a. Third sentence

    (b.) Fourth sentence

3. Does the thesis describe a plan of development?

    (a.) Yes

    b. No

4. Write the words in the thesis that announce the three major supporting points in the essay:

    a. _inconvenience of going out_

    b. _temptations of the theater_

    c. _behavior of some patrons_

Body: Supporting Paragraphs

Most essays have three supporting points, developed at length over three separate paragraphs. (Some essays have two supporting points, others four or more. For the purposes of this book, your goal will be three supporting points unless your instructor indicates otherwise.) Each of the supporting paragraphs should begin with a *topic sentence* that states the point to be detailed in that paragraph. Just as a thesis provides a focus for an entire essay, a topic sentence provides a focus for a supporting paragraph.

Activity

1. What is the topic sentence for the first supporting paragraph of the model essay?

    To begin with, I just don't enjoy the general hassle of the evening.

2. The first topic sentence is then supported by the following details (fill in the missing details):

    a. Have to drive fifteen minutes

    b. _Parking lot is always jammed_

    c. Endless ticket line

    d. _Tickets may sell out, and theater is crowded_

    e. _Tickets cost up to $8 each_

    f. Sticky floor

3. What is the topic sentence for the second supporting paragraph of the essay?

    Second, the theater offers tempting snacks that I really don't need.

4. The second topic sentence is then supported by the following details:

    a. At home only snacks are celery and carrot sticks

    b. Theater is like a Seven-Eleven with seats

        (1) fresh popcorn

        (2) *chocolate bars*

        (3) *Milk Duds*

5. What is the topic sentence for the third supporting paragraph of the essay?
Many of the other patrons are even more of a problem than the concession stand.

6. The third topic sentence is then supported by the following details:

    a. *Little kids race up and down the aisles.*

    b. *Teenagers talk back to the screen, whistle, make funny noises*

    c. Adults talk loudly and reveal plot twists

    d. People of all ages create distractions

Concluding Paragraph

The concluding paragraph often summarizes the essay by briefly restating the thesis and, at times, the main supporting points. In addition, the writer often presents a concluding thought about the subject of the paper.

Activity

1. Which two sentences in the concluding paragraph restate the thesis and supporting points of the essay?

    (a) First and second

    b. Second and third

    c. Third and fourth

2. Which sentence contains the concluding thought of the essay?

    a. Second

    b. Third

    (c) Fourth

Diagram of an Essay

The following diagram shows you at a glance the different parts of a standard college essay, also known as a *one-three-one essay*. This diagram will serve as a helpful guide when you are writing or evaluating essays.

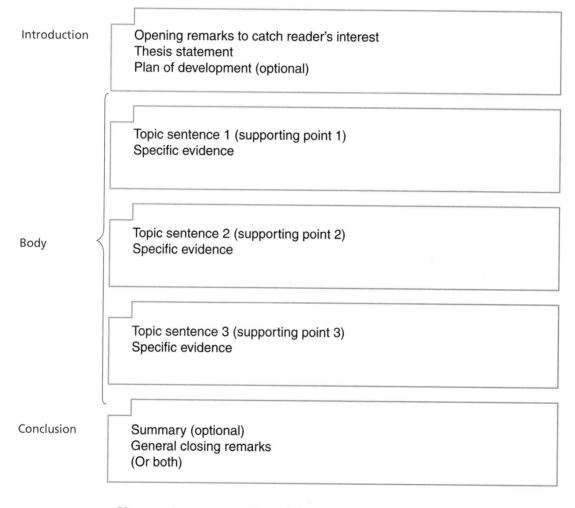

Title of the Essay

Introduction

Opening remarks to catch reader's interest
Thesis statement
Plan of development (optional)

Topic sentence 1 (supporting point 1)
Specific evidence

Body

Topic sentence 2 (supporting point 2)
Specific evidence

Topic sentence 3 (supporting point 3)
Specific evidence

Conclusion

Summary (optional)
General closing remarks
(Or both)

You now have an overview of the traditional form of the essay. In Chapter 2, you will learn just how to go about writing an effective essay. First, though, it will be helpful to consider the following: the benefits of writing traditional essays; seeing writing as both a skill and a process of discovery; and the values of journal writing and word processing.

Benefits of Writing the Traditional Essay

Writing a traditional essay offers at least three benefits. First of all, mastering the traditional essay will help make you a better writer. For other courses, you'll often do papers that will be variations on the essay form—for example, examination essays, reports, and research papers. The basic structure of the traditional essay, with its emphasis on a clear point and well-organized, logical support, will help with almost every kind of writing that you have to do.

Second, the discipline of writing an essay will strengthen your skills as a reader and listener. As a reader, you'll become more critically aware of other writers' ideas and the evidence they provide (or fail to provide) to support those ideas. Essay writing will also help you become a better speaker. You'll be more prepared to develop the three basic parts of an effective speech—an appealing introduction, a solidly developed body, and a well-rounded conclusion—because of your experience writing three-part essays.

Most important, essay writing will make you a stronger thinker. Writing a solidly reasoned traditional essay requires mental discipline and close attention to a set of logical rules. Creating an essay in which there is an overall thesis statement and in which each of three supporting paragraphs begins with a topic sentence is more challenging than writing a free-form or expressive paper. Such an essay obliges you to carefully sort out, think through, and organize your ideas. You'll learn to discover and express just what your ideas are and to develop those ideas in a logical, reasoned way. Traditional essay writing, in short, will train your mind to think clearly, and that ability will prove to be of value in every phase of your life.

Writing as a Skill

A sure way to wreck your chances of learning how to write competently is to believe that writing is a "natural gift" rather than a learned skill. People with such an attitude think that they are the only ones for whom writing is unbearably difficult. They feel that everyone else finds writing easy or at least tolerable. Such people typically say, "I'm not any good at writing" or "English was not one of my good subjects." They imply that they simply do not have a talent for writing, while others do. The result of this attitude is that people try to avoid writing, and when they do write, they don't try their best. Their attitude becomes a self-fulfilling prophecy: their writing fails chiefly because they have brainwashed themselves into thinking that they don't have the "natural talent" needed to write. Unless their attitude changes, they probably will not learn how to write effectively.

A realistic attitude about writing must build on the idea that *writing is a skill*. It is a skill like driving, typing, or cooking; and, like any skill, it can be learned.

If you have the determination to learn, this book will give you the extensive practice needed to develop your writing skills.

Many people find it difficult to do the intense, active thinking that clear writing demands. (Perhaps television has made us all so passive that the active thinking necessary in both writing and reading now seems harder than ever.) It is frightening to sit down before a blank sheet of paper and know that an hour later, nothing on it may be worth keeping. It is frustrating to discover how much of a challenge it is to transfer thoughts and feelings from one's head onto a sheet of paper. It is upsetting to find that an apparently simple writing subject often turns out to be complicated. But writing is not an automatic process: we will not get something for nothing—and we should not expect to. For almost everyone, competent writing comes from plain hard work—from determination, sweat, and head-on battle. The good news is that the skill of writing can be mastered, and if you are ready to work, you will learn what you need to know.

Writing as a Process of Discovery

In addition to believing that writing is a natural gift, many people falsely believe that writing should flow in a simple, straight line from the writer's head onto the written page. But writing is seldom an easy, one-step journey in which a finished paper comes out in a first draft. The truth is that *writing is a process of discovery* that involves a series of steps, and those steps are very often a zigzag journey. Look at the following illustrations of the writing process:

Seldom the Case

Starting point ————————————————⟶ Finished paper

Usually the Case

Starting point —⟋\⟍⟋\⟍⟋\⟍⟋\⟍— Finished paper

Very often, writers do not discover just what they want to write about until they explore their thoughts in writing. For example, Diane Woods, the author of the paragraph and essay on moviegoing, had been assigned to write about some annoyance in everyday life. She did not know what annoyance she would choose; instead, she just began writing about annoyances in general, in order to discover a topic. One of those annoyances was traffic, which seemed promising, so she began putting down ideas and details that came to her about traffic. One detail was the traffic she had to deal with in going to the movies. That made her think of the traffic in the parking lot at the theater complex. At that point, she realized that moviegoing itself was an annoyance. She switched direction in midstream and began writing down ideas and details about moviegoing.

As Diane wrote, she realized how much other moviegoers annoyed her, and she began thinking that other movie patrons might be her main idea in a paper. But when she was writing about patrons who loudly drop popcorn tubs onto the floor, she realized how much all the snacks at the concession stand tempted her. She changed direction again, thinking now that maybe she could talk about patrons and tempting snacks. She kept writing, just putting down more and more details about her movie experiences, still not having figured out exactly how she would fit both patrons and snacks into the paper. She was not worried because her paper had not quite jelled; she knew that if she kept writing, it would eventually come together.

The point is that writing is often a process of continuing discovery; as you write, you may suddenly switch direction or double back. You may be working on a topic sentence and realize suddenly that it could be your concluding thought. Or you may be developing a supporting idea and then decide that it should be the main point of your paper. Chapter 2 will treat the writing process more directly. What is important to remember here is that writers frequently do not know their exact destination as they begin to write. Very often they discover the direction and shape of a paper during the process of writing.

Writing a Journal

Because writing is a skill, it makes sense that the more you practice writing, the better you will write. One excellent way to get practice in writing, even before you begin composing essays, is to keep a daily or almost daily journal. Writing a journal will help you develop the habit of thinking on paper and will show you how ideas can be discovered in the process of writing. A journal can make writing a familiar part of your life and can serve as a continuing source of ideas for papers.

At some point during the day—perhaps during a study period after your last class of the day, or right before dinner, or right before going to bed—spend fifteen minutes or so writing in your journal. Keep in mind that you do not have to plan what to write about, or be in the mood to write, or worry about making mistakes as you write; just write down whatever words come out. You should write at least one page in each session.

You may want to use a notebook that you can easily carry with you for on-the-spot writing. Or you may decide to write on loose-leaf paper that can be transferred later to a journal folder on your desk. No matter how you proceed, be sure to date all entries.

Your instructor may ask you to make journal entries a specific number of times a week, for a specific number of weeks. He or she may have you turn in your journal every so often for review and feedback. If you are keeping the journal on your own, try to make entries three to five times a week every week of the semester.

Using a Computer

If you don't yet write on a computer, it's time to start. In today's world, word processing is an essential mechanical skill, just as effective writing is a vital communication skill.

The computer can be a real aid in the writing process. You can quickly add or delete anything, from a word to an entire section. You can "cut" material and "paste" it elsewhere in seconds. A word-processing program makes it easy to set margins, space lines, and number pages. It can also help you check your spelling, your grammar, and to some extent your style. And at any point during your work, you can print out one or more copies of your text.

Word processing is not hard to learn. Just as you don't need to know how a car works to drive one, you don't need to understand how a computer functions to use it. With a few simple keystrokes under your belt, you can begin. You do not even need to own your own computer. Nearly every college has at least one computer center, complete with rows of computers and staff members to provide assistance. Free classes in word processing may be available as well.

Some Tips on Using a Computer

- If you are using your school's computer center, allow enough time. You may have to wait for a computer or printer to be free. In addition, you may need several sessions at the computer and printer to complete your paper.

- Every word-processing program allows you to "save" your writing by hitting one or more keys. Save your work frequently as you work on a draft. Work that is saved is preserved by the computer. Work that is not saved is lost when the file you are working on is closed, when the computer is turned off—or if there's a power or system failure.

- Keep your work in two places—the hard drive or disk you are working on and a backup disk. At the end of each session with the computer, copy your work onto the backup disk. Then if the hard drive or working disk becomes damaged, you'll have the backup copy.

- Print out your work at least at the end of every session. Then not only will you have your most recent draft to work on away from the computer; you'll also have a copy in case something should happen to your disks.

- Work in single spacing so that you can see as much of your writing on the screen at one time as possible. Just before you print out your work, change to double spacing.

- Before making major changes in a paper, create a copy of your file. For example, if your file is titled "Worst Job," create a file called "Worst Job 2." Then make all your changes in that new file. If the changes don't work out, you can always go back to the original file.

Using a Computer at Each Stage of the Writing Process

Following are some ways to make word processing a part of your writing. Note that this section may be more meaningful *after* you have worked through Chapter 2 of the book.

Prewriting

If you're a fast typist, many kinds of prewriting will go well on the computer. With freewriting in particular, you can get ideas onto the screen almost as quickly as they occur to you. A passing thought that could be productive is not likely to get lost. You may even find it helpful, when freewriting, to dim the screen of your monitor so that you can't see what you're typing. If you temporarily can't see the screen, you won't have to worry about grammar or spelling or typing errors (all of which do not matter in prewriting); instead, you can concentrate on getting down as many ideas and details as possible about your subject.

After any initial freewriting, questioning, and list-making on a computer, it's often very helpful to print out a hard copy of what you've done. With a clean printout in front of you, you'll be able to see everything at once and revise and expand your work with handwritten comments in the margins of the paper.

If you have prepared a list of items, you may be able to turn that list into an outline right on the screen. Delete the ideas you feel should not be in your paper (saving them at the end of the file in case you change your mind), and add any new ideas that occur to you. Then use the cut and paste functions to shuffle the supporting ideas around until you find the best order for your paper.

Word processing also makes it easy for you to experiment with the wording of the point of your paper. You can try a number of versions in a short time. After you have decided on the version that works best, you can easily delete the other versions—or simply move them to a temporary "leftover" section at the end of the paper.

Writing Your First Draft

Like many writers, you may want to write out your first draft by hand and then type it into the computer for revision. Even as you type your handwritten draft, you may find yourself making some changes and improvements. And once you have a draft on the screen, or printed out, you will find it much easier to revise than a handwritten one.

If you feel comfortable composing directly on the screen, you can benefit from the computer's special features. For example, if you have written an anecdote in your freewriting that you plan to use in your paper, simply copy the story from your freewriting file and insert it where it fits in your paper. You can refine it then or later. Or if you discover while typing that a sentence is out of place, cut it out from where it is and paste it wherever you wish. And if while writing you realize that an earlier sentence can be expanded, just move your cursor back to that point and type in the added material.

Revising

It is during revision that the virtues of word processing really shine. All substituting, adding, deleting, and rearranging can be done easily within an existing file. All changes instantly take their proper places within the paper, not scribbled above the line or squeezed into the margin. You can concentrate on each change you want to make, because you never have to type from scratch or work on a messy draft. You can carefully go through your paper to check that all your supporting evidence is relevant and to add new support as needed here and there. Anything you decide to eliminate can be deleted in a keystroke. Anything you add can be inserted precisely where you choose. If you change your mind, all you have to do is delete or cut and paste. Then you can sweep through the paper, focusing on other changes, such as improving word choice, increasing sentence variety, eliminating wordiness, and so on.

If you are like many students, you will find it convenient to print out a hard copy of your file at various points throughout the revision. You can then revise in longhand—adding, crossing out, and indicating changes—and later quickly make those changes in the document.

Editing and Proofreading

Editing and proofreading also benefit richly from word processing. Instead of crossing or whiting out mistakes, or rewriting an entire paper to correct numerous errors, you can make all necessary changes within the most recent draft. If you find editing or proofreading on the screen hard on your eyes, print out a copy. Mark any corrections on that copy, and then transfer them to the final draft.

If the word-processing package you're using includes spelling and grammar checks, by all means use them. The spell-check function tells you when a word is not in the computer's dictionary. Keep in mind, however, that the spell-check cannot tell you how to spell a name correctly or when you have mistakenly used, for example, *their* instead of *there*. To a spell-check, *Thank ewe four the complement* is as correct as *Thank you for the compliment*. Also, use the grammar check with caution. Any errors it doesn't uncover are still your responsibility.

A word-processed paper, with its clean look and handsome formatting, looks so good that you may feel it is in better shape than it really is. Do not be fooled by your paper's appearance. Take sufficient time to carefully review your grammar, punctuation, and spelling.

Even after you hand in your paper, save the computer file. Your teacher may ask you to do some revising, and then the file will save you from having to type the paper from scratch.

Review Activities

Activity 1

Answering the following questions will help you evaluate your attitude about writing.

Answers will vary.

1. How much practice were you given writing compositions in high school?

   _____ Much   _____ Some   _____ Little

2. How much feedback (positive or negative comments) from teachers were you given on your compositions?

   _____ Much   _____ Some   _____ Little

3. How did your teachers seem to regard your writing?

   _____ Good   _____ Fair   _____ Poor

4. Do you feel that some people simply have a gift for writing and others do not?

   _____ Yes   _____ Sometimes   _____ No

5. When do you start writing a paper?

   _____ Several days before it is due

   _____ About a day before it is due

   _____ At the last possible minute

Many people who answer *Little* to questions 1 and 2 often answer *Poor, Yes,* and *At the last possible minute* to questions 3, 4, and 5. On the other hand, people who answer *Much* or *Some* to questions 1 and 2 also tend to have more favorable responses to the other questions. The point is that people with little practice in the skill of writing often have understandably negative feelings about their writing ability. They need not have such feelings, however, because writing is a skill that they can learn with practice.

6. Did you learn to write traditional essays (introductory paragraph, supporting paragraphs, concluding paragraph) in high school?

    _____ Yes   _____ No

7. If so, did your teacher explain to you the benefits of writing such essays?

    _____ Yes, very clearly

    _____ Maybe, but not that I remember

    _____ No

If you answered *Maybe* or *No* to question 7, you may not be looking forward to taking the course in which you are using this book. It will be worth your while to read and consider again (on page 12) the enormous benefits that can come from practice in writing traditional essays.

8. In your own words, explain what it means to say that writing is often a zigzag journey rather than a straight-line journey.

    _____

    _____

    _____

    _____

    _____

Activity 2

Following is an excerpt from one student's journal. As you read, look for a general point and supporting material that could be the basis for an interesting paper.

September 6

   My first sociology class was tonight. The parking lot was jammed when I got there. I thought I was going to be late for class. A guard had us park on a field next to the regular lot. When I got to the room, it had the usual painted-cinder-block construction. Every school I have ever been in since first grade seems to be made of cinder block. The students all sat there without saying anything, waiting for the instructor to arrive. I think they were all a bit nervous like me. I hoped there wasn't going to be a ton of work in the course. I think I was also afraid of looking foolish somehow. This goes back to grade school, when I wasn't a very good student and teachers sometimes embarrassed me in class. I didn't like grade school, and I hated high school. Now here I am six years later—in college, of all places. Who would have thought I would end up here? The instructor appeared—a woman who I think was a bit nervous herself. I think I like her. Her name is Barbara Hanlin. She says we should call her Barbara. We got right into it, but it was interesting stuff. I like the fact that she asks questions but then she lets you volunteer. I always hated it when teachers would call on you whether you wanted to answer or not. I also like the fact that she answers the questions and doesn't just leave you hanging. She takes the time to write important ideas on the board. I also like the way she laughs. This class may be OK.

1. If the writer of the journal entry above was looking for ideas for an essay, he could probably find several in this single entry. For example, he might write a story about the roundabout way he apparently wound up in college. See if you can find in the entry an idea that might be the basis for an interesting essay, and write your point in the space below.

    Answers will vary. _____

2. Take fifteen minutes now to write a journal entry on this day in your life. On a separate sheet of paper, just start writing about anything that you have seen, said, heard, thought, or felt today, and let your thoughts take you where they may.

Using This Text

Here is a suggested sequence for using this book if you are working on your own.

1 After completing this introduction, read Chapters 4 through 6 in Part One and work through as many of the activities as you need to master the ideas in these chapters. By the end of Part One, you will have covered all the basic theory needed to write effective papers.

2 Work through some of the chapters in Part Two, which describes a number of traditional patterns for organizing and developing essays. You may want to include "Examples," "Process," "Comparison and Contrast," and "Argumentation." Each chapter opens with a brief introduction to a specific pattern, followed by two student essays and one professional essay written in that pattern. Included are a series of questions so that you can evaluate the essays in terms of the basic principles of writing explained in Part One. Finally, a number of writing topics are presented, along with hints about prewriting and revising to help you plan and write an effective paper.

3 Turn to Part Three as needed for help with types of writing you will do in college: exam essays, summaries, reports, the résumé and job application letter, and the research paper. You will see that these kinds of writing are variations of the essay form you have already learned.

4 In addition, refer to Part Four as needed for review and practice in the skills needed to write effective, error-free sentences.

For your convenience, the book includes the following:

- On the inside front cover, there is a checklist of the four basic steps in effective writing.
- On the inside back cover, there is a list of commonly used correction symbols.

Get into the habit of referring to these guides on a regular basis; they'll help you produce clearly thought-out, well-written essays.

College Writing Skills will help you learn, practice, and apply the thinking and writing skills you need to communicate effectively. But the starting point must be your own determination to do the work needed to become a strong writer. The ability to express yourself clearly and logically can open doors of opportunity for you, both in school and in your career. If you decide—and only you can decide—that you want such language power, this book will help you reach that goal.

2 THE WRITING PROCESS

> **This chapter will explain and illustrate:**
>
> - the sequence of steps in writing an effective essay
> - prewriting
> - revision
> - editing

Chapter 1 introduced you to the essay form and to some basics of writing. This chapter will explain and illustrate the sequence of steps in writing an effective essay. In particular, the chapter will focus on prewriting and revising—strategies that can help with every paper that you write.

For many people, writing is a process that involves the following steps:

1 Discovering a thesis—often through prewriting.
2 Developing solid support for the thesis—often through more prewriting.
3 Organizing the thesis and supporting material and writing it out in a first draft.
4 Revising and then editing carefully to ensure an effective, error-free paper.

Learning this sequence will help give you confidence when the time comes to write. You'll know that you can use prewriting as a way to think on paper and to gradually discover just what ideas you want to develop. You'll understand that there are four clear-cut goals—unity, support, organization, and error-free sentences—to aim for in your writing. You'll realize that you can use revision to rework a paper until it is a strong and effective piece of writing. And you'll be able to edit a paper so that your sentences are clear and error-free.

Prewriting

If you are like many people, you may have trouble getting started with writing. A mental block may develop when you sit down before a blank sheet of paper. You may not be able to think of an interesting topic or thesis. Or you may have trouble coming up with relevant details to support a possible thesis. And even after starting a paper, you may hit snags—moments when you wonder "What else can I say?" or "Where do I go next?"

The following pages describe five techniques that will help you think about and develop a topic and get words on paper: (1) freewriting, (2) questioning, (3) making a list, (4) diagramming, and (5) preparing a scratch outline. These prewriting techniques help you think about and create material, and they are a central part of the writing process.

Technique 1: Freewriting

Freewriting means jotting down in rough sentences or phrases everything that comes to mind about a possible topic. See if you can write nonstop for ten minutes or more. Do not worry about spelling or punctuating correctly, about erasing mistakes, about organizing material, or about finding exact words. Instead, explore an idea by putting down whatever pops into your head. If you get stuck for words, repeat yourself until more words come. There is no need to feel inhibited, since mistakes *do not count* and you do not have to hand in your paper.

Freewriting will limber up your writing muscles and make you familiar with the act of writing. It is a way to break through mental blocks about writing. Since you do not have to worry about mistakes, you can focus on discovering what you want to say about a subject. Your initial ideas and impressions will often become clearer after you have gotten them down on paper, and they may lead to other impressions and ideas. Through continued practice in freewriting, you will develop the habit of thinking as you write. And you will learn a technique that is a helpful way to get started on almost any paper.

Freewriting: A Student Model

Diane Woods's essay "The Hazards of Moviegoing" on pages 7–8 was developed in response to an assignment to write about some annoyance in everyday life. Diane began by doing some general freewriting and thinking about things that annoy her. Here is her freewriting:

> There are lots of things I get annoyed by. One of them that comes to mind is politishans, in fact I am so annoyed by them that I don't want to say anything about them the last thing I want is to write about them. Another thing that bothers me are people who keep complaining about everything. If you're having trouble, do something about it just don't keep complaining and just talking. I am really annoyed by traffic. There are too many cars in

our block and its not surprising. Everyone has a car, the parents have cars and the parents are just too induljent and the kids have cars, and theyre all coming and going all the time and often driving too fast. Speeding up and down the street. We need a speed limit sign but here I am back with politiks again. I am really bothered when I have to drive to the movies all the congestion along the way plus there are just so many cars there at the mall. No space even though the parking lot is huge it just fills up with cars. Movies are a bother anyway because the people can be annoying who are sitting there in the theater with you, talking and dropping popcorn cups and acting like they're at home when they're not.

At this point, Diane read over her notes and, as she later commented, "I realized that I had several potential topics. I said to myself, 'What point can I make that I can cover in an essay? What do I have the most information about?' I decided that maybe I could narrow my topic down to the annoyances involved in going to the movies. I figured I would have more details for that topic." Diane then did more focused freewriting to accumulate details for a paper on problems with moviegoing:

I really find it annoying to go see movies anymore. Even though I love films. Traffic to Cinema Six is awful. I hate looking for a parking place, the lot isn't big enough for the theaters and other stores. You just keep driving to find a parking space and hoping someone will pull out and no one else will pull in ahead of you. Then you don't want there to be a long line and to wind up in one of the first rows with this huge screen right in front of you. Then I'm in the theater with the smell of popcorn all around. Sitting there smelling it trying to ignore it and just wanting to pour a whole bucket of popcorn with melted butter down my throat. I can't stop thinking about the choclate bars either. I love the stuff but I don't need it. The people who are there sometimes drive me nuts. Talking and laughing, kids running around, packs of teens hollaring, who can listen to the movie? And I might run into my old boyfriend—the last thing I need. Also sitting thru all the previews and commercals. If I arrive late enough to miss that junk the movie may be selled out.

Comment

Notice that there are errors in spelling, grammar, and punctuation in Diane's freewriting. Diane is not worried about such matters, nor should she be. At this stage, she just wants to do some thinking on paper and get some material down on the page. She knows that this is a good first step, a good way of getting started, and that she will then be able to go on and shape the material.

You should take the same approach when freewriting: explore your topic without worrying at all about being "correct." Figuring out what you want to say and getting raw material down on the page should have all of your attention at this early stage of the writing process.

Activity

To get a sense of the freewriting process, take a sheet of paper and freewrite about some of the everyday annoyances in your life. See how much material you can accumulate in ten minutes. And remember not to worry about "mistakes"; you're just thinking on paper.

Answers will vary.

Technique 2: Questioning

In *questioning*, you generate ideas and details by asking as many questions as you can think of about your subject. Such questions include *Why? When? Where? Who?* and *How?*

Here are some questions that Diane Woods might have asked while developing her paper.

Questioning: A Student Model

Questions	Answers
<u>Why</u> don't I like to go to the theater?	Just too many problems involved.
<u>When</u> is going to the movies a problem?	Could be any time—when a movie is popular, the theater is too crowded; when traffic is bad, the trip is a drag.
<u>Where</u> are problems with moviegoing?	On the highway, in the parking lot, at the concession stand, in the theater itself.
<u>Who</u> creates the problems?	I do by wanting to eat too much. The patrons do by creating disturbances. The theater owners do by not having enough parking space and showing too many commercials.
<u>How</u> can I deal with the problem?	I can stay home and watch movies on video or cable TV.

Comment

Asking questions can be an effective way of getting yourself to think about a topic from a number of different angles. The questions can really help you generate details about a topic.

Activity

To get a sense of the questioning process, use a sheet of paper to ask yourself a series of questions about a good or bad experience that you have had recently. See how many details you can accumulate in ten minutes. And remember again not to be concerned about "mistakes," because you are just thinking on paper.
Answers will vary.

Technique 3: Making a List

In *making a list*, also known as *brainstorming*, you collect a list of ideas and details that relate to your subject. Pile these items up, one after another, without trying to sort out major details from minor ones or trying to put the details in any special order. Your goal is just to make a list of everything about your subject that occurs to you.

After Diane did her freewriting about moviegoing, she made up the following list of details.

Making a List: A Student Model

Traffic is bad between my house and theater

Noisy patrons

Don't want to run into Jeremy

Hard to be on a diet

Kids running in aisles

I'm crowded into seats between strangers who push me off armrests

Not enough parking

Parking lot needs to be expanded

Continued

Too many previews

Can't pause or fast-forward as you can with a VCR

Long lines

High ticket prices

Too many temptatons at snack stand

Commercials for food on the screen

Can prepare healthy snacks for myself at home

Tubs of popcorn with butter

Huge choclate bars

Candy has always been my downfall

Movie may be sold out

People who've seen movie before talk along with actors and give away plot twists

People coughing and sneezing

Icky stuff on floor

Teenagers yelling and showing off

Comment

One detail led to another as Diane expanded her list. Slowly but surely, more details emerged, some of which she could use in developing her paper. By the time she was done with her list, she was ready to plan an outline of her paragraph and then to write her first draft.

Activity

To get a sense of list-making, use a sheet of paper to list a series of realistic goals, major or minor, that you would like to accomplish between today and one year from today. Your goals can be personal, academic, and career-related.

Technique 4: Diagramming

Diagramming, also known as *clustering* or *mapping*, is another strategy that can be used to generate material for a paper. This method is helpful for people who like to do their thinking in a visual way. In diagramming, you use lines, boxes, arrows, and circles to show relationships among the ideas and details that occur to you.

Begin by stating your subject in a few words in the center of a blank sheet of paper. Then, as ideas and details come to you, put them in boxes or circles around the subject and draw lines to connect them to each other and to the subject. Put minor ideas or details in smaller boxes or circles, and use connecting lines to show how they relate as well.

Keep in mind that there is no right or wrong way of diagramming or clustering. It is a way to think on paper about how various ideas and details relate to one another. Below is an example of what Diane might have done to develop her ideas.

Diagramming: A Student Model

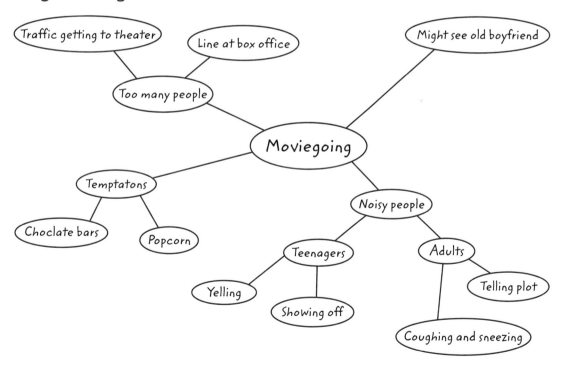

Comment

In addition to helping generate material, diagramming can provide an early sense of how ideas and details relate to one another. For example, the cluster above suggests that different kinds of noisy people could be the focus of one paragraph and that different kinds of temptations could be the focus of another paragraph.

Activity

Use diagramming or clustering to organize the list of year-ahead goals that you created for the previous activity (page 28).

Answers will vary.

Technique 5: Preparing a Scratch Outline

A *scratch outline* is an excellent sequel to the first four prewriting techniques. A scratch outline often follows freewriting, questioning, list-making, or diagramming; or it may gradually emerge in the midst of these strategies. In fact, trying to make a scratch outline is a good way to see if you need to do more prewriting. If you cannot come up with a solid outline, then you know you need to do more prewriting to clarify your main point or its several kinds of support.

In a scratch outline, you think carefully about the point you are making, the supporting items for that point, and the order in which you will arrange those items. The scratch outline is a plan or blueprint to help you achieve a unified, supported, well-organized composition.

When you are planning a traditional essay consisting of an introduction, three supporting paragraphs, and a conclusion, a scratch outline is especially important. It may be only a few words, but it will be the framework on which your whole essay will be built.

Scratch Outline: A Student Model

As Diane was working on her list of details, she suddenly realized what the plan of her essay could be. She could organize many of her details into one of three supporting groups: (1) annoyances in going out; (2) too many tempting snacks; and (3) other people. She then went back to the list, crossed out items that she now saw did not fit, and numbered the items according to the group where they fit. Here is what Diane did with her list:

1 Traffic is bad between my house and theater

3 Noisy patrons

~~Don't want to run into Jeremy~~

2 Hard to be on a diet

3 Kids running in aisles

3 I'm crowded into seats between strangers who push me off armrests

1 Not enough parking

1 Parking lot needs to be expanded

1 Too many previews

~~Can't pause or fast-forward as you can with a VCR~~

1 Long lines

1 High ticket prices

2 Too many temptatons at snack stand

~~Commercials for food on the screen~~

2 Can prepare healthy snacks for myself at home

2 Tubs of popcorn with butter

2 Huge choclate bars

~~Candy has always been my downfall~~

1 Movie may be sold out

3 People who've seen movie before talk along with actors and give away plot twists

3 People coughing and sneezing

1 Icky stuff on floor

3 Teenagers yelling and showing off

Under the list, Diane was now able to prepare her scratch outline:

Going to the movies offers some real problems.

1. Inconvenience of going out

2. Tempting snacks

3. Other moviegoers

Comment

After all her prewriting, Diane was pleased. She knew that she had a promising paper—one with a clear point and solid support. She saw that she could organize the material into a traditional essay consisting of an introduction, several supporting paragraphs, and a conclusion. She was now ready to write the first draft of her paper, using her outline as a guide. Chances are that if you do enough prewriting and thinking on paper, you will eventually discover the point and support of your essay.

Activity

Create a scratch outline that could serve as a guide if you were to write an essay on your year-ahead goals.
Answers will vary.

Writing a First Draft

When you write a first draft, be prepared to put in additional thoughts and details that did not emerge during prewriting. And don't worry if you hit a snag. Just leave a blank space or add a comment such as "Do later" and press on to finish the paper. Also, don't worry yet about grammar, punctuation, or spelling. You don't want to take time correcting words or sentences that you may decide to remove later. Instead, make it your goal to state your thesis clearly and develop the content of your paper with plenty of specific details.

Writing a First Draft: A Student Model

Here is Diane's first draft:

> Even though I love movies, my friends have stopped asking me to go. There are just too many problems involved in going to the movies.
>
> There are no small theaters anymore, I have to drive fifteen minutes to a big multaplex. Because of a supermarket and restarants, the parking lot is filled. I have to keep driving around to find a space. Then I have to stand in a long line. Hoping that they do not run out of tickets. Finally, I have to pay too much money for a ticket. Putting out that much money, I should not have to deal with a floor that ~~is sticky~~ seems coated with rubber cement. By the end of a movie, my shoes are often sealed to a mix of spilled soda, bubble gum, and other stuff.
>
> The theater offers temptatons in the form of snacks I really don't need. Like most of us I have to worry about weight gain. At home I do pretty well by simply watching what I keep in the house and not buying stuff that is bad for me. I can make do with healthy snacks because there is nothing in the house. Going to the theater is like spending my evening in a ~~market~~ Seven-Eleven that's been equiped with a movie screen and there are seats which are comfortable. I try to convince myself to just have a diet soda. The smell of popcorn soon overcomes me. My friends are as bad as I am. Choclate bars seem to jump into your hands, I am eating enormous mouthfuls of milk duds. By the time I leave the theater I feel sick and tired of myself.
>
> Some of the other moviegoers are the worst problem. There are teenagers who try to impress their friends in one way or another. Little kids race up and down the aisles, gigling and laughing. Adults act as if they're watching the movie at home. They talk loudly about the ages of the stars and give away the plot. Other people are droping popcorn tubs or cups of ~~soda~~ crushed ice and soda on the floor. Also coughing a lot and doing other stuff—bs!
>
> I decided one night that I was not going to be a moviegoer anymore. I joined a local video store, and I'll watch movies comfortable in my own living room.

Comment

After Diane finished the first draft, she was able to put it aside until the next day. You will benefit as well if you can allow some time between finishing a draft and starting to revise. See if you can fill in the missing words in the following explanation of Diane's first draft.

Activity

1. Diane has a very brief introduction—no more than an opening sentence and a second sentence that states the ___thesis___. She knows she can develop the introduction more fully in a later draft.

2. Of Diane's three supporting paragraphs, only the ___first___ paragraph lacks a topic sentence. She realizes that this is something to work on in the next draft.

   (answers may vary)

3. There are some misspellings—for example, ___equiped___. Diane doesn't worry about spelling at this point. She just wants to get down as much of the substance of her paper as possible.

4. There are various punctuation errors, especially the several run-ons in the ___third___ paragraph. Again, Diane is focusing on content; she knows she can attend to punctuation and grammar later.

5. At several points in the essay, Diane revises on the spot to make images more ___specific___: she changes "is sticky" to "seems coated with rubber cement," "market" to "Seven-Eleven," and "cups of soda" to "cups of crushed ice and soda."

6. Near the end of her essay, Diane can't think of added details to insert so she simply puts the letters "___bs___" at that point to remind herself to "be specific" in the next draft. She then goes on to finish her first draft.

7. Her ___conclusion___ is as brief as her introduction. Diane knows she can round off her essay more fully during revision.

Revision

Revising is as much a stage in the writing process as prewriting, outlining, and doing the first draft. *Revising* means rewriting a paper, building on what has already been done, in order to make it stronger. One writer has said about revision, "It's like cleaning house—getting rid of all the junk and putting things in the right order." It is not just "straightening up"; instead, you must be ready to roll up your sleeves and do whatever is needed to create an effective paper. Too many students think that the first draft *is* the paper. They start to become writers when they realize that revising a rough draft three or four times is often at the heart of the writing process.

Here are some quick hints that can help make revision easier. First, set your first draft aside for a while. A few hours is fine, but a day or two is best. You can then come back to it with a fresh, more objective point of view. Second, work from typed or printed text. You'll be able to see the paper more impartially in this way than if you were just looking at your own familiar handwriting. Next, read your draft aloud. Hearing how your writing sounds will help you pick up problems with meaning as well as with style. Finally, as you do all these things, add your thoughts and changes above the lines or in the margins of your paper. Your written comments can serve as a guide when you work on the next draft.

There are three stages to the revising process:

- Revising content
- Revising sentences
- Editing

Revising Content

To revise the content of your essay, ask the following questions:

1 Is my paper **unified?**
  - Do I have a thesis that is clearly stated or implied in the introductory paragraph of my essay?
  - Do all my supporting paragraphs truly support and back up my thesis?

2 Is my paper **supported?**
  - Are there three separate supporting points for the thesis?
  - Do I have *specific* evidence for each of the three supporting points?
  - Is there *plenty of* specific evidence for each supporting point?

3 Is my paper **organized?**
  - Do I have an interesting introduction, a solid conclusion, and an accurate title?
  - Do I have a clear method of organizing my paper?
  - Do I use transitions and other connecting words?

Chapters 3 and 4 will give you practice in achieving **unity, support,** and **organization** in your writing.

Revising Sentences

To revise sentences in your essay, ask the following questions:

1 Do I use parallelism to balance my words and ideas?
2 Do I have a consistent point of view?
3 Do I use specific words?
4 Do I use active verbs?
5 Do I use words effectively by avoiding slang, clichés, pretentious language, and wordiness?
6 Do I vary my sentences?

Chapter 5 will give you practice in revising sentences.

Editing

After you have revised your paper for content and style, you are ready to *edit*—check for and correct—errors in grammar, punctuation, and spelling. Students often find it hard to edit a paper carefully. They have put so much, or so little, work into their writing that it's almost painful for them to look at the paper one more time. You may simply have to *will* yourself to perform this important closing step in the writing process. Remember that eliminating sentence-skills mistakes will improve an average paper and help ensure a strong grade on a good paper. Further, as you get into the habit of checking your papers, you will also get into the habit of using the sentence skills consistently. They are an integral part of clear and effective writing.

Chapter 5 and Part Four of this book will serve as a guide while you are editing your paper for mistakes in **sentence skills.**

An Illustration of the Revising and Editing Processes

Revising with a Second Draft: A Student Model

Since Diane Woods was using a word-processing program on a computer, she was able to print out a double-spaced version of her movie essay, leaving her plenty of room for revisions. Here is one of her revised paragraphs:

Secondly,

The theater offers ~~temptatons in the form of~~ *tempting* snacks I really don't need.

Like most of us I have to ~~worry about weight gain~~ *battle an expanding waistline*. At home I do pretty well

by simply ~~watching what I keep in the house and~~ not buying stuff that is bad

for me. I can make do with ~~healthy~~ snacks *like celery and carrot sticks* because there is ~~nothing~~ *no ice cream* in the

freezer. Going to the theater is *however* like spending my evening in a Seven-Eleven

that's been equiped with a movie screen and ~~there are~~ seats ~~which are~~

~~comfortable.~~ *As* I try to convince myself to just have a diet soda/ ~~T~~*t*he smell of

fresh popcorn *dripping with butter* soon overcomes me. ~~My friends are as bad as I am.~~ Choclate

bars seem to jump into ~~your~~ *my* hands. ~~I am eating~~ *risk pulling out my fillings as I chew* enormous mouthfuls of milk

duds. By the time I leave the theater I feel ~~out of sorts~~ *disgusted* with myself.

Comment

Diane made her changes in longhand as she worked on the second draft. As you will see when you complete the activity below, her revision serves to make the paragraph more unified, better supported, and better organized.

Activity

Fill in the missing words.

1. To achieve better organization, Diane adds at the beginning of the paragraph the transitional phrase "___Second,___" making it very clear that the second of her supporting ideas is tempting snacks.

2. Diane also adds the transition "___however___" to clearly show the difference between being at home and being in the theater.

3. In the interest of (*unity, support, organization*) _____unity_____, Diane crosses out the sentence "___My friends are as bad as I am___." She realizes this sentence is not a relevant detail but really another topic idea.

4. To add more (*unity, support, organization*) _____support_____, Diane changes "healthy snacks" to "___snacks like celery and carrot sticks___"; she changes "nothing in the freezer" to "___no ice cream in the freezer___"; she adds "___dripping with butter___" after "popcorn"; and she changes "am eating" to "___risk pulling out my fillings as I chew___."

5. In the interest of eliminating wordiness, she removes the words "___watching what I keep in the house___" from the third sentence.

6. In the interest of parallelism, Diane changes "and there are seats which are comfortable" to "___comfortable seats___."

7. For greater sentence variety, Diane combines two short sentences, beginning the first sentence with the subordinating word "_____As_____."

8. To create a consistent point of view, Diane changes "jump into your hands" to "___jump into my hands___."

9. Finally, Diane replaces the vague "out of sorts" with the more precise "___disgusted___."

Editing: A Student Model

After typing into her word-processing file all the changes in her second draft, Diane printed out another clean draft of the paper. The paragraph on tempting snacks required almost no more revision, so Diane turned her attention mostly to editing changes, illustrated below with her work on the second supporting paragraph:

Secondly, the theater offers tempting snacks I really don't need. Like most

of us, I have to battle an expanding waistline. At home I do pretty well by

simply not buying stuff that is bad for me. I can make do with healthy snacks

like celery and carrot sticks because there is no ice cream in the freezer.

Going to the theater, however, is like spending my evening in a Seven-Eleven

equipped
that's been ~~equiped~~ with a movie screen and comfortable seats. As I try to

Coke
convince myself to just have a diet ~~soda,~~ the smell of fresh popcorn dripping

Chocolate   the size of small automobiles
with butter soon overcomes me. ~~Choclate~~ bars seem to jump into my hands.

M   D
I risk pulling out my fillings as I chew enormous mouthfuls of ~~m~~ilk ~~d~~uds. By

the time I leave the theater, I feel disgusted with myself.

Comment

Once again, Diane makes her changes in longhand right on the printout of her paper. To note these changes, complete the activity below.

Activity

Fill in the missing words.

1. As part of her editing, Diane checked and corrected the ____*spelling*____ of two words, *equipped* and *chocolate*.

2. She added ____*commas*____ to set off two introductory phrases ("Like most of us" in the second sentence and "By the time I leave the theater" in the final sentence) and also to set off the interrupting word *however* in the fourth sentence.

3. She realized that "milk duds" is a brand name and added ____*capital letters*____ to make it "Milk Duds."

4. And since revision can occur at any stage of the writing process, including editing, she makes one of her details more vivid by adding the descriptive words "____*the size of small automobiles*____."

Review Activities

You now have a good overview of the writing process, from prewriting to first draft to revising to editing. The remaining chapters in Part One will deepen your sense of the four goals of effective writing: unity, support, organization or coherence, and sentence skills.

To reinforce much of the information about the writing process that you have learned in this chapter, you can now work through the following activities:

1 Taking a writing inventory

2 Outlining practice

3 Prewriting

4 Revision

1 Taking a Writing Inventory

Activity

Answer the questions below to evaluate your approach to the writing process. This activity is not a test, so try to be as honest as possible. Becoming aware of your writing habits will help you realize changes that may be helpful.

Answers will vary.

1. When you start work on a paper, do you typically do any prewriting?

    _____ Yes   _____ Sometimes   _____ No

2. If so, which of the prewriting techniques do you use?

    _____ Freewriting   _____ Diagramming

    _____ Questioning   _____ Scratch outline

    _____ List making   _____ Other (please describe)

3. Which prewriting technique or techniques work best for you, or which do you think will work best for you?

4. Many students have said they find it helpful to handwrite a first draft and then type that draft on a computer. They then print the draft out and revise it by hand. Describe the way you proceed in drafting and revising a paper.

5. After you write the first draft of a paper, do you have time to set it aside for a while, so you can come back to it with a fresh eye?

_____ Yes   _____ No

6. How many drafts do you typically write when doing a paper?

_____

7. When you revise, are you aware that you should be working toward a paper that is unified, solidly supported, and clearly organized? Has this chapter given you a better sense that unity, support, and organization are goals to aim for?

8. Do you revise a paper for the effectiveness of its sentences as well as for its content?

_____ Yes   _____ No

9. Do you typically do any editing of the almost-final draft of a paper, or do you tend to "hope for the best" and hand it in without careful checking?

_____ Edit   _____ Hope for the best

10. What (if any) information has this chapter given you about prewriting that you will try to apply in your writing?

11. What (if any) information has this chapter given you about revising that you will try to apply in your writing?

12. What (if any) information has this chapter given you about editing that you will try to apply in your writing?

2 Prewriting

Activity

Below are examples of how the five prewriting techniques could be used to develop the topic "Problems of Combining Work and College." Identify each technique by writing F (for freewriting), Q (for questioning), L (for the list), D (for the diagram), or SO (for the scratch outline) in the answer space.

_____L_____ Never enough time
Miss campus parties
Had to study (only two free hours a night)
Give up activities with friends
No time to rewrite papers
Can't stay at school to play video games or talk to friends
Friends don't call me to go out anymore
Sunday no longer relaxed day—have to study
Missing sleep I should be getting
Grades aren't as good as they could be
Can't watch favorite TV shows
Really need the extra money
Tired when I sit down to study at nine o'clock

_____Q_____ <u>What</u> are some of the problems of combining work and school?

Schoolwork suffers because I don't have time to study or rewrite papers. I've had to give up things I enjoy, like sleep and touch football. I can't get into the social life at college, because I have to work right after class.

<u>How</u> have these problems changed my life?

My grades aren't as good as they were when I didn't work. Some of my friends have stopped calling me. My relationship with a girl I liked fell apart because I couldn't spend much time with her. I miss TV.

<u>What</u> do I do in a typical day?

I get up at 7 to make an 8 A.M. class. I have classes till 1:30, and then I drive to the supermarket where I work. I work till 7 P.M., and then I drive home and eat dinner. After I take a shower and relax for a half hour, it's about 9. This gives me only a couple of hours to study—read textbooks, do math exercises, write essays. My eyes start to close well before I go to bed at 11.

<u>Why</u> do I keep up this schedule?   I can't afford to go to school without working, and I need a degree to get the accounting job I want. If I invest my time now, I'll have a better future.

SO

Juggling a job and college has created major difficulties in my life.
1. Little time for studying
    a. Not reading textbooks
    b. No rewriting papers
    c. Little studying for tests
2. Little time for enjoying social side of college
    a. During school
    b. After school
3. No time for personal pleasures
    a. Favorite TV shows
    b. Sunday football games
    c. Sleeping late

D

_____F_____ It's hard working and going to school at the same time. I never realized how much I'd have to give up. I won't be quitting my job because I need the money. And the people are friendly at the place where I work. I've had to give up a lot more than I thought. We used to play touch football games every Sunday. They were fun and we'd go out for drinks afterwards. Sundays now are for catch-up work with my courses. I have to catch up because I don't get home every day until 7, I have to eat dinner first before studying. Sometimes I'm so hungry I just eat cookies or chips. Anyway, by the time I take a shower it's 9 P.M. or later and I'm already feeling tired. I've been up since 7 A.M. Sometimes I write an English paper in twenty minutes and don't even read it over. I feel that I'm missing out on a lot in college. The other day some people I like were sitting in the cafeteria listening to music and talking. I would have given anything to stay and not have to go to work. I almost called in sick. I used to get invited to parties, I don't much anymore. My friends know I'm not going to be able to make it, so they don't bother. I can't sleep late on weekends or watch TV during the week.

3 Outlining

As already mentioned (see page 30), outlining is central to writing a good paper. An outline lets you see, and work on, the bare bones of a paper, without the distraction of a clutter of words and sentences. It develops your ability to think clearly and logically. Outlining provides a quick check on whether your paper will be *unified*. It also suggests right at the start whether your paper will be adequately *supported*. And it shows you how to plan a paper that is *well organized*.

The following two exercises will help you develop the outlining skills so important to planning and writing a solid essay.

Activity 1

One key to effective outlining is the ability to distinguish between major ideas and details that fit under those ideas. In each of the four lists below, major and supporting items are mixed together. Put the items into logical order by filling in the outline that follows each list. In items 3 and 4, one of the three major ideas is missing and must be added.

1. Thesis: My high school had three problem areas.

    Involved with drugs   a. _Students_
    Leaky ceilings   (1) _Involved with drugs_
    Students   (2) _Formed cliques_
    Unwilling to help after class
    Formed cliques   b. _Teachers_
    Teachers   (1) _Much too strict_
    Buildings   (2) _Unwilling to help after class_
    Ill-equipped gym
    Much too strict   c. _Buildings_
                                                     (1) _Leaky ceilings_
                                                     (2) _Ill-equipped gym_

2. Thesis: Working as a dishwasher in a restaurant was my worst job.

    Ten-hour shifts   a. _Working conditions_
    Heat in kitchen   (1) _Heat in kitchen_
    Working conditions   (2) _Noisy work area_
    Minimum wage
    Hours changed every week   b. _Hours_
    No bonus for overtime   (1) _Ten-hour shifts_
    Hours   (2) _Hours changed every week_
    Pay
    Noisy work area   c. _Pay_
                                                     (1) _Minimum wage_
                                                     (2) _No bonus for overtime_

3. Thesis: Joining an aerobics class has many benefits.

    Make new friends   a. _Physical benefits_
    Reduces mental stress   (1) _Strengthens heart_
    Social benefits   (2) _Tones muscles_
    Strengthens heart
    Improves self-image   b. _Mental benefits_
    Mental benefits   (1) _Reduces mental stress_
    Tones muscles   (2) _Improves self-image_
    Meet interesting instructors
    Physical benefits   c. _Social benefits_
                                                     (1) _Make new friends_
                                                     (2) _Meet interesting instructors_

4.   Thesis: My favorite times in school were the days before holiday vacations.

Lighter workload
Teachers more relaxed
Pep rallies
Less work in class
Friendlier atmosphere
Less homework
Holiday concerts
Students happy about vacation
Appealing activities

a. _Lighter workload_
  (1) _Less work in class_
  (2) _Less homework_

b. _Friendlier atmosphere_
  (1) _Teachers more relaxed_
  (2) _Students happy about vacation_

c. _Appealing activities_
  (1) _Pep rallies_
  (2) _Holiday concerts_

Activity 2

Read the essay on the following pages and outline it in the spaces provided. Write out the central point and topic sentences, and summarize in a few words the supporting material that fits under each topic sentence. One item is summarized for you as an example.

Losing Touch

Steve, a typical American, stays home on workdays. He plugs into a computer terminal in order to hook up with the office, and he sends and receives work during the day by electronic mail and a fax-modem. Evenings, he puts on his stereo headphones, watches a movie on his VCR, or logs back onto the computer to visit the Internet. On many days, Steve doesn't talk to any other human beings, and he doesn't see any people except those on television. Steve is imaginary, but his lifestyle is very common. More and more, the inventions of modern technology seem to be cutting us off from contact with our fellow human beings.

Thesis: _More and more, the inventions of modern technology seem to be cutting us off from contact with our fellow human beings._

The world of business is one area in which technology is isolating us. Many people now work alone at home. With access to a large central computer, employees such as secretaries, insurance agents, and accountants do their jobs at display terminals in their own homes. They no longer actually have to see the people they're dealing with. In addition, employees are often paid in an impersonal way. Workers' salaries are automatically credited to their bank accounts, eliminating the need for paychecks. Fewer people stand in line with their coworkers to receive their pay or cash their checks. Finally, personal banking is becoming a detached process. Customers interact with machines rather than people to deposit or withdraw money from their accounts. Even some bank loans are approved or rejected, not in an interview with a loan officer, but through a display on a computer screen.

First topic sentence: The world of business is one area in which technology is isolating us.

Support: 1.   Many people now work alone at home.

       2.   Workers' salaries are automatically credited to their bank accounts.

       3.   Personal banking is becoming a detached process.

         a.   Customers interact with machines to make deposits and withdrawals.

         b.   Some loans are accepted or rejected by computers, not loan officers.

Another area that technology is changing is entertainment. Music, for instance, was once a group experience. People listened to music in concert halls or at small social gatherings. For many people now, however, music is a solitary experience. Walking along the street or sitting in their living rooms, they wear headphones to build a wall of music around them. Movie entertainment is changing, too. Movies used to be social events. Now, some people are not going out to see a movie. Some are choosing to wait for a film to appear on cable television. Instead of being involved with the laughter, applause, or hisses of the audience, viewers watch movies in the isolation of their own living rooms.

Second topic sentence: Another area that technology is changing is entertainment.

Support: 1.   Music is a solitary experience.

       2.   Fewer people go out to see movies.

Education is a third important area in which technology is separating us from others. From elementary schools to colleges, students spend more and more time sitting by themselves in front of computers. The computers give them feedback, while teachers spend more time tending the computers and less time interacting with their classes. A similar problem occurs in homes. As more families buy computers, increasing numbers of students practice their math and reading skills with software programs instead of with their friends, brothers and sisters, and parents. Last, alienation is occurring as a result of another high-tech invention, videotapes. People are buying videocassette tapes on subjects such as cooking, real estate investment, speaking, and speed-reading. They then practice their skills at home rather than by taking group classes in which a rich human interaction can occur.

Third topic sentence: _Education is a third important area in which technology is separating us from others._

Support: 1. _Students sit alone in front of computers at school._

2. _Students use software at home instead of interacting with others._

3. _Videotapes are replacing class instruction._

Technology, then, seems to be driving human beings apart. Soon, we may no longer need to communicate with other human beings in order to do our work, entertain ourselves, or pursue an education. Machines will be the coworkers and companions of the future.

4 Revising

Activity

Following is the second supporting paragraph from an essay called "Problems of Combining School and Work." The paragraph is shown in four different stages of development: (1) first full draft, (2) revised second draft, (3) edited next-to-final draft, (4) final draft. The four stages appear in scrambled order. Write the number 1 in the answer blank for the first full draft and number the remaining stages in sequence.

_2_

I have also given up some personal pleasures in my life. On sundays for example I used to play softball or football, now I use the entire day to study. Good old-fashioned sleep is another lost pleasure for me now. I never get as much as I like because their just isn't time. Finally I miss having the chance to just sit in front of the TV, on weeknights. In order to watch the whole lineup of movies and sports that I used to watch regularly. These sound like small pleasures, but you realize how important they are when you have to give them up.

_1_

I've had to give up pleasures in my life. I use to spend sundays playing games, now I have to study. Im the sort of person who needs a lot of sleep, but I dont have the time for that either. Sleeping nine or ten hours a night woul'dnt be unusual for me. Psycologists say that each individual need a different amount of sleep, some people need as little as five hours, some need as much as nine or ten. So I'm not unusual in that. But Ive given up that pleasure too. And I can't watch the TV shows I use to enjoy. This is another personal pleasure Ive lost because of doing work and school. These may seem like small things, but you realize how good they are when you give them up.

_4_

Besides missing the social side of college life, I've also had to give up some of my special personal pleasures. I used to spend Sunday afternoons, for example, playing lob-pitch softball or touch football depending on the season. Now I use Sunday as a catch-up day for my studies. Another pleasure I've lost is sleeping late on days off and weekends. I once loved mornings when I could check the clock, bury my head in the pillow, and drift off for another hour. These days I'm forced to crawl out of bed the minute the alarm lets out its piercing ring. Finally, I no longer have the chance to just sit watching the movies and sports programs that I enjoy. A leisurely night of <u>Monday Night Football</u> or a network premiere of a Harrison Ford movie is a pleasure of the past for me now.

_3_

Besides missing the social side of college life, I've also had to give up some of my special personal pleasures. I used to spend sunday afternoons, for example playing lob-pitch softball or touch football depending on the season. Now I use the day as a catchup day for my studies. Another pleasure I've lost is sleeping late on days off and weekends. I once loved mornings when I could check the clock, then burying my head in the pillow, and you drift off to sleep for another hour. These days I'm forced to get out of bed the minute the alarm lets out it's ring. Finally I no longer have the chance to just sit watching the movies and also programs with sports that I enjoy. A leisurely night of Monday Night Football or a network premiere of a Harrison Ford movie is a pleasure of the past for me now.

3 The First and Second Steps in Essay Writing

This chapter will show you how to

- start an essay with a point, or thesis
- support that point, or thesis, with specific evidence

Chapter 2 emphasized how prewriting and revising can help you become an effective writer. This chapter will focus on the first two steps in writing an effective essay:

1 Begin with a point, or thesis.
2 Support the thesis with specific evidence.

The chapters that follow will then focus on the third step and fourth steps in writing:

3 Organize and connect the specific evidence (pages 77–102);
4 Write clear, error-free sentences (pages 103–137).

Step 1: Begin with a Point, or Thesis

Your first step in writing is to discover what point you want to make and to write that point out in a single sentence. There are two reasons for doing this. You want to know right from the start if you have a clear and workable thesis. Also, you will be able to use the thesis as a guide while writing your essay. At any stage you can ask yourself, "Does this support my thesis?" With the thesis as a guide, the danger of drifting away from the point of the essay is greatly reduced.

Writing a Good Thesis

To write a good thesis, you must begin with a subject that is neither too broad nor too narrow. Suppose, for example, that an instructor asks you to write a paper on marriage. A topic such as marriage is obviously too broad to cover in a five-hundred-word essay. You would have to write a book to support adequately any point you might make about the general subject of marriage. What you need to do, then, is limit your subject. Narrow it down until you have a thesis that you can deal with specifically in about five hundred words. In the box that follows are (1) several general subjects, (2) limited versions of those general subjects, and (3) thesis statements about the limited subjects.

General Subject	Limited Subject	Thesis
Marriage	Honeymoon	A honeymoon is perhaps the worst way to begin a marriage.
Family	Older sister	My older sister helped me overcome my shyness.
Television	TV preachers	TV evangelists use sales techniques to promote their messages.
Children	Disciplining of children	My husband and I have several effective ways of disciplining our children.
Sports	Players' salaries	Players' high salaries are bad for the game, for the fans, and for the values our children are developing.

Activity

Sometimes a subject must go through several stages of limiting before it is narrow enough to write about. Below are four lists reflecting several stages that writers went through in moving from a general subject to a narrow thesis statement. Number the stages in each list from 1 to 5, with 1 marking the broadest stage and 5 marking the thesis.

List 1

___2___ Teachers

___1___ Education

___3___ Math teacher

___5___ My high school math teacher was incompetent.

___4___ High school math teacher

List 2

___3___ Bicycles

___4___ Dangers of bike riding

___1___ Recreation

___2___ Recreational vehicles

___5___ Bike riding in the city is a dangerous activity.

List 3

___1___ Retail companies

___2___ Supermarkets

___4___ Dealing with customers

___3___ Working in a supermarket

___5___ I've learned how to handle unpleasant supermarket customers.

List 4

___3___ Camping

___4___ First camping trip

___2___ Summer vacation

___5___ My first camping trip was a disastrous experience.

___1___ Vacations

Later in this chapter, you will get more practice in narrowing general subjects to thesis statements.

Common Errors in Writing a Thesis

When writing thesis statements, people often make mistakes that undermine their chances of producing an effective essay. One mistake is to simply announce the subject rather than state a true thesis idea. A second mistake is to write a thesis that is too broad, and a third is to write a thesis that is too narrow. A fourth mistake is to write a thesis containing more than one idea. Following are examples of these four errors.

1 Announcements Rather Than Statements

The subject of this paper will be my parents.

I want to talk about the crime wave in our country.

The "baby boom" generation is the concern of this essay.

In this first group, the sentences are not thesis statements but just announcements of a topic. For instance, "The subject of this paper will be my parents" does not make a point *about* the parents but merely tells, in a rather weak and unimaginative way, the writer's general subject. A thesis statement must advance a point about a limited subject.

2 Statements That Are Too Broad

My parents have been the most influential people in my life.

Crime is a major concern of everyone in our country.

The "baby boom" generation has changed history.

In this second group, all the statements are too broad to be supported adequately in a student essay. For example, "My parents have been the most influential people in my life" could not be supported with specific details in five hundred words or less. There are many autobiographies in which entire chapters detail the influence of parents on the author's life.

3 Statements That Are Too Narrow

My parents had only one child.

In the last year there have been over twenty robberies in our neighborhood.

The members of the post-World War II "baby boom" make up the largest single age group in the United States.

In this third group, there is no room in any of the three statements for support to be given. For instance, "My parents had only one child" is too narrow to be expanded into a paper. It is a simple fact that does not require much support. Such a statement is sometimes called a *dead-end statement;* there is no place to go with it. On the other hand, "My parents helped me grow in three important ways" is a point that you could support with specific ideas in an essay.

4 Statements That Contain More Than One Idea

My parents helped me grow in important ways, although in other respects I was limited.

The problem of overcrowded American prisons must be solved, and judges must start handing out tougher sentences.

The "baby boom" generation has had many advantages, but it also faces many problems.

In this fourth group, each statement contains more than one idea. For instance, "My parents helped me grow in important ways, although in other respects I was limited" appears to have two separate ideas ("parents helped me grow" *and* "in other respects I was limited"). The reader is asked to focus on two quite separate points, each of which more logically belongs in an essay of its own.

Activity

Part A: Write TN in the space next to each statement that is too narrow to be developed in an essay. Write TB beside each statement that is too broad to be covered in an essay.

TB	1. The way our society treats elderly people is unbelievable.
TN	2. The first car that I owned was a Ford.
TB	3. Computers have changed our society.
TN	4. People who eat a lot of red meat are almost three times more likely to get colon cancer than people who eat mostly fish and chicken.
TB	5. Action must be taken against drugs.

Part B: Write A beside each sentence that is an announcement rather than a thesis statement. Write 2 beside each statement that contains more than one idea.

2	6. My last car was dependable, but many American cars are poorly made.
A	7. The subject of this essay is daily prayer in our public schools.
2	8. Soap operas show many stereotyped characters, although they also portray real problems in American life.
A	9. I am going to write on my ideas concerning "F" grades.
2	10. The strangest teacher I ever had taught me a lesson I will never forget.

Step 2: Support the Thesis with Specific Evidence

The first essential step in writing a successful essay is to formulate a clearly stated thesis. The second basic step is to support the thesis with specific reasons or details.

To ensure that your essay will have adequate support, you may find an informal outline very helpful. Write down a brief version of your thesis idea and then work out and jot down the three points that will support the thesis.

Here is the scratch outline that was prepared by the author of the earlier essay on moviegoing:

Moviegoing is a problem.
1. Inconvenience of going out
2. Tempting snacks
3. Other moviegoers

A scratch outline like this one looks simple, but developing it often requires a great deal of careful thinking. The time spent on developing a logical outline is invaluable, though. Once you have planned out the steps that logically support your thesis, you will be in an excellent position to go on to write an effective essay.

Activities in this section will give you practice in the crucial skill of planning an essay clearly.

Activity

Following are six informal outlines. Complete any five of them by adding a third logical supporting point *(c)* that will parallel the two already provided *(a* and *b).*
Answers will vary; examples are shown.

1. The first day on a new job can be nerve-racking.
    a. Meeting new people
    b. Finding your way around a new place
    c. *Learning new rules and procedures*

2. My stepmother has three qualities I admire.
    a. Patience
    b. Thoughtfulness
    c. *Sense of humor*

3. At our school, the library is the worst place to study.
    a. Uncomfortable chairs and tables
    b. Little privacy
    c. *Too cold in the winter*

4. College students should live at home.
    a. Stay in touch with family
    b. Avoid distractions of dorm or apartment life
    c. *Save money*

5. _____ is the worst job I've ever had.
   a. Difficult boss
   b. Poor pay
   c. _Long hours_____

6. College is a stressful situation for many people.
   a. Worry about grades
   b. Worry about being accepted
   c. _Worry about finances_____

The Importance of *Specific* Details

Just as a thesis must be developed with three supporting points, those supporting points must be developed with specific details. Specific details are valuable in two key ways. First, details excite the reader's interest. They make writing a pleasure to read, for we all enjoy learning particulars about people, places, and things. Second, details serve to explain a writer's points. They give the evidence needed for us to see and understand general ideas.

All too often, the body paragraphs in essays contain only vague generalities, rather than the specific supporting details that are needed to engage and convince a reader. Here is what one of the paragraphs in "The Hazards of Moviegoing" would have looked like if the writer had not detailed her supporting evidence vividly.

Some of the other patrons are even more of a problem than the theater itself. Many people in the theater often show themselves to be inconsiderate. They make noises and create disturbances at their seats. Included are people in every age group, from the young to the old. Some act as if they were at home in their own living room watching the TV set. And people are often messy, so that you're constantly aware of all the food they're eating. People are also always moving around near you, creating a disturbance and interrupting your enjoyment of the movie.

The following box contrasts the vague support in the preceding paragraph with the specific support in the essay.

Vague Support	Specific Support
1. Many people in the theater show themselves to be inconsiderate. They make noises and create disturbances at their seats. Included are people in every age group, from the young to the old. Some act as if they were at home in their own living room watching the TV set.	1. Little kids race up and down the aisles, usually in giggling packs. Teenagers try to impress their friends by talking back to the screen, whistling, and making what they consider to be hilarious noises. Adults act as if they were at home in their own living room and comment loudly on the ages of the stars or why movies aren't as good anymore.
2. And people are often messy, so that you're constantly aware of all the food they're eating.	2. And people of all ages crinkle candy wrappers, stick gum on their seats, and drop popcorn tubs or cups of crushed ice and soda on the floor.
3. People are also always moving around near you, creating a disturbance and interrupting your enjoyment of the movie.	3. They also cough and burp, squirm endlessly in their seats, file out for repeated trips to the rest rooms or concession stand, and elbow you out of the armrest on either side of your seat.

The effective paragraph from the essay provides details that make vividly clear the statement that patrons are a problem in the theater. The writer specifies the exact age groups (little kids, teenagers, and adults) and the offenses of each (giggling, talking and whistling, and loud comments). She specifies the various food excesses (crinkled wrappers, gum on seats, dropped popcorn and soda containers). Finally, she provides concrete details that enable us to see and hear other disturbances (coughs and burps, squirming, constant trips to bathroom, jostling for elbow room). The ineffective paragraph asks us to guess about these details; the effective paragraph describes the details in a specific and lively way.

In the strong paragraph, then, sharp details capture our interest and enable us to share the writer's experience. They provide pictures that make each of us feel, "I am there." The particulars also enable us to understand clearly the writer's point that patrons are a problem. Aim to make your own writing equally convincing by providing detailed support.

Activity

Write S in front of the two selections below that provide specific evidence to support the opening point. Write X in front of the two selections in which the opening point is followed by vague, general, wordy sentences.

___S___ 1. Building a wooden deck can be an enjoyable project only if you take certain precautions.

Get a building permit before you start. If you don't have one, you may have to tear down everything you've built when the town's building inspector learns of your project. Also, purchase pressure-treated lumber for any posts that will be set into the ground. Ordinary wood, not treated with preservatives, will eventually rot from contact with soil and moisture.

___X___ 2. My mother was a harsh disciplinarian.

When I did something wrong, no matter how small, she would inflict serious punishment. She had expectations that I was to live up to, and she never changed her attitude. When I did not behave as I should, I was dealt with severely. There were no exceptions as far as my mother was concerned.

___S___ 3. Some things are worse when they're "improved."

A good cheesecake, for one thing, is perfect. It doesn't need pineapple, cherries, blueberries, or whipped cream smeared all over it. Plain old American blue jeans, the ones with five pockets and copper rivets, are perfect too. Manufacturers only made them worse when they added flared legs, took away the pockets, tightened the fit, and plastered white logos and designers' names all over them.

___X___ 4. Pets can be more trouble than children.

My dog, unlike my children, has never been completely housebroken. When he's excited or nervous, he still has an occasional problem. My dog, unlike my children, has never learned how to take care of himself when we're away, despite the fact that we've given him plenty of time to do so. We don't have to worry about our grown children anymore. However, we still have to hire a dog-sitter.

The Importance of *Adequate* Details

One of the most common and most serious problems in students' writing is inadequate development. You must provide *enough* specific details to fully support the point in a body paragraph of an essay. You could not, for example, include a paragraph about a friend's unreliability and provide only a one- or two-sentence example. You would have to extend the example or add several other examples showing your friend as an unreliable person. Without such additional support, your paragraph would be underdeveloped.

Students may try to disguise unsupported paragraphs through repetition and generalities. Do not fall into this "wordiness trap." Be prepared to do the plain hard work needed to ensure that each paragraph has solid support.

Activity 1

Both of the following body paragraphs were written on the same topic, and each has a clear opening point. Which paragraph is adequately developed? Which one has only several particulars and uses mostly vague, general, wordy sentences to conceal the fact that it is starved for specific details?

First paragraph is adequately developed.

Eternal Youth?—No Thanks

I wouldn't want to be a teenager again, first of all, because I wouldn't want to worry about talking to girls. I still remember how scary it was to call up a girl and ask her out. My heart would race, my pulse would pound, and perspiration would trickle down my face, adding to my acne by the second. I never knew whether my voice would come out deep and masculine, like a television anchorman's, or squeaky, like a little boy's. Then there were the questions: Would she be at home? If she was, would she want to talk to me? And if she did, what would I say? The one time I did get up the nerve to take a girl in my homeroom to a movie, I was so tongue-tied that I stared silently at the box of popcorn in my lap until the feature finally started. Needless to say, I wasn't very interesting company.

Terrors of My Teenage Years

I wouldn't want to be a teenager again, first of all, because I wouldn't want to worry about talking to girls. Calling up a girl to ask her out was something that I completely dreaded. I didn't know what words to express or how to express them. I would have all the symptoms of nervousness when I got on the phone. I worried a great deal about how I would sound, and I had a lot of doubts about the girl's reaction. Once, I managed to call up a girl to go out, but the evening turned out to be a disaster. I was too unsure of myself to act in a confident way. I couldn't think of anything to say and just kept quiet. Now that I look back on it, I really made a fool of myself. Agonizing over my attempts at relationships with the opposite sex made adolescence a very uncomfortable time.

The first paragraph offers a series of well-detailed examples of the author's nerve-racking experiences, as a teenager, with girls. The second paragraph, on the other hand, is underdeveloped. For instance, the second paragraph makes only the general observation, "I would have all the symptoms of nervousness when I got on the phone"; but the first paragraph states, "My heart would race, my pulse would pound, and perspiration would trickle down my face."

The second paragraph makes the general statement "I worried a great deal about how I would sound," but in the first paragraph the author wonders if his voice will "come out deep and masculine, like a television anchorman's, or squeaky, like a little boy's." And in the second paragraph, there is no specific description of the evening that turned into a disaster. In summary, the second paragraph lacks the full, detailed support needed to develop its opening point convincingly.

Activity 2

Take a few minutes to write a paragraph supporting the point "My room is a mess." Afterward, you and your classmates, perhaps working in small groups, should read your paragraphs aloud. The best-received paragraphs are almost sure to be those with plenty of specific details.

Answers will vary.

Practice in Advancing and Supporting a Thesis

You now know the two most important steps in competent essay writing: (1) advancing a point, or thesis, and (2) supporting that thesis. The purpose of this section is to expand and strengthen your understanding of these two basic steps. You will first work through a series of activities on *developing* a thesis:

1 Identifying the parts of an essay
2 Evaluating thesis statements
3 Completing thesis statements
4 Writing a thesis statement
5 Limiting a topic and writing a thesis

You will then sharpen your understanding of how to *support* a thesis effectively by working through the following activities:

6 Providing specific evidence

7 Identifying adequate supporting evidence

8 Adding details to complete an essay

1 Identifying the Parts of an Essay

Activity

This activity will sharpen your sense of the parts of an essay. "Coping with Old Age" has no indentations between paragraphs. Read this essay carefully, and then double-underline the thesis and single-underline the topic sentence for each of the three supporting paragraphs and the first sentence of the conclusion. Write the numbers of those sentences in the spaces provided at the end.

Coping with Old Age

[1]I recently read about an area of the former Soviet Union where many people live to be well over a hundred years old. [2]Being 115 or even 125 isn't considered unusual there, and these old people continue to do productive work right up until they die. [3]The United States, however, isn't such a healthy place for older people. [4]Since I retired from my job, I've had to cope with the physical, mental, and emotional stresses of being "old." [5]For one thing, I've had to adjust to physical changes. [6]Now that I'm over sixty, the trusty body that carried me around for years has turned traitor. [7]Aside from the deepening wrinkles on my face and neck, and the wiry gray hairs that have replaced my brown hair, I face more frightening changes. [8]I don't have the energy I used to. [9]My eyes get tired. [10]Once in a while, I miss something that's said to me. [11]My once faithful feet seem to have lost their comfortable soles, and I sometimes feel I'm walking on marbles. [12]In order to fight against this slow decay, I exercise whenever I can. [13]I walk, I stretch, and I climb stairs. [14]I battle constantly to keep as fit as possible. [15]I'm also trying to cope with mental changes. [16]My mind was once as quick and sure as a champion gymnast. [17]I never found it difficult to memorize answers in school or to remember the names of people I met. [18]Now, I occasionally have to search my mind for the name of a close neighbor or favorite television show. [19]Because my mind needs exercise, too, I challenge it as much as I can. [20]Taking a college course like this English class, for example, forces me to concentrate. [21]The mental gymnast may be a little slow and out of shape, but he can still do a back flip or turn a somersault when he has to. [22]Finally, I must deal with the emotional impact of being old. [23]Our society typecasts old people. [24]We're supposed to be unattractive, senile, useless leftovers.

[25]We're supposed to be the crazy drivers and the cranky customers. [26]At first, I was angry and frustrated that I was considered old at all. [27]And I knew that people were wrong to stereotype me. [28]Then I got depressed. [29]I even started to think that maybe I was a cast-off, one of those old animals that slow down the rest of the herd. [30]But I have now decided to rebel against these negative feelings. [31]I try to have friends of all ages and to keep up with what's going on in the world. [32]I try to remember that I'm still the same person who sat at a first-grade desk, who fell in love, who comforted a child, who got a raise at work. [33]I'm not "just" an old person. [34]Coping with the changes of old age has become my latest full-time job. [35]Even though it's a job I never applied for, and one for which I had no experience, I'm trying to do the best I can.

Thesis statement in "Coping with Old Age":   ___4___

Topic sentence of first supporting paragraph: ___5___

Topic sentence of second supporting paragraph: ___15___

Topic sentence of third supporting paragraph: ___22___

First sentence of the conclusion: ___34___

2 Evaluating Thesis Statements

As was explained on pages 53–54, some writers use an announcement of a subject instead of stating a true thesis idea. Others write a dead-end thesis statement that is too narrow to need support or development. Contrasting with such a dead-end statement is the statement that is wide open—too broad to be adequately supported in the limited space of a five-hundred-word essay. Other thesis statements are vague or contain more than one idea. They suggest that the writer has not thought out the main point sufficiently.

Activity 1

Write A beside each sentence that is an announcement rather than a thesis statement. Write OK beside the statement in each pair that is a clear, limited point which could be developed in an essay.

1. ___A___   a.   This essay will discuss the people you meet in exercise class.

   ___OK___   b.   The kinds of workout clothes worn in my aerobics class identify "jocks," "strugglers," and "princesses."

2. __OK__ a. I made several mistakes in the process of trying to win the respect and affection of my teenage stepson.

   __A__ b. My thesis in this paper is relationships between stepparents and stepchildren.

3. __OK__ a. A period of loneliness can teach you to use your creativity, sort out your values, and feel empathy for others.

   __A__ b. Loneliness is the subject of this paper.

4. __A__ a. This paper will be about sharing housework.

   __OK__ b. Deciding who will perform certain unpleasant household chores can be the crisis that makes or breaks a marriage.

5. __A__ a. My concern here is to discuss "near-death" experiences reported by some patients.

   __OK__ b. There are several possible explanations for the similar "near-death" experiences reported by some patients.

Activity 2

Write TN beside each statement that is too narrow to be developed in an essay. Write OK beside the statement in each pair that is a clear, limited point.

1. __TN__ a. I had squash, tomatoes, and corn in my garden last summer.

   __OK__ b. Vegetable gardening can be a frustrating hobby.

2. __TN__ a. The main road into our town is lined with billboards.

   __OK__ b. For several reasons, billboards should be abolished.

3. __TN__ a. There are now more single-parent households in our country than ever before.

   __OK__ b. Organization is the key to being a successful single parent.

4. __OK__ a. In my first job, I learned that I had several bad work habits.

   __TN__ b. Because I was late for work yesterday, I lost an hour's pay and was called in to see the boss.

5. __OK__ a. Americans abuse alcohol because it has become such an important part of our personal and public celebrations.

   __TN__ b. Consumption of wine, beer, and hard liquor increases in the United States every year.

Activity 3

Write TB beside each statement that is too broad to be developed in an essay. Write OK beside the statement in each pair that is a clear, limited point.

1. __TB__ a. In many ways, sports are an important part of American life.

   __OK__ b. Widespread gambling has changed professional football for the worse.

2. __TB__ a. Modern life makes people suspicious and unfriendly.

   __OK__ b. A frightening experience in my neighborhood has caused me to be a much more cautious person in several ways.

3. __OK__ a. Toy ads on television teach children to be greedy, competitive, and snobbish.

   __TB__ b. Advertising has bad effects on all of society.

4. __TB__ a. Learning new skills can be difficult and frustrating.

   __OK__ b. Learning to write takes work, patience, and a sense of humor.

5. __TB__ a. I didn't get along with my family, so I did many foolish things.

   __OK__ b. Running away from home taught me that my parents weren't as terrible as I thought.

Activity 4

For each pair, write 2 beside the statement that contains more than one idea. Write OK beside the statement that is a clear, limited point.

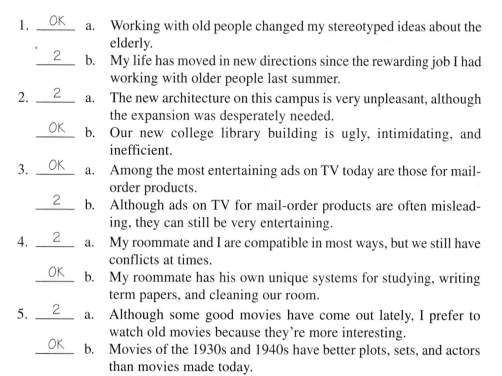

1. __OK__ a. Working with old people changed my stereotyped ideas about the elderly.

   __2__ b. My life has moved in new directions since the rewarding job I had working with older people last summer.

2. __2__ a. The new architecture on this campus is very unpleasant, although the expansion was desperately needed.

   __OK__ b. Our new college library building is ugly, intimidating, and inefficient.

3. __OK__ a. Among the most entertaining ads on TV today are those for mail-order products.

   __2__ b. Although ads on TV for mail-order products are often misleading, they can still be very entertaining.

4. __2__ a. My roommate and I are compatible in most ways, but we still have conflicts at times.

   __OK__ b. My roommate has his own unique systems for studying, writing term papers, and cleaning our room.

5. __2__ a. Although some good movies have come out lately, I prefer to watch old movies because they're more interesting.

   __OK__ b. Movies of the 1930s and 1940s have better plots, sets, and actors than movies made today.

3 Completing Thesis Statements

Activity

Complete the following thesis statements by adding a third supporting point that will parallel the two already provided. You might first want to check the section on parallelism in Chapter 5 (page 103) to make sure you understand parallel form.
Answers will vary; examples are given.

1. Because I never took college preparatory courses in high school, I entered college deficient in mathematics, study skills, and _____science_____.

2. A good salesperson needs to like people, to be aggressive, and _____to be enthusiastic_____.

3. Rather than blame myself for failing the course, I blamed the instructor, my adviser, and even _____my boyfriend_____.

4. Anyone who buys an old house planning to fix it up should be prepared to put in a lot of time, hard work, and _____money_____.

5. Our old car eats gas, makes funny noises, and _____fails to start on cold mornings_____.

6. My mother, my boss, and my _____coach_____ are three people who are very important in my life right now.

7. Getting married too young was a mistake because we hadn't finished our education, we weren't ready for children, and _____we weren't able to commit ourselves to each other_____.

8. Some restaurant patrons seem to leave their honesty, their cleanliness, and their _____manners_____ at home.

9. During my first semester at college, I had to learn how to manage my time, my diet, and _____my relationships with others_____.

10. Three experiences I wish I could forget are the time I fell off a ladder, the time I tried to fix my parents' lawn mower, and _____the time I performed in a piano recital_____.

4 Writing a Thesis Statement

Activity

Write a thesis for each group of supporting statements. This activity will give you practice in writing an effective essay thesis—one that is neither too broad nor too narrow. It will also give you practice in understanding the logical relationship between a thesis and its supporting details.

Wording of thesis may vary.

1. Thesis: *My cars have reflected stages in my life.*
   a. My first car was a rebellious-looking one which matched the way I felt and acted as a teenager.
   b. My next car reflected my more mature and practical adult self.
   c. My latest car seems to tell me that I'm aging; it shows my growing concern with comfort and safety.

2. Thesis: *A two-year college has certain advantages.*
   a. All the course credits that are accumulated can be transferred to a four-year school.
   b. Going to a two-year college can save a great deal of money in tuition and other fees.
   c. If the college is nearby, there are also significant savings in everyday living expenses.

3. Thesis: *I have tried several ways to give up snacks.*
   a. First, I tried simply avoiding the snacks aisle of the supermarket.
   b. Then I started limiting myself to only five units of any given snack.
   c. Finally, in desperation, I began keeping the cellophane bags of snacks in a padlocked cupboard.

4. Thesis: *Halloween is not all fun.*
   a. The holiday can be very frightening for little children.
   b. Children can be struck by cars while wearing vision-obstructing masks and dark costumes.
   c. There are always incidents involving deadly treats: fruits, cookies, and candies that contain razor blades or even poison.

5. Thesis: *Three factors contributed to my heart attack.*
   a. First of all, I was a typical "type A" personality: anxious, impatient, and hard-driving.
   b. I also had a family history of relatives with heart trouble.
   c. My unhealthy lifestyle, though, was probably the major factor.

5 Limiting a Topic and Writing a Thesis

The following two activities will give you practice in distinguishing general from limited subjects and in writing a thesis.

Activity 1

Look carefully at the ten general subjects and ten limited subjects below. Then see if you can write a thesis for any five of them.

Hint: To create a thesis for a limited subject, ask yourself, "What point do I want to make about _____ (*my limited subject*)?"

General Subject
1. Apartment
2. Self-improvement
3. Family
4. Eating
5. Automobiles
6. Health
7. Owning a house
8. Baseball
9. Parenthood
10. Pollution

Limited Subject
1. Sharing an apartment with a roommate
2. Behavior toward others
3. My mother
4. Fast-food restaurants
5. Bad driving habits
6. Regular exercise
7. Do-it-yourself home repairs
8. Free-agent system
9. Being a single parent
10. Noise pollution

Thesis statements for five of the limited subjects:

Answers will vary; examples are given.

1. Sharing an apartment with a roommate calls for goodwill, a sense of give-and-take, and plenty of intelligence.

2. To improve your behavior toward others, learn to listen, to sympathize, and to share.

5. Three potentially deadly driving habits are inattention, a "tough guy" attitude, and a short temper.

6. Regular exercise is a good way to reduce stress, worry, and your waistline.

10. Interestingly, sources of noise pollution can be loud, moderate, or even very faint.

Activity 2

Here is a list of ten general subjects. Limit five of the subjects. Then write thesis statements about each of the five limited subjects.

General Subject	Limited Subject
	Answers will vary; examples are given.
1. Pets	Beagles
2. Teenagers	Teenage motherhood
3. Television	Sports announcers on television
4. Work	Working at home
5. College	Your first week at college
6. Doctors	Our family doctor
7. Vacations	Disastrous vacations
8. Cooking	Cooking for one
9. Money	Unusual things used as money
10. Shopping	Shopping for a wedding gown

Thesis statements for five of the limited subjects:

Answers will vary; examples are given.

1. Beagles make great pets because they are loving, cheerful, and sturdy.

2. Teenage motherhood can be harmful to the mother herself, to her child, and to society.

3. Working at home is a sensible alternative for many people, including parents of young children; older people; and technology wizards.

5. A few simple tips will help you survive your first week at college.

8. Cooking for one person—yourself—can be remarkably pleasant.

6 Providing Specific Evidence

Activity

Provide three details that logically support each of the following points. Your details can be drawn from your own experience, or they can be invented. In each case, the details should show *specifically* what the point expresses only generally. State your details briefly in several words rather than in complete sentences.

Example   We quickly spruced up the apartment before our guest arrived.

1. Hid toys and newspapers in spare closet
2. Vacuumed pet hairs off sofa
3. Sprayed air freshener around living room

Answers will vary; examples are given.

1. The dinner was a disaster.

   Guests arrived two hours late

   Roast was burned

   Host and hostess got into a huge fight

2. My seven-year-old nephew has some disgusting habits.

   Collects dead frogs, birds, and worms

   Loves to dunk pizza in his chocolate milk

   Combs his hair with his toothbrush

3. There are several reasons why I put off studying.

   Too tired.

   Too hungry.

   Too disorganized.

4. My parents never allowed me to think for myself.

   Chose my friends for me

   Chose my clothes for me

   Chose my college for me

5. I have several ways in which I can earn extra cash.

   Baby-sitting

   Gardening

   Baking cookies

6. My car needs repairs.

New ignition
_____

New brakes
_____

New heater
_____

7. Friday evening, I didn't sit still for a minute.

Cat got sick
_____

Kids got sick
_____

Roof started to leak
_____

8. Mr. (or Ms. _____) was the worst teacher I ever had.

Slept at his desk
_____

Gave six hours of homework per night
_____

Had a filthy temper
_____

7 Identifying Adequate Supporting Evidence

Activity

The following body paragraphs were taken from student essays. Two of the paragraphs provide sufficient details to support their topic sentences convincingly. Write AD for *adequate development* beside those paragraphs. Three paragraphs use vague, wordy, general, or irrelevant sentences instead of real supporting details. Write U for *underdeveloped* beside those paragraphs.

___AD___   1.   Another consideration in adopting a dog is the cost. Initial fees for shots and a license might add up to $40. Annual visits to the vet for heartworm pills, rabies or distemper shots, and general checkups could cost $50 or more. Then there is the cost of food. A twenty-five-pound bag of dry food (the cheapest kind) costs around $10. A large dog can eat that much in a couple of weeks.

___U___   2.   People can be cruel to pets simply by being thoughtless. They don't think about a pet's needs, or they simply ignore those needs. It never occurs to them that their pet can be experiencing a great deal of discomfort as a result of their failure to be sensitive. The cruelty is a result of the basic lack of attention and concern—qualities that should be there, but aren't.

_____U_____ 3.   If I were in charge of the nighttime programming on a TV network, I would make changes. I would completely eliminate some shows. In fact, all the shows that proved to be of little interest would be canceled. Commercials would also change, so that it would be possible to watch them without wanting to turn off the TV set. I would expand the good shows so that people would come away with an even better experience. My ideal network would be a great improvement over the average lineup we see today on any of the major networks.

_____AD_____ 4.   A friend's rudeness is much more damaging that a stranger's. When a friend says sharply, "I don't have time to talk to you just now," you feel hurt instead of angry. When a friend shows up late for lunch or a shopping trip, with no good reason, you feel that you're being taken for granted. Worst, though, is when a friend pretends to be listening to you but his or her wandering eyes show a lack of attention. Then you feel betrayed. Friends, after all, are supposed to make up for the thoughtless cruelties of strangers.

_____U_____ 5.   Giving my first shampoo and set to a real person, after weeks of practicing on wigs, was a nerve-racking experience. The customer was a woman who acted very sure about what she came for. She tried to describe what she wanted, and I tried without much success to understand what she had in mind. Every time I did something, she seemed to be indicating in one way or another that it was not what she wanted. I got more and more nervous as I worked on her hair, and the nervousness showed. The worst part of the ordeal happened at the very end, when I added the final touches. Nothing, to this woman, had turned out right.

8 Adding Details to Complete an Essay

Activity

In the following essay, specific details are needed to back up the ideas in the supporting paragraphs. Using the spaces provided, add a sentence or two of clear, convincing details for each supporting idea. This activity will give you practice at supplying specific details and an initial feel for writing an essay.
Answers will vary.

Life Without Television

Introduction

When my family's only television set went to the repair shop the other day, my parents, my sister, and I thought we would have a terrible week. How could we get through the long evenings in such a quiet house? What would it be like without all the shows to keep us company? We soon realized, though, that living without television for a while was a stroke of good fortune. It became easy for each of us to enjoy some activities alone, to complete some postponed chores, and to spend rewarding time with each other and friends.

First supporting paragraph

First of all, with no television to compete for our time, we found plenty of hours for personal interests. We all read more that week than we had read during the six months before. _____

_____

_____

We each also enjoyed some hobbies we had ignored for ages. _____

_____

_____

_____

In addition, my sister and I both stopped procrastinating with our homework. _____

_____

_____

_____

Second supporting paragraph

Second, we did chores that had been hanging over our heads for too long. There were many jobs around the house that had needed attention for some time. _____

_____

_____

We also had a chance to do some long-postponed shopping. _____

_____

_____

And each of us also did some letter writing or other paperwork that was long overdue. _____

_____

_____

Third supporting paragraph

Finally, and probably most important, we spent time with each other. Instead of just being in the same room together while we stared at a screen, we actually talked for many pleasant hours. _____

_____

_____

Moreover, for the first time in years my family played some games together. _____

_____

_____

And because we didn't have to worry about missing this or that show, we had some family friends over on a couple of evenings and spent an enjoyable time with them. _____

_____

_____

Conclusion

> Once our television set returned, we were not prepared to put it in the attic. But we had a sense of how it can take over our lives if we are not careful. We are now more selective. We turn on the set for our favorite shows, certain sports events, and the news, but we don't leave it running all night. As a result, we find we can enjoy television and still have time left over for other activities and interests.

4 The Third Step in Essay Writing

> This chapter will show you how to
>
> - organize and connect specific evidence in the body paragraphs of an essay
> - begin and end an essay with effective introductory and concluding paragraphs

You know from Chapter 3 that the first two steps in writing an effective essay are advancing a thesis and supporting it with specific evidence. This chapter will deal with the third step. You'll learn the chief ways to organize and connect the supporting information in a paper. You'll then see how to start an essay with a suitable introductory paragraph and how to finish it with a well-rounded concluding paragraph.

Step 3: Organize and Connect the Specific Evidence

As you are generating the specific details needed to support a thesis, you should be thinking about ways to organize and connect those details. All the details in your essay must *cohere,* or stick together, so that your reader will be able to move smoothly and clearly from one bit of supporting information to the next. This section will show you how to organize and connect supporting details by the use of (1) common methods of organization, (2) transitions, and (3) other connecting words.

Common Methods of Organization

Two common methods used to organize the supporting material in an essay are time order and emphatic order. (You will learn more specific methods of development in Part Two of this book.)

Time, or *chronological, order* simply means that details are listed as they occur in time. *First* this is done; *next* this; *then* this; *after* that, this; and so on. Here is an outline of an essay in this book in which time order is used.

Thesis

To exercise successfully, you should follow a simple plan consisting of arranging the time, making preparations, and warming up properly.

1. To begin with, set aside a regular hour for exercise.

2. Next, prepare for your exercise session.

3. Finally, do a series of warm-up activities.

Fill in the missing word: The topic sentences in the essay use the words _____To begin with_____, _____Next_____, and _____Finally_____ to help show time order.

Here is one supporting paragraph from the essay:

Next, prepare for your exercise session. You do this, first, by not eating or drinking anything for an hour before the session. Why risk an upset stomach? Then, dress comfortably in something that allows you to move freely. Because you'll be in your own home, there's no need to invest in a high-fashion dance costume. A loose T-shirt and shorts are good. A bathing suit is great in summer, and in winter long underwear is warm and comfortable. If your hair tends to flop in your eyes, pin it back or wear a headband or scarf. After dressing, prepare the exercise area. Turn off the phone and lock the door to prevent interruptions. Shove the coffee table out of the way so you won't bruise yourself on it. Finally, get out the simple materials you'll need to exercise on.

Fill in the missing words: The paragraph uses the following words to help show time order: _____Next_____, _____First_____, _____Then_____, _____After_____, and _____Finally_____.

Emphatic order is sometimes described as "saving the best till last." It is a way to put *emphasis* on the most interesting or important detail by placing it in the last part of a paragraph or in the final supporting paragraph of an essay. (In cases where all the details seem equal in importance, the writer should impose a personal order that seems logical or appropriate.) The last position in a paper is the most emphatic position because the reader is most likely to remember the last thing read. *Finally, last of all,* and *most important* are typical words or phrases showing emphasis. Here is an outline of an essay in this book that uses emphatic order:

Thesis   Celebrities lead very stressful lives.

1. For one thing, celebrities don't have the privacy an ordinary person does.

2. In addition, celebrities are under constant pressure.

3. Most important, celebrities must deal with the stress of being in constant danger.

Fill in the missing words: The topic sentences in the essay use the words ___For one thing___, ___In addition___, and ___Most important___ to help show emphatic order.

Here is the third supporting paragraph from the essay:

> Most important, celebrities must deal with the stress of being in constant danger. The friendly grabs, hugs, and kisses of enthusiastic fans can quickly turn into uncontrolled assaults on a celebrity's hair, clothes, and car. Celebrities often get strange letters from people who become obsessed with their idols or from people who threaten to harm them. Worst of all, threats can turn into deeds. The attempt to kill Ronald Reagan and the murder of John Lennon came about because two unbalanced people tried to transfer the celebrity's fame to themselves. Famous people must live with the fact that they are always fair game—and never out of season.

Fill in the missing words: The words ___Worst of all___ are used to mark the most emphatic detail in the paragraph.

Some essays use a combination of time order and emphatic order. For example, the essay on moviegoing in Chapter 1 includes time order: the writer first describes getting to the theater, then the theater itself, and finally the behavior of patrons during the movie. At the same time, the writer uses emphatic order, ending with the most important reason for her dislike of moviegoing: "Some of the other patrons are even more of a problem than the theater itself."

Activity

Part A: Read the essays listed below and identify their method of organizing details—time order, emphatic order, or a combination of both.

1. "Adopting a Handicap" (page 195)
    <u>time order</u>

2. "A Vote for McDonald's (page 267)
    <u>emphatic order</u>

3. "Everyday Cruelty" (page 211)
    <u>combination</u>

Part B: Now see if you can complete the explanations that follow.

The essay titled "Adopting a Handicap" uses (*add the missing word*) <u>time</u> order. The author begins with the challenge of learning to sit properly in the wheelchair, then moves on to learning to move in the wheelchair, and ends with several problems that occurred next, during the church service. "A Vote for McDonald's" uses (*add the missing word*) <u>emphatic</u> order. The writer presents three advantages of eating at McDonald's and ends with the most important one: reasonable prices. "Everyday Cruelty" uses a combination of (*add the missing words*) <u>time</u> and <u>emphatic</u> order. It moves from the beginning to the end of a particular workday. It also ends with the "worst incident of mean-spiritedness" that the writer witnessed that day.

Transitions

Transitional Words

Transitions signal the direction of a writer's thought. They are like the road signs that guide travelers. In the box below are some common transitions, grouped according to the kind of signal they give to readers. Note that certain words provide more than one kind of signal.

Addition signals: one, first of all, second, the third reason, also, next, another, and, in addition, moreover, furthermore, finally, last of all

Time signals: first, then, next, after, as, before, while, meanwhile, soon, now, during, finally

Space signals: next to, across, on the opposite side, to the left, to the right, above, below, near, nearby

Change-of-direction signals: but, however, yet, in contrast, although, otherwise, still, on the contrary, on the other hand

Illustration signals: for example, for instance, specifically, as an illustration, once, such as

Conclusion signals: therefore, consequently, thus, then, as a result, in summary, to conclude, last of all, finally

Activity

1.   Underline the three *addition* signals in the following selection:

To create the time you need to pass difficult courses, find some easy courses. These are the ones that combine the least amount of work with the fewest tests and the most lenient professors. <u>One</u> way to find such classes is to ask friends and classmates about courses in which they received A's after attending only 25 percent of the classes. <u>Also</u>, inquire around to see which instructors lecture with the same notes every year and give the same tests. Photocopies of the class notes are usually cheap and widely available. <u>Another</u> great way of finding simple courses is to pick up a copy of the master schedule and study it carefully. Find the telltale course titles that signal an easy glide through a painless subject. Look for titles like "History of the Animated Cartoon," "Arts and Crafts for Beginners," and "Rock Music of the 1950s."

2.   Underline the four *time* signals in the following selection:

<u>After</u> you've snagged the job of TV sports reporter, you have to begin working on the details of your image. <u>First</u>, invest in two or three truly loud sports jackets. Look for gigantic plaid patterns in odd color combinations like purple and green or orange and blue. These should become familiar enough to viewers so that they will associate that crazy jacket with that dynamic sportscaster. <u>Next</u>, try to cultivate a distinctive voice that will be just annoying enough to be memorable. A nasal whine or a gravelly growl

will do it. Be sure to speak only in tough, punchy sentences that seem to be punctuated with imaginary exclamation points. <u>Finally,</u> you must share lots of pompous, obnoxious opinions with your viewers. Your tone of voice must convey the hidden message, "I dare anyone to disagree with me." If the home teams lose, call them bums. If players strike, talk sarcastically about the good old days. If a sports franchise leaves town, say, "Good riddance."

3.   Underline the three *space* signals in the following selection:

The vegetable bin of my refrigerator contained an assortment of weird-looking items. <u>Next</u> to a shriveled, white-coated lemon were two oranges covered with blue fuzz. <u>To the right</u> of the oranges was a bunch of carrots that had begun to sprout points, spikes, knobs, and tendrils. The carrots drooped into U shapes as I picked them up with the tips of my fingers. <u>Near</u> the carrots was a net bag of onions; each onion had sent curling shoots through the net until the whole thing resembled a mass of green spaghetti. The most horrible item, though, was a head of lettuce that had turned into a pool of brown goo. It had seeped out of its bag and coated the bin with a sticky, evil-smelling liquid.

4.   Underline the two *change-of-direction* signals in the following selection:

Taking small children on vacation, for instance, sounds like a wonderful experience for the entire family. <u>But</u> vacations can be scary or emotionally overwhelming times for children. When children are taken away from their usual routine and brought to an unfamiliar place, they can become very frightened. That strange bed in the motel room or the unusual noises in Grandma's spare bedroom may cause nightmares. On vacations, too, children usually clamor to do as many things in one day as they can and to stay up past their usual bedtime. And, since it is vacation time, parents may decide to give in to the children's demands. A parental attitude like this, <u>however,</u> can lead to problems. After a sixteen-hour day of touring the amusement park, eating in a restaurant, and seeing a movie, children can experience sensory and emotional overload. They become cranky, unhappy, or even rebellious and angry.

5.   Underline the two *illustration* signals in the following selection:

Supermarkets also use psychology to encourage you to buy. <u>For example,</u> in most supermarkets, the milk and the bread are either at opposite ends of the store or located far away from the first aisle. Even if you've stopped at the market only for staples like these, you must pass hundreds of items in order to reach them. The odds are that instead of leaving with just a quart of milk, you'll leave with additional purchases as well. Special displays, <u>such as</u> a pyramid of canned green beans in an aisle and a large end display of cartons of paper towels, also increase sales. Because you assume that these items are a good buy, you may pick them up. However, they may not even be on sale! Store managers know that the customer is automatically attracted to a display like this, and they will use it to move an overstocked product.

6. Underline the two *conclusion* signals in the following selection:

<u>Finally</u>, my grandmother was extremely thrifty. She was one of those people who hoard pieces of used aluminum foil after carefully scraping off the cake icing or beef gravy. She had a drawer full of old eyeglasses that dated back at least thirty years. The lens prescriptions were no longer accurate, but Gran couldn't bear to throw away "a good pair of glasses." She kept them "just in case," but we could never figure out what situation would involve a desperate need for a dozen pairs of old eyeglasses. We never realized the true extent of Gran's thriftiness, though, until after she died. Her house was to be sold, and <u>therefore</u> we cleaned out its dusty attic. In one corner was a cardboard box filled with two- and three-inch pieces of string. The box was labeled, in Gran's spidery hand, "String too short to be saved."

Transitional Sentences

Transitional, or *linking, sentences* are used between paragraphs to help tie together the supporting paragraphs in an essay. They enable the reader to move smoothly and clearly from the idea in one paragraph to the idea in the next paragraph.

Here is the linking sentence used in the essay on moviegoing:

Many of the other patrons are even more of a problem than the concession stand.

The words *concession stand* remind us of the point of the first supporting paragraph, while *Many of the other patrons* presents the point to be developed in the second supporting paragraph.

Activity

Below is a brief sentence outline of an essay. The second and third topic sentences serve as transitional, or linking, sentences. Each reminds us of the point in the preceding paragraph and announces the point to be developed in the current paragraph. In the spaces provided, add the words needed to complete the second and third topic sentences.

Thesis

The most helpful values I learned from my parents are the importance of family support, of hard work, and of a good education.

First supporting paragraph

First, my parents taught me that family members should stick together, especially in time of trouble. . . .

Second supporting paragraph

In addition to teaching me about the importance of _family support_ _____,

my parents taught me the value of _____ hard work _____

_____ . . . .

Third supporting paragraph

Along with the value of _____ hard work _____,

my parents emphasized the benefits of _____ a good education _____

_____ . . . .

Other Connecting Words

In addition to transitions, there are three other kinds of connecting words that help tie together the specific evidence in a paper: *repeated words, pronouns,* and *synonyms.* Each will be discussed in turn.

Repeated Words

Many of us have been taught—correctly—not to repeat ourselves in writing. However, repeating *key* words helps tie together the flow of thought in a paper. Below, repeated words remind readers of the selection's central idea.

> One reason for studying <u>psychology</u> is to help you deal with your children. Perhaps your young daughter refuses to go to bed when you want her to and bursts into tears at the least mention of "lights out." A little knowledge of <u>psychology</u> comes in handy. Offer her a choice of staying up until 7:30 with you or going upstairs and playing until 8:00. Since she gets to make the choice, she does not feel so powerless and will not resist. <u>Psychology</u> is also useful in rewarding a child for a job well done. Instead of telling your ten-year-old son what a good boy he is when he makes his own bed, tell him how neat it looks, how happy you are to see it, and how proud of him you are for doing it by himself. The <u>psychology</u> books will tell you that being a good boy is much harder to live up to than doing one job well.

Pronouns

Pronouns (*he, she, it, you, they, this, that,* and others) are another way to connect ideas. Also, using pronouns in place of other words can help you avoid needless repetition. (Note, however, that pronouns should be used with care to avoid the problems described on pages 460–462.) Here is a selection that makes good use of pronouns:

> Another way for people to economize at an amusement park is to bring <u>their</u> own food. If <u>they</u> pack a nourishing, well-balanced lunch of cold chicken, carrot sticks, and fruit, <u>they</u> will avoid having to pay high prices for hamburgers and hot dogs. <u>They</u> will also save on calories. Also, instead of filling up on soft drinks, <u>they</u> should bring a thermos of iced tea. Iced tea is more refreshing than soda, and <u>it</u> is a great deal cheaper. Every dollar that is not spent at a refreshment stand is <u>one</u> that can be spent on another ride.

Synonyms

Synonyms are words alike in meaning. Using synonyms can also help move the reader easily from one thought to the next. In addition, the use of synonyms increases variety and interest by avoiding needless repetition.

Note the synonyms for *method* in the following selection:

There are several methods of fund-raising that work well with small organizations. One technique is to hold an auction, with everyone either contributing an item from home or obtaining a donation from a sympathetic local merchant. Because all the merchandise and the services of the auctioneer have been donated, the entire proceeds can be placed in the organization's treasury. A second fund-raising procedure is a car wash. Club members and their children get together on a Saturday and wash all the cars in the neighborhood for a few dollars apiece. A final, time-tested way to raise money is to hold a bake sale, with each family contributing homemade cookies, brownies, layer cakes, or cupcakes. Sold by the piece or by the box, these baked goods will satisfyingly fill both the stomach and the pocketbook.

Activity

Read the selection below and then answer the questions about it that follow:

[1]When I think about my childhood in the 1930s, life today seems like the greatest of luxuries. [2]In our house, we had only a wood-burning cookstove in the kitchen to keep us warm. [3]In the morning, my father would get up in the icy cold, go downstairs, and light a fire in the black iron range. [4]When he called us, I would put off leaving my warm bed until the last possible minute and then quickly grab my school clothes. [5]The water pitcher and washing basin in my room would be layered with ice, and my breath would come out as white puffs as I ran downstairs. [6]My sisters and I would all dress—as quickly as possible—in the chilly but bearable air of the kitchen. [7]Our schoolroom, once we had arrived, didn't provide much relief from the cold. [8]Students wore woolen mitts which left their fingers free but covered their palms and wrists. [9]Even with these, we occasionally suffered chilblains. [10]The throbbing swellings on our hands made writing a painful process. [11]When we returned home in the afternoon, we spent all our indoor hours in the warm kitchen. [12]We hated to leave it at bedtime in order to make the return trip to those cold bedrooms and frigid sheets. [13]My mother made up hot-water bottles and gave us hot bricks to tuck under the covers, but nothing could eliminate the agony of that penetrating cold when we first slid under the bedclothes.

1. How many times is the key word *cold* used? _____4_____

2. Write here the pronoun that is used for *father* (sentence 4): _____he_____

3. Write here the words in sentence 3 that are used as a synonym for *cookstove:* _____iron range_____; write in the words in sentence 10 that are used as a synonym for *chilblains:* __throbbing swellings__; write in the word in sentence 12 that is used as a synonym for *cold:* _____frigid_____.

Introductions, Conclusions, and Titles

So far, this chapter has discussed ways to organize and connect the supporting paragraphs of an essay. A well-organized essay, however, also needs a strong introductory paragraph, an effective concluding paragraph, and a good title.

Introductory Paragraph

Functions of the Introduction

A well-written introductory paragraph performs several important roles:

1 It attracts the reader's interest, encouraging him or her to continue reading the essay.

2 It supplies any background information that may be needed to understand the essay.

3 It presents a thesis statement. This clear, direct statement of the main idea of the paper usually appears near the end of the introductory paragraph.

4 It indicates a plan of development. In this "preview," the major supporting points for the thesis are listed in the order in which they will be presented. In some cases, the thesis and plan of development appear in the same sentence. However, writers sometimes choose not to describe the plan of development.

Common Methods of Introduction

Here are some common methods of introduction. Use any one method, or a combination of methods, to introduce your subject in an interesting way to the reader.

1 *Begin with a broad, general statement of your topic and narrow it down to your thesis statement.* Broad, general statements ease the reader into your thesis statement by first introducing the topic. In the example below, the writer talks generally about diets and then narrows down to comments on a specific diet.

> Bookstore shelves today are crammed with dozens of different diet books. The American public seems willing to try any sort of diet, especially the ones that promise instant, miraculous results. And authors are more than willing to invent new fad diets to cash in on this craze. Unfortunately, some of these fad diets are ineffective or even unsafe. One of the worst fad diets is the "Palm Beach" plan. It is impractical, doesn't achieve the results it claims, and is a sure route to poor nutrition.

2 *Start with an idea or situation that is the opposite of the one you will develop.* This approach works because your readers will be surprised, and then intrigued, by the contrast between the opening idea and the thesis that follows it.

> When I decided to return to school at age thirty-five, I wasn't at all worried about my ability to do the work. After all, I was a grown woman who had raised a family, not a confused teenager fresh out of high school. But when I started classes, I realized that those "confused teenagers" sitting around me were in much better shape for college than I was. They still had all their classroom skills in bright, shiny condition, while mine had grown rusty from disuse. I had to learn how to locate information in a library, how to write a report, and even how to speak up in class discussions.

3 *Explain the importance of your topic to the reader.* If you can convince your readers that the subject in some way applies to them, or is something they should know more about, they will want to keep reading.

> Diseases like scarlet fever and whooping cough used to kill more young children than any other cause. Today, however, child mortality due to disease has been almost completely eliminated by medical science. Instead, car accidents are the number one killer of our children. And most of the children fatally injured in car accidents were not protected by car seats, belts, or restraints of any kind. Several steps must be taken to reduce the serious dangers car accidents pose to our children.

4 *Use an incident or brief story.* Stories are naturally interesting. They appeal to a reader's curiosity. In your introduction, an anecdote will grab the reader's attention right away. The story should be brief and should be related to your main idea. The incident in the story can be something that happened to you, something you have heard about, or something you have read about in a newspaper or magazine.

> Early Sunday morning the young mother dressed her little girl warmly and gave her a candy bar, a picture book, and a well-worn stuffed rabbit. Together, they drove downtown to a Methodist church. There the mother told the little girl to wait on the stone steps until children began arriving for Sunday school. Then the young mother drove off, abandoning her five-year-old because she couldn't cope with being a parent anymore. This incident is one of thousands of cases of child neglect and abuse that occur annually. Perhaps the automatic right to become a parent should no longer exist. Would-be parents should be forced to apply for parental licenses for which they would have to meet three important conditions.

5 *Ask one or more questions.* You may simply want the reader to think about possible answers, or you may plan to answer the questions yourself later in the paper.

> What is love? How do we know that we are really in love? When we meet that special person, how can we tell that our feelings are genuine and not merely infatuation? And, if they are genuine, will these feelings last? Love, as we all know, is difficult to define. But most people agree that true and lasting love involves far more than mere physical attraction. Love involves mutual respect, the desire to give rather than take, and the feeling of being wholly at ease.

6 *Use a quotation.* A quotation can be something you have read in a book or article. It can also be something that you have heard: a popular saying or proverb ("Never give advice to a friend"), a current or recent advertising slogan ("Reach out and touch someone"), or a favorite expression used by friends or family ("My father always says . . ."). Using a quotation in your introductory paragraph lets you add someone else's voice to your own.

> "Fish and visitors," wrote Benjamin Franklin, "begin to smell after three days." Last summer, when my sister and her family came to spend their two-week vacation with us, I became convinced that Franklin was right. After only three days of my family's visit, I was thoroughly sick of my brother-in-law's corny jokes, my sister's endless complaints about her boss, and their children's constant invasions of our privacy.

Activity

The box below summarizes the six kinds of introduction. Read the introductions that follow it and, in the space provided, write the letter of the kind of introduction used in each case.

A. General to narrow	D. Incident or story
B. Starting with an opposite	E. Questions
C. Stating importance of topic	F. Quotation

_____ B _____   1.   The ad, in full color on a glossy magazine page, shows a beautiful kitchen with gleaming counters. In the foreground, on one of the counters, stands a shiny new food processor. Usually, a feminine hand is touching it lovingly. Around the main picture are other, smaller shots. They show mounds of perfectly sliced onion rings, thin rounds of juicy tomatoes, heaps of matchstick-sized potatoes, and piles of golden, evenly grated cheese. The ad copy tells you how wonderful, how easy, food preparation will be with a processor. Don't believe it. My processor turned out to be expensive, difficult to operate, and very limited in its use.

_____ F _____   2.   My father stubbornly says, "You *can* often tell a book by its cover," and when it comes to certain paperbacks, he's right. When you're browsing in the drugstore or supermarket and you see a paperback featuring an attractive young woman in a low-cut dress fleeing from a handsome dark figure in a shadowy castle, you know exactly what you're getting. Every romance novel has the same elements: an innocent heroine, an exotic setting, and a cruel but fascinating hero.

_____ A _____   3.   We Americans are incredibly lazy. Instead of cooking a simple, nourishing meal, we pop a frozen dinner into the oven. Instead of studying a daily newspaper, we are contented with the capsule summaries on the network news. Worst of all, instead of walking even a few blocks to the local convenience store, we jump into our cars. This dependence on the automobile, even for short trips, has robbed us of a valuable experience— walking. If we drove less and walked more, we would save money, become healthier, and discover fascinating things about our surroundings.

Concluding Paragraph

A concluding paragraph is your chance to remind the reader of your thesis idea and bring the paper to a natural and graceful end.

Common Methods of Conclusion

Any one of the methods below, or a combination of methods, may be used to round off your paper.

1 *End with a summary and final thought.* When army instructors train new recruits, each of their lessons follows a three-step formula:

  a Tell them what you're going to tell them.

  b Tell them.

  c Tell them what you've told them.

An essay that ends with a summary is not very different. After you have stated your thesis ("Tell them what you're going to tell them") and supported it ("Tell them"), you restate the thesis and supporting points ("Tell them what you've told them"). However, don't use the exact wording you used before. Here is a summary conclusion:

> Catalog shopping at home, then, has several advantages. Such shopping is convenient, saves you money, and saves you time. It is not surprising that growing numbers of devoted catalog shoppers are welcoming those full-color mail brochures that offer everything from turnip seeds to televisions.

Note that the summary is accompanied by a final comment that "rounds off" the paper and brings the discussion to a close. This combination of a summary and a final thought is the most common method of concluding an essay.

2 *Include a thought-provoking question or short series of questions.* A question grabs the reader's attention. It is a direct appeal to your reader to think further about what you have written. A question should follow logically from the points you have already made in the paper. A question must deal with one of these areas:

a Why the subject of your paper is important

b What might happen in the future

c What should be done about this subject

d Which choice should be made

In your conclusion, you may provide an answer to your question. Be sure, though, that the question is closely related to your thesis. Here is an example:

> What, then, will happen in the twenty-first century when most of the population will be over sixty years old? Retirement policies could change dramatically, with the age-sixty-five testimonial dinner and gold watch postponed for five or ten years. Even television would change as the Metamucil generation replaces the Pepsi generation. Glamorous gray-haired models would sell everything from toilet paper to televisions. New soap operas and situation comedies would reveal the secrets of the "sunset years." It will be a different world indeed when the young find themselves outnumbered.

3 *End with a prediction or recommendation.* Like questions, predictions and recommendations also involve your readers. A prediction states what may happen in the future:

If people stopped to think before acquiring pets, there would be fewer instances of cruelty to animals. Many times, it is the people who adopt pets without considering the expense and responsibility involved who mistreat and neglect their animals. Pets are living creatures. They do not deserve to be treated as carelessly as one would treat a stuffed toy.

A recommendation suggests what should be done about a situation or problem:

Stereotypes such as the helpless homemaker, harried executive, and dotty grandparent are insulting enough to begin with. In magazine ads or television commercials, they become even more insulting. Now these unfortunate characters are not just being laughed at; they are being turned into hucksters to sell products to an unsuspecting public. Consumers should boycott companies whose advertising continues to use such stereotypes.

Activity

In the space provided, note whether each concluding paragraph ends with a summary and final thought (write S in the space), ends with a prediction or recommendation (write P/R), or ends with a question (write Q).

_P/R_   1. Disappointments are unwelcome, but regular, visitors in everyone's life. We can feel depressed about them, or we can try to escape from them. The best thing, though, is to accept a disappointment and then try to use it somehow: step over the unwelcome visitor and then get on with life.

_Q_   2. Holidays, it is clear, are often not the fulfilling experience they are supposed to be. They can, in fact, be very stressful. But would we rather have a holiday-free calendar?

_S_   3. Some people dream of starring roles, their names in lights, and their pictures on the cover of People magazine. I'm not one of them, though. A famous person gives up private life, feels pressured all the time, and is never completely safe. So let someone else have that cover story. I'd rather lead an ordinary, but calm, life than a stress-filled one.

Titles

A title is usually a very brief summary of what your paper is about. It is often no more than several words. You may find it easier to write the title *after* you have completed your paper.

Following are the introductory paragraphs for two of the essays in this text, along with the titles of the essays.

Introductory
Paragraph

I'm not just a consumer—I'm a victim. If I order a product, it is sure to arrive in the wrong color, size, or quantity. If I hire people to do repairs, they never arrive on the day scheduled. If I owe a bill, the computer is bound to overcharge me. Therefore, in self-defense, I have developed the following consumer's guide to complaining effectively.

Title: How to Complain

Introductory
Paragraph

Schools divide people into categories. From first grade on up, students are labeled "advanced" or "deprived" or "remedial" or "antisocial." Students pigeonhole their fellow students, too. We've all known the "brain," the "jock," the "dummy," and the "teacher's pet." In most cases, these narrow labels are misleading and inaccurate. But there is one label for a certain type of college student that says it all: "zombie."

Title: Student Zombies

Note that you should not underline the title. Nor should you put quotation marks around it. On the other hand, you should capitalize all but small connecting words in the title. Also, you should skip a space between the title and the first line of the text. (See "Manuscript Form," page 485.)

Activity

Write an appropriate title for each of the introductory paragraphs that follow. Answers may vary.

1. For my birthday this month, my wife has offered to treat me to dinner at the restaurant of my choice. I think she expects me to ask for a meal at the Chalet, the classiest, most expensive restaurant in town. However, I'm going to eat my birthday dinner at McDonald's. When I compare the two restaurants, the advantages of eating at McDonald's are clear.

   Title: Advantages of McDonald's

2. I've been in lots of diners, and they've always seemed to be warm, busy, friendly, happy places. That's why, on a recent Monday night, I stopped at a diner for a cup of coffee. I was returning home after an all-day car trip and needed something to help me make the last forty-five miles. A diner at midnight, however, was not the place I had expected. It was different—and lonely.

   Title: A Lonely Diner

3. If you see rock-concert audiences only on television or in newspaper photos, the people at these events may all seem to be excited teenagers. However, if you attended a few rock shows, you would see that several kinds of people make up the crowd. At any concert, you would find the typical fan, the out-of-place person, and the troublemaker.

Title: <u>Audiences at Rock Concerts</u>

Practice in Organizing and Connecting Specific Evidence

You now know the third step in effective writing: organizing the specific evidence used to support the thesis of a paper. This closing section will expand and strengthen your understanding of the third step in writing. You will work through the following series of activities:

1 Organizing through time or emphatic order
2 Providing transitions
3 Identifying transitions and other connecting words
4 Completing transitional sentences
5 Identifying introductions and conclusions

1 Organizing Through Time or Emphatic Order

Activity 1

Use time order to organize the scrambled lists of supporting ideas below. Write 1 beside the supporting idea that should come first in time, 2 beside the idea that logically follows, and 3 beside the idea that comes last in time.

1. Thesis: When I was a child, Disney movies frightened me more than any other kind.

    _1_ As a five-year-old, I was terrified by the movie *Pinocchio,* about a puppet transformed into a boy.

    _3_ Although I saw *Bambi* when I was old enough to begin poking fun at "baby movies," the scene during which Bambi's mother is killed has stayed with me to this day.

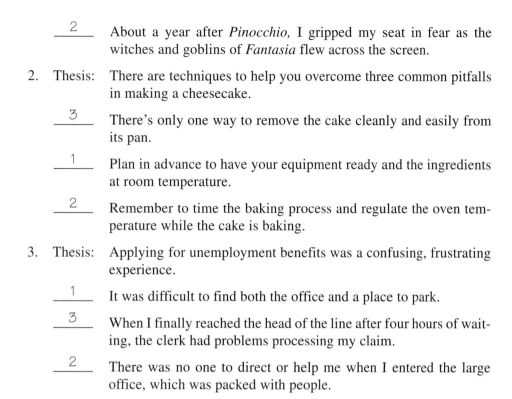

__2__ About a year after *Pinocchio,* I gripped my seat in fear as the witches and goblins of *Fantasia* flew across the screen.

2. Thesis: There are techniques to help you overcome three common pitfalls in making a cheesecake.

__3__ There's only one way to remove the cake cleanly and easily from its pan.

__1__ Plan in advance to have your equipment ready and the ingredients at room temperature.

__2__ Remember to time the baking process and regulate the oven temperature while the cake is baking.

3. Thesis: Applying for unemployment benefits was a confusing, frustrating experience.

__1__ It was difficult to find both the office and a place to park.

__3__ When I finally reached the head of the line after four hours of waiting, the clerk had problems processing my claim.

__2__ There was no one to direct or help me when I entered the large office, which was packed with people.

Activity 2

Use emphatic order (order of importance) to arrange the following scrambled lists of supporting ideas. For each thesis, write 1 in the blank beside the point that is perhaps less important or interesting than the other two, 2 beside the point that appears more important or interesting, and 3 beside the point that should be most emphasized.

1. Thesis: My after-school job has been an invaluable part of my life this year.

__2__ Better yet, it has taught me how to get along with many kinds of people.

__1__ Since it's in the morning, it usually keeps me from staying up too late.

__3__ Without it, I would have had to drop out of school.

2. Thesis: We received some odd gifts for our wedding.

__3__ The winner in the odd-gift category was a large wooden box with no apparent purpose or function.

    __1__   Someone gave us a gift certificate for a massage.

    __2__   Even stranger, my uncle gave me his favorite bowling ball.

3. Thesis: Donna is my most loyal friend.

    __2__   She has taken time to do special favors for me.

    __3__   She's always there in real emergencies or emotional crises.

    __1__   She once lent me her favorite necklace to wear on a date.

2 Providing Transitions

Activity

In the spaces provided, add appropriate transitions to tie together the sentences and ideas in the following essay. Draw from the words given in the boxes above the paragraphs. Use each word only once.

Annoying People

    President Richard Nixon used to keep an "enemies list" of all the people he didn't especially like. I'm ashamed to confess it, but I, too, have an enemies list—a mental one. On this list are all the people I would gladly live without, the ones who cause my blood pressure to rise to the boiling point. The top three places on the list go to people with annoying nervous habits, people who talk in movie theaters, and people who talk on car phones while driving.

For example	First of all	Another	However

    ___First of all___, there are the people with annoying nervous habits. ___For example___, there are the ones who make faces. When in deep thought, they twitch, squint, and frown, and they can be a real distraction when I'm trying to concentrate during an exam. ___Another___ type of nervous character makes useless designs. These people bend paper clips into abstract sculptures or string the clips into necklaces as they talk. ___However___, neither of these groups is as bad as the people who make noises. These individuals, when they are feeling uncomfortable, bite their fingernails or crack their knuckles. If they have a pencil in their hands, they tap it rhythmically against whatever surface is handy—a desk, a book, a head. Lacking a pencil to play with, they jingle the loose change or keys in their pockets. These people make me wish I were hard of hearing.

On the contrary	Then	As a result	After	second

A _____second_____ category of people I would gladly do away with is the ones who talk in movie theaters. These people are not content to sit back, relax, and enjoy the film they have paid to see. _____On the contrary_____, they feel compelled to comment loudly on everything from the hero's hairstyle to the appropriateness of the background music. _____As a result_____, no one hears a word of any dialog except theirs. _____After_____ they have been in the theater for a while, their interest in the movie may fade. _____Then_____ they will start discussing other things, and the people around them will be treated to an instant replay of the latest family scandal or soap opera episode. These stories may be entertaining, but they don't belong in a movie theater.

In addition	But	Last of all

_____Last of all_____, there are the people who talk on the phone while they're driving. One of the things that irritate me about them is the way they seem to be showing off. They're saying, "Look at me! I'm so important I have to make phone calls in my *car.*" _____In addition_____, such behavior is just plain dangerous. Instead of concentrating on adjusting carefully to ever-changing traffic conditions, they're weaving all over the road or getting much too close to the car in front of them as they gossip with a friend, make an appointment with a doctor, or order a pizza.

So long as murder remains illegal, the nervous twitchers, movie talkers, and car-phone users of the world are safe from me. _____But_____ if ever I am granted the power of life or death, these people had better think twice about annoying me. They might not have long to live.

3 Identifying Transitions and Other Connecting Words

Activity

The following items use connecting words to help tie ideas together. The connecting words you are to identify are set off in italics. In the space, write T for *transition*, RW for *repeated word*, S for *synonym*, or P for *pronoun*.

___S___   1.   Kate wears a puffy, quilted, down-filled jacket. In this *garment*, she resembles a stack of inflated inner tubes.

___P___   2.   Plants like poinsettias and mistletoe are pretty. *They* are also poisonous.

___T___   3.   A strip of strong cloth can be used as an emergency fan-belt replacement. *In addition*, a roll of duct tape can be used to patch a leaky hose temporarily.

___S___   4.   Newspapers may someday be brought to your home, not by paper carriers, but by computers. Subscribers will simply punch in a code, and the *machines* will display the desired pages.

___P___   5.   I'm always losing my soft contact lenses, which resemble little circles of thick Saran Wrap. One day I dropped both of *them* into a cup of hot tea.

___RW___   6.   The molded plastic chairs in the classrooms are hard and uncomfortable. When I sit in one of these *chairs*, I feel as if I were sitting in a bucket.

___P___   7.   One way to tell if your skin is aging is to pinch a fold of skin on the back of your hand. If *it* doesn't smooth out quickly, your skin is losing its youthful tone.

___P___   8.   I never eat sloppy joes. *They* look as if they've already been eaten.

___T___   9.   Clothing intended just for children seems to have vanished. *Instead*, children wear scaled-down versions of everything adults wear.

___RW___   10.   Some successful salespeople use voice tones and hand gestures that are almost hypnotic. Customers are not conscious of this *hypnotic* effect but merely feel an urge to buy.

___S___   11.   The giant cockroaches in Florida are the subject of local legends. A visitor, according to one tale, saw one of the *insects*, thought it was a Volkswagen, and tried to drive it away.

___T___ 12. Some thieves scour garbage cans for credit-card receipts. *Then* they use the owner's name and card number to order merchandise by phone.

___P___ 13. When the phone rang, I dropped the garden hose. *It* whipped around crazily and squirted water through the kitchen screen door.

___RW___ 14. There are many phobias other than the ones described in psychology textbooks. I have *phobias,* for instance, about toasters and lawn mowers.

___T___ 15. My mother believes that food is love. *Therefore,* when she offers homemade cookies or cupcakes, I hate to hurt her feelings by refusing them.

4 Completing Transitional Sentences

Activity

Following are brief sentence outlines from two essays. In each outline, the second and third topic sentences serve as transitional, or linking, sentences. Each reminds us of the point in the preceding paragraph and announces the point to be developed in the current paragraph. In the spaces provided, add the words needed to complete the second and third topic sentences.

Thesis 1

In order to set up a day-care center in your home, you must make sure your house will conform to state regulations, obtain the necessary legal permits, and advertise your service in the right places.

First supporting paragraph

First of all, as a potential operator of a home day-care center, you must make sure your house will conform to state regulations. . . .

Second supporting paragraph

After making certain that ___your house conforms to regulations___

_____

you must obtain ___legal permits___ . . . .

Third supporting paragraph	Finally, once you have the necessary _____*legal permits*_____ you can begin to _____*advertise*_____.

Thesis 2	Cheaper cost, greater comfort, and superior electronic technology make watching football at home more enjoyable than attending a game at the stadium.

First supporting paragraph	For one thing, watching the game on TV eliminates the cost of attending the game. . . .

Second supporting paragraph	In addition to saving me money, watching the game at home is more _____*comfortable*_____ than sitting in a stadium. . . .

Third supporting paragraph	Even more important than _____*cost*_____ and _____*comfort*_____, though, is the _____*technology*_____ which makes a televised game better than the "real thing." . . .

5 Identifying Introductions and Conclusions

Activity

The box on the next page lists six common kinds of introductions and three common kinds of conclusions. Read the three pairs of introductory and concluding paragraphs that follow. Then, in the space provided, write the letter of the kind of introduction and conclusion used in each case.

> ### Introductions
> A. General to narrow
> B. Starting with an opposite
> C. Stating importance of topic
> D. Incident or story
> E. Question(s)
> F. Quotation
>
> ### Conclusions
> G. Summary and final thought
> H. Question(s)
> I. Prediction or recommendation

Pair 1

_____D_____

Shortly before Easter, our local elementary school sponsored a fund-raising event at which classroom pets and their babies—hamsters, guinea pigs, and baby chicks—were available for adoption. Afterward, as I was driving home, I saw a hand drop a baby hamster out of the car ahead of me. I couldn't avoid running over the tiny creature. One of the parents had taken the pet, regretted the decision, and decided to get rid of it. Such people have never stopped to consider the several real obligations involved in owning a pet.

_____I_____

A pet cannot be thrown onto a trash heap when it is no longer wanted or tossed into a closet if it begins to bore its owner. A pet, like us, is a living thing that needs attention and care. Would-be owners, therefore, should think seriously about their responsibilities before they acquire a pet.

Pair 2

_____E_____

What would life be like if we could read each other's minds? Would communications be instantaneous and perfectly clear? These questions will never be answered unless mental telepathy becomes a fact of life. Until then, we will have to make do with less perfect means of communication. Letters, telephone calls, and e-mail messages do have serious drawbacks.

_____G_____

Neither letters, phone calls, nor e-mails guarantee perfect communication. With all our sophisticated skills, we human beings often communicate less effectively than howling wolves or chattering monkeys. We always seem to find some way to foul up the message.

Pair 3

_____F_____   "Few things are harder to put up with," said Mark Twain, "than the annoyance of a good example." Twain obviously knew the problems faced by siblings cursed with older brothers or sisters who are models of perfection. All our lives, my older sister Shelley and I have been compared. Unfortunately, in competition with my sister's virtues, my looks, talents, and accomplishments always ended up on the losing side.

_____G_____   Although I always lost in the sibling contests of looks, talents, and accomplishments, Shelley and I have somehow managed not to turn into deadly enemies. Feeling like the Edsel of the family, in fact, helped me to develop a drive to succeed and a sense of humor. In our sibling rivalry, we both managed to win.

5 The Fourth Step in Essay Writing

This chapter will show you how to

- revise so that your sentences flow smoothly and clearly
- edit so that your sentences are error-free

Up to now this book has emphasized the first three goals in effective writing: unity, support, and coherence. This chapter will focus on the fourth goal of writing effectively: sentence skills. You'll learn how to revise an essay so that your sentences flow smoothly and clearly. Then you'll review how to edit a paper for mistakes in grammar, punctuation, and spelling.

Revising Sentences

The following strategies will help you to revise your sentences effectively.

- Use parallelism.
- Use a consistent point of view.
- Use specific words.
- Use active verbs.
- Use concise words.
- Vary your sentences.

Use Parallelism

Words in a pair or a series should have parallel structure. By balancing the items in a pair or a series so that they have the same kind of structure, you will make the sentence clearer and easier to read. Notice how the parallel sentences that follow read more smoothly than the nonparallel ones.

Nonparallel (Not Balanced)	Parallel (Balanced)
My job includes checking the inventory, initiating the orders, and *to call* the suppliers.	My job includes checking the inventory, initiating the orders, and calling the suppliers. (A balanced series of *-ing* words: *checking, initiating, calling*)
The game-show contestant was told to be cheerful, charming, and *with enthusiasm.*	The game-show contestant was told to be cheerful, charming, and enthusiastic. (A balanced series of descriptive words: *cheerful, charming, enthusiastic*)
Grandmother likes to read mystery novels, to do needlepoint, and *browsing* the Internet on her home computer.	Grandmother likes to read mystery novels, to do needlepoint, and to browse the Internet on her home computer. (A balanced series of *to* verbs: *to read, to do, to browse*)
We painted the trim in the living room; *the wallpaper was put up by a professional.*	We painted the trim in the living room; a professional put up the wallpaper. (Balanced verbs and word order: *We painted . . . ; a professional put up . . .*)

Balanced sentences are not a skill you need worry about when writing first drafts. But when you rewrite, you should try to put matching words and ideas into matching structures. Such parallelism will improve your writing style.

Activity

Cross out and revise the unbalanced part of each of the following sentences.

Example   Chocolate makes me gain weight, lose my appetite, and ~~breaking~~ out in hives.   *break*

1. The novelty store sells hand buzzers, plastic fangs, and insects ~~that are fake~~.   *fake*

2. Many people share the same three great fears: being in high places, working with numbers, and ^speeches.   *making*

3. To decide on a career, students should think closely about their interests, hobbies, and ~~what they are skilled at~~.   *skills*

4. At the body shop, the car was sanded down to the bare metal, painted with
sprayed with
primer, and red enamel. ~~was sprayed on.~~

5. In order to become a dancer, Lola is taking lessons, working in amateur
auditioning
shows, and ~~auditioned~~ for professional companies.

6. Juan's last job offered security; a better chance for advancement. *his new job offers* ~~is offered~~
~~by his new job.~~

7. People in today's world often try to avoid silence, whether on the job, in
school, or ~~when relaxing~~ at home.

8. Because the dying woman was dignified and ~~with courage,~~ *courageous* she won
everyone's respect.

9. The politician trusted no one, rewarded loyalty, and ~~was dependent~~ *depended* only on
his own instincts.

10. If we're not careful, we'll leave the next generation polluted air, contaminated
dying
water, and forests. ~~that are dying.~~

Use a Consistent Point of View

Consistency with Verbs

Do not shift verb tenses unnecessarily. If you begin writing a paper in the present tense, do not shift suddenly to the past. If you begin in the past, do not shift without reason to the present. Notice the inconsistent verb tenses in the following example:

Jean *punched* down the risen yeast dough in the bowl. Then she *dumps* it onto the floured worktable and *kneaded* it into a smooth, shiny ball.

The verbs must be consistently in the present tense:

Jean *punches* down the risen yeast dough in the bowl. Then she *dumps* it onto the floured worktable and *kneads* it into a smooth, shiny ball.

Or the verbs must be consistently in the past tense:

> Jean *punched* down the risen yeast dough in the bowl. Then she *dumped* it onto the floured worktable and *kneaded* it into a smooth, shiny ball.

Activity

Make the verbs in each sentence consistent with the *first* verb used. Cross out the incorrect verb and write the correct form in the space at the left.

ran   Example   Aunt Helen tried to kiss her little nephew, but he ~~runs~~ out of the room.

arrived   1. An aggressive news photographer knocked a reporter to the ground as the movie stars ~~arrive~~ for the Academy Awards.

asked   2. The winning wheelchair racer in the marathon slumped back in exhaustion and ~~asks~~ for some ice to soothe his blistered hands.

slices   3. On the TV commercial for mail-order kitchen knives, an actor cuts a tree branch in half and ~~sliced~~ an aluminum can into ribbons.

goes   4. "My husband is so dumb," said Martha, "that when he ~~went~~ to Las Vegas, he tries to play the stamp machines."

tipped   5. The jeep swerved around the corner, went up on two wheels, and ~~tips~~ over on its side.

floats   6. In a zero-gravity atmosphere, water breaks up into droplets and ~~floated~~ around in space.

grabbed   7. Ralph ripped open the bag of cheese puffs with his teeth, ~~grabs~~ handfuls of the salty orange squiggles, and stuffed them into his mouth.

swoops   8. From his perch high up on the rocky cliff, the eagle spots a white-tailed rabbit and ~~swooped~~ down toward his victim.

recharge   9. Several times a year, I like to take a day off, go away by myself, and ~~recharged~~ my mental batteries.

burned   10. When the great earthquake struck San Francisco in 1906, the entire city ~~burns~~ to the ground in less than twenty-four hours.

Consistency with Pronouns

When writing a paper, you should not shift your point of view unnecessarily. Be consistent in your use of first-, second-, or third-person pronouns.

	Singular	*Plural*
First-person pronouns	I (my, mine, me)	we (our, us)
Second-person pronouns	you (your)	you (your)
Third-person pronouns	he (his, him)	they (their, them)
	she (her)	
	it (its)	

Note: Any person, place, or thing, as well as any indefinite pronoun like *one, anyone, someone,* and so on (page 461), is a third-person word.

For instance, if you start writing in the first person, *I,* do not jump suddenly to the second person, *you.* Or if you are writing in the third person, *they,* do not shift unexpectedly to *you.* Look at the examples.

Inconsistent	*Consistent*
One of the fringe benefits of my job is that *you* can use a company credit card for gasoline.	One of the fringe benefits of my job is that *I* can use a company credit card for gasoline.
(The most common mistake people make is to let a *you* slip into their writing after they start with another pronoun.)	
Though *we* like most of *our* neighbors, there are a few *you* can't get along with.	Though *we* like most of *our* neighbors, there are a few *we* can't get along with.
(The writer begins with the first-person pronouns *we* and *our,* but then shifts to the second-person *you.*)	

Activity

Cross out inconsistent pronouns in the following sentences and revise with the correct form of the pronoun above each crossed-out word.

Example When I examined the used car, ~~you~~ could see that one of the front
fenders had been replaced.

I

1. Many people are ignorant of side effects that diets can have on ~~your~~ *their* health.

2. When I buy lipstick or nail polish, ~~you~~ *I* never know how the color will actually look.

3. It is expensive for us to take public transportation to work every day, but what choice do ~~you~~ *we* have if ~~you~~ *we* can't afford a car?

4. During the border crisis, each country refused to change ~~their~~ *its* aggressive stance.

5. If you want to do well in this course, ~~one~~ *you* should plan on attending every day.

6. One of the things I love about my new apartment is that ~~you~~ *I* can own a pet.

7. Toni refuses to eat pepperoni pizza because she says it gives ~~you~~ *her* indigestion.

8. It's hard for us to pay for health insurance, but ~~you~~ *we* don't dare go without it.

9. People often take a first-aid course so that ~~we~~ *they* can learn how to help choking and heart attack victims.

10. There are several ways you can impress your new boss. For example, ~~one~~ *you* should dress well, arrive at work on time, and complete tasks efficiently.

Use Specific Words

To be an effective writer, you must use specific words rather than general words. Specific words create pictures in the reader's mind. They help capture interest and make your meaning clear. Compare the following sentences:

General

She walked down the street.

Animals came into the space.

The man signed the paper.

Specific

Anne wandered slowly along Rogers Lane.

Hungry lions padded silently into the sawdust-covered arena.

The biology teacher hastily scribbled his name on the course withdrawal slip.

The specific sentences create clear pictures in our minds. The details *show* us exactly what has happened.

Here are four ways to make your sentences specific.

1 Use exact names.

He sold his *camper.*
Vince sold his *Winnebago.*

2 Use lively verbs.

The flag *moved* in the breeze.
The flag *fluttered* in the breeze.

3 Use descriptive words (modifiers) before nouns.

A man strained to lift the crate.
A *heavyset, perspiring* man strained to lift the *heavy wooden* crate.

4 Use words that relate to the senses—sight, hearing, taste, smell, touch.

That woman jogs five miles a day.
That *fragile-looking, gray-haired* woman jogs five miles a day. (*sight*)

A noise told the crowd that there were two minutes left to play.
A *piercing whistle* told the *cheering* crowd that there were two minutes left to play. (*hearing*)

When he returned, all he found in the refrigerator was bread and milk.
When he returned, all he found in the refrigerator was *stale* bread and *sour* milk. (*taste*)

Neil stroked the kitten's fur until he felt its tiny claws on his hand.
Neil stroked the kitten's *velvety* fur until he felt its tiny, *needle-sharp* claws on his hand. (*touch*)

Fran placed a sachet in her bureau drawer.
Fran placed a *lilac-scented* sachet in her bureau drawer. (*smell*)

Activity 1

Revise the following sentences, changing vague, indefinite words into sharp, specific ones.

Example   *Several of our appliances* broke down at the same time.
  Our washer, refrigerator, and television broke . . .

Answers will vary; examples are shown.

1. *Salty snacks* are my diet downfall.
   Potato chips, pretzels, and salted peanuts . . .

2. I swept aside the *things* on my desk in order to spread out the road map.

    . . . papers, books, and magazines . . .

    _____

    _____

3. Our neighbor's family room has *a lot of electronic equipment.*

    . . . a TV, a CD player, and a computer.

    _____

    _____

4. *Several sections* of the newspaper were missing.

    The comics, the sports pages, the obituaries, and the society page . . .

    _____

    _____

5. The doctor examined *various parts of my body* before diagnosing my illness as bronchitis.

    . . . my throat, my ears, and my lungs . . .

    _____

    _____

Activity 2

Again, you will practice changing vague, indefinite writing into lively, image-filled writing that helps capture the reader's interest and makes your meaning clear. With the help of the methods described above, add specific details to the five sentences that follow. Note the two examples.

Examples   The person got off the bus.

The teenage boy bounded down the steps of the shiny yellow school bus.

She worked hard all summer.

All summer, Eva sorted peaches and blueberries in the hot, noisy canning factory.

Answers will vary; examples are shown.

1. The car would not start.

    The rusty old Buick sputtered, whined, and refused to start.

    _____

    _____

2. The test was difficult.

   The mathematics final was filled with tricky, baffling problems.

   _____

   _____

3. The boy was tired.

   Little Robbie was so exhausted that he could scarcely keep his eyes open.

   _____

   _____

4. My room needs cleaning.

   My cluttered, jumbled, dusty bedroom needs to be swept out, scrubbed,

   and reorganized.

   _____

5. A vehicle blocked traffic.

   A broken-down city bus blocked Main Street and stopped traffic for an

   hour.

   _____

Use Active Verbs

When the subject of a sentence performs the action of the verb, the verb is in the *active voice.* When the subject of a sentence receives the action of a verb, the verb is in the *passive voice.*

The passive form of a verb consists of a form of the verb *to be* (*am, is, are, was, were*) plus the past participle of the main verb (which is usually the same as its past tense form). Look at the following active and passive forms.

Passive	*Active*
The computer *was turned on* by Hakim.	Hakim *turned on* the computer.
The car's air conditioner *was fixed* by the mechanic.	The mechanic *fixed* the car's air conditioner.

In general, active verbs are more effective than passive verbs. Active verbs give your writing a simpler and more vigorous style.

Activity

Revise the following sentences, changing verbs from the passive to the active voice and making any other word changes necessary.

Example   Fruits and vegetables are painted often by artists.
Artists often paint fruits and vegetables.

1. Many unhealthy foods are included in the typical American diet.
    The typical American diet includes many unhealthy foods.

2. The family picnic was invaded by hundreds of biting ants.
    Hundreds of biting ants invaded the family picnic.

3. Antibiotics are used by doctors to treat many infections.
    Doctors use antibiotics to treat many infections.

4. The fatal traffic accident was caused by a drunk driver.
    A drunk driver caused the fatal traffic accident.

5. Final grades will be determined by the instructor on the basis of class performance.
    The instructor will determine final grades . . .

Use Concise Words

Wordiness—using more words than necessary to express a meaning—is often a sign of lazy or careless writing. Your readers may resent the extra time and energy they must spend when you have not done the work needed to make your writing direct and concise.

Here are two examples of wordy sentences:

In this paper, I am planning to describe the hobby that I enjoy of collecting old comic books.

In Ben's opinion, he thinks that cable television will change and alter our lives in the future.

Omitting needless words improves these sentences:

I enjoy collecting old comic books.

Ben thinks that cable television will change our lives.

Following is a list of some wordy expressions that could be reduced to single words.

Wordy Form	Short Form
at the present time	now
in the event that	if
in the near future	soon
due to the fact that	because
for the reason that	because
is able to	can
in every instance	always
in this day and age	today
during the time that	while
a large number of	many
big in size	big
red in color	red
five in number	five
return back	return
good benefit	benefit
commute back and forth	commute
postponed until later	postponed

Activity

Revise the following sentences, omitting needless words.
Answers will vary.

1. In conclusion, I would like to end my essay by summarizing each of the major points that were covered within my paper.

    I will conclude by summarizing my major points.
    _____

2. Controlling the quality and level of the television shows that children watch is a continuing challenge to parents that they must meet on a daily basis.

    Every day, parents must control their children's television watching.
    _____

3. In general, I am the sort of person who tends to be shy, especially in large crowds or with strangers I don't know well.

I am shy.

_____

4. Someone who is analyzing magazine advertising can find hidden messages that, once uncovered, are seen to be clever and persuasive.

Magazine advertising contains clever hidden messages.

_____

5. My greatest mistake that I made last week was to hurt my brother's feelings and then not to have the nerve to apologize and say how sorry I was.

My worst mistake last week was to hurt my brother's feelings and not

apologize.

6. In today's uncertain economic climate, it is clear that people, namely, average middle-class working people, have great difficulty saving much money or putting anything aside for emergencies.

In today's uncertain economy, the middle class finds it hard to save.

_____

7. We thought the television program that was on last night was enjoyable, whereas our parents reacted with dislike to the content of the show.

We liked last night's television show, but our parents didn't.

_____

8. Because of the bad weather, the school district felt it would be safer to cancel classes and let everyone stay home than risk people having accidents on the way to school.

The school district canceled classes because of the bad weather.

_____

9. Out of all the regrets in my life so far, one of my greatest ones to the present time is that I did not take word processing lessons when I was still in high school and had a chance to do so.

I regret not having studied word processing in high school.

_____

10. It seems obvious to me, and it should be to everyone else too, that people can be harmed as much by emotional abuse as by physical abuse, even if you don't lay a hand on them.

People are harmed by emotional as well as physical abuse.

_____

Vary Your Sentences

One part of effective writing is to vary the kinds of sentences you write. If every sentence follows the same pattern, writing may become monotonous to read. This section explains four ways you can create variety and interest in your writing style. It will also describe coordination and subordination—two important techniques for achieving different kinds of emphasis in writing.

The following are four methods you can use to revise simple sentences, making them more complex and sophisticated:

1 Add a second complete thought (coordination).

2 Add a dependent thought (subordination).

3 Begin with a special opening word or phrase.

4 Place adjectives or verbs in a series.

Revise by Adding a Second Complete Thought

When you add a second complete thought to a simple sentence, the result is a *compound* (or double) sentence. The two complete statements in a compound sentence are usually connected by a comma plus a joining or coordinating word (*and, but, for, or, nor, so, yet*).

A compound sentence is used to give equal weight to two closely related ideas. The technique of showing that ideas have equal importance is called *coordination*. Following are some compound sentences. In each case, the sentence contains two ideas that the writer considers equal in importance.

Greg worked on the engine for three hours, but the car still wouldn't start.

Bananas were on sale this week, so I bought a bunch for the children's lunches.

We laced up our roller blades, and then we moved cautiously onto the rink.

Activity

Combine the following pairs of simple sentences into compound sentences. Use a comma and a logical joining word (*and, but, for, so*) to connect each pair of statements.

Note: If you are not sure what *and, but, for,* and *so* mean, review pages 431–432.

Example   The weather was cold and windy.
            Al brought a thick blanket to the football game.

The weather was cold and windy, so Al brought a thick blanket to the football game.

1. My son can't eat peanut butter snacks or sandwiches.
    He is allergic to peanuts.

    . . . sandwiches, for he is allergic . . .

2. I tried to sleep.
    The thought of tomorrow's math exam kept me awake.

    . . . sleep, but the thought . . .

3. This diner has its own bakery.
    It has take-out service as well.

    . . . bakery, and it has . . .

4. The cardboard storage boxes were soggy.
    Rainwater had seeped into the basement during the storm.

    . . . soggy, for rainwater had . . .

5. I didn't have enough money to buy my parents an anniversary present.
    I offered to mow their lawn for the whole summer.

    . . . present, so I offered . . .

Revise by Adding a Dependent Thought

When you add a dependent thought to a simple sentence, the result is a *complex* sentence.* A dependent thought begins with one of the following subordinating words:

---

*The two parts of a complex sentence are sometimes called an *independent clause* and a *dependent clause*. A *clause* is simply a word group that contains a subject and a verb. An independent clause expresses a complete thought and can stand alone. A dependent clause does not express a complete thought in itself and "depends on" the independent clause to complete its meaning. Dependent clauses always begin with a dependent or subordinating word.

after	if, even if	when, whenever
although, though	in order that	where, wherever
as	since	whether
because	that, so that	which, whichever
before	unless	while
even though	until	who
how	what, whatever	whose

A complex sentence is used to emphasize one idea over another. Look at the following complex sentence:

Although the exam room was very quiet, I still couldn't concentrate.

The idea that the writer wishes to emphasize here—*I still couldn't concentrate*—is expressed as a complete thought. The less important idea—*Although the exam room was very quiet*—is subordinated to the complete thought. The technique of giving one idea less emphasis than another is called *subordination.*

Following are other examples of complex sentences. In each case, the part starting with the dependent word is the less emphasized part of the sentence.

Even though I was tired, I stayed up to watch the horror movie.

Before I take a bath, I check for spiders in the tub.

When Ivy feels nervous, she pulls on her earlobe.

Activity

Use logical subordinating words to combine the following pairs of simple sentences into sentences that contain a dependent thought. Place a comma after a dependent statement when it starts the sentence.

Example   Rita bit into the hard taffy.
           She broke a filling.
           When Rita bit into the hard taffy, she broke a filling.

Answers may vary.

1. I had forgotten to lock the front door.
    I had to drive back to the house.

    Because I had forgotten to lock the front door, I . . .

    _____

2. The bear turned over the rotten log.
    Fat white grubs crawled in every direction.

    When the bear turned over the rotten log, fat . . .

    _____

3. Kevin had sent away for a set of tools.
    He changed his mind about spending the money.

    After Kevin had sent away for a set of tools, he . . .

    _____

4. Some people are allergic to wool.
    They buy only sweaters made from synthetic fibers.

    Because some people are allergic to wool, they . . .

    _____

5. An older woman in my typing class can type almost one hundred words a
    minute.
    She is having trouble landing a secretarial job.

    Even though an . . . minute, she is . . .

    _____

Revise by Beginning with a Special Opening Word or Phrase

Among the special openers that can be used to start sentences are *-ed* words, *-ing*
words, *-ly* words, *to* word groups, and prepositional phrases. Here are examples
of all five kinds of openers:

-ed *word*

Concerned about his son's fever, Paul called a doctor.

-ing *word*

Humming softly, the woman browsed through the rack of dresses.

-ly *word*

Hesitantly, Sue approached the instructor's desk.

to *word group*

To protect her hair, Eva uses the lowest setting on her blow dryer.

Prepositional phrase

During the exam, drops of water fell from the ceiling.

Activity

Combine each of the following pairs of simple sentences into one sentence by using the opener shown at the left and omitting repeated words. Use a comma to set off the opener from the rest of the sentence.

Example   *-ing* word   The pelican scooped small fish into its baggy bill.
It dipped into the waves.

Dipping into the waves, the pelican scooped small fish into its baggy bill.

-ly word   1.   Shirley signed the repair contract.
She was reluctant.

Reluctantly, Shirley signed the repair contract.

_____

to word group   2.   The interns volunteered to work overtime.
They wanted to improve their chances of promotion.

To improve their chances of promotion, the interns . . .

_____

Prepositional phrase   3.   The accused murderer grinned at the witnesses.
He did this during the trial.

During the trial, the accused murderer . . .

_____

-ed word   4.   The vet's office was noisy and confusing.
It was crowded with nervous pets.

Crowded with nervous pets, the vet's office . . .

_____

-ing word   5.   Barry tried to find something worth watching.
He flipped from channel to channel.

Trying to find something worth watching, Barry flipped from channel to channel.

_____

Revise by Placing Adjectives or Verbs in a Series

Various parts of a sentence may be placed in a series. Among these parts are adjectives (descriptive words) and verbs. Here are examples of both in a series:

Adjectives

I gently applied a *sticky new* Band-Aid to the *deep, ragged* cut on my finger.

Verbs

The truck *bounced* off a guardrail, *sideswiped* a tree, and *plunged* down the embankment.

Activity

Combine the simple sentences into one sentence by using adjectives or verbs in a series and by omitting repeated words. Use a comma when necessary between adjectives or verbs in a series.

Example   Jesse spun the basketball on one finger.
He rolled it along his arms.
He dribbled it between his legs.

Jesse spun the basketball on one finger, rolled it along his arms, and dribbled it between his legs.

Answers may vary.

1.   The baby toddled across the rug.
He picked up a button.
He put the button in his mouth.

The baby toddled across the rug, picked up a button, and put the button in his mouth.

2.   Water dribbled out of the tap.
The water was brown.
The water was foul-tasting.
The tap was rusty.
The tap was metal.

Brown, foul-tasting water dribbled out of the rusty metal tap.

3. By 6 A.M. I had read the textbook chapter.
I had taken notes on it.
I had studied the notes.
I had drunk eight cups of coffee.

By 6 A.M. I had read the textbook chapter, taken notes on it, studied the notes, and drunk eight cups of coffee.

4. The exterminator approached the wasps' nests hanging under the eaves.
The nests were large.
The nests were papery.
The eaves were old.
The eaves were wooden.

. . . approached the large, papery wasps' nests hanging under the old wooden eaves.

5. Reeds bordered the pond.
The reeds were slim.
The reeds were brown.
The pond was green.
The pond was stagnant.

Slim brown reeds bordered the stagnant green pond.

Editing Sentences

After revising sentences in a paper so that they flow smoothly and clearly, you need to edit the paper for mistakes in grammar, punctuation, mechanics, usage, and spelling. Even if a paper is otherwise well-written, it will make an unfavorable impression on readers if it contains such mistakes. To edit a paper, check it against the agreed-upon rules or conventions of written English—simply called *sentence skills* in this book. Here are the most common of these conventions:

1 Write complete sentences rather than fragments.

2 Do not write run-ons.

3 Use verb forms correctly.

4 Make sure that subject, verbs, and pronouns agree.

5 Eliminate faulty modifiers.

6 Use pronoun forms correctly.

7 Use capital letters where needed.

8 Use the following marks of punctuation correctly: apostrophe, quotation marks, comma, semicolon, colon, hyphen, dash, parentheses.

9 Use correct manuscript form.

10 Eliminate slang, clichés, and pretentious words.

11 Check for possible spelling errors.

12 Eliminate careless errors.

These sentence skills are treated in detail in Part Four of this book, and they can be referred to easily as needed. Both the list of sentence skills on the inside front cover of this book and the correction symbols on the inside back cover include page references so that you can turn quickly to any skill you want to check.

Hints about Editing

Here are hints that can help you edit the next-to-final draft of a paper for sentence-skills mistakes:

1 Have at hand two essential tools: a good dictionary and a grammar handbook (you can use the one in this book beginning on page 409).

2 Use a sheet of paper to cover your essay so that you will expose only one sentence at a time. Look for errors in grammar, spelling, and typing. It may help to read each sentence out loud. If a sentence does not read clearly and smoothly, chances are something is wrong.

3 Pay special attention to the kinds of errors you tend to make. For example, if you tend to write run-ons or fragments, be especially on the lookout for those errors.

4 Try to work on a typewritten or word-processed draft, where you'll be able to see your writing more objectively than you can on a handwritten page; use a pen with colored ink so that your corrections will stand out.

Note: A series of editing tests appears on pages 550–562. You will probably find it most helpful to take these tests after reviewing the sentence skills in Part Four.

Proofreading

Proofreading means checking the final, edited draft of your paper closely for typos and other careless errors. A helpful strategy is to read your paper backward, from the last sentence to the first. This helps keep you from getting caught up in the flow of the paper and missing small mistakes. Here are six helpful proofing symbols:

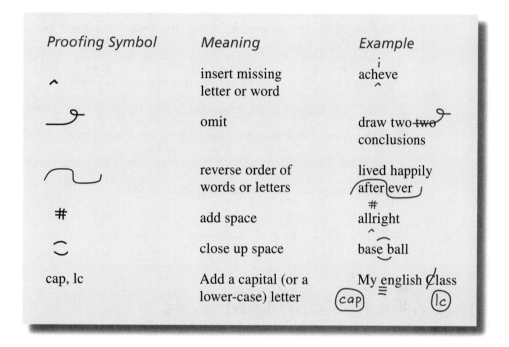

Proofing Symbol	Meaning	Example
^	insert missing letter or word	acheve
⌐ⲟ	omit	draw two ~~two~~ conclusions
⁀	reverse order of words or letters	lived happily after ever
#	add space	allright
‿	close up space	base ball
cap, lc	Add a capital (or a lower-case) letter	My english Class

If you make many corrections, retype the page or enter corrections into your word processor file and reprint the page.

Activity

In the spaces at the bottom, write the numbers of the ten word groups that contain fragments or run-ons. Then, in the spaces between the lines, edit by making the necessary corrections. One is done for you as an example.
Corrections may vary.

   [1]A unique object in my family's living room is an ashtray. [2]Which I made

in second grade. [3]I can still remember the pride I felt, [4]When I presented it

to my mother. [5]Now, I'm amazed that my parents didn't hide it away at the back of a shelf it is a remarkably ugly object. ⁶The ashtray is made out of brown clay which I had tried to mold into a perfect circle, unfortunately, my class was only forty-five minutes long. ⁷The best I could do was to shape it into a lopsided oval. ⁸Its most distinctive feature, though, was the grooves carved into its rim. ⁹I had theorized that each groove could hold a cigarette or cigar, I made at least fifty of them. ¹⁰I somehow failed to consider that the only person who smoked in my family was my father, ¹¹Who smoked about five cigars a year. ¹²Further, although our living room is decorated in sedate tans and blues, my ashtray is bright purple, ¹³My favorite color at the time. ¹⁴For variety, it has stripes around its rim they are colored neon green. ¹⁵My parents have proudly displayed my little masterpiece on their coffee table for the past ten years. ¹⁶If I ever wonder if my parents love me, ¹⁷I look at that ugly ashtray, the answer is plain to see.

1. ___2___   3. ___5___   5. ___9___   7. ___13___   9. ___16___
2. ___4___   4. ___6___   6. ___11___ 8. ___14___   10. ___17___

Practice in Revising Sentences

You now know the fourth step in effective writing: revising and editing sentences. You also know that practice in *editing* sentences is best undertaken after you have worked through the sentence skills in Part Four. The focus in this closing section, then, will be on *revising* sentences—using a variety of methods to ensure that your sentences flow smoothly and are clear and interesting. You will work through the following series of Review Tests:

1   Using parallelism
2   Using a consistent point of view
3   Using specific words
4   Using active verbs
5   Using concise words
6   Varying your sentences

Using Parallelism

■ Review Test 1

Cross out the unbalanced part of each sentence. In the space provided, revise the unbalanced part so that it matches the other item or items in the sentence.

Example   Cigarette smoking is expensive, disgusting, and ~~a health risk~~. *unhealthy*

1. Gary prefers books that are short, scary, and *filled with suspense*.
   suspenseful

2. A sale on electrical appliances, *furniture for the home office*, and stereo equipment begins this Friday.
   home office furniture

3. To escape the stresses of everyday life, I rely upon watching television, reading books, and ~~my kitchen~~.
   working in my kitchen

4. The keys to improving grades are to take effective notes in class, to plan study time, and ~~preparing~~ carefully for exams.
   to prepare

5. Qualities that I look for in friends are a sense of humor, ~~being kind~~, and dependability.
   kindness

6. My three favorite jobs were veterinary assistant, gardener, and ~~selling toys~~.
   toy salesman (or: saleswoman)

7. Housekeeping shortcuts will help you speed up doing laundry, cleaning rooms, and ~~food on the table~~.
   putting food on the table

8. Studying a little every day is more effective than ~~to cram~~.
   cramming

9. The chickens travel on a conveyor belt, where they are plucked, washed, rinsed, and ~~bags are put on them~~.
   bagged (or: put into bags)

10. The speaker impressed the audience because of his clear, reasonable presentation ~~with friendliness as well~~.
    and his friendliness

Using Parallelism

■ Review Test 2

Cross out the unbalanced part of each sentence. In the space provided, revise the unbalanced part so that it matches the other item or items in the sentence.

1. Paying college tuition and not studying is as sensible as ~~to buy~~ tickets to a movie and not watching it. _buying_

2. The best programming on television includes news programs, ~~shows on science~~, and children's series. _scientific shows_

3. Curling overgrown vines, ~~porch furniture that was rotted~~, and sagging steps were my first impressions of the neglected house. _rotting porch furniture_

4. The little girl came home from school with a tear-streaked face, a black eye, and ~~her shirt was torn~~. _a torn shirt_

5. There are two ways to the top floor: climb the stairs or ~~taking~~ the elevator. _take (or: climbing . . . taking)_

6. While waiting for the exam to start, small groups of nervous students glanced over their notes, drank coffee, and ~~were whispering~~ to each other. _whispered_

7. In many ways, starting college at forty is harder than ~~to start~~ at eighteen. _starting_

8. Interesting work is as important to me as ~~pay that is good~~. _good pay_

9. The "bag lady" shuffled along the street, bent over to pick something up, and ~~was putting~~ it in her shopping bag. _put_

10. A teamsters' strike now would mean interruptions in food deliveries, a showdown in the economy, and ~~losing~~ wages for workers. _lost_

Using a Consistent Point of View

■ Review Test 1

Change verbs as needed in the following selection so that they are consistently in the past tense. Cross out each incorrect verb and write the correct form above it, as shown in the example. You will need to make ten corrections.

My uncle's shopping trip last Thursday was discouraging to him. First of all, he had to drive around for fifteen minutes until he ~~finds~~ *found* a parking space. There was a half-price special on paper products in the supermarket, and every spot ~~is~~ *was* taken. Then, when he finally got inside, many of the items on his list were not where he expected. For example, the pickles he wanted ~~are~~ *were* not on the same shelf as all the other pickles. Instead, they were in a refrigerated case next to the bacon. And the granola was not on the cereal shelves but in the health food section. Shopping thus ~~proceeds~~ *proceeded* slowly. About halfway through his list, he knew there would not be time to cook dinner and ~~decides~~ *decided* to pick up a barbecued chicken. The chicken, he learned, was available at the end of the store he had already passed. So he ~~parks~~ *parked* his shopping cart in an aisle, ~~gets~~ *got* the chicken, and came back. After adding half a dozen more items to his cart, he suddenly ~~realizes~~ *realized* it contained someone else's food. So he retraced his steps, found his own cart, ~~transfers~~ *transferred* the groceries, and continued to shop. Later, when he began loading items onto the checkout counter, he ~~notices~~ *noticed* that the barbecued chicken was missing. He must have left it in the other cart, certainly gone by now. Feeling totally defeated, he returned to the deli counter and ~~says~~ *said* to the clerk, "Give me another chicken. I lost the first one." My uncle told me that when he saw the look on the clerk's face, he felt as if he'd flunked Food Shopping.

Using a Consistent Point of View

■ **Review Test 2**

Cross out inconsistent pronouns in the following sentences and revise with the correct form of the pronoun above each crossed-out word.

Example   Dog owners should put tags on their dogs in case ~~you~~ *they* lose their pets.

1. These days people never seem to get the recognition they deserve no matter how hard ~~you~~ *they* work.

2. All ~~you~~ *I* could hear was the maddening rattle of the heating register, even though I buried my face in the pillow.

3. When we answer the telephone at work, ~~you~~ *we* are supposed to say the company's name.

4. Each year I pay more money for my college tuition. But, despite the cost, ~~one~~ *I* must complete college in order to get a better, more meaningful job.

5. Gary bought the used car from a local dealership. The car was so clean and shiny that ~~you~~ *he* could not tell that the engine needed to be replaced.

6. I would like to go to a school where ~~one~~ *I* can meet many people who are different from me.

7. When I first began to work as a waitress, I was surprised at how rude some customers were to ~~you~~ *me*.

8. When ~~you~~ *I* drive on the highway, I get disgusted at the amount of trash I see.

9. Students may not leave the exam room unless ~~you~~ *they* have turned in the exam.

10. Nina wanted to just browse through the store, but in every department a salesperson came up and asked to help ~~you~~ *her*.

Using Specific Words

■ **Review Test 1**

Revise the following sentences, changing vague, indefinite words into sharp, specific ones.

Answers will vary; examples are shown.

1. When my marriage broke up, I felt *various emotions.*

   . . . I felt sad, angry, and worried.

2. The *food choices* in the cafeteria were unappetizing.

   The lukewarm soup, stale sandwiches, and limp salads . . .

3. *Bugs* invaded our kitchen and pantry this summer.

   Ants, moths, and spiders . . .

4. All last week, *the weather was terrible.*

   . . . it rained nonstop, with a bone-chilling wind.

5. In the car accident, our teacher suffered *a number of injuries.*

   . . . a broken arm, two broken ribs, and a concussion.

Using Specific Words

■ **Review Test 2**

With the help of the methods described on page 109, add specific details to the sentences that follow.

Answers will vary; examples are given.

1.   The salesperson was obnoxious.

     The haughty, scowling salesman told us not to waste his time with stupid

     questions.

     _____

2.   The child started to cry.

     Betty dug her fists into her eyes and shook with sobs.

     _____

     _____

3.   The game was exciting.

     The third game of the World Series was a tense pitchers' duel.

     _____

     _____

4.   The lounge area was busy.

     The airport lounge was thronged with holiday travelers.

     _____

     _____

5.   A passenger on the bus was acting strangely.

     The woman in the front seat was muttering to herself and trembling.

     _____

     _____

Using Active Verbs

■ Review Test

Revise the following sentences, changing verbs from the passive to the active voice and making any other necessary word changes.

Example   Soccer is played by children all over the world.
Children all over the world play soccer.

1. The pizza restaurant was closed by the health inspector.
   The health inspector closed the pizza restaurant.

2. Huge stacks of donated books were sorted by the workers in the library.
   The workers in the library sorted huge stacks of donated books.

3. My computer was infected by a virus.
   A virus infected my computer.

4. Gasoline prices will not be increased by oil companies this winter.
   Oil companies will not increase gasoline prices this winter.

5. High-powered bombs were dropped by our airplanes onto enemy bases.
   Our airplanes dropped high-powered bombs onto enemy bases.

6. An additional charge was placed on our phone bill by the telephone company.
   The telephone company placed an additional charge on our phone bill.

7. The community center was damaged by a group of vandals.
   A group of vandals damaged the community center.

8. Stress is relieved by physical activity, meditation, and relaxation.
   Physical activity, meditation, and relaxation relieve stress.

9. Taxes will be raised by the federal government to pay for highway improvements.
   The federal government will raise taxes to pay . . .

10. Studies show that violent behavior among young children is increased by watching violent TV programs.
    Studies show that watching violent TV programs increases violent behavior . . .

Using Concise Words

■ Review Test 1

Revise the following sentences, omitting needless words.

Answers may vary; examples are given.

1. I finally made up my mind and decided to look for a new job.

    I finally decided to look for a new job.

2. Due to the fact that the printer was out of paper, Renee went to the store for the purpose of buying some.

    Because her printer was out of paper, Renee went to buy some.

3. Tamika realized suddenly that her date had stood her up and was not going to show up.

    Tamika realized suddenly that her date had stood her up.

4. Our teacher does not know at this point in time if she will return to our school next year.

    Our teacher does not yet know if she will return next year.

5. The salesperson advised us not to buy the computer at this time because it was going to have a drop in price in the very near future.

    The salesperson advised us to wait until the price dropped before buying

    our computer.

Using Concise Words

■ **Review Test 2**

Revise the following sentences, omitting needless words.

Answers may vary; examples are given.

1. The policy at our company at the present time is that there are two coffee breaks, with each of them being fifteen minutes long.

   Our company allows two fifteen-minute coffee breaks.

2. Permit us to take this opportunity to inform you that your line of credit has been increased.

   Your line of credit has been increased.

3. I have a strong preference for candy over fruit, which, in my opinion, doesn't taste as good as candy does.

   I prefer candy to fruit.

   Or: I think candy tastes better than fruit.

4. Lynn is one of those people who rarely admit being wrong, and it is very unusual to hear her acknowledge that she has made a mistake.

   Lynn rarely admits that she has made a mistake.

5. Many people are of the opinion that children should be required by law to attend school until they reach the age of sixteen years old.

   Many people think that children should, by law, attend school until age sixteen.

Varying Your Sentences

■ Review Test 1

Combine each of the following groups of simple sentences into one longer sentence. Omit repeated words. Various combinations are often possible, so try to find a combination in each group that flows most smoothly and clearly.

Answers will vary; examples are shown.

1. Sophie had repaired her broken watchband with a paper clip.
   The clip snapped.
   The watch slid off her wrist.

   . . . with a paper clip, but the clip snapped and the watch slid . . .

2. The physical therapist watched.
   Julie tried to stand on her weakened legs.
   They crumpled under her.

   . . . watched as Julie tried to stand on her weakened legs and they

   crumpled under her.

3. There were parking spaces on the street.
   Richie pulled into an expensive garage.
   He did not want to risk damage to his new car.

   Although there were parking spaces on the street, Richie pulled . . . garage

   because he did not want . . .

4. The truck was speeding.
   The truck was brown.
   The truck skidded on some ice.
   The truck almost hit a police officer.
   The police officer was startled.
   The police officer was young.

   Speeding, the brown truck skidded on some ice and almost hit a startled

   young police officer.

5. The rainstorm flooded our basement.
   The rainstorm was sudden.
   The rainstorm was terrible.
   It knocked slates off the roof.
   It uprooted a young tree.

   A sudden terrible rainstorm flooded our basement, knocked slates off the

   roof, and uprooted a young tree.

Varying Your Sentences

■ **Review Test 2**

Combine each of the following groups of simple sentences into two longer sentences. Omit repeated words. Various combinations are often possible, so try to find combinations in each group that flow most smoothly and clearly.

Answers will vary; examples are shown.

1. A sudden cold front hit the area.
    Temperatures dropped thirty degrees in less than an hour.
    My teeth began to chatter.
    I was not wearing a warm jacket.

    When a sudden . . . area, temperatures dropped . . . hour. I was not wearing

    a warm jacket, so my teeth . . .

2. Vern works as a model.
    He has to look his best.
    He gained ten pounds recently.
    He had to take off the extra weight.
    He would have lost his job.

    Vern works as a model, so he has to look his best. When he gained ten

    pounds recently, he had to take off the extra weight, since he would have

    lost his job.

3. The ball game was about to begin.
    A dog ran onto the field.
    The dog began nipping the infielders' ankles.
    The game had to be delayed.
    The dog was chased away.

    As the ball game was about to begin, a dog ran onto the field and began

    nipping the infielders' ankles. The game had to be delayed until the dog was

    chased away.

4. The lion was hungry.
    It watched the herd of gazelle closely.
    A young or sick animal wandered away from the group.
    The lion would move in for the kill.

    The hungry lion watched the herd of gazelle closely. If a young . . . group, the

    lion would move in for the kill.

5. My aunt decided to find a helpful form of exercise.
She was suffering from arthritis.
She learned that swimming is very healthful.
It works every muscle group in the body without straining the muscles.

My aunt, suffering from arthritis, decided . . . exercise. She learned that

swimming is very helpful because it works . . .

Varying Your Sentences

■ **Review Test 3**

Combine the sentences in the following paragraph into four sentences. Omit repeated words. Try to find combinations in each case that flow as smoothly and clearly as possible.

Lena and Miles wanted a vacation. They wanted a vacation that was nice. They wanted one that was quiet. They wanted one that was relaxing. They rented a small lakeside cabin. Their first day there was very peaceful. The situation quickly changed. A large family moved into a nearby cabin. They played music at top volume. They raced around in a speedboat with a loud whining engine. Lena and Miles were no longer very relaxed. They packed up their things. They drove off. They returned to their quiet apartment.

Answers will vary. An example is shown.

Lena and Miles wanted a nice, quiet, relaxing vacation, so they rented a

small lakeside cabin. Their first day there was very peaceful, but the

situation quickly changed when a large family moved into a nearby cabin.

They played music at top volume and raced around in a speedboat with a

large whining engine. Lena and Miles, no longer very relaxed, packed up their

things, drove off, and returned to their quiet apartment.

6 Four Bases for Revising Essays

This chapter will show you how to evaluate an essay for

- unity
- support
- coherence
- sentence skills

In the preceding chapters, you learned four essential steps in writing an effective paper. The box below shows how the steps lead to four standards, or bases, you can use in revising an essay.

Four Steps ⟶	Four Bases
1 If you advance a single point and stick to that point,	your paper will have *unity*.
2 If you support the point with specific evidence,	your paper will have *support*.
3 If you organize and connect the specific evidence,	your paper will have *coherence*.
4 If you write clear, error-free sentences,	your paper will demonstrate effective *sentence skills*.

This chapter will discuss these four bases—unity, support, coherence, and sentence skills—and will show how the four bases can be used to evaluate and revise a paper.

Base 1: Unity

Understanding Unity

The following student essays are on the topic "Problems or Pleasures of My Teenage Years." Which one makes its point more clearly and effectively, and why?

Essay 1

Teenage Pranks

Looking back at some of the things I did as a teenager makes me break   1
out in a sweat. The purpose of each adventure was fun, but occasionally things got out of hand. In my search for good times, I was involved in three notable pranks, ranging from fairly harmless to fairly serious.

The first prank proved that good, clean fun does not have to be dull.   2
As a high school student, I was credited with making the world's largest dessert. With several friends, I spent an entire year collecting boxes of Jell-O. Entering our school's indoor pool one night, we turned the water temperature up as high as it would go and poured in box after box of the strawberry powder. The next morning, school officials arrived to find the pool filled with thirteen thousand gallons of the quivering, rubbery stuff. No one was hurt by the prank, but we did suffer through three days of a massive cleanup.

Not all my pranks were harmless, and one involved risking my life.   3
As soon as I got my driver's license, I wanted to join the "Fliers' Club." Membership in this club was limited to those who could make their cars fly a distance of at least ten feet. The qualifying site was an old quarry field where friends and I had built a ramp made of dirt. I drove my battered Ford Pinto up this ramp as fast as it would go. The Pinto flew ten feet, but one of the tires exploded when I landed. The car rolled on its side, and I luckily escaped with only a bruised arm.

Risking my own life was bad enough, but there was another prank where   4
other people could have been hurt, too. On this occasion, I accidentally set a valley on fire. Two of my friends and I were sitting on a hill sharing a few beers. It was a warm summer night, and there was absolutely nothing to do. The idea came like a thunderclap. We collected a supply of large plastic trash bags, emergency highway flares, and a half tank of helium left over from a science-fair experiment. Then we began to construct a fleet of UFOs. Filling the bags with helium, we tied them closed with wire and suspended several burning flares below each bag. Our UFOs leaped into the air like an army of invading Martians. Rising and darting in the blackness, they convinced even us. Our fun turned into horror, though, as we watched the balloons begin to drop onto the wooded valley of expensive homes below. Soon, a brushfire started and, quickly sobered, we hurried off to call the fire department anonymously.

Every so often, I think back on the things that I did as a teenager. I chuckle at the innocent pranks and feel lucky that I didn't harm myself or others with the not-so-innocent ones. Those years were filled with wild times. Today I'm older, wiser—and maybe just a little more boring. 5

Essay 2   **Problems of My Adolescence**

In the unreal world of television situation comedies, teenagers are carefree, smart, funny, wisecracking, secure kids. In fact, most of them are more "together" than the adults on the shows. This, however, isn't how I recall my teenage years at all. As a teen, I suffered. Every day, I battled the terrible physical, family, and social troubles of adolescence. 1

For one thing, I had to deal with a demoralizing physical problem— acne. Some days, I would wake up in the morning with a red bump the size of a taillight on my nose. Since I worried constantly about my appearance anyway, acne outbreaks could turn me into a crying, screaming maniac. Plastering on a layer of (at the time) orange-colored Clearasil, which didn't fool anybody, I would slink into school, hoping that the boy I had a crush on would be absent that day. Within the last few years, however, treatments for acne have improved. Now, skin doctors prescribe special drugs that clear up pimples almost immediately. An acne attack could shatter whatever small amount of self-esteem I had managed to build up. 2

In addition to fighting acne, I felt compelled to fight my family. As a teenager, I needed to be independent. At that time, the most important thing in life was to be close to my friends and to try out new, more adult experiences. Unfortunately, my family seemed to get in the way. My little brother, for instance, turned into my enemy. ~~We are close now, though. In fact, Eddie recently painted my new apartment for me~~. Eddie used to barge into my room, listen to my phone conversations, and read my secret letters. I would threaten to tie him up and leave him in a garbage dumpster. He would scream, my mother would yell, and all hell would break loose. My parents, too, were enemies. They wouldn't let me stay out late, wear the clothes I wanted to wear, or hang around with the friends I liked. So I tried to get revenge on them by being miserable, sulky, and sarcastic at home. 3

Worst of all, I had to face the social traumas of being a teenager. Things that were supposed to be fun, like dates and dances, were actually horrible. On the few occasions when I had a real date, I agonized over everything— my hair, my weight, my pimples. After a date, I would come home, raid the kitchen, and drown my insecurities in a sea of junk food. Dances were also stressful events. My friends and I would sneak a couple of beers just to get up the nerve to walk into the school gym. ~~Now I realize that teenage drinking is dangerous. I read recently that the number one killer of teenagers is drunk driving.~~ At dances, I never relaxed. It was too important to look exactly right, to act really cool, and to pretend I was having fun. 4

I'm glad I'm not a teenager anymore. I wouldn't ever want to feel so   5
unattractive, so confused, and so insecure again. I'll gladly accept the crow's-
feet and stomach bulge of adulthood in exchange for a little peace of mind.

Activity

Fill in the blanks.

Essay __1__ makes its point more clearly and effectively because _____
it is more unified.

_____

_____

Comment: Essay 1 is more effective because it is unified. All the details in
this essay are on target; they support and develop each of its three topic sentences
("The first prank proved that good, clean fun does not have to be dull"; "Not all
my pranks were harmless, and one involved risking my life"; and "Risking my
own life was bad enough, but there was another prank where other people could
have been hurt, too").

On the other hand, essay 2 contains some details irrelevant to its topic sentences. In the first supporting paragraph (paragraph 2), the sentences "Within the
last few years, however, treatments for acne have improved. Now, skin doctors prescribe special drugs that clear up pimples almost immediately" do not support the
writer's topic statement that she had to deal with the physical problem of acne.
Such details should be left out in the interest of unity.

The difference between these first two essays leads us to the first base or standard of effective writing: *unity*. To achieve unity is to have all the details in your
paper related to your thesis and to your three supporting topic sentences. Each time
you think of something to put into your paper, ask yourself whether it relates to
your thesis and your supporting points. If it does not, leave it out. For example,
if you were writing a paper about the problems of being unemployed and then
spent a couple of sentences talking about the pleasures of having a lot of free time,
you would be missing the first and most essential base of good writing.

Revising for Unity

Activity

Go back to essay 2 and cross out the two sentences in the second supporting paragraph (paragraph 3) and the two sentences in the third supporting paragraph (paragraph 4) that are off target and do not help support their topic sentences.

Base 2: Support

Understanding Support

The following essays were written on "Dealing with Disappointment." Both are unified, but one communicates more clearly and effectively. Which one, and why?

Essay 1   **Dealing with Disappointment**

One way to look at life is as a series of disappointments. Life can certainly 1
appear that way because disappointment crops up in the life of everyone
more often, it seems, than satisfaction. How disappointments are handled
can have a great bearing on how life is viewed. People can react negatively
by sulking or by blaming others, or they can try to understand the reasons
behind the disappointment.

Sulking is one way to deal with disappointment. This attitude—"Why 2
does everything always happen to me?"—is common because it is easy to
adopt, but it is not very productive. Everyone has had the experience of
meeting people who specialize in feeling sorry for themselves. A sulky
manner will often discourage others from wanting to lend support, and it
prevents the sulker from making positive moves toward self-help. It becomes
easier just to sit back and sulk. Unfortunately, feeling sorry for oneself does
nothing to lessen the pain of disappointment. It may, in fact, increase the
pain. It certainly does not make future disappointments easier to bear.

Blaming others is another negative and unproductive way to cope with 3
disappointment. This all-too-common response of pointing the finger at
someone else doesn't help one's situation. This posture will lead only to
anger, resentment, and, therefore, further unhappiness. Disappointment in
another's performance does not necessarily indicate that the performer is at
fault. Perhaps expectations were too high, or there could have been a
misunderstanding as to what the performer actually intended to accomplish.

A positive way to handle disappointment is to try to understand the 4
reasons behind the disappointment. An analysis of the causes of
disappointment can have an excellent chance of producing desirable results.
Often understanding alone can help alleviate the pain of disappointment
and can help prevent future disappointments. Also, it is wise to try to
remember that what would be ideal is not necessarily what is reasonable
to expect in any given situation. The ability to look disappointment squarely
in the face and then go on from there is the first step on the road back.

Continuous handling of disappointment in a negative manner can lead 5
to a negative view of life itself. Chances for personal happiness in such a state
of being are understandably slim. Learning not to expect perfection in an
imperfect world and keeping in mind those times when expectations were
actually surpassed are positive steps toward allowing the joys of life to prevail.

Essay 2   **Reactions to Disappointment**

Ben Franklin said that the only sure things in life are death and taxes.   1
He left something out, however: disappointment. No one gets through life
without experiencing many disappointments. Strangely, though, most
people seem unprepared for disappointment and react to it in negative
ways. They feel depressed or try to escape their troubles instead of using
disappointment as an opportunity for growth.

One negative reaction to disappointment is depression. For example,   2
Helen, a woman trying to win a promotion, works hard for over a year in
her department. Helen is so sure she will get the promotion, in fact, that she
has already picked out the car she will buy when her salary increase comes
through. However, the boss names one of Helen's coworkers to the spot. The
fact that all the other department employees tell Helen that she is the one
who really deserved the promotion doesn't help her deal with the crushing
disappointment. Deeply depressed, Helen decides that all her goals are
doomed to defeat. She loses her enthusiasm for her job and can barely force
herself to show up every day. Helen tells herself that she is a failure and that
doing a good job just isn't worth the work.

Another negative reaction to disappointment, and one that often   3
follows depression, is the desire to escape. Jamal fails to get into the college
his brother is attending, the college that was the focus of all his dreams,
and decides to escape his disappointment. Why worry about college at all?
Instead, he covers up his real feelings by giving up on his schoolwork and
getting completely involved with friends, parties, and "good times." Or
Carla doesn't make the varsity basketball team—something she wanted
very badly—and so refuses to play sports at all. She decides to hang around
with a new set of friends who get high every day; then she won't have to
confront her disappointment and learn to live with it.

The positive way to react to disappointment is to use it as a chance for   4
growth. This isn't easy, but it's the only useful way to deal with an inevitable
part of life. Helen, the woman who wasn't promoted, could have handled
her disappointment by looking at other options. If her boss doesn't
recognize her talent and hard work, perhaps she could transfer to another
department. Or she could ask the boss how to improve her performance
so that she would be a shoo-in for the next promotion. Jamal, the boy
who didn't get into the college of his choice, should look into other schools.
Going to another college may encourage him to be his own person, step out
of his brother's shadow, and realize that being turned down by one college
isn't a final judgment on his abilities or potential. Rather than escape into
drugs, Carla could improve her basketball skills for a year or pick up another
sport—like swimming or tennis—that would probably turn out to be more
useful to her as an adult.

Disappointments are unwelcome but regular visitors to everyone's life. We   5
can feel depressed about them, or we can try to escape from them. The best
thing, though, is to accept a disappointment and then try to use it somehow:
step over the unwelcome visitor on the doorstep and get on with life.

Activity

Fill in the blanks.

Essay __2__ makes its point more clearly and effectively because _____
it has better support for its thesis.

_____

Comment: Here, essay 2 is more effective, for it offers specific examples of
the ways people deal with disappointment. We see for ourselves the kinds of reactions people have to disappointment.

Essay 1, on the other hand, gives us no specific evidence. The writer tells us
repeatedly that sulking, blaming others, and trying to understand the reasons
behind a disappointment are the reactions people have to a letdown. However, the
writer never *shows* us any of these responses in action. Exactly what kinds of disappointments is the writer talking about? And how, for instance, does someone
analyze the causes of disappointment? Would a person write a list of causes on a
piece of paper, or review the causes with a concerned friend, or speak to a professional therapist? In an essay like this, we would want to see *examples* of how
sulking and blaming others are negative ways of dealing with disappointment.

Consideration of these two essays leads us to the second base of effective writing: *support*. After realizing the importance of specific supporting details, one student writer revised a paper she had done on being lost in the woods as the worst
experience of her childhood. In the revised paper, instead of talking about "the
terror of being separated from my parents," she referred to such specifics as "tears
streamed down my cheeks as I pictured the faces I would never see again" and "I
clutched the locket my parents had given me as if it were a lucky charm that could
help me find my way back to the campsite." All your papers should include such
vivid details!

Revising for Support

Activity   Answers will vary.

On a separate sheet of paper, revise one of the three supporting paragraphs in
"Dealing with Disappointment" by providing specific supporting examples.

Base 3: Coherence

Understanding Coherence

The following two essays were written on the topic "Positive or Negative Effects of Television." Both are unified, and both are supported. However, one communicates more clearly and effectively. Which one, and why?

Essay 1   **Harmful Effects of Watching Television**

In a recent cartoon, one character said to another, "When you think   1
of the awesome power of television to educate, aren't you glad it doesn't?"
It's true that television has the power to educate and to entertain, but
unfortunately, these benefits are outweighed by the harm it does to
dedicated viewers. Television is harmful because it creates passivity,
discourages communication, and presents a false picture of reality.

Television makes viewers passive. Children who have an electronic   2
baby-sitter spend most of their waking hours in a semiconscious state.
Older viewers watch tennis matches and basketball games with none of
the excitement of being in the stands. Even if children are watching <u>Sesame
Street</u> or <u>Barney & Friends</u>, they are being educated passively. The child
actors are going on nature walks, building crafts projects, playing with
animals, and participating in games, but the little viewers are simply
watching. Older viewers watch guests discuss issues with Oprah Winfrey,
but no one will turn to the home viewers to ask their opinion.

Worst of all, TV presents a false picture of reality that leaves viewers   3
frustrated because they don't have the beauty or wealth of the characters
on television. Viewers absorb the idea that everyone else in the United
States owns a lavish apartment, a suburban house, a sleek car, and an
expensive wardrobe. Every detective, police officer, oil baron, and lawyer,
male or female, is suitable for a pinup poster. The material possessions
on TV shows and commercials contribute to the false image of reality.
News anchors and reporters, with their perfect hair and makeup, must
fit television's standard of beauty. From their modest homes or cramped
apartments, many viewers tune in daily to the upper-middle-class world
that TV glorifies.

Television discourages communication. Families watching television do   4
very little talking except for brief exchanges during commercials. If Uncle
Bernie or the next-door neighbors drop in for a visit, the most comfortable
activity for everyone may be not conversation but watching ESPN. The family
may not even be watching the same set; instead, in some households, all the
family members head for their own rooms to watch their own sets. At

dinner, plates are plopped on the coffee table in front of the set, and the   5
meal is wolfed down during <u>NBC Nightly News</u>. During commercials, the
only communication a family has all night may consist of questions like "Do
we have any popcorn?" and "Where's the <u>TV Guide</u>?"

Television, like cigarettes or saccharine, is harmful to our health. We
are becoming isolated, passive, and frustrated. And, most frightening, the
average viewer now spends more time watching television than ever before.

Essay 2   **The Benefits of Television**

We hear a lot about the negative effects of television on the viewer.   1
Obviously, television can be harmful if it is watched constantly to the
exclusion of other activities. It would be just as harmful to listen to CDs
all the time or to eat constantly. However, when television is watched in
moderation, it is extremely valuable, as it provides relaxation,
entertainment, and education.

First of all, watching TV has the value of sheer relaxation. Watching   2
television can be soothing and restful after an eight-hour day of pressure,
challenges, or concentration. After working hard all day, people look
forward to a new episode of a favorite show or yet another showing of
<u>Casablanca</u> or <u>Red River</u>. This period of relaxation leaves viewers refreshed
and ready to take on the world again. Watching TV also seems to reduce
stress in some people. This benefit of television is just beginning to be
recognized. One doctor, for example, advises his patients with high blood
pressure to relax in the evening with a few hours of television.

In addition to being relaxing, television is entertaining. Along with   3
the standard comedies, dramas, and game shows that provide enjoyment
to viewers, television offers a variety of movies and sports events. Moreover,
in many areas, viewers can pay a monthly fee and receive special cable
programming. With this service, viewers can watch first-run movies, rock
and classical music concerts, and specialized sports events, like international
soccer and Grand Prix racing. Viewers can also buy or rent movies to show
on their television sets through videodisk players or videocassette players.
Still another growing area of TV entertainment is video games. Cartridges
are available for everything from electronic baseball to Mortal Kombat,
allowing the owner to have a video game arcade in the living room.

Most important, television is educational. Preschoolers learn colors,   4
numbers, and letters from public television programs, like <u>Sesame Street</u>,
that use animation and puppets to make learning fun. Science shows for
older children, like <u>Fun with Nature</u>, go on location to analyze everything
from volcanoes to rocket launches. Adults, too, can get an education
(college credits included) from courses given on television. Also, television
widens our knowledge by covering important events and current news.

Viewers can see and hear presidents' speeches, state funerals, natural   5
disasters, and election results as they are happening. Finally, with a phone
line and a special terminal, television allows any member of the family to
access and learn from all the information resources on the Internet.

Perhaps because television is such a powerful force, we like to criticize
it and search for its flaws. However, the benefits of television should not be
ignored. We can use television to relax, to have fun, and to make ourselves
smarter. This electronic wonder, then, is a servant, not a master.

Activity

Fill in the blanks.

Essay __2__ makes its point more clearly and effectively because _____
it is more clearly organized.

_____

Comment: In this case, essay 2 is more effective because the material is
organized clearly and logically. Using emphatic order, the writer develops three
positive uses of television, ending with the most important use: television as an
educational tool. The writer includes transitional words that act as signposts, making movement from one idea to the next easy to follow. The major transitions
include *First of all, In addition,* and *Most important;* transitions within paragraphs
include such words as *Moreover, Still another, too, Also,* and *Finally.* And this
writer also uses a linking sentence ("In addition to being relaxing, television is
entertaining") to tie the first and second supporting paragraphs together clearly.

Although essay 1 is unified and supported, the writer does not have any clear
and consistent way of organizing the material. The most important idea (signaled
by the phrase *Worst of all*) is discussed in the second supporting paragraph instead
of being saved for last. None of the supporting paragraphs organizes its details in
a logical fashion. The first supporting paragraph, for example, discusses older
viewers, then goes to younger viewers, then jumps back to older people again. The
third supporting paragraph, like the first, leaps from an opening idea (families talking only during commercials) to several intervening ideas and then back to the
original idea (talking during commercials). In addition, essay 1 uses practically
no transitional devices to guide the reader.

These two essays lead us to the third base of effective writing: *coherence.* All
the supporting ideas and sentences in a paper must be organized so that they
cohere, or "stick together." As has been discussed in Chapter 3, key techniques
for tying together the material in a paper include a clear method of organization
(such as time order or emphatic order), transitions, and other connecting words.

Revising for Coherence

Activity

On a separate sheet of paper, revise one of the three supporting paragraphs in "Harmful Effects of Watching Television" by providing a clear method of organizing the material and transitional words. Answers will vary.

Base 4: Sentence Skills

Understanding Sentence Skills

Following are the opening paragraphs from two essays. Both are unified, supported, and organized, but one version communicates more clearly and effectively. Which one, and why?

Essay 1,
First Part   **"revenge"**

[1]Revenge is one of those things that everyone enjoy. [2]People don't like   1
to talk about it, though. [3]Just the same, there is nothing more tempting,
more satisfying, or with the reward of a bit of revenge. [4]The purpose is not
to harm your victims. [5]But to let them know that you are upset about
something they are doing. [6]Careful plotting can provide you with relief from
bothersom coworkers, gossiping friends, or nagging family members.

[7]Coworkers who make comments about the fact that you are always   2
fifteen minutes late for work can be taken care of very simply. [8]The first
thing that you should do is to get up extra early one day. [9]Before the sun
comes up, drive to each coworker's house, reach under the hood of his car,
and disconnected the center wire that leads to the distrib. cap. [10]The car will
be unharmed, but it will not start, and your friends at work will all be late
for work on the same day. [11]If your lucky, your boss might notice that you
are the only one there and will give you a raise. [12]Later if you feel guilty
about your actions you can call each person anonymously and tell them how
to get the car running. . . .

Essay 2,
First Part   **A Bit of Revenge**

Revenge is one of those things that everyone enjoys. People don't like   1
to talk about it, though. Just the same, there is nothing more tempting,
more satisfying or more rewarding than a bit of revenge. The purpose is

not to harm your victims but to let them know that you are upset about something they are doing to you. Careful plotting can provide you with relief from bothersome coworkers, gossiping friends, or nagging family members.

Coworkers who make comments about the fact that you are always fifteen minutes late for work can be taken care of very simply. The first thing that you should do is to get up extra early one day. Before the sun comes up, drive to each coworker's house. Reach under the hood of your coworker's car and disconnect the center wire that leads to the distributor cap. The car will be unharmed, but it will not start, and your friends at work will all be late for work on the same day. If you're lucky, your boss might notice that you are the only one there and will give you a raise. Later, if you feel guilty about your actions, you can call your coworkers anonymously and tell them how to get their cars running again. . . .

2

Activity

Fill in the blanks.

Essay __2__ makes its point more clearly and effectively because _____
it is free of errors in grammar, spelling, and punctuation. It shows good use

of sentence skills.

Comment: Essay 2 is more effective because it uses *sentence skills*, the fourth base of competent writing. Here are the sentence-skills mistakes in essay 1:

- The title should not be set off in quotation marks.
- The first letter of the title should be capitalized.
- The singular subject *everyone* in sentence 1 should have a singular verb: *enjoy* should be *enjoys*.
- There is a lack of parallelism in sentence 3: *with the reward of* should be *rewarding*.
- Word group 5 is a fragment; it can be corrected by attaching it to the previous sentence.
- The word *bothersom* in sentence 6 is misspelled; it should be *bothersome*.
- The word *disconnected* in sentence 9 should be *disconnect* to be consistent in tense with *reach*, the other verb in the sentence.
- The word *distrib.* in sentence 9 should be spelled out in full: *distributor.*
- The first *your* in sentence 11 stands for *you are*; an apostrophe and an *e* must be added: *you're.*
- Commas must be added in sentence 12 to set off the interrupting words.

Revising for Sentence Skills

Activity

Here are the final three paragraphs from the two essays. Edit the sentences in the first essay to make the corrections needed. Note that comparing essays 1 and 2 will help you locate the mistakes. This activity will also help you identify some of the sentence skills you may want to review in Part Four.
Editing may vary slightly.

Essay 1, Last Part

. . . [13]Gossiping friends at school are also perfect targets for a simple act of revenge. [14]A way to trap either male or female friends ~~are~~ *is* to leave phony messages on their lockers. [15]If the friend that you want to get is male, leave a message that a certain girl would like him to stop by her house later that day. [16]With any luck, her boyfriend will be there. [17]The girl won't know what's going on, and the victim will be so embarrassed that he probably won't leave his home for a month. [18]The plan works just as well for female friends, too.   3

[19]When Mom and Dad and your sisters and brothers really begin to annoy you, harmless revenge may be just the way to make them ~~quite~~ *quiet* down for a while. [20]The dinner table, where most of the nagging probably happens, is a likely place. [21]Just before the meal begins, throw a handful of raisins into the food. [22]Wait about ~~5~~ *five* minutes and, after everyone has ~~began~~ *begun* to eat, clamp your hand over your mouth and begin to make odd noises.   4

[23]When they ask you what the matter is, point to a raisin and yell, "Bugs!" [24]~~Dumping the~~ *They'll all dump their* food in the disposal, *jump into* the car ~~will~~ *and* head quickly for ~~mcdonald's~~ *McDonald's*. [25]That night, you'll have your first quiet, peaceful meal in a long time.

[26]A well-planned revenge does not have to hurt anyone. [27]The object is simply to let other people know that they are beginning to bother you. [28]You should remember, though, to stay on your guard after completing your revenge. [29]The reason for this is simple. ~~coworkers,~~ *Coworkers,* friends and family can also plan revenge on you.   5

. . . Gossiping friends at school are also perfect targets for a simple act   3
of revenge. A way to trap either male or female friends is to leave phony
messages on their lockers. If the friend that you want to get is male, leave a
message that a certain girl would like him to stop by her house later that day.
With any luck, her boyfriend will be there. The girl won't know what's going
on, and the victim will be so embarrassed that he probably won't leave his
home for a month. The plan works just as well for female friends, too.

When Mom and Dad and your sisters and brothers really begin to annoy   4
you, harmless revenge may be just the way to make them quiet down for
a while. The dinner table, where most of the nagging probably happens,
is a likely place. Just before the meal begins, throw a handful of raisins into
the food. Wait about five minutes and, after everyone has begun to eat,
clamp your hand over your mouth and begin to make odd noises. When
they ask you what the matter is, point to a raisin and yell, "Bugs!" They'll
all dump their food in the disposal, jump into the car, and head quickly
for McDonald's. That night, you'll have your first quiet, peaceful meal in
a long time.

A well-planned revenge does not have to hurt anyone. The object is   5
simply to let other people know that they are beginning to bother you. You
should remember, though, to stay on your guard after completing your
revenge. The reason for this is simple. Coworkers, friends, and family can
also plan revenge on you.

Practice in Using the Four Bases

You are now familiar with four standards, or bases, of effective writing: *unity,
support, coherence,* and *sentence skills.* In this section you will expand and
strengthen your understanding of the four bases as you evaluate and revise essays
for each of them.

1 Revising Essays for Unity

Activity

Both of the following essays contain irrelevant sentences that do not relate to the
thesis of the essay or support the topic sentence of the paragraph in which they
appear. Cross out the irrelevant sentences and write the numbers of those sentences
in the spaces provided.

Essay 1   **Playing on the Browns**

1For the past three summers, I have played first base on a softball team   1
known as the Browns. 2We play a long schedule, including playoffs, and
everybody takes the games pretty seriously. 3In that respect, we're no
different from any other of the thousand or so teams in our city. 4But in
one respect, we <u>are</u> different. 5In an all-male league, we have a woman on
the team—me. 6Thus I've had a chance to observe something about human
nature by seeing how the men have treated me. 7Some have been
disbelieving; some have been patronizing; and, fortunately, some have
simply accepted me.

8One new team in the league was particularly flabbergasted to see me   2
start the game at first base. 9Nobody on the Comets had commented one
way or the other when he saw me warming up, but playing in the actual
game was another story. 10The Comets' first-base coach leaned over to me
with a disbelieving grin and said, "You mean, you're starting, and those
three guys are on the bench?" 11I nodded and he shrugged, still amazed.
12He probably thought I was the manager's wife. 13When I came up to bat,
the Comet pitcher smiled and called to his outfielders to move way in on me.
14Now, I don't have a lot of power, but I'm not exactly feeble. 15~~I used to
work out on the exercise machines at a local health club until it closed, and
now I lift weights at home a couple of times a week~~. 16I wiped the smirks off
their faces with a line drive double over the left fielder's head.

The number of the irrelevant sentence: _____15_____

17The next game, we played another new team, the Argyles, and their   3
attitude was patronizing. 18The Argyles had seen me take batting practice,
so they didn't do anything so rash as to draw their outfield way in. 19They
had respect for my ability as a player. 20However, they tried to annoy me
with phony concern. 21For example, a redheaded Argyle got on base in the
first inning and said to me, "You'd better be careful, Hon. 22When you have
your foot on the bag, somebody might step on it. 23You can get hurt in this
game." 24~~I was mad, but I have worked out several mental techniques to
control my anger because it interferes with my playing ability.~~ 25Well, this
delicate little girl survived the season without injury, which is more than
I can say for some of the "he-men" on the Argyles.

The number of the irrelevant sentence: _____24_____

26Happily, most of the teams in the league have accepted me, just as   4
the Browns did. 27The men on the Browns coached and criticized me (and
occasionally cursed me) just like anyone else. 28~~Because I'm a religious~~
~~person, I don't approve of cursing, but I don't say anything about it to my~~
~~teammates~~. 29They are not amazed when I get a hit or stretch for a wide
throw. 30My average this year was higher than the averages of several of my
teammates, yet none of them acted resentful or threatened. 31On several
occasions I was taken out late in a game for a pinch runner, but other slow
players on the team were also lifted at times for pinch runners. 32Every
woman should have a team like the Browns!

The number of the irrelevant sentence: ___28___

33Because I really had problems only with the new teams, I've concluded   5
that it's when people are faced with an unfamiliar situation that they react
defensively. 34Once a rival team has gotten used to seeing me on the field,
I'm no big deal. 35Still, I suspect that the Browns secretly feel we're a little
special. 36After all, we won the championship with a woman on the team.

Essay 2   **How to Con an Instructor**

1Enter college, and you'll soon be reminded of an old saying: "The   1
pen is mightier than the sword." 2That person behind the instructor's desk
holds your future in his or her ink-stained hands. 3So your first important
assignment in college has nothing to do with required readings, examinations,
or even the hazards of registration. 4It is, instead, how to con an instructor.
5The first step in conning an instructor is to use body language. 6You   2
may be able to convince your instructor that you are special without even
saying a word. 7When you enter the classroom, be sure to sit in the front
row. 8That way, the instructor can't possibly miss you. 9Then, as the
instructor lectures, take notes frantically. 10The instructor will be flattered
that you think so much of his or her words that you want to write them all
down. 11~~A felt-tip pen is superior to a pen or pencil; it will help you write~~
~~faster and prevent aching wrists~~. 12While you are writing, be sure to smile at
the instructor's jokes and nod violently in agreement with every major point.
13Most important, as class continues, sit with your body pitched forward and
your eyes wide open, fixed firmly, as if hypnotized, on your instructor's face.
14Make your whole body suggest that you are watching a star.

The number of the irrelevant sentence: ___11___

[15]Once you have mastered body language, it is time to move on to the second phase of conning the instructor: class participation. [16]Everyone knows that the student who is most eager to learn is the one who responds to the questions that are asked and even comes up with a few more. [17]Therefore, be sure to be responsive. [18]Questions such as, "How does this affect the future of the United States?" or "Don't you think that someday all this will be done by computer?" can be used in any class without prior knowledge of the subject matter. [19]~~Many students, especially in large classes, get lost in the crowd and never do anything to make themselves stand out.~~ [20]Another good participation technique is to wait until the instructor has said something that sounds profound and then ask him or her to repeat it slowly so you can get it down word for word in your notes. [21]No instructor can resist this kind of flattery.

3

The number of the irrelevant sentence: ___19___

[22]However, the most advanced form of conning an instructor happens after class. [23]Don't be like the others who slap their notebooks closed, snatch up their books, and rush out the door before the echoes of the final bell have died away. [24]~~Did you ever notice how students begin to get restless about five minutes before class ends, even if there's no clock on the wall?~~ [25]Instead, be reluctant to leave. [26]Approach the instructor's desk hesitantly, almost reverently. [27]Say that you want to find out more about the topic. [28]Is there any extra reading you can do? [29]Even better, ask if the instructor has written anything on the topic—and whether you could borrow it. [30]Finally, compliment your instructor by saying that this is the most interesting course you've ever taken. [31]Nothing beats the personal approach for making an instructor think you care.

4

The number of the irrelevant sentence: ___24___

[32]Body language, questions, after-class discussions—these are the secrets of conning an instructor that every college student should know. [33]~~These kinds of things go on in high school, too, and they're just as effective on that level.~~ [34]Once you master these methods, you won't have to worry about a thing—until the final exam.

5

The number of the irrelevant sentence: ___33___

2 Revising Essays for Support

Activity

Both of the essays below lack supporting details at certain key points. In each essay, identify the spots where details are needed.

Essay 1   **Formula for Happiness**

1   ¹Everyone has his or her own formula for happiness. ²As we go through life, we discover the activities that make us feel best. ³I've already discovered three keys to happiness. ⁴I depend on karate, music, and self-hypnosis.

2   ⁵Karate helps me feel good physically. ⁶Before taking karate lessons, I was tired most of the time, my muscles felt like foam rubber, and I was twenty pounds overweight. ⁷After three months of these lessons, I saw an improvement in my physical condition. ⁸Also, my endurance has increased. ⁹At the end of my workday, I used to drag myself home to eat and watch television all night. ¹⁰Now, I have enough energy to play with my children, shop, or see a movie. ¹¹Karate has made me feel healthy, strong, and happy.

The spot where supporting details are needed occurs after sentence ___7___.

3   ¹²Singing with a chorus has helped me achieve emotional well-being by expressing my feelings. ¹³In situations where other people would reveal their feelings, I would remain quiet. ¹⁴Since joining the chorus, however, I have an outlet for joy, anger, or sadness. ¹⁵When I sing, I pour my emotions into the music and don't have to feel shy. ¹⁶For this reason, I most enjoy singing certain kinds of music, since they demand real depth of feeling.

The first spot where supporting details are needed occurs after sentence ___13___.

The second spot occurs after sentence ___16___.

4   ¹⁷Self-hypnosis gives me peace of mind. ¹⁸This is a total relaxation technique, which I learned several years ago. ¹⁹Essentially I breathe deeply and concentrate on relaxing all my muscles. ²⁰I then repeat a key suggestion to myself. ²¹Through self-hypnosis, I have gained control over several bad habits that have long been haunting me. ²²I have also learned to reduce the stress that goes along with my secretarial job. ²³Now I can handle the boss's demands or unexpected work without feeling tense.

The first spot where supporting details are needed occurs after sentence ___20___.

The second spot occurs after sentence ___21___.

[24]In short, my physical, emotional, and mental well-being have been   5
greatly increased through karate, music and self-hypnosis. [25]These activities
have become important elements in my formula for happiness.

Essay 2   **Problems of a Foreign Student**

[1]About ten months ago I decided to leave my native country and come to   1
the United States to study. [2]When I got here, I suddenly turned into someone
labeled "foreign student." [3]A foreign student, I discovered, has problems.
[4]Whether from Japan, like me, or from some other country, a foreign student
has to work twice as hard as Americans do to succeed in college.

[5]First of all, there is the language problem. [6]American students have the   2
advantage of comprehending English without working at it. [7]But even they
complain that some professors talk too fast, mumble, or use big words. [8]As a
result, they can't take notes fast enough to keep up, or they misunderstand
what was said. [9]Now consider my situation. [10]I'm trying to cope with a
language that is probably one of the hardest in the world to learn. [11]Dozens
of English slang phrases—"mess around," "hassle," "get into"—were totally
new to me. [12]Other language problems gave me trouble, too.

The spot where supporting details are needed occurs after sentence ___12___.

[13]Another problem I face has to do with being a stranger to American   3
culture. [14]For instance, the academic world is much different in Japan. [15]In
the United States, instructors seem to treat students as equals. [16]Many
classes are informal, and the relationship between instructor and student
is friendly; in fact, students call some instructors by their first names. [17]In
Japan, however, the instructor-student relationship is different. [18]Lectures,
too are more formal, and students show respect by listening quietly and
paying attention at all times. [19]This more casual atmosphere occasionally
makes me feel uncomfortable in class.

The spot where supporting details are needed occurs after sentence ___17___.

[20]Perhaps the most difficult problem I face is social. [21]American students   4
may have some trouble making new friends or may feel lonely at times.
[22]However, they usually manage to find other people with the same
background, interests, or goals. [23]It is twice as hard to make friends, though,
if a person has trouble making the small talk that can lead to a relationship.
[24]I find it difficult to become friends with other students because I don't
understand some aspects of American life. [25]Students would rather talk to
someone who is familiar with these things.

The spot where supporting details are needed occurs after sentence ___24___.

²⁶Despite all the handicaps that I, as a foreign student, have to   5
overcome, I wouldn't give up this chance to go to school in the United
States. ²⁷Each day, the problems seem a little bit less overwhelming. ²⁸Like
a little child who is finally learning to read, write, and make sense of things,
I am starting to enjoy my experience of discovering a brand-new world.

3 Revising Essays for Coherence

Activity

Both of the essays that follow could be revised to improve their coherence. Answer
the questions about coherence that come after each essay.

Essay 1   **Noise Pollution**

¹Natural sounds—waves, wind, birdsongs—are so soothing that companies   1
sell tapes of them to anxious people seeking a relaxing atmosphere at home
or in the car. ²One reason why "environmental sounds" are big business is the
fact that ordinary citizens, especially city dwellers, are bombarded by noise
pollution. ³On the way to work, on the job, and on the way home, the typical
urban resident must cope with a continuing barrage of unpleasant sounds.

⁴The noise level in an office can be unbearable. ⁵From nine to five o'clock,   2
phones and fax machines ring, modems sound, computer keyboards chatter,
intercoms buzz, and copy machines thump back and forth. ⁶Every time the
receptionists can't find people, they resort to a nerve-shattering public
address system. ⁷And because the managers worry about the employees'
morale, they graciously provide the endless droning of canned music. ⁸This
effectively eliminates any possibility of a moment of blessed silence.

⁹Traveling home from work provides no relief from the noisiness of the   3
office. ¹⁰The ordinary sounds of blaring taxi horns and rumbling buses are
occasionally punctuated by the ear-piercing screech of car brakes. ¹¹Taking
a shortcut through the park will bring the weary worker face to face with
chanting religious cults, freelance musicians, screaming children, and barking
dogs. ¹²None of these sounds can compare with the large radios many park
visitors carry. ¹³Each radio blasts out something different, from heavy-metal
rock to baseball, at decibel levels so strong that they make eardrums throb
in pain. ¹⁴If there are birds singing or wind in the trees, the harried
commuter will never hear them.

¹⁵Even a trip to work at 6 or 7 A.M. isn't quiet. ¹⁶No matter which route   4
a worker takes, there is bound to be a noisy construction site somewhere
along the way. ¹⁷Hard hats will shout from third-story windows to warn their
coworkers below before heaving debris out and sending it crashing to earth.
¹⁸Huge front-end loaders will crunch into these piles of rubble and back up,
their warning signals letting out loud, jarring beeps. ¹⁹Air hammers begin an

ear-splitting chorus of rat-a-tat-tat sounds guaranteed to shatter sanity as well as concrete. [20]Before reaching the office, the worker is already completely frazzled.

[21]Noise pollution is as dangerous as any other kind of pollution. [22]The   5
endless pressure of noise probably triggers countless nervous breakdowns, vicious arguments, and bouts of depression. [23]And imagine the world problems we could solve, if only the noise stopped long enough to let us think.

1. In "Noise Pollution," what is the number of the sentence to which the transition word *Also* could be added in paragraph 2? ___6___

2. In the last sentence of paragraph 2, to what does the pronoun *This* refer? _endless droning of canned music_____

3. What is the number of the sentence to which the transition word *But* could be added in paragraph 3? ___12___

4. What is the number of the sentence to which the transition word *Then* could be added in paragraph 4? ___18___

5. What is the number of the sentence to which the transition word *Meanwhile* could be added in paragraph 4? ___19___

6. What word is used as a synonym for *debris* in paragraph 4? ___rubble___

7. How many times is the key word *sounds* used in the essay? ___six times___

8. The time order of the three supporting paragraphs is confused. Which supporting paragraph should come first? ___4___ Second? ___2___ Third? ___3___

Essay 2   **Weight Loss**

[1]The big fraternity party turned out to be the low point of my first year   1
at college. [2]I was in heaven until I discovered that my date with handsome Greg, the fraternity vice president, was a hoax: he had used me to win the "ugliest date" contest. [3]I ran sobbing back to the dorm, wanting to resign from the human race. [4]Then I realized that it was time to stop kidding myself about my weight. [5]Within the next two years, I lost forty-two pounds and turned my life around. [6]Losing weight gave me self-confidence socially, emotionally, and professionally.

[7]I am more outgoing socially. [8]Just being able to abandon dark colors,   2
overblouses, and tent dresses in favor of bright colors, T-shirts, and designer jeans made me feel better in social situations. [9]I am able to do more things. [10]I once turned down an invitation for a great camping trip with my best friend's family, making up excuses about sun poisoning and allergies. [11]Really, I was too embarrassed to tell them that I couldn't fit into the

bathroom in their Winnebago! ¹²I made up for it last summer when I was one of the organizers of a college backpacking trip through the Rockies.

¹³Most important, losing weight helped me seek new professional goals. ³ ¹⁴When I was obese, I organized my whole life around my weight, as if it were a defect I could do nothing about. ¹⁵With my good grades, I could have chosen almost any major the college offered, but I had limited my goal to teaching kindergarten because I felt that little children wouldn't judge how I looked. ¹⁶Once I was no longer fat, I realized that I love working with all sorts of people. ¹⁷I became a campus guide and even had small parts in college theater productions. ¹⁸As a result, last year I changed my major to public relations. ¹⁹The area fascinates me, and I now have good job prospects there.

²⁰I have also become more emotionally honest. ²¹Rose, at the college ⁴ counseling center, helped me see that my "fat and jolly" personality had been false. ²²I was afraid others would reject me if I didn't always go along with their suggestions. ²³I eventually put Rose's advice to the test. ²⁴My roommates were planning an evening at a Greek restaurant. ²⁵I loved the restaurant's atmosphere, but there wasn't much I liked on the menu. ²⁶Finally, in a shaky voice I said, "Actually, I'm not crazy about lamb. ²⁷How about Chinese food?" ²⁸They scolded me for not mentioning it before, and we had dinner at a Chinese restaurant. ²⁹We all agreed it was one of our best evenings out.

³⁰Fortunately, the low point of my first year turned out to be the turning ⁵ point leading to what promises to be an exciting senior year. ³¹Greg's cruel joke became a strange sort of favor, and I've gone from wanting to resign from the human race to welcoming each day as a source of fresh adventure and self-discovery.

1. In "Weight Loss," what is the number of the sentence to which the transition words *For one thing* could be added in paragraph 2? ___8___

2. What is the number of the sentence to which the transition word *Also* could be added in paragraph 2? ___9___

3. What is the number of the sentence to which the transition word *But* could be added in paragraph 2? ___12___

4. In sentence 11, to what does the pronoun *them* refer? __my best friend's family__

5. What is the number of the sentence to which the transition word *However* could be added in paragraph 3? ___16___

6. What word is used as a synonym for *obese* in paragraph 3? ___fat___

7. How many times is the key word *weight* used in the essay? ___four times___

8. Which supporting paragraph should be placed in the emphatic final position? ___3___

4 Revising Essays for All Four Bases: Unity, Support, Coherence, and Sentence Skills

Activity

In this activity, you will evaluate and revise two essays in terms of all four bases: unity, support, coherence, and sentence skills. Comments follow each supporting paragraph. Circle the letter of the *one* statement that applies in each case.

Essay 1   **Chiggers**

I had lived my whole life not knowing what chiggers are. I thought they were probably a type of insect Humphrey Bogart encountered in <u>The African Queen</u>. I never had any real reason to care, until one day last summer. Within twenty-four hours, I had vividly experienced what chigger bites are, learned how to treat them, and learned how to prevent them.

1

First of all, I learned that chiggers are the larvae of tiny mites found in the woods and that their bites are always multiple and cause intense itching. A beautiful summer day seemed perfect for a walk in the woods. I am definitely not a city person, for I couldn't stand to be surrounded by people, noise, and concrete. As I walked through the ferns and pines, I noticed what appeared to be a dusting of reddish seeds or pollen on my slacks. Looking more closely, I realized that each speck was a tiny insect. I casually brushed off a few and gave them no further thought. I woke up the next morning feeling like a victim staked to an anthill by an enemy wise in the ways of torture. Most of my body was speckled with measlelike bumps that at the slightest touch burned and itched like a mosquito bite raised to the twentieth power. When antiseptics and calamine lotion failed to help, I raced to my doctor for emergency aid.

2

a. Paragraph 2 contains an irrelevant sentence.
b. Paragraph 2 lacks supporting details at one key spot.
c. Time order in paragraph 2 is confused.
d. Paragraph 2 contains two run-ons.

Healing the bites of chiggers, as the doctor diagnosed them to be, is not a simple procedure. It seems that there is really no wonder drug or commercial product to help. The victim must rely on a harsh and primitive home remedy and mostly wait out the course of the painful bites. First, the doctor explained, the skin must be bathed carefully in alcohol. An

3

antihistamine spray applied several hours later will soothe the intense itching and help prevent infection. Before using the spray, I had to saturate each bite with gasoline or nail polish to kill any remaining chiggers. A few days after the treatment, the bites finally healed. Although I was still in pain, and desperate for relief, I followed the doctor's instructions. I carefully applied gasoline to the bites and walked around for an hour smelling like a filling station.

a. Paragraph 3 contains an irrelevant sentence.
b. Paragraph 3 lacks supporting details at one key spot.
c. Time order in paragraph 3 is confused.
d. Paragraph 3 contains one fragment.

Most important of all, I learned what to do to prevent getting chigger bites in the future. Mainly, of course, stay out of the woods in the summertime. But if the temptation is too great on an especially beautiful day, I'll be sure to wear the right type of clothing, like a long-sleeved shirt, long pants, knee socks, and closed shoes. In addition, I'll cover myself with clouds of superstrength insect repellent. I will then shower thoroughly as soon as I get home, I also will probably burn all my clothes if I notice even one suspicious red speck.

4

a. Paragraph 4 contains an irrelevant sentence.
b. Paragraph 4 lacks supporting details at one key spot.
c. Paragraph 4 lacks transitional words.
d. Paragraph 4 contains a run-on and a fragment.

I will never forget my lessons on the cause, cure, and prevention of chigger bites. I'd gladly accept the challenge of rattlesnakes and scorpions in the wilds of the West but will never again confront a siege of chiggers in the pinewoods.

5

Essay 2   **The Hazards of Being an Only Child**

Many people who have grown up in multichild families think that being an only child is the best of all possible worlds. They point to such benefits as the only child's annual new wardrobe and the lack of competition for parental love. But single-child status isn't as good as people say it is. Instead of having everything they want, only children are sometimes denied certain basic human needs.

1

Only children lack companionship. An only child can have trouble making friends, since he or she isn't used to being around other children.

2

Often, the only child comes home to an empty house; both parents are working, and there are no brothers or sisters to play with or to talk to about the day. At dinner, the single child can't tell jokes, giggle, or throw food while the adults discuss boring adult subjects. An only child always has his or her own room but never has anyone to whisper to half the night when sleep doesn't come. Some only children thrive on this isolation and channel their energies into creative activities like writing or drawing. Owing to this lack of companionship, an only child sometimes lacks the social ease and self-confidence that come from being part of a closely knit group of contemporaries.

a. Paragraph 2 contains an irrelevant sentence.
b. Paragraph 2 lacks supporting details at one key spot.
c. Paragraph 2 lacks transitional words.
d. Paragraph 2 contains one fragment and one run-on.

Second, only children lack privacy. An only child is automatically the center of parental concern. There's never any doubt about which child tried to sneak in after midnight on a weekday. And who will get the lecture the next morning. Also, whenever an only child gives in to a bad mood, runs into his or her room, and slams the door, the door will open thirty seconds later, revealing an anxious parent. Parents of only children sometimes don't even understand the child's need for privacy. For example, they may not understand why a teenager wants a lock on the door or a personal telephone. After all, the parents think, there are only the three of us, there's no need for secrets.

3

a. Paragraph 3 contains an irrelevant sentence.
b. Paragraph 3 lacks supporting details at one key spot.
c. Paragraph 3 lacks transitional words.
d. Paragraph 3 contains one fragment and one run-on.

Most important, only children lack power. They get all the love; but if something goes wrong, they also get all the punishment. When a bottle of perfume is knocked to the floor or the television is left on all night, there's no little sister or brother to blame it on. Moreover, an only child has no recourse when asking for a privilege of some kind, such as permission to stay out late or to take an overnight trip with friends. There are no other siblings to point to and say, "You let them do it. Why won't you let me?" With no allies their own age, only children are always outnumbered, two to one. An only child hasn't a chance of influencing any major family decisions, either.

4

a. Paragraph 4 contains an irrelevant sentence.
b. Paragraph 4 lacks supporting details at one key spot.
c. Paragraph 4 lacks transitional words.
d. Paragraph 4 contains one fragment and one run-on.

Being an only child isn't as special as some people think. It's no fun   5
being without friends, without privacy, and without power in one's own
home. But the child who can triumph over these hardships grows up self-
reliant and strong. Perhaps for this reason alone, the hazards are worth it.

Part Two

Patterns of Essay Development

7 Introduction to Essay Development

Traditionally, essay writing has been divided into the following patterns of development:

- Description
- Narration
- Exposition

Examples	Comparison and contrast
Process	Definition
Cause and effect	Division and classification

- Argumentation

A *description* is a verbal picture of a person, place, or thing. In *narration*, a writer tells the story of something that happened.

In *exposition*, the writer provides information about and explains a particular subject. Patterns of development within exposition include giving *examples*, detailing a *process* of doing or making something, analyzing *causes and effects*, *comparing and contrasting*, *defining* a term or concept, and *dividing* something into parts or *classifying* it into categories.

Finally, in *argumentation*, a writer attempts to support a controversial point or to defend a position on which there is a difference of opinion.

The pages ahead present individual chapters on each pattern. You will have a chance, then, to learn nine different patterns or methods for organizing material in your papers. Each pattern has its own internal logic and provides its own special strategies for imposing order on your ideas. As you practice each pattern, you should keep two points in mind.

- *Point 1:* While each essay that you write will involve one predominant pattern, very often one or more additional patterns may be involved as well. For example, consider the two student essays in the chapter on "Examples." The first essay there, "Everyday Cruelty" (page 211), is developed through a series of *examples*. But there is also an element of *narration*, because the writer presents examples that occur as he proceeds through his day. In the second essay, "Altered States" (page 213), use of *examples* is again the predominant pattern, but in a lesser way the author is also explaining the *causes* of altered states of mind.

- *Point 2:* No matter which pattern or patterns you use, each essay will probably involve some form of argumentation. You will advance a point and then go on to support that point. In "Everyday Cruelty," for instance, the author uses *examples* to support his point that people inflict little cruelties on each other. In an essay that appears earlier, a writer supports the point that a particular diner is depressing by providing a number of *descriptive details* (see page 176). Another writer claims that a certain experience in his life was frightening and then uses a *narrative* to persuade us of the truth of this statement (see page 196). And yet another author states that a fast-food restaurant can be preferable to a fancy one and then supplies *comparative information* about both to support his statement (see page 267). Much of your writing, in short, will have the purpose of persuading your reader that the idea you have advanced is valid.

The Progression in Each Chapter

In Chapters 8 through 16, after each type of essay development is explained, student essays and a professional essay illustrating that type are presented, followed by questions about the essays. The questions relate to unity, support, and coherence—principles of effective writing explained earlier in this book. You are then asked to write your own essay. In most cases, the first assignment is fairly structured and provides a good deal of guidance for the writing process. The other assignments offer a wide choice of writing topics. In each case, one assignment involves writing an essay with a specific purpose and for a specific audience. And in three instances (examples, cause-effect, and comparison or contrast), the final assignments require outside reading of literary works; a student model is provided for each of these assignments.

Important Considerations in Essay Development

Before you begin to work on particular types of essays, there are several general considerations about writing to keep in mind. They will be discussed in turn.

Understanding the Nature and Length of an Assignment

In all likelihood, there will be a good deal of variety in your college writing assignments. Sometimes you will able to write on a topic of your own choosing, or on a point you discover within a given topic; at other times you may be given a very specific assignment. In any case, do not start writing a paper until you know just what is expected.

First of all, be clear about the *kind of paper* that the instructor has in mind. Should it be primarily a research summary of other people's ideas? Should it consist entirely of your own ideas? Should it consist of a comparison of your ideas with those of a given author? Should it be something else? If you are not sure about the nature of an assignment, other students may be confused as well. Do not hesitate, then, to ask an instructor about an assignment. Most instructors are more than willing to provide an explanation. They would rather spend a few minutes of class time explaining an assignment than spend hours reading student essays that miss the mark.

Second, find out right at the start *how long* a paper is expected to be. Many instructors will indicate the approximate length of the papers they assign. Knowing the expected length of a paper will help you decide just how detailed your treatment of a subject should be.

Knowing Your Subject

Whenever possible, try to write on a subject that interests you. You will then find it easier to put more time into your work. Even more important, try to write on a subject that you already know something about. If you do not have direct experience with the subject, you should at least have indirect experience—knowledge gained through thinking, reading, or talking about the subject as well as from prewriting.

If you are asked to write on a topic about which you have no experience or knowledge, you should do whatever research is required to gain the background information you may need. Chapter 21, "Using the Library and the Internet," will show you how to look up relevant information. Without direct or indirect experience, or the information you gain through research, you may not be able to provide the specific evidence needed to develop an essay.

Knowing Your Purpose and Audience

The three most common purposes of writing are to inform, to persuade, and to entertain. As noted above, much of the writing you do in this book will involve some form of argumentation or persuasion. You will advance a point or thesis and then support it in a variety of ways. To some extent, also, you will write papers to inform—to provide readers with information about a particular subject. And since, in practice, writing often combines purposes, you might also find yourself at times providing vivid or humorous details in order to entertain your readers.

Your audience will be primarily your instructor and sometimes other students. Your instructor is really a symbol of the larger audience you should see yourself writing for—educated adult readers who expect you to present your ideas in a clear, direct, organized way. If you can learn to write to persuade or inform such a general audience, you will have accomplished a great deal.

It will also be helpful for you to write some papers for a more specific audience. By doing so, you will develop an ability to choose words and adopt a tone and point of view that are just right for a given audience. This part of the book includes assignments asking you to write with very specific purposes in mind, and for very specific audiences.

Determining Your Point of View

When you write, you can take any of three approaches, or points of view: first-person, second-person, or third-person.

First-Person Approach

In the first-person approach—a strongly individualized point of view—you draw on your own experience and speak to your audience in your own voice, using pronouns like *I, me, mine, we, our*, and *us*.

The first-person approach is most common in narrative essays based on personal experience. It also suits other essays where most of the evidence presented consists of personal observation.

Here is a first-person supporting paragraph from an essay on camping:

> First of all, I like comfort when I'm camping. My GMC motor home, with its completely equipped kitchen, shower stall, toilet, double bed, and color television, resembles a mobile motel room. I can sleep on a real mattress, clean sheets, and fluffy pillows. Next to my bed are devices that make me feel at home: a radio, an alarm clock, and a TV remote-control unit. Unlike the poor campers huddled in tents, I don't have to worry about cold, rain, heat, or annoying insects. After a hot shower, I can slide into my best nightgown, sit comfortably on my down-filled quilt, and read the latest best-seller while a thunderstorm booms outside.

Second-Person Approach

In the second-person approach, the writer speaks directly to the reader, using the pronoun *you*. The second-person approach is considered appropriate for giving direct instructions and explanations to the reader. That is why *you* is used throughout this book.

You should expect to use the second-person approach only when writing a process essay. Otherwise, as a general rule, *never* use the word *you* in writing. (If doing so has been a common mistake in your writing, you should review the rule about pronoun point of view on pages 106–107.)

Third-Person Approach

The third-person approach is by far the most common point of view in academic writing. In the third person, the writer includes no direct references to the reader (*you*) or the self (*I, me*). Third person gets its name from the stance it suggests—that of an outsider or "third person" observing and reporting on matters of public rather than private importance. In this approach, you draw on information that you have gotten through observation, thinking, or reading.

Here is the paragraph on camping, recast in the third person. Note the third-person pronouns *their, them,* and *they,* which all refer to *campers* in the first sentence.

First of all, modern campers bring complete bedrooms with them. Winnebagos, GMC motor homes, and Airstream trailers lumber into America's campgrounds every summer like mobile motel rooms. All the comforts of home are provided inside. Campers sleep on real mattresses with clean sheets and fluffy pillows. Next to their beds are the same gadgets that litter their night tables at home—radios, alarm clocks, and TV remote-control units. It's not necessary for them to worry about annoyances like cold, heat, rain, or buzzing insects, either. They can sit comfortably in bed and read the latest best-sellers while a thunderstorm booms outside.

Using Peer Review

In addition to having your instructor as an audience for your writing, you will benefit from having another student in your class as an audience. On the day a paper is due, or on a day when you are writing papers in class, your instructor may ask you to pair up with another student. That student will read your paper, and you will read his or her paper.

Ideally, read the other paper aloud while your peer listens. If that is not practical, read it in a whisper while your peer looks on. As you read, both you and your peer should look and listen for spots where the paper does not read smoothly and clearly. Check or circle the trouble spots where your reading snags.

Your peer should then read your paper, marking possible trouble spots. Then each of you should do three things.

1 Identification

At the top of a separate sheet of paper, write the title and author of the paper you have read. Under it, write your name as the reader of the paper.

2 Scratch Outline

"X-ray" the paper for its inner logic by making up a scratch outline. The scratch outline need be no more than twenty words or so, but it should show clearly the logical foundation on which the essay is built. It should identify and summarize the overall point of the paper and the three areas of support for the point.

Your outline can look as follows.

Point: _____

Support:

(1) _____

(2) _____

(3) _____

For example, here is a scratch outline of the essay on moviegoing on pages 6–7:

Point: _Moviegoing is a problem._____

Support:

(1) _Inconvenience of going out_____

(2) _Tempting snacks_____

(3) _Other patrons_____

3 Comments

Under the outline, write a heading: "Comments." Here is what you should comment on:

- Look at the spots where your reading of the paper snagged. Are words missing or misspelled? Is there a lack of parallel structure? Are there mistakes with punctuation? Is the meaning of a sentence confused? Try to figure out what the problems are and suggest ways of fixing them.
- Are there spots in the paper where you see problems with *unity*, *support*, or *organization*? (You'll find it helpful to refer to the checklist on the inside front cover of this book.) If so, offer comments. For example, you might say, "More details are needed in the first supporting paragraph," or, "Some of the details in the last supporting paragraph don't really back up your point."
- Finally, note something you really liked about the paper, such as good use of transitions or an especially realistic or vivid specific detail.

After you have completed your evaluation of the paper, give it to your peer. Your instructor may give you the option of rewriting a paper in light of the feedback you get. Whether or not you rewrite, be sure to hand in the peer evaluation form with your paper.

Doing a Personal Review

1 While you're writing and revising an essay, you should be constantly evaluating it in terms of *unity, support,* and *organization.* Use as a guide the detailed checklist on the inside front cover of the book.

2 After you've finished the next-to-final draft of an essay, check it for the *sentence skills* listed on the inside front cover. It may also help to read the paper out loud. If a given sentence does not sound right—that is, if it does not read clearly and smoothly—chances are something is wrong. Then revise or edit as needed until your paper is complete.

8 Description

When you describe someone or something, you give your readers a picture in words. To make the word picture as vivid and real as possible, you must observe and record specific details that appeal to your readers' senses (sight, hearing, taste, smell, and touch). More than any other type of essay, a descriptive paper needs sharp, colorful details.

Here is a sentence in which there is almost no appeal to the senses: "In the window was a fan." In contrast, here is a description rich in sense impressions: "The blades of the rusty window fan clattered and whirled as they blew out a stream of warm, soggy air." Sense impressions in this second example include sight (*rusty window fan, whirled*), hearing (*clattered*), and touch (*warm, soggy air*). The vividness and sharpness provided by the sensory details give us a clear picture of the fan and enable us to share the writer's experience.

In this chapter, you will be asked to describe a person, place, or thing sharply, by using words rich in sensory details. To prepare for this assignment, first read the student essays and the professional essay that follow and work through the questions that accompany the essays.

Student Essays to Consider

Family Portrait

My mother, who is seventy years old, recently sent me a photograph   1
of herself that I had never seen before. While cleaning out the attic of her
Florida home, she came across a studio portrait she had had taken about
a year before she married my father. This picture of my mother as a twenty-
year-old girl and the story behind it have fascinated me from the moment
I began to consider it.

The young woman in the picture has a face that resembles my own in   2
many ways. Her face is a bit more oval than mine, but the softly waving
brown hair around it is identical. The small, straight nose is the same model
I was born with. My mother's mouth is closed, yet there is just the slightest
hint of a smile on her full lips. I know that if she had smiled, she would have
shown the same wide grin and down-curving "smile lines" that appear in
my own snapshots. The most haunting feature in the photo, however, is my
mother's eyes. They are an exact duplicate of my own large, dark-brown
ones. Her brows are plucked into thin lines, which are like two pencil strokes
added to highlight those fine, luminous eyes.

I've also carefully studied the clothing and jewelry in the photograph.   3
My mother is wearing a blouse and skirt that, although the photo was taken
fifty years ago, could easily be worn today. The blouse is made of heavy
eggshell-colored satin and reflects the light in its folds and hollows. It has
a turned-down cowl collar and smocking on the shoulders and below the
collar. The smocking (tiny rows of gathered material) looks hand-done. The
skirt, which covers my mother's calves, is straight and made of light wool
or flannel. My mother is wearing silver drop earrings. They are about two
inches long and roughly shield-shaped. On her left wrist is a matching
bracelet. My mother can't find this bracelet now, despite the fact that we
spent hours searching through the attic for it. On the third finger of her
left hand is a ring with a large, square-cut stone.

The story behind the picture is as interesting to me as the young woman   4
it captures. Mom, who was earning twenty-five dollars a week as a file clerk,
decided to give her boyfriend (my father) a picture of herself. She spent
almost two weeks' salary on the skirt and blouse, which she bought at a
fancy department store downtown. She borrowed the earrings and bracelet
from her older sister, my Aunt Dorothy. The ring she wore was a present
from another young man she was dating at the time. Mom spent another
chunk of her salary to pay the portrait photographer for the hand-tinted
print in old-fashioned tones of brown and tan. Just before giving the picture
to my father, she scrawled at the lower left, "Sincerely, Beatrice."

When I study this picture, I react in many ways. I think about the trouble   5
that Mom went to in order to impress the young man who was to be my
father. I laugh when I look at the ring, which was probably worn to make my
father jealous. I smile at the serious, formal inscription my mother used at
this stage of the budding relationship. Sometimes, I am filled with a mixture
of pleasure and sadness when I look at this frozen long-ago moment. It is a
moment of beauty, of love, and—in a way—of my own past.

The Diner at Midnight

I've been in lots of diners, and they've always seemed to be warm, busy,   1
friendly, happy places. That's why, on a recent Monday night, I stopped in a
diner for a cup of coffee. I was returning home after an all-day car trip and
needed something to help me get through the last forty-five miles. I'd been
visiting my cousins, whom I try to get together with at least twice a year.
A diner at midnight, however, was not the place I had expected—it was
different, and lonely.

Even the outside of the diner was uninviting. My Escort pulled to a halt   2
in front of the dreary gray aluminum building, which looked like an old
railroad car. A half-lit neon sign sputtered the message, "Fresh baked goods
daily," reflected on the surface of the rain-slick parking lot. Only a half
dozen cars and a battered pickup were scattered around the lot. An empty
paper coffee cup made a hollow scraping sound as it rolled in small circles

on one cement step close to the entrance. I pulled hard at the balky glass door, and it banged shut behind me.

The diner was quiet when I entered. As there was no hostess on duty, only the faint odor of stale grease and the dull hum of an empty refrigerated pastry case greeted me. The outside walls were lined with vacant booths which squatted back to back in their black vinyl upholstery. On each black-and-white checkerboard-patterned table were the usual accessories—glass salt and pepper shakers, ketchup bottle, sugar packets—silently waiting for the next morning's breakfast crowd. I glanced through the round windows on the two swinging metal doors leading to the kitchen. I could see only part of the large, apparently deserted cooking area, with a shiny stainless-steel range and blackened pans of various sizes and shapes hanging along a ledge.   3

I slid onto one of the cracked vinyl seats at the Formica counter. Two men in rumpled work shirts also sat at the counter, on stools several feet apart, smoking cigarettes and staring wearily into cups of coffee. Their faces sprouted what looked like daylong stubbles of beard. I figured they were probably shift workers who, for some reason, didn't want to go home. Three stools down from the workers, I spotted a thin young man with a mop of curly black hair. He was dressed in new-looking jeans with a black Gap polo shirt, unbuttoned at the neck. He wore a blank expression as he picked at a plate of limp french fries. I wondered if he had just returned from a disappointing date. At the one occupied booth sat a middle-aged couple. They hadn't gotten any food yet. He was staring off into space, idly tapping his spoon against the table, while she drew aimless parallel lines on her paper napkin with a bent dinner fork. Neither said a word to the other. The people in the diner seemed as lonely as the place itself.   4

Finally, a tired-looking waitress approached me with her thick order pad. I ordered the coffee, but I wanted to drink it fast and get out of there. My car, and the solitary miles ahead of me, would be lonely. But they wouldn't be as lonely as that diner at midnight.   5

■ Questions

About Unity

1. In which supporting paragraph of "The Diner at Midnight" does the topic sentence appear at the paragraph's end, rather than the beginning?

   a. paragraph 2

   b. paragraph 3

   c. paragraph 4

2. Which sentence in paragraph 1 of "The Diner at Midnight" should be eliminated in the interest of paragraph unity? *(Write the opening words.)*

   I'd been visiting my cousins . . .

3. Which of the following sentences from paragraph 3 of "Family Portrait" should be omitted in the interest of paragraph unity?
   a. My mother is wearing a blouse and skirt that, although the photo was taken fifty years ago, could easily be worn today.
   b. It has a turned-down cowl collar and smocking on the shoulders and below the collar.
   c. My mother can't find this bracelet now, despite the fact that we spent hours searching the attic for it.
   d. On the third finger of her left hand is a ring with a large, square-cut stone.

About Support

4. How many separate items of clothing and jewelry are described in paragraph 3 of "Family Portrait"?
   a. four
   b. five
   c. six

5. Label as sight, touch, hearing, or smell all the sensory details in the following sentences taken from the two essays. The first one is done for you as an example.
   a.   *sight*   *smell*
      "As there was no hostess on duty, only the faint odor of stale grease and
         hearing   *sight*
      the dull hum of an empty refrigerated pastry case greeted me."
   b.   *sight*   *hearing*
      "He was staring off into space, idly tapping his spoon against the table,
                                    sight
      while she drew aimless parallel lines on her paper napkin with a bent
      dinner fork."
   c.   *touch*   *sight*   *sight*
      "The blouse is made of heavy eggshell-colored satin and reflects the light
         sight
      in its folds and hollows."
   d.   *touch*   *sight*   *sight*
      Her brows are plucked into thin lines, which are like two pencil strokes
                     sight
      added to highlight those fine, luminous eyes.

6. What are three details in paragraph 3 of "The Diner at Midnight" that reinforce the idea of "quiet" expressed in the topic sentence?

   . . . dull hum . . .

   . . . silently waiting . . .

   . . . deserted cooking area . . .

About Coherence

7. Which method of organization does paragraph 2 of "Family Portrait" use?

    a.   Time order

    (b.) Emphatic order

8. Which sentence in paragraph 2 of "Family Portrait" suggests the method of organization? *(Write the opening words.)*

    The most haunting feature in the photo, . . .

9. The last paragraph of "The Diner at Midnight" begins with a word that serves as which type of signal?

    (a.) time

    b.   addition

    c.   contrast

    d.   illustration

About the Introduction and Conclusion

10. Which statement best describes the introduction to "The Diner at Midnight"?

    (a.) It starts with an idea that is the opposite of the one then developed.

    b.   It explains the importance of the topic to its readers.

    c.   It begins with a general statement of the topic and narrows it down to a thesis statement.

    d.   It begins with an anecdote.

Developing a Descriptive Essay

Development Through Prewriting

Because the function of a descriptive essay is to provide readers with a vivid picture in words, you must choose a topic that appeals strongly to at least one of your senses. It's possible to write a descriptive essay, maybe even a good one, about a boiled potato. But it would be easier (not to mention more fun) to describe a bowl of potato salad, with its contrasting textures of soft potato and crisp celery, its creamy dressing, and its tangy seasonings. Likewise, as you choose a topic for your essay, you should pick one that gives you plenty to work with in terms of sensory detail.

When Cindy, the author of "Family Portrait," sat down to think about a topic for her essay, she looked around her apartment for inspiration. First she thought about describing her own bedroom. But she had moved into the apartment only recently and hadn't done much in the way of decorating, so the room struck her as too bare and sterile. Then she looked out her window, thinking of describing the view. That seemed much more promising: she noticed the sights and sounds of children playing on the sidewalks and a group of older men playing cards, as well as smells—neighbors' cooking and exhaust from passing traffic. She was jotting down some details for such an essay when she glanced up at the framed portrait of her mother on her desk. "I stopped and stared at it, as I often do, wondering again about this twenty-year-old girl who became my mother," she said. "While I sat there studying it, I realized that the best topic of all was right under my nose."

As she looked at the photograph, Cindy began to freewrite. This is what she wrote:

> Mom is twenty in the picture. She's wearing a beautiful skirt and blouse and jewelry she borrowed from Dorothy. Looks a lot like me—nose, eyes, mouth. She's shorter than I am but you really can't tell in picture. Looks a lot like old photos I've seen of Grandma too—all the Diaz women resemble each other. Earrings and bracelet are of silver and they match. Ring might be amber or topaz? We've laughed about the "other man" who gave it to her. Her brown hair is down loose on her shoulders. She's smiling a little. That doesn't really look like her—her usual smile is bigger and opens her mouth. Looking at the photo makes me a little sad even though I really like it. Makes me realize how much older she's getting and I wonder how long she'll be with us. It's funny to see a picture of your parent at a younger age than you are now—stirs up all kinds of weird feelings. Picture was taken at a studio in Houston to give to Dad. Signed "Sincerely, Beatrice." So serious! Hard to imagine them being so formal with each other.

Cindy looked over her notes and thought about how she might organize her essay. First she thought only of describing how the photograph *looked*. With that in mind, she thought her main points might be (1) what her mother's face looked like and (2) what her mother was wearing. But she was stuck for a third main point.

Studying her notes again, Cindy noticed two other possible main points. One was her own emotional reaction to the photo—how it made her feel. The other was the story of the photo—how and why it was taken. Not sure which of those two she would use as her third main point, she began to write. This is her first draft.

First Draft   **Family Portrait**

> I have a photograph of my mother that was taken fifty years ago, when she was only twenty. She sent it to me only recently, and I find it very interesting.
>
> In the photo, I see a girl who looks a good deal like I do, even though it's been a long time since I was twenty. Like most of the women in her

family, including me, the girl in the picture has a short, straight nose, waving brown hair, and large brown eyes. Her mouth is closed and she is smiling slightly. That isn't my mother's usual big grin that shows her teeth and her "smile lines."

In the photo, Mom is wearing a very pretty skirt and blouse. They look like something that would be fashionable today. The blouse is made of heavy satin. The satin falls in lines and hollows that reflect the light. It has a turned-down cowl collar and smocking on the shoulders and under the collar. Her skirt is below her knees and looks like it is made of light wool. She is wearing jewelry. Her silver earrings and bracelet match. She had borrowed them from her sister. Dorothy eventually gave them both to her, but the bracelet has disappeared. On her left hand is a ring with a big yellow stone.

When I look at this photo, I feel conflicting emotions. It gives me pleasure to see Mom as a pretty young woman. It makes me sad, too, to think how quickly time passes and realize how old she is getting. It amuses me to read the inscription to my father, her boyfriend at the time. She wrote, "Sincerely, Beatrice." It's hard for me to imagine Mom and Dad ever being so formal with each other.

Mom had the photograph taken at a studio near where she worked in Houston. She spent nearly two weeks' salary on the outfit she wore for it. She must have really wanted to impress my father to go to all that trouble and expense.

Development Through Revision

Cindy showed this first draft to her classmate Elena, who read it and returned it with these notes jotted in the margin:

Reader's Comments

Was this the first time you'd seen it? Where's it been? And "very interesting" doesn't really say anything. Be more specific about why it interests you.

the "Diaz family nose" isn't helpful for someone who doesn't know the Diaz family—describe it!

Nice beginning, but I still can't quite picture her. Can you add more specific detail? Does anything about her face really stand out?

Family Portrait

I have a photograph of my mother that was taken fifty years ago, when she was only twenty. She sent it to me only recently, and I find it very interesting.

In the photo, I see a girl who looks a good deal like I do, even though it's been a long time since I was twenty. Like most of the women in her family, including me, she's got the Diaz family nose, waving brown hair, and large brown eyes. Her mouth is closed and she is smiling slightly. That isn't my mother's usual big grin that shows her teeth and her "smile lines."

Color?

This is nice—I can picture the material.

What is smocking?

How—what are they like?

It'd make more sense for the main points of the essay to be about your mom and the photo. How about making this—your reaction—the conclusion of the essay?

This is interesting stuff—she really did go to a lot of trouble to have the photo taken. I think the story of the photograph deserves to be a main point.

In the photo, Mom is wearing a very pretty skirt and blouse. They look like something that would be fashionable today. The blouse is made of heavy satin. The satin falls in lines and hollows that reflect the light. It has a turned-down cowl collar and smocking on the shoulders and under the collar. Her skirt is below her knees and looks like it is made of light wool. She is wearing jewelry. Her silver earrings and bracelet match. She had borrowed them from her sister. Dorothy eventually gave them both to her, but the bracelet has disappeared. On her left hand is a ring with a big yellow stone.

When I look at this photo, I feel conflicting emotions. It gives me pleasure to see Mom as a pretty young woman. It makes me sad, too, to think how quickly time passes and realize how old she is getting. It amuses me to read the inscription to my father, her boyfriend at the time. She wrote, "Sincerely, Beatrice." It's hard for me to imagine Mom and Dad ever being so formal with each other.

Mom had the photograph taken at a studio near where she worked in Houston. She spent nearly two weeks' salary on the outfit she wore for it. And I think she wore the ring, which another boy had given her, to make Dad jealous. She must have really wanted to impress my father to go to all that trouble and expense.

Making use of Elena's comments and her own reactions upon rereading her essay, Cindy wrote the final draft that appears on page 175.

A Professional Essay to Consider

Read the following professional essay. Then answer the questions and read the comments that follow.

Lou's Place

by Beth Johnson

Imagine a restaurant where your every whim is catered to, your every   1
want satisfied, your every request granted without hesitation. The people on
the staff live to please you. They hover anxiously as you sample your selection, waiting for your judgment. Your pleasure is their delight, your dissatis-
faction their dismay.

Lou's isn't that kind of place.   2

At Lou's Kosy Korner Koffee Shop, the mock abuse flows like a cup of   3
spilled Folgers. Customers are yelled at, lectured, blamed, mocked, teased,
and ignored. They pay for the privilege of pouring their own coffee and
scrambling their own eggs. As in a fond but dysfunctional family, Lou displays
his affection through criticism and insults, and his customers respond in kind.
If Lou's had a slogan, it might be, "If I'm polite to you, ask yourself what's
wrong."

Lou's is one of three breakfast joints located in the business district of a   4
small mid-Atlantic town. The county courthouse is nearby, supplying a steady
stream of lawyers, jurors, and office workers looking for a bite to eat. A local
trucking firm also provides Lou with customers as its drivers come and go in
town. Lou's is on the corner. Beside it is a jewelry shop ("In Business Since
1946—Watch Repairs Our Speciality") and an upscale home accessories store
that features bonsai trees and hand-painted birdhouses in its window.
There's a bus stop in front of Lou's. Lou himself has been known to storm out
onto the sidewalk to shoo away people who've dismounted from the bus and
lingered too long on the corner.

The sign on Lou's front door says "Open 7 A.M.–3 P.M." But by 6:40 on a   5
brisk spring morning, the restaurant's lights are on, the door is unlocked, and
Lou is settled in the booth nearest the door. The *Philadelphia Inquirer* spread
over the table, Lou is sunk deep into the booth's brown vinyl seat, its rips
neatly mended with silver duct tape. He is studying the box scores from the
night before as a would-be customer pauses on the sidewalk, unsure whether
to believe the sign or her own eyes. She opens the door enough to stick her
head in.

"Are you open?" she asks.   6

Without lifting his eyes from the paper, Lou answers. "I'm here, aren't I?"   7

Unsure how to interpret this remark, the woman enters and sits at a   8
booth. Lou keep studying the paper. He begins to hum under his breath. The
woman starts tracing a pattern on the glass-topped table with her fingernail.
She pulls out her checkbook and pretends to balance it. After a few long minutes, Lou apparently reaches a stopping point in his reading. He rises, his eyes
still on the folded newspaper he carries with him. His humming breaks into
low-volume song as he trudges behind the counter. "Maaaaaaaake someone
happy . . . Make-make-maaaaaaake someone happy," he croons as he lifts the

steaming pot that has infused the room with the rich aroma of freshly brewed coffee. He carries it to the woman's table, fills her cup, and drops two single-serving containers of half-and-half nearby. He then peers over the tops of his reading glasses at his customer. "You want anything else, dear?" he asks, his bushy gray eyebrows rising with the question.

She shakes her head. "I'm meeting someone. I'll order when he gets here." 9

Lou nods absently, his eyes back on his paper. As he shuffles back to his seat, he mutters over his shoulder, "Hope he shows up before three. I close then." 10

Lou reads his paper; the woman drinks her coffee and gazes around the room. It's a small restaurant: just an eight-seat counter and seven padded booths. A grill, coffeepots, and a huge stainless-steel refrigerator line the wall behind the counter. Under the glass top of the tables is the breakfast menu: it offers eggs, pancakes, home fries, bacon, and sausage. A wall rack holds Kellogg's Jumbo Packs of single-serving cereals: smiling toucans and cheerful tigers offer Froot Loops and Frosted Flakes. 11

Two poster-size photographs hang side by side at the far wall. One is of Lou and his wife on their wedding day. The pair appears to be in their mid-twenties. He is slim, dark-haired, beaming; his arm circles the shoulders of his fair-haired bride. The other photo shows the same couple in an identical pose—only in this one, Lou looks much as he is today. His short white hair is parted at the side; a cropped white beard emphasizes his prominent red mouth. His formerly slim figure now expands to take up much of the photograph. But the smile is the same as he embraces his silver-haired wife. 12

The bell at the door tinkles; two sleepy-eyed men in flannel shirts, work boots, and oil-company caps walk in. Lou glances up and grunts at them; they nod. One picks up an *Inquirer* from the display stand and leaves two quarters on the cash register. They drop onto seats at the counter, simultaneously swivel to look at the woman in the booth behind them, and then turn back. For a few minutes, they flip through the sports section. Lou doesn't move. One man rises from his seat and wanders behind the counter to find cups and the coffeepot. He fills the cups, returns to his seat, and immerses himself in the paper. There is no noise but the occasional slurping of men sipping hot coffee. 13

Minutes pass. Finally one of the men speaks. "Lou," he says. "Can I maybe get some breakfast?" 14

"I'm reading the paper," says Lou. "Eggs are in the refrigerator." 15

The man sighs and lumbers behind the counter again. "In some restaurants, they actually cook for ya," he says, selecting eggs from the carton. 16

Lou doesn't raise his eyes. "In some restaurants, they wouldn't let a guy with a face like yours in." 17

The room falls silent again, except for the splatter of grease on the grill and the scrape of the spatula as the customer scrambles his eggs. He heaps 18 them onto his plate, prepares some toast, and returns to his seat. The bell at the door begins tinkling as the breakfast rush begins—men, mostly, about half in work clothes and the rest in suits. They pour in on a wave of talk and laughter. Lou reluctantly rises and goes to work behind the counter, volleying comments with the regulars:

"Three eggs, Lou," says one.   19

"Three eggs. One heart attack wasn't enough for you? You want some   20
bacon grease on top of that?"

A large red-haired man in blue jeans and a faded denim shirt walks in   21
with a newspaper, which he reads as he waits for his cup of takeout coffee. "Anything good in the paper, Dan?" Lou asks.

"Not a thing," drawls Dan. "Not a *damn* thing. The only good thing is   22
that the machine down the street got my fifty cents instead of you."

Lou flips pancakes as the restaurant fills to capacity. The hum of voices   23
fills the room as the aromas of coffee, bacon, eggs, and toasting bread mingle in the air. A group of suits from the nearby courthouse slide into the final empty booth. After a moment one rises, goes behind the counter, and rummages in a drawer.

"Whatcha need, Ben?" Lou asks, pouring more batter.   24

"Rag," Ben answers. He finds one, returns to the booth, and wipes crumbs   25
off the tabletop. A minute later he is back to drop a slice of ham on the hot grill. He and Lou stand side by side attending to their cooking, as comfortable in their silence as an old married couple. When the ham is sizzling and its rich fragrance reaches the far corners of the room, Ben slides it onto a plate and returns to his booth.

Filled plate in hand, Lou approaches a woman sitting at the counter. Her   26
golden hair contrasts with her sunken cheeks and her wrinkled lips sucking an unfiltered Camel. "You wanna I put this food in your ashtray, or are you gonna move it?" Lou growls. The woman moves the ashtray aside.

"Sorry, Lou," she says.   27

"I'm not really yelling at you, dear," he answers.   28

"I know," says the woman. "I'm glad *you're* here this morning." She   29
lowers her voice. "That girl you've got working here sometimes, Lou—she doesn't *like* me." Lou rolls his eyes, apparently at the poor taste of the waitress, and moves down to the cash register. As he rings up a bill, a teenage girl enters and walks by silently. Lou glares after her. "Start the day with a 'Good morning,' please," he instructs.

"Good morning, Lou," she replies obediently.   30

"*Very* nice," he mutters, still punching the cash-register buttons. "Thank   31
you *so* much for your concern. I get up at the crack of dawn to make your breakfast, but don't bother saying 'good morning' to *me*."

The day's earliest arrival, the woman in the booth, has been joined by a   32
companion. They order eggs and hash browns. As Lou slides the filled plates

before them, he reverts briefly to the conventional manners he saves for first-timers. "Enjoy your meal," he says.

"Thank you," says the woman. "May I have some hot sauce?"   33

Lou's reserve of politeness is instantly exhausted. "Hot sauce. Jeez. She   34
wants *hot sauce*!" he announces to the room at large. "Anything else? Some
caviar on the side, maybe?" He disappears behind the counter, reemerging
with an enormous red bottle. "Here you are. It's a new bottle. Don't use it
all, please. I'd like to save a little for other customers. Hey, on second thought,
use it all if you want. Then I'll know you'll like my chili." Laughing loudly at
his own joke, he refills the woman's coffee cup without being asked. Golden-
brown coffee splashes into her saucer. Lou ignores it.

Lou's waitress, Stacy, has arrived, and begins taking orders and deliver-   35
ing meals. Lou alternates between working the grill and clearing tables.
Mid-stride, he halts before the golden-haired woman at the counter, who has
pushed her plate aside and is lighting another cigarette. "What? What is
this?" he demands.

"Looouuu . . . " she begins soothingly, a stream of smoke jetting from her   36
mouth with the word.

"Don't 'Lou' me," he retorts. "You don't eat your toast, you don't eat   37
your potatoes, you barely touch your eggs. Whatcha gonna live on? Camels?"

"Awww, Lou," she says, but she pulls her plate back and eats a few more   38
bites.

As the rush of customers slows to a trickle, Lou returns to the register,   39
making change and conversation, talking Phillies and the weather. One of the
flannel-shirted men rises from his counter seat and heads for the door, dropping his money on the counter. "'Bye, Stacy," he says to the waitress. "Have
a nice day."

"'Bye, Mel," she replies. "You too."   40

"What about me?" Lou calls after Mel.   41

Mel doesn't pause. "Who cares what kind of a day *you* have?"   42

Mel disappears into the morning sunshine; the Camel lady pulls a cross-   43
word puzzle out of her purse and taps an unlit cigarette rapidly against the
counter. Stacy wipes the tables and empties a wastebasket of its load of dark,
wet coffee grounds. Lou butters a piece of toast and returns to his favorite
booth. He spreads out his newspaper again, then glances up to catch the eye
of the hot-sauce woman. "Where's your friend?" he asks.

"He left," she replies.   44

"He left you, eh?" Lou asks.   45

"No, he didn't *leave* me. He just had to go to work . . . "   46

"Dump him," Lou responds automatically. "And now, if you don't mind   47
very much, I would like to finish my newspaper."

■ Questions

About Unity

1. What is the thesis of Johnson's essay? If it is stated directly, locate the relevant sentence or sentences. If it is implied, state the thesis in your own words.
    Lou's coffee shop is like "a fond but dysfunctional family." (Wording may vary.)

2. Which statement would best serve as a topic sentence for paragraph 13?
    a. Many of Lou's customers are, like him, interested in the Philadelphia sports teams.
    b. Lou doesn't mind if customers serve themselves coffee.
    c. Lou apparently disliked the two men in oil-company caps who came into the restaurant.
    d. Regular customers at Lou's are used to taking care of themselves while Lou reads his paper.

About Support

3. In paragraph 3, Johnson claims that Lou and his customers are fond of one another. How does she support that claim in the case of the golden-haired woman who is first mentioned in paragraph 26?
    Lou is concerned that she is smoking rather than eating.

4. Which of these sentences from "Lou's Place" best supports the idea that customers enjoy the unusual atmosphere at the coffee shop?
    a. "The bell at the door tinkles; two sleepy-eyed men in flannel shirts, work boots, and oil-company caps walk in."
    b. "He and Lou stand side by side attending to their cooking, as comfortable in their silence as an old married couple."
    c. "As [Lou] rings up a bill, a teenage girl enters and walks by silently."
    d. "Mid-stride, [Lou] halts before the golden-haired lady at the counter, who has pushed her plate aside and is lighting another cigarette."

5. Check each sense appealed to in the passage below from "Lou's Place."

    "Maaaaaaaake someone happy . . . Make-make-maaaaaaake someone happy," he croons as he lifts the steaming pot that has infused the room with the rich aroma of freshly brewed coffee. He carries it to the woman's table, fills her cup, and drops two single-serving containers of half-and-half nearby.

    Sight __✓__ Hearing __✓__ Taste _____ Smell __✓__ Touch _____

About Coherence

6. Which of the following sentences contains a change-of-direction signal?
    a. " 'You want anything else, dear?' he asks, his bushy gray eyebrows rising with the question."
    b. "In some restaurants, they wouldn't let a guy with a face like yours in."
    c. "After a moment one rises, goes behind the counter and rummages in a drawer."
    d. "I get up at the crack of dawn to make your breakfast, but don't bother saying 'good morning' to *me*."

7. Which sentence in paragraph 23 begins with a time signal? (*Write the opening words of that sentence.*)

    <u>After a moment . . .</u>

8. The sentence that makes up paragraph 38 includes which of the following types of transition?
    a. time
    b. addition
    c. change of direction
    d. conclusion

About the Introduction and Conclusion

9. Which statement describes the style of Johnson's introduction?
    a. It presents a situation that is the opposite of the one that will be developed.
    b. It explains the importance of the topic to the reader.
    c. It asks a question.

10. Which statement describes the conclusion of "Lou's Place"?
    a. It summarizes its description of the coffee shop.
    b. It ends with a comment of Lou's that characterizes the mood of his shop.
    c. It ends with a prediction of the future of the coffee shop.

Writing a Descriptive Essay

■ Writing Assignment 1

Write an essay about a particular place that you can observe carefully or that you already know well. You might choose one of the following, or another place that you think of:

Pet shop

Doctor's waiting room

Laundromat

Bar or nightclub

Video arcade

Library study area

Your bedroom or the bedroom of someone you know

Locker room after the winning or loss of an important game

Waiting room at train station, bus terminal, or airport

Antique shop or some other small shop

Prewriting

a Remember that, like all essays, a descriptive paper must have a thesis. Your thesis should state a dominant impression about the place you are describing. Write a short single sentence in which you name the place you want to describe and the dominant impression you want to make. Don't worry if your sentence doesn't seem quite right as a thesis—you can refine it later. For now, you just want to find and express a workable topic. Here are some examples of such sentences:

The study area was noisy.

The bedroom was well-organized.

The pet shop was crowded.

The restaurant was noisy.

The bus terminal was frightening.

The locker room was glum.

The exam room was tense.

b Once you have written your sentence, make a list of as many details as you can to support that general impression. For example, this is the list made by the writer of "The Diner at Midnight":

Tired workers at counter

Rainy parking lot

Vacant booths

Quiet

Few cars in lot

Dreary gray building

Lonely young man

Silent middle-aged couple

Out-of-order neon sign

No hostess

Couldn't see anyone in kitchen

Tired-looking waitress

c   Organize your paper according to one or a combination of the following:

Physical order—move from left to right or from far to near, or follow some other consistent order.

Size—Begin with large features or objects and work down to smaller ones.

A special order—Use an order that is appropriate to your subject.

For example, the writer of "The Diner at Midnight" builds his essay around the dominant impression of loneliness. The paper is organized in terms of physical order (from the parking lot to the entrance to the interior); a secondary method of organization is size (large parking lot to smaller diner to still smaller people).

d   Use as many senses as possible in describing a scene. Chiefly you will use sight, but to an extent you may be able to use touch, hearing, smell, and perhaps even taste as well. Remember that it is through the richness of your sense impressions that the reader will gain a picture of the scene.

e   Proceed to write the first draft of your essay.

Rewriting

After you have completed the first draft of the paper, set it aside for a while—if possible, until the next day. When you review the draft, try to do so as critically as you would if it were not your own work. Ask yourself these questions:

- Does my paper have a clearly stated thesis, including a dominant impression?
- Have I provided rich, specific details that appeal to a variety of senses (sight, hearing, smell, taste, touch)?
- Is there any irrelevant material that should be eliminated or rewritten?
- Have I organized my essay in some consistent manner—physical order, size, time progression, or another way that is appropriate to my subject?
- Have I used transition words to help readers follow my train of thought?
- Do I have a concluding paragraph that provides a summary, a final thought, or both?

As you revise your essay through one or more additional drafts, continue to refer to this list until you can answer "yes" to each question. Then be sure to check the next-to-final draft of the paper for the sentence skills listed on the inside front cover.

■ Writing Assignment 2

Write an essay about a family portrait. (The picture may be of an individual or a group.)

a Decide how you will organize your essay. Your decision will depend on what seems appropriate for the photograph. Two possibilities are these:

As in "Family Portrait," you might use the first supporting paragraph to describe the subjects' faces, the second to describe their clothing and jewelry, and the third to describe the story behind the picture.

Another possible order might be, first, the people in the photograph (and how they look); second, the relationships among the people (and what they are doing in the photo); and third, the story behind the picture (time, place, occasion, other circumstances).

b Make a scratch outline for your essay, based on the organization you have chosen.

c Using your scratch outline as a guide, make a list of details that support each of your main points. As practice in doing this, complete this list of details based on "Family Portrait":

A. Mother's face

Small, straight nose
Slight smile on her full lips
Large, dark eyes

Plucked eyebrows

Oval face

Wavy brown hair

B.   Mother's clothing and jewelry

Blouse of heavy satin
Blouse is eggshell-colored
Cowl collar
Smocking on blouse
Light wool skirt

Silver earrings

Bracelet

Ring

C.   Story behind the photo

Mother spent two weeks' salary on clothing
Borrowed jewelry from sister

Ring from another man

Signature ("Sincerely . . .")

d Use your scratch outline and list of details to write your first draft.

Rewriting

Refer to the guidelines for rewriting provided on page 190 with Assignment 1.

■ Writing Assignment 3

In this descriptive essay, you will write with a specific purpose and for a specific audience. Imagine that you have subscribed to a video dating service. Clients of the service are asked to make a five-minute presentation which will be recorded on videotape. Write a paper in which you describe yourself. Your goal is to give interested members of the dating service a good sense of what you are like.

Prewriting

a Decide how you will organize your presentation. What aspects of yourself will you describe? Remember, your presentation will be recorded on videotape, so viewers of the tape will see for themselves what you look like. Therefore it won't be necessary to describe your appearance.

You might organize your presentation in terms of describing your attitudes and beliefs, your interests, and your personal habits. Other ideas you might use as main points could be your hopes for the future, how you spend a typical day, or your imaginary perfect date.

b Focus on each of the main points you've decided to write on and brainstorm to generate details to support each one. For example, if you were going to write about your perfect date, you would ask yourself questions like these:

Where would I go?

What would I do?

What time of day would the date occur?

Why would I enjoy this date so much?

How would I travel to my destination?

Continue brainstorming until you have a number of rich, specific, sensory details to support each of your main points.

c Plan a brief introductory paragraph that will indicate to your viewer how you'll organize your presentation . For instance, one student might write, "I'm Terry Jefferson. I'm going to tell you something about what I believe, what I enjoy doing, and what I hope to accomplish in the future."

d Write the first draft of your presentation.

Rewriting

Once you have the first draft of your paper completed, review it with these questions in mind:

- Does my introduction indicate a clear plan of development?
- Is my presentation clearly organized according to three main points?
- Have I filled each of my supporting paragraphs with rich, descriptive details that help the viewer vividly imagine me?
- Have I rounded off my presentation with an appropriate concluding paragraph?
- Have I proofread my presentation, referring to the list of sentence skills on the inside front cover?

■ Writing Assignment 4

Write an essay describing a person. First, decide on your dominant impression of the person, and then use only those details which will add to it. Here are some examples of interesting types of people you might want to write about:

Campus character	Competitor	Drunk
Dentist	Clergyman	Employer
Bus driver	Clergywoman	TV or movie personality
Close friend	Teacher	Street person
Rival	Child	Older person
White-collar crook	Bum	Hero

9 Narration

Children beg to hear a beloved story read again and again. Over dinner, tired adults tell each other about their day. A restless class is hushed when a teacher says, "Let me tell you something strange that happened to me once." Whatever our age, we never outgrow our hunger for stories. Just as our ancestors entertained and instructed each other with tales of great hunts and battles, of angry gods and foolish humans, we still love to share our lives and learn about others through storytelling.

Narration is storytelling, whether we are relating a single story or several related ones. Through narration, we make a statement clear by relating in detail something that has happened to us. In the story we tell, we present the details in the order in which they happened. A person might say, for example, "I was really embarrassed the day I took my driver's test," and then go on to develop that statement with an account of the experience. If the story is sharply detailed, we will be able to see and understand just why the speaker felt that way.

In this section, you'll be asked to tell a story that illustrates some point. To prepare for this assignment, first read the student essays and the professional essay that follow and work through the questions that accompany the essays. All three essays use narratives to develop their points.

Student Essays to Consider

Adopting a Handicap

My church recently staged a "Sensitivity Sunday" to make our congregation more aware of the problems faced by people with physical disabilities. We were asked to "adopt a disability" for several hours one Sunday morning. Some members, like me, chose to use wheelchairs. Others wore sound-blocking earplugs, hobbled around on crutches, or wore blindfolds.

1

Just sitting in the wheelchair was instructive. I had never considered before how awkward it would be to use one. As soon as I sat down, my weight made the chair begin to roll. Its wheels were not locked, and I fumbled clumsily to correct that. Another awkward moment occurred when I realized I had no place to put my feet. I fumbled some more to turn the metal footrest into place. I felt psychologically awkward as well, as I took my

2

first uneasy look at what was to be my only means of transportation for several hours. I realized that for many people, "adopting a wheelchair" is not a temporary experiment. That was a sobering thought as I sank back into my seat.

Once I sat down, I had to learn how to cope with the wheelchair. I   3
shifted around, trying to find a comfortable position. I thought it might be restful, even kind of nice, to be pushed around for a while. I glanced around to see who would be pushing me and then realized I would have to navigate the contraption by myself! My palms reddened and my wrist and forearm muscles started to ache as I tugged at the heavy metal wheels. I realized as I veered this way and that that steering and turning were not going to be easy tasks. Trying to make a right-angle turn from one aisle to another, I steered straight into a pew. I felt as though everyone was staring at me and commenting on my clumsiness.

When the service started, other problems cropped up to frustrate me   4
further. Every time the congregation stood up, my view was blocked. I could not see the minister, the choir, or the altar. Also, as the church's aisles were narrow, I seemed to be in the way no matter where I parked myself. For instance, the ushers had to squeeze by me to pass the collection plate. This made me feel like a nuisance. Thanks to a new building program, however, our church will soon have the wide aisles and well-spaced pews that will make life easier for the disabled. After the service ended, when people stopped to talk to me, I had to strain my neck and look up at them. This made me feel like a little child being talked down to and added to my sense of powerlessness.

My wheelchair experiment was soon over. It's true that it made an   5
impression on me. I no longer resent large tax expenditures for ramp-equipped buses, and I wouldn't dream of parking my car in a space marked "Handicapped Only." But I also realize how little I know about the daily life of a truly disabled person. A few hours of voluntary "disability" gave me only a hint of the challenges, both physical and emotional, that people with handicaps must overcome.

A Night of Violence

According to my history instructor, Adolf Hitler once said that he wanted   1
to sign up "brutal youths" to help him achieve his goals. If Hitler were still alive, he wouldn't have any trouble recruiting the brutal youths he wanted; he could get them right here in the United States. I know, because I was one of them. As a teenager, I ran with a gang. And it took a frightening incident for me to see how violent I had become.

The incident was planned one Thursday night when I was out with my   2
friends. I was still going to school once in a while, but most of my friends weren't. We spent our days on the streets, talking, showing off, sometimes

shoplifting a little or shaking people down for a few dollars. My friends and I were close, maybe because life hadn't been very good to any of us. On this night, we were drinking wine and vodka on the corner. For some reason, we all felt tense and restless. One of us came up with the idea of robbing one of the old people who lived in the high-rise close by. We would just knock him or her over, grab the money, and party with it.

The robbery did not go as planned. After about an hour, and after more   3
wine and vodka, we spotted an old man. He came out of the glass door of the building and started up the street. Pine Street had a lot of antique stores as well as apartment buildings. Stuffing our bottles in our jacket pockets, we closed in behind him. Suddenly, the old man whipped out a homemade wooden club from under his jacket and began swinging. The club thudded loudly against Victor's shoulder, making him yelp with pain. When we heard that, we went crazy. We smashed our bottles over the old man's head. Not content with that, Victor kicked him savagely, knocking him to the ground. As we ran, I kept seeing him sprawled on the ground, blood from our beating trickling into his eyes. Victor, the biggest of us, had said, "We want your money, old man. Hand it over."

Later, at home, I had a strong reaction to the incident. My head would   4
not stop pounding, and I threw up. I wasn't afraid of getting caught; in fact, we never did get caught. I just knew I had gone over some kind of line. I didn't know if I could step back, now that I had gone so far. But I knew I had to. I had seen plenty of people in my neighborhood turn into the kind of people who hated their lives, people who didn't care about anything, people who wound up penned in jail or ruled by drugs. I didn't want to become one of them.

That night, I realize now, I decided not to become one of Hitler's "brutal   5
youths." I'm proud of myself for that, even though life didn't get any easier and no one came along to pin a medal on me. I just decided, quietly, to step off the path I was on. I hope my parents and I will get along better now, too. Maybe the old man's pain, in some terrible way, had a purpose.

■ Questions

About Unity

1. Which essay lacks an opening thesis statement?

   "Adopting a Handicap"

2. Which sentence in paragraph 4 of "Adopting a Handicap" should be omitted in the interest of paragraph unity? (*Write the opening words.*)

   Thanks to a new building program . . .

3. What sentence in paragraph 3 of "A Night of Violence" should be omitted in the interest of paragraph unity? *(Write the opening words)*

    Pine Street had a lot of antique stores . . .

4. What sentence in the final paragraph of "A Night of Violence" makes the mistake of introducing a new topic and so should be eliminated?

    I hope my parents and I . . .

About Support

5. Label as *sight, touch, hearing,* or *smell* all the sensory details in the following sentences taken from the essays.

            sight   *touch*

    a. "My palms reddened and my wrist and forearm muscles started to ache
        sight   *touch*
    as I tugged at the heavy metal wheels."

            sight

    b. "I could not see the minister, the choir, or the altar."

        hearing   *hearing*

    c. "The club thudded loudly against Victor's shoulder, making him yelp

    with pain."

                                                            sight

    d. "As we ran, I kept seeing him sprawled on the ground, blood from our

    beating trickling into his eyes."

6. In a narrative, the main method of organization is time order. Which sentence in paragraph 3 of "A Night of Violence" is placed out of order?

    "Victor, the biggest of us . . ."

7. In "Adopting a Handicap," how many examples support the topic sentence of paragraph 4, "When the service started, other problems cropped up to frustrate me further"?   *three*

About Coherence

8. The first stage of the writer's experience in "Adopting a Handicap" might be called *sitting down in the wheelchair*. What are the other two stages of the experience?

    Coping with the wheelchair

    Dealing with additional problems in the wheelchair

9. List three time transitions used in the third paragraph of "A Night in Violence."

       After   *When*   *As*

About the Introduction and Conclusion

10. What method of introduction forms the first paragraph of "A Night of Violence"? Circle the appropriate letters.

   (a.) Broad, general statement narrowing to a thesis

   b.   Idea that is the opposite of the one to be developed

   c.   Questions

Developing a Narrative Essay

Development Through Prewriting

When you write a narrative essay, you are essentially telling a story. Most likely, you will develop that story in chronological order—from what happened first to what happened next, and so on. The challenge in creating a successful narrative is twofold: to decide on the point of your essay, and to make sure that all the material in the essay contributes to that point.

Freewriting is a particularly helpful prewriting technique as you're planning your narrative essay. (For more about freewriting, see pages 24–26.) As you think about the story you want to relate, many ideas will crowd into your mind. Simply writing them down in free-form style will jog loose details you may have forgotten and also help you determine what the central point of your story really is.

Lisa, the writer of "Adopting a Handicap," spent a half-hour freewriting before she wrote the first draft of her essay. Here is what she came up with:

> Our church was planning a building renovation to make the church more accessible to handicapped people. Some people thought it was a waste of money and that the disabled could get along all right in the church the way it was. Not many disabled people come to our church anyway. Pastor Henry gave a sermon about disabilities. He suggested that we spend one Sunday pretending to be disabled ourselves. We got to choose our disability. Some people pretended to be blind or deaf or in need of crutches. I chose to use a wheelchair. I thought it might be fun to have someone push me around. It was a lot scarier and more disturbing than I expected. We borrowed wheelchairs and crutches from the local nursing home. I didn't like sitting down in the wheelchair. I didn't know how to work it right. It rolled when I didn't want it to. I felt clumsy trying to make it move. I even ran into a pew. I felt silly pretending to be disabled and also sort of disrespectful because for most people sitting in a wheelchair isn't a choice. It also bothered me to think what it'd be like if I couldn't get up again. It turned out that nobody was going to push me around. I thought Paula

would but instead she put on a blindfold and pretended to be blind. She knocked over a cup of coffee before the morning was over. She told me later she felt really panicky when that happened. Sitting down so low in the wheelchair was weird. I couldn't see much of anything. People ignored me or talked to me like I was a little kid. I was glad when the morning was over. Making the wheels turn hurt my hands and arms.

As Lisa read over her freewriting passage, she decided that the central point of her story was her new realization of how challenging it would be to truly be disabled. In order to support that central point, she realized, she would need to concentrate on details that demonstrated the frustrations she felt. She created a scratch outline for the first draft of her essay:

Thesis statement: A church experiment led to my spending the morning in a wheelchair.

1. Sitting in the wheelchair
   a. Awkward because it rolled
   b. Awkward because footrest was out of place
   c. Psychologically awkward

2. Moving the wheelchair
   a. I thought someone would push me
   b. It was hard to make the chair move and it hurt my hands
   c. Difficult to steer

c. Ways the wheelchair affected me
   a. Couldn't see
   b. I felt in the way
   c. I felt funny talking to people as they bent down over me

---

Lisa based her first draft on her scratch outline. Here is the draft:

First Draft   **Adopting a Handicap**

The pastor at our church suggested that we each "adopt a disability" for a few hours on Sunday morning. Some members, like me, chose to use wheelchairs. Others wore earplugs, used crutches, or wore blindfolds.

It surprised me that I felt nervous about sitting down in my wheelchair. I'm not sure why I felt scared about it. I guess I realized that most people who use wheelchairs don't do it by choice—they have to.

When I sat down, I thought my friend Paula would push me around. We had talked about her doing that earlier. But she decided instead to "adopt" her own disability and she pretended to be blind. I saw her with a blindfold on, trying to fix herself a cup of coffee and knocking it off the table as she stirred it. So I had to figure out how to make the chair move by myself. It wasn't so easy. Pushing the wheels made my hands and arms sore. I also kept bumping into things. I felt really awkward. I even had trouble locking the wheels and finding the footrest.

I couldn't see well as I sat down low in my chair. When the rest of the congregation stood up, I could forget about seeing entirely. People would nod or chuckle at something that had happened up at the front of the church and I could only guess what was going on. Instead of sitting in the pew with everyone else, I was parked out in the aisle, which was really too narrow for the chair. The new building program our church is planning will make that problem better by widening the aisles and making the pews farther apart. It's going to be expensive, but it's a worthwhile thing. Another thing I disliked was how I felt when people talked to me. They had to lean down as though I was a kid, and I had to stare up at them as though I was too. One person I talked to who seemed to understand what I was experiencing was Don Henderson, who mentioned that his brother-in-law uses a wheelchair.

Development Through Revision

Lisa read over her first draft. Then she showed it to her roommate. After hearing her roommate's comments, Lisa read the essay again. This time she made a list of comments about how she thought it could be improved:

- The introduction should explain <u>why</u> the pastor wanted us to adopt disabilities.
- The second paragraph is sort of weak. Instead of saying "I'm not sure why I felt scared," I should try put into specific words what was scary about the experience.
- The stuff about Paula doesn't really add to my main point. The story is about me, not Paula.
- Maybe I shouldn't talk so much about the new building program. It's related to people with disabilities, but it doesn't really support the idea that my morning in a wheelchair was frustrating.
- Eliminate the part about Don Henderson. It doesn't contribute to my feeling frustrated.
- The essay ends too abruptly. I need to wrap it up with some sort of conclusion.

With that list of comments in hand, Lisa returned to her essay. She then wrote the version that appears on page 195.

A Professional Essay to Consider

Read the following professional essay. Then answer the questions and read the comments that follow.

The Yellow Ribbon

by Pete Hamill

They were going to Fort Lauderdale, the girl remembered later. There   1
were six of them, three boys and three girls, and they picked up the bus
at the old terminal on 34th Street, carrying sandwiches and wine in paper
bags, dreaming of golden beaches and the tides of the sea as the gray cold
spring of New York vanished behind them. Vingo was on board from the
beginning.

As the bus passed through Jersey and into Philly, they began to notice   2
that Vingo never moved. He sat in front of the young people, his dusty face
masking his age, dressed in a plain brown ill-fitting suit. His fingers were
stained from cigarettes and he chewed the inside of his lip a lot, frozen into
some personal cocoon of silence.

Somewhere outside of Washington, deep into the night, the bus   3
pulled into a Howard Johnson's, and everybody got off except Vingo. He sat
rooted in his seat, and the young people began to wonder about him, trying
to imagine his life: Perhaps he was a sea captain, maybe he had run away
from his wife, he could be an old soldier going home. When they went back
to the bus, the girl sat beside him and introduced herself.

"We're going to Florida," the girl said brightly. "You going that far?"   4

"I don't know," Vingo said.   5

"I've never been there," she said. "I hear it's beautiful."   6

"It is," he said quietly, as if remembering something he had tried to for-   7
get.

"You live there?"   8

"I did some time there in the Navy. Jacksonville."   9

"Want some wine?" she said. He smiled and took the bottle of   10
Chianti and took a swig. He thanked her and retreated again into silence.
After a while, she went back to the others, as Vingo nodded into sleep.

In the morning they awoke outside another Howard Johnson's, and this   11
time Vingo went in. The girl insisted that he join them. He seemed
very shy and ordered black coffee and smoked nervously, as the young
people chattered about sleeping on the beaches. When they went back
on the bus, the girl sat with Vingo again, and after a while, slowly and
painfully and with great hesitation, he began to tell his story. He had been
in jail in New York for the last four years, and now he was going home.

"Four years!" the girl said. "What did you do?"   12

"It doesn't matter," he said with quiet bluntness. "I did it and I went to 13
jail. If you can't do the time, don't do the crime. That's what they say and
they're right."

"Are you married?"   14

"I don't know."   15

"You don't know?" she said.   16

"Well, when I was in the can I wrote to my wife," he said. "I told her,   17
I said, Martha, I understand if you can't stay married to me. I told her that.
I said I was gonna be away a long time, and that if she couldn't stand it, if
the kids kept askin' questions, if it hurt her too much, well, she could just
forget me. Get a new guy—she's a wonderful woman, really something—and
forget about me. I told her she didn't have to write me or nothing. And she
didn't. Not for three and a half years."

"And you're going home now, not knowing?"   18

"Yeah," he said shyly. "Well, last week, when I was sure the parole was   19
coming through I wrote her. I told her that if she had a new guy, I understood.
But if she didn't, if she would take me back she should let me know. We used
to live in this town, Brunswick, just before Jacksonville, and there's a great
big oak tree just as you come into town, a very famous tree, huge. I told
her if she would take me back, she should put a yellow handkerchief on the
tree, and I would get off and come home. If she didn't want me, forget it,
no handkerchief, and I'd keep going on through."

"Wow," the girl said. "Wow."   20

She told the others, and soon all of them were in it, caught up in the   21
approach of Brunswick, looking at the pictures Vingo showed them of his
wife and three children, the woman handsome in a plain way, the children
still unformed in a cracked, much-handled snapshot. Now they were twenty
miles from Brunswick and the young people took over window seats on the
right side, waiting for the approach of the great oak tree. Vingo stopped
looking, tightening his face into the ex-con's mask, as if fortifying himself
against still another disappointment. Then it was ten miles, and then five and
the bus acquired a dark hushed mood, full of silence, of absence, of lost years,
of the woman's plain face, of the sudden letter on the breakfast table, of the
wonder of children, of the iron bars of solitude.

Then suddenly all of the young people were up out of their seats, scream- 22
ing and shouting and crying, doing small dances, shaking clenched fists in
triumph and exaltation. All except Vingo.

Vingo sat there stunned, looking at the oak tree. It was covered with   23
yellow handkerchiefs, twenty of them, thirty of them, maybe hundreds, a tree
that stood like a banner of welcome blowing and billowing in the wind,
turned into a gorgeous yellow blur by the passing bus. As the young people
shouted, the old con slowly rose from his seat, holding himself tightly, and
made his way to the front of the bus to go home.

■ Questions

About Unity

1. The thesis of Hamill's essay is implied rather than stated directly. See if you can state the thesis in your own words.

    Answers will vary. On a very simple level, the theme could be stated: Vingo

    returned from prison to find that his wife still loved him.

2. Which statement best expresses the implied point of paragraph 2?

    a. Vingo sat very still in his seat.

    (b.) Something about Vingo made the young people curious.

    c. Vingo appeared to be a nervous person.

    d. Vingo was the most unusual person the young people had ever seen.

3. Which statement would best serve as a topic sentence for paragraph 11?

    (a.) The girl's friendliness finally caused Vingo to confide in her.

    b. The group woke up outside of a Howard Johnson's.

    c. Vingo had been in jail for four years.

    d. The girl persisted in being friendly to Vingo.

About Support

4. "His fingers were stained from cigarettes and he chewed the inside of his lip a lot, frozen in some personal cocoon of silence." This line from paragraph 2 supports the idea that

    a. Vingo had been drinking.

    (b.) Vingo was nervous.

    c. Vingo was a hostile person.

    d. Vingo knew the young people were watching him.

5. Hamill writes in paragraph 11 that Vingo "seemed very shy." Find at least two pieces of evidence in the essay to support the idea that Vingo was shy.

    Answers may vary; examples are given.

    1. He tells his story "slowly and painfully and with great hesitation."

    2. He asks his wife to leave a signal (the handkerchief), rather than

    confront her directly.

6. Hamill implies that despite his crime, Vingo was an honorable man. Find evidence that supports that point.

Doesn't express any self-pity about being in jail; owns up to his crime.

Offers his wife her freedom.

About Coherence

7. The story in this essay takes place on a trip, so it's especially appropriate that Hamill uses geographical and place names to signal the passing of the time and miles. List at least four of the specific places named. *Any four answers:*

Fort Lauderdale,	*New Jersey,*	*Washington,*	*Jacksonville*
34th Street terminal in New York,		*Philadelphia,*	*Brunswick*

8. What sentence in paragraph 19 begins with a transition word that indicates contrast? *(Write the opening words.)*

But if she didn't . . .

About the Introduction and Conclusion

9. The introductory paragraph indicates that Hamill

   a. was one of the young people on the bus.

   b. heard the story from Vingo years later.

   c. was a friend of Vingo's wife.

   (d) interviewed one of the young girls who'd been on the bus.

10. Hamill has concluded his narrative with

   a. a summary.

   b. a thought-provoking question.

   c. a recommendation.

   (d) the last event of his narrative.

Writing a Narrative Essay

■ Writing Assignment 1

Write an essay narrating an experience in which a certain emotion was predominant. The emotion might be disappointment, embarrassment, happiness, frustration, any of the following, or some other:

Fear	Shock	Nervousness	Loss
Pride	Love	Hate	Sympathy
Jealousy	Anger	Surprise	Violence
Sadness	Nostalgia	Shyness	Bitterness
Terror	Relief	Silliness	Envy
Regret	Greed	Disgust	Loneliness

The experience should be limited in time. Note that each of the three essays presented in this chapter describes an experience that occurred within a relatively short period. One writer described her frustration in acting like a disabled person at a morning church service; another detailed the terror of a minute's mugging that had lifelong consequences; Pete Hamill described an overnight bus trip and its thrilling conclusion.

Prewriting

a Think of an experience or event in your life in which you felt a certain emotion. Then spend at least ten minutes freewriting about that experience. Do not worry at this point about such matters as spelling or grammar or putting things in the right order; instead, just try to get down as many details as you can think of that seem related to the experience.

b This preliminary writing will help you decide whether your topic is promising enough to continue working on. If it is not, choose another emotion. If it is, do three things:

First, write out your thesis in a single sentence, underlining the emotion you will focus on. For example, "My first day in kindergarten was one of the scariest days of my life."

Second, think about just what creates the conflict—the source of tension—in your story. What details can you add that will build up enough tension to "hook" readers and keep them interested?

Third, make up a long list of all the details involved in the experience. Then arrange those details in chronological (time) order.

c Using your list as a guide, prepare a rough draft of your paper.

Rewriting

Once you have a first draft of your essay completed, consider the following as you work on a second draft:

a *To achieve unity:* Do you state the thesis of your narrative in the introductory paragraph? If it is not stated, have you clearly implied it somewhere in the essay? Ask yourself if there are any portions of the essay that do not support the thesis and therefore should be eliminated or rewritten.

b *To achieve support:* Do you have enough details, including dialogue? Notice how dialogue in Pete Hamill's essay adds drama and immediacy and helps a situation come alive. See if during this revision you can add more vivid, exact details that will help your readers experience the event as it actually happened.

c *To achieve coherence:* See if you can add time signals such as *first, then, next, after, while, during,* and *finally* to help connect details as you move from the beginning to the middle to the end of the narrative.

Also, see if you can divide the story into separate stages (what happened first, what happened next, what finally happened). Put each stage into a separate paragraph. In narratives, it is sometimes difficult to write a topic sentence for each supporting paragraph. You may, therefore, want to start new paragraphs at points where natural shifts or logical breaks in the story seem to occur.

d *To achieve sentence skills:* Use the checklist on the inside front cover to edit and proofread your next-to-final draft for sentence-skills mistakes, including spelling.

■ Writing Assignment 2

Think of an experience in your life that supports one of the statements below:

If you never have a dream, you'll never have a dream come true.—popular saying

"For fools rush in where angels fear to tread."—Alexander Pope

"Before I got married I had six theories about bringing up children; now I have six children and no theories."—John Wilmot, Earl of Rochester

"There are some things you learn best in calm, and some in storm."—Willa Cather

"Success is 99 percent perspiration and 1 percent inspiration."—Thomas Edison

"Lying is an indispensable part of making life tolerable."—Bergen Evans

"What a tangled web we weave/When first we practice to deceive."—Walter Scott

"There's a sucker born every minute."—P.T. Barnum

"We lie loudest when we lie to ourselves."—Eric Hoffer

"All marriages are happy. It's the living together afterward that causes all the trouble."—Raymond Hull

"Hoping and praying are easier but do not produce as good results as hard work."—Andy Rooney

"A little learning is a dangerous thing."—Alexander Pope

"Nothing is as good as it seems beforehand."—George Eliot

"You don't like weak women/You get bored too quick/And you don't like strong women/'Cause they're hip to your tricks."—Joni Mitchell

"Give a pig a finger, and he'll take the whole hand."—folk saying

"Life shrinks or expands in proportion to one's courage."—Anais Nin

"When I got to the end of my long journey in life/ I realized I was the architect of my own destiny."—Amado Nervo

"A fool and his money are soon parted."—popular saying

"From what we get, we can make a living; what we give, however, makes a life."—Arthur Ashe

"No matter how lovesick a woman is, she shouldn't take the first pill that comes along."—Dr. Joyce Brothers

"Fear not those who argue but those who dodge."—Marie von Ebner-Eschenback

"Trust in Allah, but tie your camel."—old Muslim proverb

Think of an experience you have had that demonstrates the truth of one of the above statements or another noteworthy saying—perhaps one that has been a guidepost for your life. Then, using one of these statements as your thesis, write a narrative essay about that experience. As you develop your essay, refer to the suggestions in the following prewriting strategies and rewriting strategies.

Prewriting

The key to the success of your essay will be your choice of an incident from your life that illustrates the truth of the statement you have chosen. Here are some guidelines to consider as you choose such an incident:

- The incident should be one that includes a *conflict*, or source of tension. That conflict does not need to be dramatic, such as a fistfight between two characters. Equally effective is a quieter conflict, such as a conflict between a person's conscience and desires, or a decision that must be made, or a difficult situation which has no clear resolution.

- The incident should be limited in time. It would be difficult to do justice in such a brief essay to an experience that continued over several weeks or months.
- The incident should evoke a definite emotional response in you, so that it might draw a similar response from your reader.
- The incident must *fully support* the statement you have chosen, not merely be linked by some of the same ideas. Do not, for example, take the statement "We lie loudest when we lie to ourselves" and then write about an incident in which someone just told a lie. The essay should demonstrate the cost of being untruthful to oneself.

Here is how one adult student tested whether her plan for her narrative essay was a good one.

- What statement have I chosen as my thesis?

    "The chains of habit are too weak to be felt until they are too strong to be broken." — Samuel Johnson

- Does the incident I have chosen include some kind of tension?

    Yes. I am going to write about a day when I overheard my little daughter make a remark that made me realize she was aware of my alcohol abuse. The tension is between my fantasy, which was that my drinking was a secret, and the truth, which was that even a little child knew about it.

- Is the incident limited in time?

    Yes. I am going to write about events that happened in one afternoon.

- Does the incident evoke an emotional response in me?

    Yes. I was ashamed, embarrassed, and angry at myself.

- Does the incident support the statement I have chosen?

    Yes. My "habit" was drinking, and I did not realize I was caught in its "chains" until I was unable to stop without help.

Rewriting

Once you have a first draft of your essay completed, you should review it with these questions in mind:

- Have I included the essay's thesis (my chosen statement) in my introductory paragraph, or is it clearly implied?
- Does each paragraph, and each sentence within that paragraph, help either to keep the action moving or to reveal important things about the characters?
- Do transitional words and phrases, and linking sentences between paragraphs, help make the sequence of events clear?

- Should I break up the essay by using bits of interesting dialogue instead of narration?
- Are there portions of the essay that do not support my thesis, and therefore should be eliminated or rewritten?

■ Writing Assignment 3

In this narrative essay, you will write with a specific purpose and for a specific audience.

Option 1:   Imagine that you are in a town fifty miles from home, that your car has broken down several miles from a gas station, and that you are carrying no money. You're afraid you are going to have a terrible time, but the friendly people who help you turn your experience into a positive one. It is such a good day, in fact, that you don't want to forget what happened.

Write a narrative of the day's events in your diary, so that you can read it ten years from now and remember exactly what happened. Begin with the moment you realize your car has broken down and continue until you're safely back home. Include a thesis at either the beginning or the end of your narration.

Option 2:   Imagine that a friend or sister or brother has to make a difficult decision of some kind. Perhaps he or she must decide how to deal with a troubled love affair, or a problem with living at home, or a conflict with a boss or coworker. Write a narrative from your own experience that will teach him or her something about the decision that must be made.

10 Examples

In our daily conversations, we often provide examples—details, particulars, and specific instances—to explain statements that we make. Here are several statements and supporting examples:

The first day of school was frustrating.	My sociology course was canceled. Then, I couldn't find the biology lab. And the lines at the bookstore were so long that I went home without buying my textbooks.
That washing machine is unreliable.	The water temperature can't be predicted; it stops in midcycle; and it sometimes shreds my clothing.
My grandfather is a thrifty person.	He washes and reuses aluminum foil. He wraps gifts in newspaper. And he's worn the same Sunday suit for twenty years.

In each case, the examples help us see for ourselves the truth of the statement that has been made. In essays, too, explanatory examples help your audience fully understand your point. Lively, specific examples also add interest to your paper.

In this section, you will be asked to provide a series of examples to support your thesis. First read the student essays and the professional essay that follow and work through the questions that accompany the essays. All three essays use examples to develop their points.

Student Essays to Consider

Everyday Cruelty

Last week, I found myself worrying less about problems of world politics and national crime and more about smaller evils. I came home one day with a bad taste in my mouth, the kind I get whenever I witness the little cruelties that people inflict on each other. On this particular day, I had seen too much of the cruelty of the world.

Every day I walk from the bus stop to the office where I work. This walk   2
is my first step away from the comforts of home and into the tensions of
the city. For me, a landmark on the route is a tiny patch of ground that
was once strewn with rubbish and broken glass. The city is trying to make
a "pocket park" out of it by planting trees and flowers. Every day this
spring, I watched the skinny saplings put out tiny leaves. When I walked
past, I always noted how big the tulips were getting and made bets with
myself on when they would bloom. To pass time as I walk, I often make silly
little bets with myself, such as predicting that the next man I see will be
wearing a blue tie. But last Wednesday, as I reached the park, I felt sick.
Someone had knocked the trees to the ground and trampled the budding
tulips into the dirt. Someone had destroyed a bit of beauty for no reason.

At lunchtime on Wednesday, I witnessed more meanness. Along with   3
dozens of other hungry, hurried people, I was waiting in line at McDonald's.
Also in line was a young mother with two tired, impatient children clinging
to her legs. The mother was trying to calm the children, but it was obvious
that their whining was about to give way to full-fledged tantrums. The
lines barely moved, and the lunchtime tension was building. Then, one of
the children began to cry and scream. As people stared angrily at the
helpless mother, the little boy's bloodcurdling yells resounded through the
restaurant. Finally, one man turned to her and said, "Lady, you shouldn't
bring your kids to a public place if you can't control them." A young woman
chimed in with another piece of cruel criticism. The mother was exhausted
and hungry. Someone in line could have helped her by kneeling down to
interact on eye level with one of the kids. Instead, even though many of
the customers in the restaurant were parents themselves, they treated her
like a criminal.

The worst incident of mean-spiritedness that I saw that day happened   4
after I left work. As I walked to the bus stop, I approached an old woman
huddled in a doorway. She was wrapped in a dirty blanket and clutched a
cheap vinyl bag packed with her belongings. She was one of the "street
people" our society leaves to fend for themselves. Approaching the woman
from the opposite direction were three teenagers who were laughing and
talking in loud voices. When they saw the old woman, they began to shout
crude remarks at her. Then they did even more cruel things to torment her.
The woman stared helplessly at them, like a wounded animal surrounded by
hunters. Then, having had their fun, the teenagers went on their way.

I had seen enough of the world's coldness that day and wanted to   5
leave it all behind. At home, I huddled in the warmth of my family.
I wondered why we all contribute to the supply of petty cruelty. There's
enough of it already.

Altered States

Most Americans are not alcoholics. Most do not cruise seedy city streets   1
looking to score crack cocaine or heroin. Relatively few try to con their
doctors into prescribing unneeded mood-altering medications. And yet,
many Americans are traveling through life with their minds slightly out of
kilter. In its attempt to cope with modern life, the human mind seems to
have evolved some defense strategies. Confronted with inventions like
television, the shopping center, and the Internet, the mind will slip—all by
itself—into an altered state.

Never in the history of humanity have people been expected to sit   2
passively for hours, staring at moving pictures emanating from an electronic
box. Since too much exposure to flickering images of police officers,
detectives, and talk-show hosts can be dangerous to human sanity, the mind
automatically goes into a state of TV hypnosis. The eyes see the sitcom
or the dog food commercial, but the mind goes into a holding pattern.
None of the televised images or sounds actually enters the brain. This is
why, when questioned, people cannot remember commercials they have
seen five seconds before or why the TV cops are chasing a certain suspect.
In this hypnotic, trancelike state, the mind resembles an armored armadillo.
It rolls up in self-defense, letting the stream of televised information pass
by harmlessly.

If the TV watcher arises from the couch and goes to a shopping mall,   3
he or she will again cope by slipping into an altered state. In the mall, the
mind is bombarded with the sights, smells, and sounds of dozens of stores,
restaurants, and movie theaters competing for its attention. There are
hundreds of questions to be answered. Should I start with the upper or
lower mall level? Which stores should I look in? Should I bother with the
sweater sale at J. C. Penney? Should I eat fried chicken or try the healthier-
sounding Pita Wrap? Where is my car parked? To combat this mental
overload, the mind goes into a state resembling the whiteout experienced
by mountain climbers trapped in a blinding snowstorm. Suddenly, everything
looks the same. The shopper is unsure where to go next and cannot
remember what he or she came for in the first place. The mind enters this
state deliberately, so that the shopper has no choice but to leave. Some kids
can be in a shopping mall for hours, but they are exceptions to the rule.

But no part of everyday life so quickly triggers the mind's protective   4
shut-down mode as that favorite pastime of the new millennium: cruising
the Internet. A computer user sits down with the intention of briefly
checking his or her E-mail or looking up a fact for a research paper. But once
tapped into the immense storehouse of information, entertainment, and
seemingly intimate personal connections that the Internet offers, the user
loses all sense of time and priorities. Prospects flood the mind: Should I
explore the rise of Nazi Germany? Play a trivia game? Hear the life story
of a lonely stranger in Duluth? With a mind dazed with information

overload, the user numbly hits one key after another, leaping from topic to topic, from distraction to distraction. Hours fly by as he or she sits hunched over the terminal, unable to account for the time that has passed.

Therefore, the next time you see TV viewers, shoppers, or Internet   5
surfers with eyes as glazed and empty as polished doorknobs, you'll know these people are in a protective altered state. Be gentle with them. They are merely trying to cope with the mind-numbing inventions of modern life.

■ Questions

About Unity

1. Which sentence in paragraph 3 of "Altered States" should be omitted in the interest of paragraph unity? (*Write the opening words.*)

   Some kids can be . . .

2. Which supporting paragraph in one of the essays lacks a topic sentence?

   Paragraph 2 in "Everyday Cruelty"

3. Which sentence in paragraph 2 of "Everyday Cruelty" should be omitted in the interest of paragraph unity? (*Write the opening words.*)

   To pass time as I walk . . .

About Support

4. Which sentence in paragraph 4 of "Everyday Cruelty" needs to be followed by more supporting details? (*Write the opening words.*)

   Then they did even more cruel things . . .

5. In paragraph 3 of "Everyday Cruelty," what sentence should be followed by supporting details? (*Write the opening words.*)

   A young woman chimed in . . .

6. What three pieces of evidence does the writer of "Altered States" offer to support the statement that the Internet is an "immense storehouse of information, entertainment, and seemingly intimate personal connections"?

   . . . explore the rise of Nazi Germany . . .

   . . . Play a trivia game . . .

   . . . Hear the life story of a stranger . . .

About Coherence

7. In paragraph 3 of "Everyday Cruelty," which three *time* signals does the author begin sentences with? (*Write the three signals here.*)

   I first thought . . .   At lunchtime on Wednesday . . .   . . . after I left work . . .

8. What sentence in "Altered States" indicates that the author has used emphatic order, saving his most important point for last? (*Write the opening words.*)

But no part of everyday life . . .

About the Introduction and Conclusion

9. Of the two student essays, which indicates in its introduction the essay's plan of development? (*Write the title of the essay and the opening words of the sentence that indicates the plan.*)

"Altered States": Confronted with inventions . . .

10. Which statement best describes the concluding paragraph of "Altered States"?

    a.   It contains a prediction.

    (b)   It combines a summary with a recommendation of how to treat people in an altered state.

    c.   It refers to the point made in the introduction about alcohol and drugs.

    d.   It contains thought-provoking questions about altered states.

Developing an Examples Essay

Development Through Prewriting

When Cedric, the student author of "Altered States," was considering a topic for his example essay, he looked around his dorm for inspiration. He first considered writing about examples of different types of people: jocks, brains, spaceheads. Then he thought about examples of housekeeping in dorm rooms: the Slob Kingdom, the Neat Freak Room, and the Packrat's Place.

"But that evening I was noticing how my roommate acted as he was cruising the Internet," Cedric said. "He sat down to write his brother a brief E-mail, and three hours later he was still there, cruising from website to website. His eyes were glassy and he seemed out of touch with reality. It reminded me of how spaced out I get when I go to a busy shopping mall. I began to think about how our minds have to adjust to challenges that our grandparents didn't know anything about. I added 'watching television' as the third category, and I had a pretty good idea what my essay would be about."

Cedric had his three categories, but he needed to do some more work in order to generate supporting details for each. He used the technique of diagramming to help inspire his thinking. This is what his diagram looked like:

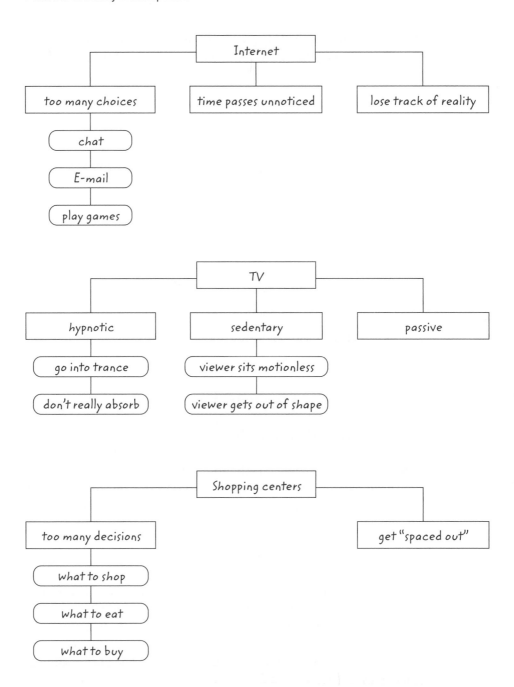

Looking at his diagram, Cedric saw that he would have no trouble support-ing the thesis that people's minds go into an "altered state" when they watch TV, go to shopping centers, or use the Internet. As he quickly jotted down details in diagram form, he had easily come up with enough ideas for his essay. He started writing and produced this first draft.

First Draft   **Altered States**

Modern life makes demands on the human mind that no other period of history has made. As society becomes more and more complex, the mind has developed some defense mechanisms. Confronted with inventions like the Internet, television, and the shopping center, the mind will slip—all by itself—into an altered state.

Cruising the Internet can quickly make the mind slip into a strange state. A computer user sits down to check his E-mail or looking up something. But once tapped into the Internet, the user loses all sense of time. He can chat with strangers, research any topic, play a game, or shop for any product. Some people begin to think of the online world and online friends as more real than the people in their own homes. While my roommate is absorbed in the Internet, he can even have brief conversations with people who come into our room, yet not be able to remember the conversations later. He sits there in a daze from information overload. He seems numb as he hits key after key, going from website to website.

Then there's TV. Our grandparents could not have imagined the idea of sitting passively for hours, staring at moving pictures emanating from a box. It's not a normal state of affairs, so the mind goes into something like a hypnotic trance. You see the sitcom or the dog food commercial, but your mind goes into a holding pattern. You don't really absorb the pictures or sounds. Five minutes after I watch a show I can't remember commercials I've seen or why the TV cops are chasing a certain suspect.

If the TV watcher arises from the couch and journeys into the real world, he often goes to the shopping center. Here, the mind is bombarded with the sights, smells, and sounds of dozens of stores, restaurants, and movie theaters competing for its attention. Dazed shoppers begin to feel like mountain climbers trapped in a blinding snowstorm. Suddenly, everything looks the same. My father is the worst of all when it comes to shopping in an altered state. He comes back from the mall looking like he'd been through a war. After about fifteen minutes of shopping, he can't concentrate enough to know what he's looking for.

Internet surfers, TV viewers, and shoppers all have one thing in common. They're just trying to cope with the mind-numbing inventions of modern life. Hopefully someday we'll turn away from such inventions and return to a simpler and more healthy way of life.

Development Through Revision

Cedric showed his first-draft essay to a classmate for her critique. She returned his essay with these comments:

Altered States

Modern life makes demands on the human mind that no other period of history has made. As society becomes more and more complex, the mind has developed some defense mechanisms. Confronted with inventions like the Internet, television, and the shopping center, the mind will slip—all by itself—into an altered state.

Take the Internet, for example. A computer user sits down to check his E-mail or look up something. But once tapped into the Internet, you lose all sense of time. You can chat with strangers, research any topic, play a game, or shop for any product. Some people begin to think of the online world and online friends as more real than the people in their own homes. While my roommate is absorbed in the Internet, he can even have brief conversations with people who come into our room, yet not be able to remember the conversations later. He sits there in a daze from information overload. He seems numb as he hits key after key, going from website to website.

This seems to me like a separate topic—people's relationships with people they meet on the Internet.

Sometimes you write about "a user," other times about "you," and then about "my roommate." It's confusing. Also, is the paragraph about your roommate on the Internet or what people in general are like?

These last two sentences are good. I'd like to read more about this "altered state" you think people go into.

Then there's TV. Our grandparents could not have imagined the idea of sitting passively for hours, staring at moving pictures emanating from a box. It's not a normal state of affairs, so the mind goes into something like a hypnotic trance. You see the sitcom or the dog food commercial, but your mind goes into a holding pattern. You don't really absorb the pictures or sounds. Five minutes after I watch a show I can't remember commercials I've seen or why the TV cops are chasing a certain suspect.

The idea of the "hypnotic trance" is interesting, but you need more details to back it up.

The point of view is a problem again. You skip from "you" to "I."

If the TV watcher arises from the couch and journeys into the real world, he often goes to the shopping center. Here, the mind is bombarded with the sights, smells, and sounds of dozens of stores, restaurants, and movie theaters competing for its attention. Dazed shoppers begin to feel like mountain climbers trapped in a blinding snowstorm. Suddenly, everything looks the same.

Good image!

I don't think this works. The essay isn't about your father. It should be about modern shoppers, not just one man.

My father is the worst of all when it comes to shopping in an altered state. He comes back from the mall looking like he'd been through a war. After about fifteen minutes of shopping, he can't concentrate enough to know what he's looking for.

This final sentence seems to introduce a new topic—that we shouldn't get caught up in TV and the Internet, etc.

Internet surfers, TV viewers, and shoppers all have one thing in common. They're just trying to cope with the mind-numbing inventions of modern life. Hopefully someday we'll turn away from such inventions and return to a simpler and more healthy way of life.

Cedric read his classmate's comments and reviewed the essay himself. He agreed with her criticisms about point of view and the need for stronger supporting details. He also decided that the Internet was his strongest supporting point and should be saved for the last paragraph. He then wrote the final version of his essay, the version that appears on page 213.

A Professional Essay to Consider

Read the following professional essay. Then answer the questions and read the comments that follow.

Dad

by Andrew H. Malcolm

The first memory I have of him—of anything, really—is his strength. 1
It was in the late afternoon in a house under construction near ours. The unfinished wood floors had large, terrifying holes whose yawning darkness I knew led to nowhere good. His powerful hands, then age thirty-three, wrapped all the way around my tiny arms, then age four, and easily swung me up to his shoulders to command all I surveyed.

The relationship between a son and his father changes over time. It may 2
grow and flourish in mutual maturity. It may sour in resented dependence or independence. With many children living in single-parent homes today, it may not even exist.

But to a little boy right after World War II, a father seemed a god   3
with strange strengths and uncanny powers enabling him to do and know
things that no mortal could do or know. Amazing things, like putting a bicycle
chain back on, just like that. Or building a hamster cage. Or guiding a jigsaw
so it formed the letter F; I learned the alphabet that way in those pre-
television days, one letter or number every other evening plus a review of
the collection. (The vowels we painted red because they were special
somehow.)

He seemed to know what I thought before I did. "You look like you could   4
use a cheeseburger and a chocolate shake," he would say on hot Sunday
afternoons. When, at the age of five, I broke a neighbor's garage window
with a wild curveball and waited in fear for ten days to make the announcement, he seemed to know about it already and to have been waiting for
something.

There were, of course, rules to learn. First came the handshake. None of   5
those fishy little finger grips, but a good firm squeeze accompanied by an
equally strong gaze into the other's eyes. "The first thing anyone knows
about you is your handshake," he would say. And we'd practice it each night
on his return from work, the serious toddler in the battered Cleveland Indians
cap running up to the giant father to shake hands again and again until it
was firm enough.

When my cat killed a bird, he defused the anger of a nine-year-old   6
with a little chat about something called "instinked." The next year, when
my dog got run over and the weight of sorrow was just too immense to stand,
he was there, too, with his big arms and his own tears and some thoughts
on the natural order of life and death, although what was natural about a
speeding car that didn't stop always escaped me.

As time passed, there were other rules to learn. "Always do your   7
best." "Do it now." "NEVER LIE!" And, most important, "You can do whatever
you have to do." By my teens, he wasn't telling me what to do anymore,
which was scary and heady at the same time. He provided perspective, not
telling me what was around the great corner of life but letting me
know there was a lot more than just today and the next, which I hadn't
thought of.

When the most important girl in the world—I forget her name now—   8
turned down a movie date, he just happened to walk by the kitchen phone.
"This may be hard to believe right now, he said, "but someday you won't
even remember her name."

One day, I realize now, there was a change. I wasn't trying to please him   9
so much as I was trying to impress him. I never asked him to come to my football games. He had a high-pressure career, and it meant driving through most
of Friday night. But for all the big games, when I looked over at the sideline,
there was that familiar fedora. And, by God, did the opposing team captain
ever get a firm handshake and a gaze he would remember.

Then, a school fact contradicted something he said. Impossible that   10
he could be wrong, but there it was in the book. These accumulated over
time, along with personal experiences, to buttress my own developing
sense of values. And I could tell we had each taken our own, perfectly normal
paths.

I began to see, too, his blind spots, his prejudices, and his weaknesses.   11
I never threw these up at him. He hadn't to me, and, anyway, he seemed to
need protection. I stopped asking his advice; the experiences he drew from
no longer seemed relevant to the decisions I had to make. On the phone, he
would go on about politics at times, why he would vote the way he did or
why some incumbent was a jerk. And I would roll my eyes to the ceiling and
smile a little, though I hid it in my voice.

He volunteered advice for a while. But then, in more recent years, politics   12
and issues gave way to talk of empty errands and, always, to ailments—his
friends', my mother's, and his own, which were serious and included heart
disease. He had a bedside oxygen tank, and he would ostentatiously retire
there during my visits, asking my help in easing his body onto the mattress.
"You have very strong arms," he once noted.

From his bed, he showed me the many sores and scars on his   13
misshapen body and all the bottles of medicine. He talked of the pain
and craved much sympathy. He got some. But the scene was not attractive.
He told me, as the doctor had, that his condition would only deteriorate.
"Sometimes," he confided, "I would just like to lie down and go to sleep and
not wake up."

After much thought and practice ("You can do whatever you have to   14
do"), one night last winter, I sat down by his bed and remembered for an
instant those terrifying dark holes in another house thirty-five years before.
I told my father how much I loved him. I described all the things people were
doing for him. But, I said, he kept eating poorly, hiding in his room, and vio-
lating other doctor's orders. No amount of love could make someone else care
about life, I said: it was a two-way street. He wasn't doing his best. The decision was his.

He said he knew how hard my words had been to say and how proud he   15
was of me. "I had the best teacher," I said. "You can do whatever you have
to do." He smiled a little. and we shook hands, firmly, for the last time.

Several days later, at about 4 A.M., my mother heard Dad shuffling   16
about their dark room. "I have some things I have to do," he said. He paid a
bundle of bills. He composed for my mother a long list of legal and financial
what-to-do's "in case of emergency." And he wrote me a note.

Then he walked back to his bed and laid himself down. He went to   17
sleep, naturally. And he did not wake up.

■ Questions

About Unity

1. The story about Malcolm and his father is an example of his thesis. Which sentence expresses that thesis?

    a. The last sentence of paragraph 1

    (b) The first sentence of paragraph 2

    c. The last sentence of paragraph 2

    d. The first sentence of paragraph 3

2. Which statement would best serve as a topic sentence for paragraph 6?

    a. My dad loved my dog as much as I did.

    b. Pets were a subject that drew my dad and me together.

    (c) My dad helped me make sense of life's tragedies.

    d. I was angry at my cat for killing a bird.

3. Which statement would best serve as a topic sentence for paragraph 10?

    a. School set the author against his father.

    b. The author came to see more and more that his father was usually wrong.

    c. It is best for father and son to see eye to eye.

    (d) Some of the author's ideas gradually came to differ from those of his father.

About Support

4. How many supporting details does the author use in paragraph 3 to support the idea that his father "seemed a god with strange strengths and uncanny powers"?

    a. one

    b. two

    (c) three

5. With which sentence does Malcolm support his statement in paragraph 14 that his father "wasn't doing his best"? *(Write the opening words.)*

    But, I said, he kept . . .
    _____

6. Which of these points is supported by the anecdote in paragraph 8?
    a. "As time passed, there were other rules to learn."
    (b) "He provided perspective . . . letting me know there was a lot more than just today and the next . . . "
    c. "One day, I realize now, there was a change."
    d. "I wasn't trying to please him so much as I was trying to impress him."

About Coherence

7. Initially, Malcolm saw his father as all-wise and all-powerful. Which paragraph in the essay signals the turning point at which he began seeing his father in more realistic, less idealized terms? ___10___
8. In paragraph 6, find each of the following:
    a. two time transition signals
        _____When_____   _____The next year_____
    b. one addition transition signal
        _____too_____
    c. one change-of-direction transition signal
        _____although_____
9. Which method of organization does Malcolm use in his essay?
    (a) Time
    b. Emphatic

About the Conclusion

10. The conclusion of "Dad" is made up of
    a. a summary of the narrative and a final thought.
    b. a question about fatherhood.
    (c) the last event of the story about Malcolm and his father.
    d. a prediction of what kind of father Malcolm hopes to be himself.

Writing An Examples Essay

- ■ **Writing Assignment 1**

   For this assignment, you will complete an unfinished essay by adding appropriate supporting examples. Here is the incomplete essay:

Problems with My Apartment

> When I was younger, I fantasized about how wonderful life would be when I moved into my own apartment. Now I'm a bit older and wiser, and my dreams have turned into nightmares. My apartment has given me nothing but headaches. From the day I signed the lease, I've had to deal with an uncooperative landlord, an incompetent janitor, and inconsiderate neighbors.

> First of all, my landlord has been uncooperative. . . .

> I've had a problem not only with my landlord but also with an incompetent janitor. . . .

> Perhaps the worst problem has been with the inconsiderate neighbors who live in the apartment above me. . . .

> Sometimes, my apartment seems like a small, friendly oasis surrounded by hostile enemies. I never know what side trouble is going to come from next: the landlord, the janitor, or the neighbors. Home may be where the heart is, but my sanity is thinking about moving out.

Note: If you do not have experience with living in an apartment, write instead about problems of living in a dormitory or problems of living at home. Revise the introduction and conclusion so that they fit your topic. Problems of living in a dorm might include these:

Restrictive dorm regulations

Inconsiderate students on your floor

A difficult roommate

Problems of living at home might be these:

Lack of space

Inconsiderate brothers and sisters

Conflict with your parent or parents

Prewriting

a   Generate details for your paper by using brainstorming as a prewriting technique. Brainstorm by writing down answers to the following questions. (Use separate paper.)   Answers will vary.

How has the landlord been uncooperative?

In what ways have you been inconvenienced?

Has he (or she) been uncooperative more than once?

How have you reacted to the landlord's lack of cooperation?

What has been the landlord's reaction?

What kinds of things have you said to each other?

What is the most uncooperative thing the landlord has done?

Who is the janitor?

What has he (or she) tried to fix in the apartment?

In what ways has the janitor been incompetent?

How has the janitor inconvenienced you?

Has the janitor's incompetence cost you money?

What is the worst example of the janitor's incompetence?

Who are the neighbors?

How long have they lived upstairs?

What kind of problems have you had with them?

Have these problems occurred more than once?

If you have spoken to the neighbors about the problems, how did they respond?

What is the worst problem with these neighbors?

b Use the details generated by your brainstorming to flesh out the three paragraphs with details and examples. Remember that you may use one extended example in each paragraph (as in "Everyday Cruelty") or several brief examples (as in "Altered States").

c As you write your first draft, keep asking yourself these questions:

Do my examples truly show my landlord as *uncooperative*?

Do my examples truly show the janitor as *incompetent*?

Do my examples truly show my neighbors as *inconsiderate*?

d Proceed to write the first draft of your essay.

Rewriting

After you have completed the first draft of the paper, set it aside for a while if you can. When you review it, try to do so as critically as you would if it were not your own work. Ask yourself these questions:

- Do I have a clearly stated (or implied) thesis?
- Have I provided *relevant* specific details for the landlord's uncooperativeness, the janitor's incompetence, and the neighbors' inconsiderateness?
- Have I provided *enough* specific details to support each of the three qualities?
- Have I used transitions, including transitions between paragraphs, to help readers follow my train of thought?
- Do I have a concluding paragraph that provides a summary or final thought or both?

As you revise your essay through one or more additional drafts, continue to refer to this list until you can answer "yes" to each question. Then be sure to check the next-to-final draft of the paper for the sentence skills listed on the inside front cover.

■ Writing Assignment 2

Write an examples essay on the outstanding qualities (good or bad) of a person you know well. This person might be a member of your family, a friend, a roommate, a boss, a neighbor, an instructor, or someone else.

You may approach this assignment in one of two ways. You may choose to write about three related qualities of one person. For example, "My brother is stubborn, bad-tempered, and suspicious." Or you may write about one quality that is apparent in three different aspects of a person's life. For example, "My sister's patience is apparent in her relationships with her students, her husband, and her teenage son."

Just to jog your thinking, here are some descriptive words that can be applied to people. You are *not* restricted to writing about these qualities. Write about whatever qualities the person you choose possesses.

Honest	Persistent	Flirtatious	Spineless
Bad-tempered	Shy	Irresponsible	Good-humored
Ambitious	Sloppy	Stingy	Cooperative
Prejudiced	Hardworking	Aggressive	Disciplined
Considerate	Outgoing	Trustworthy	Sentimental
Argumentative	Supportive	Courageous	Defensive
Softhearted	Suspicious	Compulsive	Dishonest
Energetic	Lazy	Jealous	Insensitive
Patient	Cynical	Modest	Neat
Reliable	Independent	Sarcastic	
Generous	Stubborn	Self-centered	

Prewriting

a   Brainstorm to come up with supporting details for your thesis. For instance, if you are writing about your sentimental father, you would ask yourself questions like these:

Why do I think of Dad as being sentimental?

When have I seen him be sentimental?

What sort of occasions make him sentimental?

Where are some places he's become sentimental about?

Whom does Dad become sentimental about?

What are some memorable examples of Dad's acting sentimental?

b   Look over the material generated by your brainstorming and decide what your three main points will be.

c   Decide on the order of your supporting paragraphs. If one of your main points seems stronger than the others, consider making it the final point in the body of the essay.

d   Decide whether to use one extended example or two or three brief examples to support each main point.

e   Prepare a scratch outline for your essay, drawing your main points and supporting examples from details generated by your brainstorming.

f   Write the first draft of your essay.

Rewriting

Refer to the guidelines for rewriting provided on page 226.

■ Writing Assignment 3

In this examples essay, you will write with a specific purpose and for a specific audience. Imagine that you have completed a year of college and have agreed to take part in your college's summer orientation program for incoming students. You will be meeting with a small group of new students to help them get ready for college life.

Prepare a presentation to the new students in which you make the point that college is more demanding than high school. Make vividly clear—using several hypothetical students as examples—just what the consequences of being unprepared for those demands can be. Focus on three areas of college and the demands of each. Some areas you might consider are these: instructors, class attendance, time control, class note-taking, studying a textbook, work habits, balancing work and social life, and getting help when needed. Each of the areas you choose should be developed in a separate paragraph. Each paragraph should have its own detailed examples.

■ Writing Assignment 4

Write an examples essay based on an outside reading. It might be a selection recommended by your instructor, or it might be a piece by one of the following authors, all of whom have written books of essays that should be available in your college library.

Annie Dillard	Amy Tan
Ellen Goodman	Deborah Tannen
Molly Ivins	Henry David Thoreau
Maxine Hong Kingston	Calvin Trillin
George Orwell	Alice Walker
Richard Rodriguez	E. B. White
Andy Rooney	Marie Winn

Base your essay on some idea in the selection you have chosen and provide a series of examples to back up your idea. A student model follows.

Paying Attention to a Death

In "A Hanging," George Orwell describes the execution of a man in a Burmese prison. The prisoner, a Hindu, is marched from his cell, led to a gallows, and killed when the drop opens and the noose tightens. The entire procedure takes eight minutes. As he depicts this incident, Orwell uses a series of details that make us sharply aware of the enormity of killing a human being.   1

The moments leading up to the hanging are filled with tension. Six tall guards, two of them armed with rifles, surround the prisoner, "a puny wisp of a man." The guards not only handcuff the man but also chain his handcuffs to their belts and lash his arms to his sides. The guards, nervous about fulfilling their duty, treat the Hindu like "a fish which is still alive and may jump back into the water." Meanwhile, the jail superintendent prods the head jailer to get on with the execution. The superintendent's irritability is a mask for his discomfort. Then, the procession toward the gallows is interrupted by the appearance of a friendly dog, "wagging its whole body, wild with glee at finding so many human beings together." This does not ease the tension but increases it. The contrast of the lively dog licking the doomed man's face momentarily stuns the guards and arouses in the superintendent a sense of angry urgency.   2

Next, in the gallows scene, Orwell uses vivid details that emphasize the life within the man who is about to die. The condemned prisoner, who has been walking steadily up to this point, moves "clumsily" up the ladder. And until now, he has been utterly silent. But, after the noose is placed around his neck, he begins "crying out to his god." The repeated cry of "Ram! Ram! Ram!" is "like the tolling of a bell," a death knell. The dog begins to whine at the sound, and the guards go "grey," their bayonets trembling. It is as if the hooded, faceless man on the wooden platform has suddenly become a human being, a soul seeking aid and comfort. The superintendent, who has been hiding his emotions behind a stern face, gives the execution order "fiercely." The living man of moments ago simply ceases to be.   3

After the hanging, Orwell underscores the relief people feel when the   4
momentous event is over. The jail superintendent checks to be sure that the
prisoner is dead and then blows out "a deep breath" and loses his "moody
look." "One felt an impulse," Orwell says, "to sing, to break into a run, to
snigger." Suddenly, people are talking and chattering, even laughing. The
head jailer's story about a condemned prisoner who clung to the bars of his
cell so tightly that it took six men to move him sets off a gale of laughter. On
the road outside the prison, everyone who participated in the execution has
a whiskey. The men, having been so close to death, need to reassure
themselves of the fact that they are alive. They must laugh and drink, not
because they are insensitive, but because they are shaken. They must try to
forget that the dead man is only a hundred yards away.

"A Hanging" sets out to create a picture of death in the midst of life.   5
Orwell tries to make us see, through the details he chooses, that killing a
person results in "one mind less, one world less." Such an act—"cutting a life
short when it is in full tide"—violates the laws of life and nature.

11 PROCESS

Every day we perform many activities that are *processes*, that is, series of steps carried out in a definite order. Many of these processes are familiar and automatic: for example, loading film into a camera, diapering a baby, or making an omelet. We are thus seldom aware of the sequence of steps making up each activity. In other cases—for example, when someone asks us for directions to a particular place, or when we try to read and follow directions for a new table game that someone has given us—we may be painfully conscious of the whole series of steps involved in the process.

In this section, you will be asked to write a process essay—one that explains clearly how to do or make something. To prepare for this assignment, you should first read the student process papers and the professional essay and then answer the questions that follow them.

Student Essays to Consider

Successful Exercise

Regular exercise is something like the weather—we all talk about it, but we tend not to do anything about it! Exercise classes on television and exercise programs on videos and CDs—as well as the instructions in books, magazines, and pamphlets—now make it easy to have a personal, low-cost exercise program without leaving home. However, for success in exercise, you should follow a simple plan consisting of arranging time, making preparations, and starting off at a sensible pace.

Everyone has an excuse for not exercising: a heavy schedule at work or school; being rushed in the morning and exhausted at night; too many other responsibilities. However, one solution is simply to get up half an hour earlier in the morning. Look at it this way: if you're already getting up too early, what's an extra half hour? Of course, that time could be cut to fifteen minutes earlier if you could lay out your clothes, set the breakfast table, fill the coffee maker, and gather your books and materials for the next day before you go to bed.

Next, prepare for your exercise session. To begin with, get yourself ready by not eating or drinking anything before exercising. Why risk an upset stomach? Then, dress comfortably in something that allows you to move freely. Since you'll be in your own home, there's no need to invest in a high-fashion dance costume. A loose T-shirt and shorts are good. A bathing suit is great in summer, and in winter long underwear is warm

1

2

3

231

and comfortable. If your hair tends to flop in your eyes, pin it back or wear a headband or scarf. Prepare the exercise area, too. Turn off the phone and lock the door to prevent interruptions. Shove the coffee table out of the way so you won't bruise yourself on it or other furniture. Then get out the simple materials you'll need to exercise with.

Finally, use common sense in getting started. Common sense isn't so common, as anyone who reads the newspapers and watches the world can tell you. If this is your first attempt at exercising, begin slowly. You do not need to do each movement the full number of times at first, but you should <u>try</u> each one. After five or six sessions, you should be able to do each one the full number of times. Try to move in a smooth, rhythmic way; this will help prevent injuries and pulled muscles. Pretend you're a dancer and make each move graceful, even if it's just getting up off the floor. After the last exercise, give yourself five minutes to relax and cool off—you have earned it. Finally, put those sore muscles under a hot shower and get ready for a great day. 4

Establishing an exercise program isn't difficult, but it can't be achieved by reading about it, talking about it, or watching models exercise on television. It happens only when you get off that couch and do something about it. As my doctor likes to say, "If you don't use it, you'll lose it." 5

How to Complain

I'm not just a consumer—I'm a victim. If I order a product, it is sure to arrive in the wrong color, size, or quantity. If I hire people to do repairs, they never arrive on the day scheduled. If I owe a bill, the computer is bound to overcharge me. Therefore, in self-defense, I have developed the following consumer's guide to complaining effectively. 1

The first step is getting organized. I save all sales slips and original boxes. Also, I keep a special file for warranty cards and appliance guarantees. This file does not prevent a product from falling apart the day after the guarantee runs out. One of the problems in our country is the shoddy workmanship that goes into many products. However, these facts give me the ammunition I need to make a complaint. I know the date of the purchase, the correct price (or service charge), where the item was purchased, and an exact description of the product, including model and serial numbers. When I compose my letter of complaint, I find it is not necessary to exaggerate. I just stick to the facts. 2

The next step is to send the complaint to the person who will get results quickly. My experience has shown that the president of the company is the best person to contact. I call the company to find out the president's name and make sure I note the proper spelling. Then I write directly to that person, and I usually get prompt action. For example, the head of AMF arranged to replace my son's ten-speed "lemon" when it fell apart piece by piece in less than a year. Another time, the president of a Philadelphia 3 department store finally had a twenty-dollar overcharge on my bill corrected after I had spent three months arguing uselessly with a computer.

If I get no response to a written complaint within ten days, I follow   4
through with a personal telephone call. When I had a new bathtub installed a few years ago, the plumber left a gritty black substance on the bottom of the tub. No amount of scrubbing could remove it. I tried every cleanser on the supermarket shelf, but I still had a dirty tub. The plumber shrugged off my complaints and said to try Comet. The manufacturer never answered my letter. Finally, I made a personal phone call to the president of the firm. Within days a well-dressed executive showed up at my door. In a business suit, white shirt, striped tie, and rubber gloves, he cleaned the tub. Before he left, he scolded me in an angry voice: "You didn't have to call the president." The point is, I did have to call the president. No one else cared enough to solve the problem.

Therefore, my advice to consumers is to keep accurate records, and   5
when you have to complain, go right to the top. It has always worked for me.

■ Questions

About Unity

1. The (*fill in the correct answer:* first, second, third) _____ first _____ supporting paragraph of "Successful Exercise" lacks a topic sentence. Write a topic sentence that expresses its main point:

   Answers may vary in wording.

   First, arrange time for exercise.

2. Which of the following sentences from paragraph 4 of "Successful Exercise" should be omitted in the interest of paragraph unity?

   a. Finally, use common sense in getting started.

   b. Common sense isn't so common, as anyone who reads the newspaper and watches the world can tell you.

   c. If this is your first attempt at exercising, begin slowly.

   d. You do not need to do each movement the full number of times at first, but you should <u>try</u> each one.

3. Which sentence in paragraph 2 of "How to Complain" should be omitted in the interest of paragraph unity? (*Write the opening words.*)

   One of the problems . . .

About Support

4. Which sentence in paragraph 3 of "Successful Exercise" needs to be followed by more supporting details? *(Write the opening words.)*

    Then get out the simple materials . . .

5. Which supporting paragraph in "How to Complain" uses one extended example? Write the number of that paragraph and tell (in just a few words) what the example was about. *Wording of answers may vary.*

    Paragraph 4 describes an incident with a plumber who left a bathtub dirty.

6. Which supporting paragraph in "How to Complain" depends on two short examples? Write the number of that paragraph and tell (in just a few words) what each example was about. *Wording of answers may vary.*

    Paragraph 3 describes an incident with a "lemon" bicycle and an incident

    about an overcharge by a department store.

About Coherence

7. Read paragraph 3 of "Successful Exercise" and find the four sentences that begin with time signals. Write those four signals here.

Next	*Then*
To begin with	*Then*

8. "In How to Complain," which time transition word is used in the topic sentence of paragraph 2? ___*first*___ In the topic sentence of paragraph 3? ___*next*___

About the Introduction and Conclusion

9. Which statement best describes the introduction of "Successful Exercise"?

    (a.) It begins with a couple of general points about the topic and then narrows down to the thesis.

    b. It explains the importance of daily exercise to the reader.

    c. It uses a brief story about the author's experience with exercise.

    d. It asks a question about the role of exercise in life.

10. Which method of conclusion is used in both "Successful Exercise" and "How to Complain"?

   a.   Summary

   b.   Thought-provoking question

   c.   Prediction

   (d) Recommendation

Developing a Process Essay

Development Through Prewriting

A process essay requires the writer to think through the steps involved in an activity. As Marian, the author of "How to Complain," thought about possible topics for her essay, she asked herself, "What are some things I do in a methodical, step-by-step way?" A number of possibilities occurred to her, including getting herself and her children ready for school in the morning, shopping for groceries (from preparing a shopping list to organizing her coupons), and the one she finally settled on: effective complaining. "People tell me I'm 'so organized' when it comes to getting satisfaction on things I buy," Marian said. "I realized that I do usually get results when I complain because I go about complaining in an organized way. In order to write my essay, I just needed to put those steps into words."

Marian began by making a list of the steps she follows when she makes a complaint. This is what she wrote:

Save sales slips and original boxes

Engrave items with ID number in case of burglary

Write letter of complaint

Make photocopy of letter

Create file of warranties and guarantees

Send complaint letter directly to president

Call company for president's name

Follow through with telephone call if no response

Make thank-you call after action is taken

Next, she numbered those steps in the order in which she performs them. She struck out some items she realized weren't really necessary to the process of complaining:

1   Save sales slips and original boxes
~~Engrave items with ID number in case of burglary~~
4   Write letter of complaint
~~Make photocopy of letter~~
2   Create file of warranties and guarantees
5   Send complaint letter directly to president
3   Call company for president's name
6   Follow through with telephone call if no response
~~Make thank-you call after action is taken~~

Next, she decided to group her items into three steps. The steps she determined would work were (1) getting organized, (2) sending the complaint to the president, and (3) following up with further action.

With that preparation done, Marian wrote her first draft.

First Draft   **How to Complain**

Because I find that a consumer has to watch out for herself and be ready to speak up if a product or service isn't satisfactory, I have developed the following consumer's guide to complaining effectively.

The first step is getting organized. I save all sales slips, original boxes, warranty cards, and appliance guarantees. This file does not prevent a product from falling apart the day after the guarantee runs out. One of the problems in our country is the shoddy workmanship that goes into many products. That way I know the date of the purchase, the correct price, where the item was purchased, and an exact description of the product.

The next step is to send the complaint to the person who will get results quickly. I call the company to find out the president's name and then I write directly to that person. For example, the head of AMF arranged to replace my son's bike. Another time, the president of a Philadelphia department store finally had a twenty-dollar overcharge on my bill corrected.

If I get no response to a written complaint within ten days, I follow though with a personal telephone call. When I had a new bathtub installed a few years ago, the plumber left a gritty black substance on the bottom of the tub. I tried everything to get it off. Finally, I made a personal phone call to the president of the firm. Within days a well-dressed executive showed up at my door. In a business suit, white shirt, striped tie, and rubber gloves, he cleaned the tub. Before he left, he said, "You didn't have to call the president."

Therefore, my advice to consumers is to keep accurate records, and when you have to complain, go right to the top. It has always worked for me.

Development Through Reading

After she had written the first draft, Marian set it aside for several days. When she reread it, she was able to look at it more critically. These are her comments:

> I think this first draft is OK as the "bare bones" of an essay, but it needs to be fleshed out everywhere. For instance, in paragraph 1, I need to explain <u>why</u> it's important to know the date of purchase etc. And in paragraph 2, I need to explain more about <u>what happened</u> with the bike and the department store overcharge. In paragraph 3, especially, I need to explain <u>how</u> I tried to solve the problem with the bathtub before I called the president. I want to make it clear that I don't immediately go to the top as soon as I have a problem—I give the people at a lower level a chance to fix it first. All in all, my first draft looks as if I just rushed to get the basic ideas down on paper. Now I need to take the time to back up my main points with better support.

With that self-critique in mind, Marian wrote the version of "How to Complain" that appears on page 232.

A Professional Essay to Consider

Read the following professional essay. Then answer the questions and read the comments that follow.

How to Do Well on a Job Interview

by Glenda Davis

Ask a random selection of people for a listing of their least favorite   1
activities, and right up there with "getting my teeth drilled" is likely to be
"going to a job interview." The job interview is often regarded as a confusing,
humiliating, and nerve-racking experience. First of all, you have to wait for
your appointment in an outer room, often trapped there with other people
applying for the same job. You sit there nervously, trying not to think about
the fact that only one of you may be hired. Then you are called into the interviewer's office. Faced with a complete stranger, you have to try to act both
cool and friendly as you are asked all sorts of questions. Some questions are
personal: "What is your greatest weakness?" Others are confusing: "Why
should we hire you?" The interview probably takes about twenty minutes but
seems like two hours. Finally, you go home and wait for days and even weeks.
If you get the job, great. But if you don't, you're rarely given any reason why.

The job-interview "game" may not be much fun, but it is a game you *can*   2
win if you play it right. The name of the game is standing out of the crowd—
in a positive way. If you go to the interview in a Bozo the Clown suit, you'll
stand out of the crowd, all right, but not in a way that is likely to get you
hired.

Here are guidelines to help you play the interview game to win: 3

Present yourself as a winner. Instantly, the way you dress, speak, and   4
move gives the interviewer more information about you than you would
think possible. You doubt that this is true? Consider this: a professional
job recruiter, meeting a series of job applicants, was asked to signal the
moment he decided *not* to hire each applicant. The thumbs-down decision
was often made *in less than forty-five seconds—even before the applicant
thought the interview had begun.*

How can you keep from becoming a victim of an instant "no" decision?   5

- *Dress appropriately.* This means business clothing: usually a suit and tie or
  a conservative dress or skirt suit. Don't wear casual student clothing. On
  the other hand, don't overdress: you're going to a job interview, not a
  party. If you're not sure what's considered appropriate business attire, do
  some spying before the interview. Walk past your prospective place of
  employment at lunch or quitting time and check out how the employees

are dressed. Your goal is to look as though you would fit in with that group of people.

- *Pay attention to your grooming.* Untidy hair, body odor, dandruff, unshined shoes, a hanging hem, stains on your tie, excessive makeup or cologne, a sloppy job of shaving—if the interviewer notices any of these, your prospect of being hired takes a probably fatal hit.
- *Look alert, poised, and friendly.* When that interviewer looks into the waiting room and calls your name, he or she is getting a first impression of your behavior. If you're slouched in your chair, dozing or lost in the pages of a magazine; if you look up with an annoyed "Huh?"; if you slowly get up and wander over with your hands in your pockets, he or she will not be favorably impressed. What *will* earn you points is rising promptly and walking briskly toward the interviewer. Smiling and looking directly at that person, extend your hand to shake his or hers, saying, "I'm Lesley Brown. Thank you for seeing me today."
- *Expect to make a little small talk.* This is not a waste of time; it is the interviewer's way of checking your ability to be politely sociable, and it is your opportunity to cement the good impression you've already made. The key is to follow the interviewer's lead. If he or she wants to chat about the weather for a few minutes, do so. But don't drag it out; as soon as you get a signal that it's time to talk about the job, be ready to get down to business.

Be ready for the interviewer's questions. The same questions come up 6 again and again in many job interviews. *You should plan ahead for all these questions!* Think carefully about each question, outline your answer, and memorize each outline. Then practice reciting the answers to yourself. Only in this way are you going to be prepared. Here are common questions, what they really mean, and how to answer them:

- *"Tell me about yourself."* This question is raised to see how organized you are. The *wrong* way to answer it is to launch into a wandering, disjointed response or—worse yet—to demand defensively, "What do you want to know?" or "What do you mean?" When this question comes up, you should be prepared to give a brief summary of your life and work experience—where you grew up, where your family lives now, where you went to school, what jobs you've had, and how you happen to be here now looking for the challenge of a new job.
- *"What are your strengths and weaknesses?"* In talking about your strong points, mention traits that will serve you well in this particular job. If you are well-organized, a creative problem-solver, a good team member, or a quick learner, be ready to describe specific ways those strengths have served you in the past. Don't make the mistake of saying, "I don't have any real weaknesses." You'll come across as more believable if you admit a

flaw—but make it one that an employer might actually like. For instance, admit that you are a workaholic or a perfectionist.

- *"Why should we hire you?"* Remember that it is up to *you* to convince the interviewer that you're the man or woman for this job. If you just sit there and hope that the interviewer will magically discern your good qualities, you are likely to be disappointed. Don't be afraid to sell yourself. Tell the recruiter that from your research you have learned that the interviewer's company is one you would like to work for, and that you believe the company's needs and your skills are a great match.

- *"Why did you leave your last job?"* This may seem like a great opportunity to cry on the interviewer's shoulder about what a jerk your last boss was or how unappreciated you were. It is not. The experts agree: never badmouth *anyone* when you are asked this question. Say that you left in order to seek greater responsibilities or challenges. Be positive, not negative. No matter how justified you may feel about hating your last job or boss, if you give voice to those feelings in an interview, you're going to make the interviewer suspect that you're a whiner and hard to work with.

- *"Do you have any questions?"* This is the time to stress one last time how interested you are in this particular job. Ask a question or two about specific aspects of the job, pointing out again how well your talents and the company's needs are matched. Even if you're dying to know how much the job pays and how much vacation you get, don't ask. There will be time enough to cover those questions after you've been offered the job. Today, your task is to demonstrate what a good employee you would be.

Send a thank-you note. Once you've gotten past the interview, there is 7 one more chance for you to make a fine impression. As soon as you can—certainly no more than one or two days after the interview—write a note of thanks to your interviewer. In it, briefly remind him or her of when you came in and what job you applied for. As well as thanking the interviewer for seeing you, reaffirm your interest in the job and mention again why you think you are the best candidate for it. Make the note courteous, businesslike, and brief—just a paragraph or two. If the interviewer is wavering between several equally qualified candidates, such a note could tip the scales in your favor.

No amount of preparation is going to make interviewing for a job your 8 favorite activity. But if you go in well prepared and with a positive attitude, your potential employer can't help thinking highly of you. And the day will come when you are the one who wins the job.

■ Questions

About Unity

1. Either of two sentences in "How to Do Well on a Job Interview" might serve as the thesis. Write the opening words of either of these sentences:

   The job-interview "game" may not be much fun, but . . . you can win

   if you play it right.

   Here are guidelines to help you play the interview game to win.

2. Which statement would make the best topic sentence for paragraph 4?

   a. Beauty is only skin-deep.

   b. Interviewers care only about how applicants dress.

   c. Professional job recruiters meet many applicants for a single job.

   (d.) You should present yourself as a winner because first impressions count a lot.

3. In paragraph 6, which statement would best serve as a topic sentence for the list item about strengths and weaknesses?

   a. A quality such as perfectionism or workaholism can be seen as both a strength and a weakness.

   (b.) As you talk about your strengths and weaknesses, tailor what you say to the job you're applying for.

   c. Claiming to be a "creative problem-solver" is a good idea as you apply for almost any position.

   d. The interviewer is not likely to be impressed if you claim to have no major weaknesses.

About Support

4. In paragraph 5, the supporting details for the list item "dress appropriately" are:

   a. reasons for dressing appropriately.

   b. quotations of experts on how to dress for job interviews.

   (c.) ideas on how to dress appropriately.

   d. statistics on how people who are interviewed dress and how well they succeeded.

5. Which sentence from paragraph 7 best provides a *reason* for the author's suggestion about "sending a thank-you note?

    a. As soon as you can—certainly no more than one or two days after the interview—write a note of thanks to your interviewer.

    b. In it, briefly remind him or her of when you came in and what job you applied for.

    c. Make the note courteous, businesslike, and brief—just a paragraph or two.

    d. If the interviewer is wavering between several equally qualified candidates, such a note could tip the scales in your favor.

About Coherence

6. In paragraph 1, what three transitional words or phrases are used to begin sentences as the author describes the process of interviewing?

    _____First of all_____   _____Then_____   _____Finally_____

7. The main method of organization of paragraph 1 is

    a. time order.

    b. emphatic order.

8. In paragraph 5, find the "change of direction" signal that begins a sentence in the first list item. Write the opening words of that sentence here.

    On the other hand
    _____

About the Introduction and Conclusion

9. Which statement best describes the introductory paragraph of "How to Do Well on a Job Interview"?

    a. It begins with a broad, general statement about job interviews and narrows it down to the thesis statement.

    b. It describes a typical job interview and its aftermath.

    c. It explains the importance of doing well on a job interview.

    d. It asks a series of questions that encourage readers to think about how they prepare for a job interview.

10. Which statement best describes the concluding paragraph of "How to Do Well on a Job Interview"?

    a.   It ends with a summary of the article.

    (b)   It ends with a prediction of what will happen if advice in the article is followed.

    c.   It ends with a series of questions that prompt the reader to think further about what's been written.

Writing a Process Essay

■ Writing Assignment 1

Choose a topic from the list below to use as the basis for a process essay.

How to shop for groceries in a minimum of time

How to shop for a car, rent an apartment, or buy a house

How to do household cleaning efficiently

How to gain or lose weight

How to get over a broken heart

How to plan an event (party, wedding, garage sale, etc.)

How to choose a pet

How to quit smoking (or another bad habit)

How to cook a favorite dish

Prewriting

a Freewrite for ten minutes on the topic you have tentatively chosen. Don't worry about spelling, grammar, organization, or anything other than getting your thoughts down on the page. If ideas are still flowing at the end of ten minutes, keep on writing. This freewriting will give you a base of raw material that you can draw on in the next phase of your work. Judging from your freewriting, do you think you have enough material available to you to support a process essay? If so, keep following the steps below. If not, choose another topic and freewrite about *it* for ten minutes.

b Develop a single clear sentence that will serve as your thesis. Your thesis can either (1) say it is important that your readers know about this process ("Knowing how to choose a pet wisely can ensure that the two of you have a happy relationship") or (2) state your opinion of this process ("Quitting smoking is the most important single thing you can do for your health").

c   Make a list of the steps you are describing. Here, for example, is the list prepared by the author of "Successful Exercise."

Wear comfortable, loose clothing

Clear an area for exercise

Lock the door and turn off the phone

Tie hair back

Move smoothly and gracefully

Start slowly

Hot shower afterward

Make time—get up early, give up a TV show

Get out weights or other equipment

Turn on music

Cool down

---

d   Number your items in time order. Strike out items that do not fit in the list; add others as they occur to you. Thus:

---

2   Wear comfortable, loose clothing

4   Clear an area for exercise

6   Lock the door and turn off the phone

3   Tie hair back

8   Move smoothly and gracefully

7   Start slowly

10   Hot shower afterward

1   Make time—get up early, give up a TV show

5   Get out weights or other equipment

~~Turn on music~~

9   Cool down

---

e   After making the list, decide how the items can be grouped into a minimum of three steps. For example, with "Successful Exercise," you might divide the process into (1) setting a regular time, (2) preparing for exercise, and (3) the exercise itself. With a topic like "How to Quit Smoking," you might divide the process into (1) keeping a journal of your smoking, (2) mental and physical preparation, and (3) getting through the first days.

f Use your list as a guide to write the first rough draft of your paper. Do not expect to finish your paper in one draft. You should be ready to write a series of drafts as you work toward the goals of unity, support, and coherence.

Rewriting

After you have completed the first draft of the paper, set it aside for a while if you can. Then read the paper out loud to a friend or classmate whose judgment you respect. Keep these points in mind as you hear your own words, and ask your friend to respond to them as well.

- It's essential for a process paper to describe a series of activities in a way that is easy to follow. Does this paper describe the steps in a clear, logical way? Have I used transitions such as *first*, *next*, *also*, *then*, *after*, *now*, *during*, and *finally* to make the paper move smoothly and clearly from one step to another?

- Does the paper describe the necessary steps so that a reader could perform the task described, or is essential information missing?

- Do I have a concluding paragraph that provides a summary or final thought or both?

- Is the paper free of sentence-skills mistakes?

As you revise your essay through one or more additional drafts, continue to refer to this list until you can answer "yes" to each question. Then be sure to proof-read the next-to-final draft of the paper for the sentence skills listed on the inside front cover.

■ Writing Assignment 2

Everyone is an expert at something. Write a process essay on some skill that you can perform very well. Write from the point of view that "This is how _____ *should* be done." Remember that your skill need not be unusual. It can be anything from "making a perfect pie crust" to "hooking up a car stereo" to "dealing with unpleasant customers" to "programming a VCR to record."

Prewriting

a If possible, perform the task and, as you go along, take notes on what you're doing. If that's not possible (as in "dealing with unpleasant customers"), think through a particular time you had to deal with such a task and make notes about just what you did.

b Look over your notes and make a list of the steps you followed.

c Considering your list, decide how you can divide the items listed into at least three steps. For instance, look at the follow list of items for the process of "Cooking a Pot Roast." Then fill in the blanks in the scratch outline that follows:

---

1 Marinate the roast for thirty minutes with Adolph's Marinade
2 Sprinkle the roast with seasoned flour
3 Heat oil in a heavy pot
4 Brown roast on all sides in the hot oil
5 Cover the roast with one-third water, one-third beef broth, and one-third red wine
6 Bring roast and liquid to boil
7 Cover pot
8 Turn down heat and simmer for an hour
9 Taste broth and add seasonings as desired—salt, pepper, Worcestershire sauce
10 Peel potatoes and carrots and cut into chunks
11 Cut onions into chunks
12 Add vegetables to pot for the last half-hour of cooking
13 Cook until meat flakes easily when you stick a fork in it
14 Remove meat and vegetables from broth
15 Dissolve two tablespoons of flour in half-cup cold water
16 Stir flour mixture into boiling broth to thicken into gravy
17 Serve gravy with the meat and vegetables

Step 1: Preparing and cooking the meat
         Items __1__ through __9__
Step 2: Preparing and cooking the vegetables
         Items __10__ through __12__
Step 3: Preparing the gravy and serving
         Items __13__ through __17__

d Prepare such a scratch outline of your main points. Use it as your guide as you write the rough draft of your paper.

Rewriting

As you read through your first draft and subsequent drafts, ask yourself these questions:

- Have I introduced my essay with either a statement of the importance of the process or my opinion of the process?
- Have I provided a clear, step-by-step description of the process?
- Have I divided the items in the process into at least three logical steps (main points of the essay)?
- Have I used transition words such as *first*, *next*, *then*, *during*, and *finally* to help readers follow my train of thought?

As you revise your essay through one or more additional drafts, continue to refer to this list until you can answer "yes" to each question. Then be sure to check the next-to-final draft of the paper for the sentence skills listed on the inside front cover.

■ Writing Assignment 3

In this process essay, you will write with a specific purpose and for a specific audience. Imagine that you have a younger brother or sister who has asked you to be a guest editor of his or her high school paper. Prepare an informal essay in which you summarize, in your own words, the steps involved in successfully managing your time in college or in preparing for and taking an essay exam.

■ Writing Assignment 4

Any one of the topics below can be written as a process paper. Follow the steps suggested for writing assignment 1. Note that some of these topics invite a humorous point of view.

How to break a bad habit

How to live with a two-year-old, a teenager, or a parent

How to make someone like you

How to make excuses

How to fall out of love

How to improve your reading skills

How to care for an aging relative

How to improve a school or a place of work

12 Cause and Effect

Why did Gail decide to move out of her parents' house? What made you quit a well-paying job? Why are horror movies so popular? Why has Ben acted so depressed lately? Why did our team fail to make the league play-offs?

Every day we ask questions like these and look for answers. We realize that many actions do not occur without causes, and we realize also that a given action can have a series of effects—for good or bad. By examining the causes or effects of an action, we seek to understand and explain things that happen in our lives.

You will be asked in this section to do some detective work by examining the cause of something or the effects of something. First read the student essays and the professional essay that follow and work through the questions that accompany the essays. All three essays support their thesis statements by explaining a series of causes or a series of effects.

Student Essays to Consider

The Joys of an Old Car

Some of my friends can't believe that my car still runs. Others laugh when they see it parked outside the house and ask if it's an antique. But they aren't being fair to my fourteen-year-old Toyota Corolla. In fact, my "antique" has opened my eyes to the rewards of owning an old car. 1

One obvious reward of owning my old Toyota is economy. Fourteen years ago, when my husband and I were newly married and nearly broke, we bought the car—a shiny red year-old leftover—for a mere $4,200. Today it would cost four times as much. We save money on insurance, since it's no longer worthwhile for us to have collision coverage. Old age has even been kind to the Toyota's engine, which required only three major repairs in the last several years. And it still delivers twenty-eight miles per gallon in the city and forty-one on the highway—not bad for a senior citizen. 2

I've heard that when a Toyota passes the twenty-thousand-mile mark with no problems, it will probably go on forever. I wouldn't disagree. Our Toyota breezed past that mark many years ago. Since then, I've been able to count on it to sputter to life and make its way down the driveway on the coldest, snowiest mornings. When my boss got stuck with his brand-new BMW in the worst snowstorm of the year, I sauntered into work on time. The single time my Toyota didn't start, unfortunately, was the day I had a final exam. The Toyota may have the body of an old car, but beneath its elderly hood hums the engine of a teenager. 3

Last of all, having the same car for many years offers the advantage of   4
familiarity. When I open the door and slide into the driver's seat, the soft
vinyl surrounds me like a well-worn glove. I know to the millimeter exactly
how much room I have when I turn a corner or back into a curbside parking
space. When my gas gauge points to "empty," I know that 1.3 gallons are
still in reserve, and I can plan accordingly. The front wheels invariably begin
to shake when I go more than fifty-five miles an hour, reminding me that
I am exceeding the speed limit. With the Toyota, the only surprises I face
come from other drivers.

I prize my fourteen-year-old Toyota's economy and dependability, and   5
most of all, its familiarity. It is faded, predictable, and comfortable, like a
well-worn pair of jeans. And, like a well-worn pair of jeans, it will be
difficult to throw away.

Stresses of Being a Celebrity

A woman signing herself "Wants the Truth in Westport" wrote to Ann   1
Landers with a question she just had to have answered. "Please find out
for sure," she begged the columnist, "whether or not Oprah Winfrey has
had a face-lift." Fortunately for Ms. Winfrey's privacy, Ann Landers refused
to answer the question. But the incident was disturbing. How awful it would
be to be a celebrity, always in the public eye. Celebrities lead very stressful
lives, for no matter how glamorous or powerful they are, they have too little
privacy, too much pressure, and no safety.

For one thing, celebrities don't have the privacy an ordinary person has.   2
The most personal details of their lives are splashed all over the front pages
of the National Enquirer and the Globe so that bored supermarket shoppers
can read about "Leonardo DiCaprio's Awful Secret" or "The Heartbreak
Behind Winona Ryder's Smile." Even a celebrity's family is hauled into the
spotlight. A teenage son's arrest for pot possession or a wife's drinking
problem becomes the subject of glaring headlines. Photographers hound
celebrities at their homes, in restaurants, and on the street, hoping to get
a picture of Halle Berry in curlers or Jim Carrey guzzling a beer. When
celebrities try to do the things that normal people do, like eat out or attend
a football game, they run the risk of being interrupted by thoughtless
autograph hounds or mobbed by aggressive fans.

In addition to the loss of privacy, celebrities must cope with the constant   3
pressure of having to look great and act right. Their physical appearance is
always under observation. Famous women, especially, suffer from the
spotlight, drawing remarks like "She really looks old" or "Boy, has she put
on weight." Unflattering pictures of celebrities are photographers' prizes
to be sold to the highest bidder; this increases the pressure on celebrities
to look good at all times. Famous people are also under pressure to act

calm and collected under any circumstances. Because they are constantly observed, they have no freedom to blow off steam or to do something just a little crazy.

Most important, celebrities must deal with the stress of being in constant danger. The friendly grabs, hugs, and kisses of enthusiastic fans can quickly turn into uncontrolled assaults on a celebrity's hair, clothes, and car. Most people agree that photographers bear some responsibility for the death of one of the leading celebrities of the 1990s—Princess Diana. Whether or not their pursuit caused the crash that took her life, it's clear she was chased as aggressively as any escaped convict by bloodhounds. And celebrity can lead to even more deliberately lethal attacks. The attempt to kill Ronald Reagan and the murder of John Lennon came about because two unbalanced people became obsessed with these world-famous figures. Famous people must live with the fact that they are always fair game—and never out of season.

Some people dream of starring roles, their name in lights, and their picture on the cover of <u>People</u> magazine. But the cost is far too high. A famous person gives up private life, feels pressured to look and act certain ways all the time, and is never completely safe. An ordinary, calm life is far safer and saner than a life of fame.

■ Questions

About Unity

1. Which supporting paragraph in "The Joys of an Old Car" lacks a topic sentence?

   a. 2

   b. 3

   c. 4

2. Which sentence in paragraph 3 of "The Joys of an Old Car" should be omitted in the interest of paragraph unity? *(Write the opening words.)*
   The single time . . .

3. Rewrite the thesis statement of "The Joys of an Old Car" to include a plan of development. Wording of answers may vary.
   In fact, my "antique" has opened my eyes to the advantages of owning an

   old car: economy, reliability, and familiarity.

About Support

4. In paragraph 4 of "Stresses of Being a Celebrity," the author supports the idea that "celebrities must deal with the stress of being in constant danger" with (*circle the letters of the two answers that apply*)

    a. statistics.

    (b) an explanation.

    c. a quotation by an expert.

    (d) examples.

5. After which sentence in paragraph 3 of "Stresses of Being a Celebrity" are more specific details needed? (*Write the opening words.*)

    Because they are constantly observed . . .

6. In "The Joys of an Old Car," how many examples are given to support the topic sentence "One obvious reward is economy"?

    a. two

    b. three

    (c) four

    d. five

About Coherence

7. Which topic sentence in "Stresses of Being a Celebrity" functions as a linking sentence between paragraphs? (*Write the opening words.*)

    In addition to the loss of privacy . . .

8. Paragraph 3 of "Stresses of Being a Celebrity" includes two main transition words or phrases. List those words or phrases.

    In addition   also

9. What are the two transition words or phrases in "The Joys of an Old Car" that signal two major points of support for the thesis?

    One   Last of all

About the Introduction and Conclusion

10. Which method is used in the conclusion of "The Joys of an Old Car"?

    (a) Summary and final thought

    b. Thought-provoking question

    c. Recommendation

Developing a Cause-Effect Essay

Development Through Prewriting

The best essays are often those written about a topic that the author genuinely cares about. When Janine, the author of "The Joys of an Old Car," was assigned a cause-effect essay, she welcomed the assignment. She explains: "My husband and I believe in enjoying what we have and living simply, rather than 'keeping up with the Joneses.' Our beat-up old car is an example of that way of life. People often say to me, 'Surely you could buy a nicer car!' I enjoy explaining to them why we keep our old 'clunker.' So when I heard 'cause-effect essay,' I immediately thought of the car as a topic. Writing this essay was just an extension of a conversation I've had many times."

Although Janine had often praised the virtues of her old car to friends, she wasn't sure how to divide what she had to say into three main points. In order to get started, she made a list of all the good things about her car. Here is what she wrote:

Starts reliably

Has needed few major repairs

Reminder of Bill's and my first days of marriage

Gets good gas mileage

Don't need to worry about scratches and scrapes

I know exactly how much room I need to turn and park

Saves money on insurance

I'm very comfortable in it

No car payments

Cold weather doesn't seem to bother it

Don't worry about its being stolen

Uses regular gas

Can haul anything in it—dog, plants—and not worry about dirt

Know all its little tics and shimmies and don't worry about them

---

When Janine reviewed her list, she saw that the items fell into three major categories. There was (1) the car's economy, (2) its familiarity, and (3) its dependability. She went back and noted which category each of the items best fit. Then she crossed out those items that didn't seem to belong in any of the categories.

3 Starts reliably

1 Has needed few major repairs

~~Reminder of Bill's and my first days of marriage~~

1 Gets good gas mileage

~~Don't need to worry about scratches and scrapes~~

2 I know exactly how much room I need to turn and park

1 Saves money on insurance

2 I'm very comfortable in it

1 No car payments

3 Cold weather doesn't seem to bother it

~~Don't worry about its being stolen~~

1 Uses regular gas

~~Can haul anything in it—dog, plants—and not worry about dirt~~

2 Know all its little tics and shimmies and don't worry about them

Now Janine had three main points and several items to support each point. She produced this as a first draft.

First Draft

The Joys of an Old Car

When people see my beat-up old car, they sometimes laugh at it. But I tell them that owning a fourteen-year-old Toyota has its good points.

One obvious reward is economy. My husband and I bought the car when we were newly married. We paid $4,200 for it. That seemed like a lot of money then, but today we'd spend four times that much for a similar car. We also save money on insurance, since it's no longer worthwhile for us to have collision coverage. In the fourteen years we've had it, the Toyota has needed only a few major repairs. It even gets good gas mileage.

I like the familiar feel of the car. I'm so used to it that driving anything else feels very strange. When I visited my sister recently I drove her new Plymouth to the grocery store. Everything was so unfamiliar! I couldn't even figure out how to turn on the radio. I was relieved to get back to my own car.

Finally, my car is very dependable. No matter how cold and snowy it is, I know the Toyota will start quickly and get me where I need to go. Unfortunately, one day it didn't start, and naturally that day I had a final exam. But otherwise it just keeps on going and going.

My Toyota reminds me of a favorite piece of clothing that you wear forever and can't bear to throw away.

Development Through Revision

Janine traded first-draft copies with a classmate, Sharon, and each critiqued the other's work before it was revised. Here is Janine's first draft again, with Sharon's comments in the margins.

Reader's Comments

How? Is the insurance less expensive just because the car is old?

Here would be a good place for a specific detail—how good is the mileage?

This topic sentence doesn't tie in with the others—shouldn't it say "Second," or "Another reason I like the car..."

This is too much about your sister's car and not enough about yours.

This is a good comparison. But draw it out more—how is the car like comfortable old clothes?

The Joys of an Old Car

When people see my beat-up old car, they sometimes laugh at it. But I tell them that owning a fourteen-year-old Toyota has its good points.

One obvious reward is economy. My husband and I bought the car when we were newly married. We paid $4,200 for it. That seemed like a lot of money then, but today we'd spend four times that much for a similar car. We also save money on insurance. In the fourteen years we've had it, the Toyota has needed only a few major repairs. It even gets good gas mileage.

I like the familiar feel of the car. I'm so used to it that driving anything else feels very strange. When I visited my sister recently I drove her new Plymouth to the grocery store. Everything was so unfamiliar! I couldn't even figure out how to turn on the radio. I was relieved to get back to my own car.

Finally, my car is very dependable. No matter how cold and snowy it is, I know the Toyota will start quickly and get me where I need to go. Unfortunately, one day it didn't start, and naturally that day I had a final exam. But otherwise it just keeps on going and going.

My Toyota reminds me of a favorite piece of clothing that you wear forever and can't bear to throw away.

Making use of Sharon's comments, Janine wrote the final version of "The Joys of an Old Car" that appears on page 249.

A Professional Essay to Consider

Read the following professional essay. Then answer the questions and read the comments that follow.

Why Do Most Mothers Cradle Their Babies in the Left Arm?

by Desmond Morris

One of the strangest features of motherhood is that the vast majority of mothers prefer to cradle their babies in the left arm. Why should this be? The obvious explanation is that the majority of mothers are right-handed and they wish to keep their right hand free. Unfortunately, this explanation cannot apply, because left-handed mothers also favor their left arm for holding their babies. The precise figures are 83 percent for right-handed mothers and 78 percent for left-handed mothers. 1

The most likely explanation is that the mother's heart is on the left side and, by holding the baby in her left arm, she is unconsciously bringing her infant closer to the sound of the heartbeat. This is the sound which the baby heard when it was inside the mother's womb and which is therefore associated with peace, comfort, and security. 2

Tests were carried out in nurseries where some babies were played the recorded sound of a human heartbeat, and, sure enough, those babies were lulled off to sleep twice as quickly as the others. We also know that the sound of the mother's heart is quite audible inside the womb and that the unborn baby has well-developed hearing. The constant dull thud of the heart, beating so close to the fetus, second by second, must become the single most intrusive message from the outside world that a fetus can experience. So it is little wonder that traces of this imprinting appear later on, in babyhood. 3

It is interesting that fathers show less of this left-side bias than mothers, suggesting that the human female is better programmed than her partner for carrying a baby. Alternatively, she may be more sensitive to the mood of her baby and may unconsciously adjust her holding behavior to make her baby feel more secure. 4

Some new observations on our closest animal relatives, the chimpanzees and gorillas, have revealed that they too show a strong bias for holding their babies on the left side. The precise figures were 84 percent for chimpanzees and 82 percent for gorillas, remarkably close to the human percentages. Significantly, these apes do not show the strong right-handedness of the human species when using implements, which confirms the fact that left-holding has nothing to do with having a dominant right hand. 5

Recently a possible additional value in cradling babies on the left side   6
has been suggested. It has been pointed out that, because the two sides of
the brain are concerned with different aspects of behavior, it is possible that
the mother, in cradling the baby to her left, is showing the baby her "best
side." It is claimed that emotions are expressed more strongly on the left side
of the human face and that she therefore gives the baby a better chance to
read her emotional mood changes as it gazes up at her. Furthermore, the
mother's left eye and ear are more tuned in to emotional changes in her baby
than her right eye and ear would be. So in addition to the baby's seeing the
more expressive part of its mother, there is the further advantage that the
mother herself is more sensitive to the left-held baby. This may sound far-
fetched, but just possibly, it could provide a slight extra benefit for those
mothers displaying the strange one-sided bias when cradling their infants.

How does the bias occur? Do the mothers have an instinctive preference   7
for it, or do they learn it by trial and error, unconsciously adjusting the
position of their babies until the babies are more calm? The surprising answer
is that it seems to be the baby and not the mother who controls the bias.
Observations of newborn infants when they were only a few hours old
revealed that they come into the world with a preprogrammed tendency to
turn their head to the right. If the newborn's head is gently held in a dead
central position and then released, it naturally swings to the right far more
often than to the left. This happens in nearly 70 percent of babies. It means
that when the mother goes to feed her infant, she finds its head more likely
to turn that way, and this may well influence her decision concerning which
side is best for it. If it prefers turning its head to the right, it will, of course,
feel more at ease when it is held in the crook of her left arm. This will bring
mother and baby more "face to face." This may be only part of the explanation, because the holding bias is 80 percent and not 70 percent, but it adds
a further intriguing chapter to the story.

■ Questions

About Unity

1. What is the thesis of "Why Do Most Mothers Cradle Their Babies in the Left
    Arm?" If it is stated directly, locate the relevant sentence. If it is implied, state
    the thesis in your own words.

    Implied in sentence 1 and 2. It could be stated: There are various possible

    reasons why mothers tend to hold a baby in the left arm.

2. Which statement would best serve as a topic sentence for paragraph 3?

    a. An unborn baby hears well and must be constantly aware of its mother's heartbeat.

    b. Babies who listened to recordings of a human heartbeat went to sleep more quickly than those who did not.

    c. Experiences that a baby has while in the womb can have surprising effects later on.

    (d) Two pieces of evidence support the idea that babies are soothed by the sound of their mothers' heartbeat.

3. Which statement best expresses the main idea of paragraph 6?

    a. The left side of the human face is thought to express emotions more strongly than the right.

    (b) Holding her baby in her left arm may improve a mother's emotional communication with the child.

    c. A mother's left eye and ear are more sensitive to the emotional communication of her baby.

    d. A baby may be more able to "read" its mother's emotions than was previously believed.

About Support

4. Paragraph 3 supports the point made in paragraph

    (a) 2.

    b. 4.

    c. 5.

5. What evidence does the author provide that mothers may be instinctively better equipped than fathers for carrying babies?
   Fathers show less left-side bias than mothers.

6. The essay is about one main effect and several possible causes. What is the one main effect? What are two of the possible causes discussed?

    The effect: Left-side bias.

    Two possible causes: Answers may vary. Any two of the following: Mother's heart is on left side; "left brain" is more "emotional"; baby usually turns head to right.

About Coherence

7. Which cause-effect word is used in the last sentence of paragraph 2?

   therefore

8. Find the addition signal that begins a sentence in paragraph 6. Write the opening words of that sentence here.

   Recently a possible additional value . . .

About the Introduction and Conclusion

9. Which statement best describes the introductory paragraph of "Why Do Most Mothers Cradle Their Babies in the Left Arm?"

   a. It begins with a broad, general statement that narrows to a thesis.

   b. It explains the importance of understanding why mothers tend to hold their babies with the left arm.

   c. It tells a brief story about mothers and their tendency to hold their babies on their left side.

   d. It asks a question, then surprises the reader by indicating that the obvious answer is incorrect.

10. Which statement best describes the concluding paragraph of "Why Do Most Mothers Cradle Their Babies in the Left Arm?"

   a. It ends with a summary of the research on mothers and babies.

   b. It ends with a final piece of evidence and the suggestion that there is still more to learn.

   c. It ends with a series of questions about why mothers and babies interact with one another as they do.

Writing a Cause-Effect Essay

■ Writing Assignment 1

In scratch-outline form, on a separate piece of paper, provide brief causes or effects for at least *four* of the ten statements below. The first item is done for you as an example. Make sure that you have three *separate* and *distinct* items for each statement—don't provide two rewordings that say essentially the same thing. Also, indicate whether the items you have listed are causes or effects.

When you have finished your four scratch outlines, decide which of them would provide the best basis for a cause-effect essay that you will write.

1. Many youngsters are terrified of school.

   Causes:

   a. *Afraid of not being liked by other students*

   b. *Afraid of failing tests*

   c. *Intimidated by teachers*

   Answers will vary.

2. Having more mothers in the workforce has changed the way many kids grow up.

3. Society would benefit if nonviolent criminals were punished in ways other than jail time.

4. Americans tend to get married later in life than they used to.

5. Among winners of prestigious academic awards, a high percentage are children of immigrant families recently arrived in this country.

6. It is easy to fall into an unhealthy diet in our society.

7. Growing up in my family has influenced my life in significant ways.

8. A bad (or good) teacher can have long-lasting impact on a student.

9. The average workweek should be no more than thirty hours.

10. My relationship with (*name a relative or friend*) _____ has changed over time.

Prewriting

a Look at the outline you produced in the previous step. You will now use it as the basis for a cause-and-effect essay. The statement will serve as your thesis, and the three causes or effects will function as your main points. Make sure that each of your main points is a *separate* and *distinct* point, not a restatement of one of the other points.

b Decide whether you will support each of your main points with several examples or with one extended example. You may want to freewrite about each of these examples for a few minutes, or you may want to make up a list of as many details as you think of that would go with each of the examples.

c Write a first draft of an introduction that attracts the reader's interest, states your thesis, and presents a plan of development.

Rewriting

After you have completed the first draft of the paper, set it aside for a while (if possible). When you reread what you have written, prepare for rewriting by asking yourself the following questions.

- Does the paper have a clearly stated thesis?
- Have I backed up each main point with one extended example or several shorter examples? Do I have enough detailed support?
- Is there any irrelevant material that should be eliminated or rewritten?
- Have I used transition words to help readers follow my train of thought?
- Have I provided a concluding paragraph to wrap up the essay?

As you revise your essay through one or more additional drafts, continue to refer to this list until you can answer "yes" to each question. Then be sure to check the next-to-final draft of the paper for the sentence skills listed on the inside front cover.

■ Writing Assignment 2

If friendly aliens from a highly developed civilization decided to visit our planet, they would encounter a contradictory race of beings—us. We humans would have reasons to feel both proud and ashamed of the kind of society the aliens would encounter. Write an essay explaining whether you would be proud or ashamed of the state of the human race today. Give reasons for your feelings.

Prewriting

a You will probably have an instant, gut reaction to the question, "Am I more proud of or ashamed of the human race?" Go with that reaction; you will find it easier to come up with supporting points for the thesis that occurred to you immediately.

b Generate supporting details for your thesis by making a list. Title it "Reasons I am proud of the human race" or "Reasons I am ashamed of the human race." Then list as many items as you can think of. Don't worry about whether the reasons are important or silly, significant or trivial. Just write down as many as possible.

c Review your list and ask yourself if some of the items could be grouped into one category. For instance, a list of reasons to be proud of humanity might include items such as, "We've come up with cures for major diseases," "We've developed the computer," "We've invented wonderful communication devices like the telephone, radio, movies, and TV." All these could be grouped into a category called "Important inventions." That category, in turn, could serve as a main supporting point in your essay.

d As described in step *c*, decide on three supporting points. Write a scratch outline that includes those points and the examples (one extended example or several shorter ones). The point described in step *c* would be outlined like this:

Point: The human race has come up with wonderful inventions that benefit
all society.

1. Cures for diseases

2. Computers

3. Communication devices, including radio and TV

e Using your scratch outline, write a first draft of the paper. Include an introduction that states your thesis and plan of development, and a conclusion that
reminds readers of your thesis and leaves them with a final point to consider.

Rewriting

As you work through subsequent drafts, ask yourself these questions:

- Have I introduced my essay with a clearly stated thesis and plan of
development?
- Is each of my main points supported by solid, specific details?
- Have I used transition words such as *first, another, in addition,* and *also*?
- Have I checked my writing for the sentence skills listed on the inside front
cover?

■ Writing Assignment 3

In this cause-and-effect essay, you will write with a specific purpose and for a specific audience. Imagine that several friends of yours say they are having a hard
time learning anything in a class taught by Professor X. You volunteer to attend
the class and see for yourself. You also get information from your friends about
the course requirements.

Afterward, you write a letter to Professor X, politely calling attention to what
you see as causes of the learning problems that students are having in the class.
To organize your essay, you might develop each of these causes in a separate supporting paragraph. In the second part of each supporting paragraph, you might
suggest changes that Professor X could make to deal with each problem.

■ Writing Assignment 4

Write a cause-effect essay in which you advance an idea about a poem, story, play,
literary essay, or novel. The work you choose may be assigned by your instructor or may require your instructor's approval. To develop your idea, use a series
of two or more reasons and specific supporting evidence for each reason. A student model follows.

Paul's Suicide

Paul, the main character in Willa Cather's short story "Paul's Case," is a young man on a collision course with death. As Cather reveals Paul's story, we learn about elements of Paul's personality that inevitably come together and cause his suicide. Paul takes his own life as a result of his inability to conform to his society, his passive nature, and his emotional isolation.   1

First of all, Paul cannot conform to the standards of his own society. At school, Paul advertises his desire to be part of another, more glamorous world by wearing fancy clothes that set him apart from the other students. At home on Cordelia Street, Paul despises everything about his middle-class neighborhood. He hates the houses "permeated by kitchen odors," the "ugliness and commonness of his own home," and the respectable neighbors sitting on their front stoops every Sunday, "their stomachs comfortably protruding." Paul's father hopes that Paul will settle down and become like the young man next door, a nearsighted clerk who works for a corporate steel magnate. Paul, however, is repelled by the young man and all he represents. It seems inevitable, then, that Paul will not be able to cope with the office job his father obtains for him at the firm of Denny & Carson; and this inability to conform will, in turn, lead to Paul's theft of $1,000.   2

Paul's suicide is also due, in part, to his passive nature. Throughout his life, Paul has been an observer and an onlooker. Paul's only escape from the prison of his daily life comes from his job as an usher at Pittsburgh's Carnegie Hall; he lives for the moments when he can watch the actors, singers, and musicians. However, Paul has no desire to <u>be</u> an actor or musician. As Cather says, "What he wanted was to see, to be in the atmosphere, float on the wave of it, to be carried out . . . away from everything." Although Paul steals the money and flees to New York, these uncharacteristic actions underscore the desperation he feels. Once at the Waldorf in New York, Paul is again content to observe the glamorous world he has craved for so long: "He had no especial desire to meet or to know any of these people; all he demanded was the right to look on and conjecture, to watch the pageant." During his brief stay in the city, Paul enjoys simply sitting in his luxurious rooms, glimpsing the show of city life through a magical curtain of snow. At the end, when the forces of ordinary life begin to close in again, Paul kills himself. But it is typical that he does not use the gun he has bought. Rather, more in keeping with his passive nature, Paul lets himself fall under the wheels of a train.   3

Finally, Paul ends his life because he is emotionally isolated. Throughout the story, not one person makes any real contact with Paul. His teachers do not understand him and merely resent the attitude of false bravado that he uses as a defense. Paul's mother is dead; he cannot even remember her. Paul is completely alienated from his father, who obviously cares for him but who cannot feel close to this withdrawn, unhappy son. To Paul, his father is only the man waiting at the top of the stairs, "his hairy legs sticking out of his   4 nightshirt," who will greet him with "inquiries and reproaches." When Paul meets a college boy in New York, they share a night on the town. But the "champagne friendship" ends with a "singularly cool" parting. Paul is not the kind of person who can let himself go or confide in one of his peers. For the most part, Paul's isolation is self-imposed. He has drifted so far into his fantasy life that people in the "real" world are treated like invaders. As he allows no one to enter his dream, there is no one Paul can turn to for understanding.

The combination of these personality factors—inability to conform,   5
passivity, and emotional isolation—makes Paul's tragic suicide inevitable. Before he jumps in front of the train, Paul scoops a hole in the snow and buries the carnation that he has been wearing in his buttonhole. Like a hothouse flower in the winter, Paul has a fragile nature that cannot survive in its hostile environment.

13 Comparison and Contrast

Comparison and contrast are two thought processes we go through constantly in everyday life. When we *compare* two things, we show how they are similar; when we *contrast* two things, we show how they are different. We may compare or contrast two brand-name products (for example, Pepsi and Coca-Cola), two television shows, two cars, two teachers, two jobs, two friends, or two possible solutions to a problem we are facing. The purpose of comparing or contrasting is to understand each of the two things more clearly and, at times, to make judgments about them.

You will be asked in this chapter to write a paper of comparison or contrast. To prepare for this assignment, first read about the two methods of development you can use in writing your paper. Then read the student essays and the professional essay that follow and work through the questions that accompany the essays.

Methods of Development

A comparison or contrast essay calls for one of two types of development. Details can be presented *one side at a time* or *point by point*. Each format is illustrated below.

One Side at a Time

Look at the following supporting paragraph from "A Vote for McDonald's," one of the model essays that will follow.

> For one thing, going to the Chalet is more difficult than going to McDonald's. The Chalet has a jacket-and-tie rule, which means I have to dig a sport coat and tie out of the back of my closet, make sure they're semiclean, and try to steam out the wrinkles somehow. The Chalet also requires reservations. Since it is downtown, I have to leave an hour early to give myself time to find a parking space within six blocks of the restaurant. The Chalet cancels reservations if a party is more than ten minutes late. Going to McDonald's, on the other hand, is easy. I can feel comfortable wearing my jeans or warm-up suit. I don't have to do any advance planning. I can leave my house whenever I'm ready and pull into a doorside parking space within fifteen minutes.

The first half of this paragraph fully explains one side of the contrast (the difficulty of going to the Chalet). The second half of the paragraph deals entirely with the other side (the ease of going to McDonald's). When you use this method, be sure to follow the same order of points of contrast (or comparison) for each side. An outline of the paragraph shows how the points for each side are developed in a consistent sequence.

Outline   **One Side at a Time**

Thesis: Going to the Chalet is more difficult than going to McDonald's.
1. Chalet
    a. Dress code
    b. Advance reservations
    c. Leave an hour early
    d. Find parking space
2. McDonald's
    a. Casual dress
    b. No reservations
    c. Leave only fifteen minutes ahead of time
    d. Plenty of free parking

Point by Point

Now look at the supporting paragraph below, which is taken from another essay you will read, "Studying: Then and Now":

Ordinary studying during the term is another area where I've made changes. In high school, I let reading assignments go. I told myself that I'd have no trouble catching up on two hundred pages during a fifteen-minute ride to school. College courses have taught me to keep pace with the work. Otherwise, I feel as though I'm sinking into a quicksand of unread material. When I finally read the high school assignment, my eyes would run over the words but my brain would be plotting how to get the car for Saturday night. Now, I use several techniques that force me to really concentrate on my reading.

The paragraph contrasts two styles of studying point by point. The outline below illustrates the point-by point-method.

Outline   **Point by Point**

Thesis: Studying is something I do differently in college than in high
school.
1. Keeping up with reading assignments
    a. High school
    b. College
2. Concentration while reading
    a. High school
    b. College

When you begin writing a comparison or contrast paper, you should decide right
away which format you will use: one side at a time or point by point. Use that format as you create the outline for your paper. Remember that an outline is an essential step in planning and writing a clearly organized paper.

Student Essays to Consider

A Vote for McDonald's

For my birthday this month, my wife has offered to treat me to dinner
at the restaurant of my choice. I think she expects me to ask for a meal at
the Chalet, the classiest, most expensive restaurant in town. However, I'm
going to eat my birthday dinner at McDonald's. When I compare the two
restaurants, the advantages of eating at McDonald's are clear.

For one thing, going to the Chalet is more difficult than going to
McDonald's. The Chalet has a jacket-and-tie rule, which means I have to
dig a sport coat and tie out of the back of my closet, make sure they're
semiclean, and try to steam out the wrinkles somehow. The Chalet also
requires reservations. Since it is downtown, I have to leave an hour early to
give myself time to find a parking space within six blocks of the restaurant.
The Chalet cancels reservations if a party is more than ten minutes late.
Going to McDonald's, on the other hand, is easy. I can feel comfortable
wearing my jeans or warm-up suit. I don't have to do any advance planning.
I can leave my house whenever I'm ready and pull into a doorside parking
space within fifteen minutes.

1

2

The Chalet is a dimly lit, formal place. While I'm struggling to see what's   3
on my plate, I worry that I'll knock one of the fragile glasses off the table.
The waiters at the Chalet can be uncomfortably formal, too. As I awkwardly
pronounce the French words on the menu, I get the feeling that I don't
quite live up to their standards. Even the other diners can make me feel
uncomfortable. And though the food at the Chalet is gourmet, I prefer
simpler meals. I don't like unfamiliar food swimming in a pasty white sauce.
Eating at the Chalet is, to me, less enjoyable than eating at McDonald's.
McDonald's is a pleasant place where I feel at ease. It is well lighted, and
the bright-colored decor is informal. The employees serve with a smile, and
the food is easy to pronounce and identify. I know what I'm going to get
when I order a certain type of sandwich.

The most important different between the Chalet and McDonald's,   4
though, is price. Dinner for two at the Chalet, even without appetizers or
desserts, would easily cost $50. And the $50 doesn't include the cost of
parking the car and tipping the waiter, which can come to an additional
$10. Once, I forgot to bring enough money. At McDonald's, a filling meal
for two will cost around $10. With the extra $50, my wife and I can eat at
McDonald's five more times, or go to the movies three times, or buy play-off
tickets to a football game.

So, for my birthday dinner, or any other time, I prefer to eat at   5
McDonald's. It is convenient, friendly, and cheap. And with the money my
wife saves by taking me to McDonald's, she can buy me what I really want
for my birthday—a new Sears power saw.

Studying: Then and Now

One June day, I staggered into a high school classroom to take my final   1
exam in United States History IV. I had made my usual desperate effort to
cram the night before, with the usual dismal results—I had gotten only to
page seventy-five of a four-hundred-page textbook. My study habits in high
school, obviously, were a mess. But in college, I've made an attempt to
reform my note-taking, studying, and test-taking skills.

As I took notes in high school classes, I often lost interest and began   2
doodling, drawing Martians or seeing what my signature would look like
if I married the cute guy in the second row. Now, however, I try not to let
my mind wander, and I pull my thoughts back into focus when they begin
to go fuzzy. In high school, my notes often looked like something written
in Arabic. In college, I've learned to use a semiprint writing style that makes
my notes understandable. When I would look over my high school notes,
I couldn't understand them. There would be a word like "Reconstruction,"
then a big blank, then the word "important." Weeks later, I had no idea
what Reconstruction was or why it was important. I've since learned to
write down connecting ideas, even if I have to take the time to do it after
class. Taking notes is one thing I've really learned to do better since high
school days.

Ordinary studying during the term is another area where I've made   3
changes. In high school, I let reading assignments go. I told myself that I'd
have no trouble catching up on two hundred pages during a fifteen-minute
ride to school. College courses have taught me to keep pace with the work.
Otherwise, I feel as though I'm sinking into a quicksand of unread material.
When I finally read the high school assignment, my eyes would run over the
words but my brain would be plotting how to get the car for Saturday night.
Now, I use several techniques that force me to really concentrate on my
reading.

In addition to learning how to cope with daily work, I've also learned to   4
handle study sessions for big tests. My all-night study sessions in high school
were experiments in self-torture. Around 2:00 A.M., my mind, like a soaked
sponge, simply stopped absorbing things. Now, I space out exam study
sessions over several days. That way, the night before can be devoted to an
overall review rather than raw memorizing. Most important, though, I've
changed my attitude toward tests. In high school, I thought tests were
mysterious things with completely unpredictable questions. Now, I ask
instructors about the kinds of questions that will be on the exam, and I try
to "psych out" which areas or facts instructors are likely to ask about. These
practices really work, and for me they've taken much of the fear and
mystery out of tests.

Since I've reformed, note-taking and studying are not as tough as they   5
once were. And I am beginning to reap the benefits. As time goes on, my
college test sheets are going to look much different from the red-marked
tests of my high school days.

■ Questions

About Unity

1. Which supporting paragraph in "A Vote for McDonald's" has its topic sentence within the paragraph, rather than at the beginning? Write the paragraph number and the opening words of the topic sentence.

   Paragraph 3: Eating at the Chalet is . . .

2. Which sentence in paragraph 4 of "A Vote for McDonald's" should be omitted in the interest of paragraph unity? (*Write the opening words.*)

   Once, I forgot . . .

3. In which supporting paragraphs in "Studying: Then and Now" is the topic sentence at the end rather than at the beginning, where it generally belongs in student essays? 2 and 3

About Support

4. In paragraph 3 of "A Vote for McDonald's," what three points does the writer make to support his statement that, for him, dining at McDonald's is a more pleasant experience than dining at the Chalet? *Wording of answers may vary.*

   (1) Chalet is dimly lit; McDonald's is bright.

   (2) Waiters at the Chalet are formal; employees at McDonald's are friendly.

   (3) Food is unfamiliar at the Chalet; food is familiar at McDonald's.

5. In paragraph 3 of "A Vote for McDonald's," what sentence should be followed up by supporting details? *(Write the opening words of that sentence.)*

   Even the other diners . . .

6. Which sentence in paragraph 3 of "Studying: Then and Now" needs to be followed by more supporting details? *(Write the opening words.)*

   Now, I use several techniques . . .

About Coherence

7. In paragraph 2 of "A Vote for McDonald's," what "change of direction" signal does the author use to indicate that he has finished discussing the Chalet and is now going to discuss McDonald's? on the other hand

8. Write the words in paragraph 4 of "A Vote for McDonald's" that indicate the writer has used emphatic order in organizing his supporting points.

   most important

About the Introduction and Conclusion

9. Which sentence best describes the opening paragraph of "Studying: Then and Now"?

   a. It begins with a broad statement that narrows down to the thesis.

   b. It explains the importance of the topic to the reader.

   c. It uses an incident or brief story.

   d. It asks a question.

10. The conclusion of "Studying: Then and Now" falls into which category?

    a. Some observations and a prediction

    b. Summary and final thought

    c. Question or series of questions

Developing a Comparison-Contrast Essay

Development Through Prewriting

A comparison or contrast essay emphasizes how two things are alike or how they differ. When Jesse, one of the student writers featured above, had to choose two things to compare or contrast, the Chalet and McDonald's quickly came to mind: "My wife and I had been talking that morning about where I wanted to go for my birthday," he said. "I'd been thinking how I would explain to her that I'd really prefer McDonald's. So the comparisons and contrasts between the two restaurants were fresh in my mind."

To generate ideas for his paper, Jesse turned to the technique of freewriting. Without concerning himself with organization, finding the perfect word, or even spelling, he simply wrote whatever came into his mind as he asked himself, "Why would I rather eat at McDonald's than at the Chalet?" Here is what Jesse came up with.

> The Chalet is a beautiful restaurant and it's sweet of Lilly to want to take me there. But I honestly like McDonald's better. To me, food is food, and a meal at the Chalet is not five times better than a meal at McDonald's but that's what it costs. I like a plain cheeseburger better than something I can't pronounce or identify. The waiters at the Chalet are snooty and make me feel awkward—how can you enjoy eating when you're tensed up like that? Have to wear jacket and tie to the Chalet and I've gained weight; not sure jacket will even fit. Sweats or jeans are great at McDonald's. Desserts at Chalet are great, better than McCookies or whatever they're called. Parking is a hassle at the Chalet and easy at McD's. No tipping at McD's, either. I don't know why they keep it so dark at the Chalet—guess it's supposed to be relaxing, but seems creepy to me. McD's is bright and cheerful.

As Jesse looked over his freewriting, he saw that most of what he had written fell into three categories that he could use as the three supporting points of his essay. Using these three points, he prepared this first scratch outline for the essay:

I'd rather eat my special dinner at McDonald's than at the Chalet.

1. Can wear anything I want to McD's.
2. Waiters, lighting, menu at Chalet make me feel awkward.
3. Chalet is <u>much</u> more expensive than McD's.

Next, Jesse went back and inserted some supporting details that fit in with his three main points.

I'd rather eat my special dinner at McDonald's than at the Chalet.

1. Going to the Chalet is a hassle.
   a. Have to wear jacket, tie to Chalet
   b. Have to make reservations
   c. Long drive; trouble parking
2. Waiters, lighting, menu at Chalet make me feel awkward.
   a. Waiters are snooty
   b. Lighting is dim
   c. French names on menu don't mean anything to me
3. Chalet is <u>much</u> more expensive than McD's.
   a. Meal costs five times as much
   b. Parking, tips on top of that
   c. Rather spend that money on other things

Working from this scratch outline, Jesse wrote the following first draft of his essay.

First Draft   **A Vote for McDonald's**

Lilly has offered to take me anywhere I want for my birthday dinner. She thinks I'll choose the Chalet, but instead I want to eat at McDonald's.

The Chalet has a jacket-and-tie rule, and I hate wearing a jacket and tie, and the jacket's probably too tight for me anyway. I have to dig them out of the closet and get them cleaned. I can wear any old thing to McDonald's. We'd also have to leave the house early, since the Chalet requires reservations. Since it is downtown, I have to leave an hour early so I'm sure to have time to park. The Chalet cancels reservations if a party is more than ten minutes late. Going to McDonald's, on the other hand, is easy. I don't have to do any advance planning. I can leave my house whenever I'm ready.

McDonald's is a pleasant place where I feel at ease. It is bright and well lighted. The employees serve with a smile, and the food is easy to pronounce and identify. I know what I'm going to get when I order a certain type of sandwich. I like simple meals more than gourmet ones. The Chalet is dimly lit. While I'm struggling to see what's on my plate, I worry that I'll knock one of the glasses off the table. The waiters at the Chalet can be uncomfortably formal, too. I get the feeling that I don't quite live up to their standards. Even the other diners can make me feel uncomfortable.

There's a big price difference between the Chalet and McDonald's. Dinner for two at the Chalet can easily cost $50, even without any "extras" like appetizers and dessert. And the $50 doesn't include the cost of parking the car and tipping the waiter. Once, I forgot to bring enough money. At McDonald's, a meal for two will cost around $10.

So, for my birthday dinner, or any other time, I prefer to eat at McDonald's. It is convenient, friendly, and cheap.

Development Through Rewriting

Jesse put the first draft of his essay aside and took it to his writing class the next day. His instructor asked Jesse and the other students to work in small groups reading their drafts aloud and making suggestions for revision to one another. Here are the notes Jesse made on his group's comments:

- I need to explain that Lilly is my wife.
- I'm not consistent in developing my paragraphs. I forgot to do a "one side at a time" or "point by point" comparison. I think I'll try "one side at a time." I'll describe in each paragraph what the Chalet is like, then what McDonald's is like.
- I could use more support for some of my points, like when I say that the waiters at the Chalet make me uncomfortable. I should give some examples of what I mean by that.
- I want to say something about what I'd rather do with the money we save by going to McDonald's. For me that's important—we can "eat" that money at the Chalet, or do other things with it that we both enjoy.

After making these observations about his first draft, Jesse proceeded to write the version of his essay that appears on page 267.

A Professional Essay to Consider

Read the following professional essay. Then answer the questions and read the comments that follow.

American Family Life: The Changing Picture

by Donna Barron

It's another evening in an American household.   1

The door swings open at 5:30 sharp. "Hi, honey! I'm home!" In walks dear   2
old Dad, hungry and tired after a long day at the office. He is greeted by Mom
in her apron, three happy children, and the aroma of a delicious pot roast.

After a leisurely meal together, Mom does the dishes. That, after all, is   3
part of her job. The whole family then moves to the living room. There
everyone spends the evening playing Scrabble or watching TV.

Then everyone is off to bed. And the next morning Dad and the kids   4
wake up to the sounds and smells of Mom preparing pancakes and sausage
for breakfast.

What? You say that doesn't sound like life in your house? Well, you're not   5
alone. In fact, you're probably in the majority.

At one time in America, the above household might have been typical.   6
You can still visit such a home—on television. Just watch reruns of old
situation comedies. *Leave It to Beaver*, for example, shows Mom doing
housework in pearls and high heels. Dad keeps his suit and tie on all weekend.
But the families that operate like Beaver Cleaver's are fewer and fewer.
They're disappearing because three parts of our lives have changed: the way
we work, the way we eat, and the way we entertain ourselves. Becoming
aware of the effects of those changes may help us improve family life.

Let's look first at the changes in the way we work. Today the words "Hi,   7
honey! I'm home!" might not be spoken by dear old Dad. Dear old Mom is
just as likely to be saying them. A generation ago, most households could get
along on one paycheck—Dad's. Mom stayed home, at least until the children
started school. But today, over half the mothers with young children go to
work. An even greater percentage of mothers of older children are in the
workforce. And the number of single-parent homes has mushroomed in the
last thirty years.

These changes in work have affected children as well as parents. When   8
only Dad went out to work, children came home from school to Mom. (In TV
situation comedies, they came home to Mom and home-baked cookies.)
Today, we'll find them at an after-school program or a neighbor's house. Or
they may come home to no one at all. In every community, children are caring

for themselves until their parents return from work. Are these children missing out on an important part of childhood? Or are they developing a healthy sense of self-reliance? These are questions that Mrs. Cleaver never had to deal with.

In addition, Dad and now Mom are often gone from home longer than 9 ever. Not too long ago, most men worked close to home. The office or factory was just downtown. Dad often walked to work or hitched a ride with a friendly neighbor. But no more.

Today's working men and women are commuters. They travel distances to 10 work that would have made their parents gasp. Commutes of forty-five minutes or an hour are common. Workers travel on buses, subways, and crowded highways. Many leave their suburban homes at dawn and don't return until dark. No running home for lunch for today's commuter.

And speaking of lunch, there's been a second big change in American 11 family life. If both parents are away from home for long hours, who's whipping up those delicious meals in the kitchen? The answer, more and more, is nobody.

These days, few people have time to shop for and prepare "home-style" 12 meals. The Cleavers were used to dinners of pot roast or chicken. Potatoes, salad, and vegetables went with the main course, with pie or cake for dessert. But this kind of meal takes several hours to fix. People can't spend hours in the kitchen if they get home at 5:30.

So what do working families eat? They choose meals that are easy to 13 prepare or are already prepared. Fast food, takeout, and heat-and-serve dishes make up much of the modern American diet. Dad may arrive home with a bag of Big Macs and shakes. Mom may phone out for Chinese food or ask the local pizza parlor to deliver. And more and more people rely on microwaves to thaw frozen food in minutes.

One consequence of these quickly prepared meals is that families spend 14 less time dining together. And classic fast foods, like hamburgers and fries, are meant to be eaten on the run, not slowly enjoyed at the dinner table. The modern family no longer shares the evening meal. As a result, it no longer shares the day's news . . . or the feeling of togetherness.

Finally, what about after dinner? Is the family evening at least something 15 the Cleavers could relate to?

Not a chance. 16

We don't even have to look outside the home to see the changes. The 17 modern American family entertains itself in ways the Cleavers would never have dreamed of.

Thirty years ago, families gathered around a radio each evening. Later, 18 television took over. Most families had just one set, which they watched together. Today, television and computers bring a dizzying array of entertainment into the home. Cable television provides everything from aerobics classes to Shakespeare. VCRs expand the choices even more. If there's nothing good on network TV or cable, the video store offers the best and worst of Hollywood: recent movies, cartoons, "adult" films, exercise programs, travel, sports, how-to tapes. Computer games, which make viewers part of the action, also provide excitement. Players can compete in the Olympics, search out aliens, or wipe out entire civilizations on their little screens.

With all these choices, it makes sense to own more than one television 19 set. The two-or-more-TV family used to be rare. Nowadays, Dad might want to rent an action movie when Mom's cable shopping service is on. Or Junior is playing a let's-blow-up-Saturn video game while Sis wants to see *The Simpsons*. Why not invest in several sets? Then each family member can enjoy himself or herself in peace.

What's wrong with this picture of today's family? 20

Only this. Today's Cleavers spend their evenings in front of their separate 21 TV screens. Then they go to bed. The next morning, they rush off to their separate jobs (work and school). They come home at separate times. They eat separately. Finally, they return to their separate TV screens for another evening's entertainment. During all these times, when do they talk to each other or even see each other? When are they a family?

Certain realities of modern life cannot change. One is the need, in most 22 families, for both parents to bring home a paycheck. Another is the distance many of us must travel to work or to school. But must everything change? And must we lose the family structure in the process?

No one is suggesting that we go back to the 1950s. The Cleaver 23 household was a fantasy even then, not reality. But we might borrow one important lesson from the Cleavers. It is that family life is just as important as work or play. If we agree, we'll find ways of spending more time together. We'll find things to share. And then there will be something *right* with the picture.

■ Questions

About Unity

1. What is the thesis of Barron's essay? If it is stated directly, locate the relevant sentence or sentences. If it is implied, state the thesis in your own words.

   Stated in paragraph 6: ". . . the families that operate like Beaver Cleaver's

   are . . . disappearing because three parts of our lives have changed . . ."

2. Which statement is the implied topic sentence of paragraph 8?

    a. Today many mothers work outside the home.

    b. There are many single-parent homes today.

    (c) Changes in how we work affect children's lives in ways that may or may not be positive.

    d. Mrs. Cleaver never had to worry if her children were missing out on an important part of childhood.

3. Which statement is the implied topic sentence of paragraph 21?

    a. Many people today work, eat, and play under the pressure of deadlines.

    b. The "typical" family today has multiple TV sets and separate dinnertimes.

    (c) Modern families are isolated from one another by their separate schedules and activities.

    d. Adults and children today are more independent and self-reliant than people of previous generations.

About Support

4. Barron states that families today "choose meals that are easy to prepare or are already prepared." Write the sentence in which she points out the effect of that fact.

    Fast food, takeout, and heat-and-serve dishes make up much of the

    modern American diet.

5. Barron says, "The modern American family entertains itself in ways the Cleavers would never have dreamed of." What categories of home entertainment does she describe to support that statement?

    television and computers

6. In paragraph 9, Barron writes, "Not too long ago, most men worked close to home." In which paragraph does she write about a contrasting situation for today's workers? _10_

About Coherence

7. Find and write below two "time" transitional words in paragraph 3 that help the reader follow the flow of action the author describes.

    After   _then_

8. Find the sentence in paragraph 7 that uses a "change of direction" transition word to signal that the author is moving from discussion of the old-fashioned family to the modern family. (*Write the opening words.*)

    Today the words . . .

About the Introduction and Conclusion

9. What purpose do the first four paragraphs of "American Family Life" serve?

    a. They present a situation that contrasts with most families' experience today.

    b. They explain the importance of the essay's topic to the reader.

    c. They present a situation that describes life in the majority of American households.

    d. They present a broad general statement of the topic and narrow it down to a thesis statement.

10. Which statement best describes the conclusion of "American Family Life"?

    a. It asks provocative questions about how modern family life compares to that of the Cleavers.

    b. It summarizes and restates the theme of the essay.

    c. It ends with a relevant quotation from the *Leave It to Beaver* show.

    d. It recommends that we adopt one of the Cleavers' values and then predicts what would happen if we do.

Writing a Comparison or Contrast Essay

■ Writing Assignment 1

Write an essay of comparison or contrast on one of these topics:

Two teachers you've had

Two jobs you'd held

Two bosses you've worked for

Two restaurants you've eaten in

Two parenting styles you've observed

Two friends you've had

Two pets you've had or seen

Two sports you're acquainted with

Two singers or bands you've heard

Two dates you've been on

Two places you've lived

Prewriting

a As you select your topic, keep in mind that you won't merely be *describing* the two things you're writing about—you will be emphasizing the ways they are alike or different.

b Make two columns on a sheet of paper, one for each of the two things you'll write about. In the left-hand column, jot down words or phrases that describe the first of the two. Write anything that comes into your head about that half of your topic. Then go back and write a corresponding word or phrase about the item in the right-hand column. For example, here is one student's list of characteristics about two games. He began brainstorming for words and phrases to describe Scrabble.

<u>Scrabble</u>   <u>Volleyball</u>

quiet

involves words

played sitting down

involves small group of people

can let mind wander when it's
   not your turn

mental concentration, not physical

part chance—don't know what
   letters you'll get

part strategy and skill

some see as boring, egghead game

Then he wrote a corresponding list of characteristics for volleyball, which helped him add to his first list:

Scrabble	Volleyball
quiet	noisy, talking and yelling
involves words	involves ball and a net
played sitting down	played standing up, jumping
involves as few as two players	involves twelve players
can let mind wander when it's not your turn	have to stay alert every minute
mental concentration, not physical	mental and physical concentration required
part chance (what letters you get), part strategy and skill	mostly skill, strategy; little chance
some see as boring, egghead game	seen as glamorous—stars get advertising contracts
players' size doesn't matter	being tall helps

c   Your list of characteristics will help you decide if the two things you are writing about are more alike (in which case you'll write an essay *comparing* them) or different (in which case you'll emphasize how they *contrast*).

d   As you look over your lists, think how the characteristics you've written down (and others that occur to you) could fit into three categories that can serve as your supporting points. Prepare a scratch outline for your essay based on these three supporting points.

   For instance, the student writing about Scrabble and volleyball came up with these three groupings of characteristics. Fill in the blanks in his outline to indicate the supporting points.

Wording of answers may vary.

   Thesis: Although they are two of my favorite activities, Scrabble and volleyball could hardly be more different.

   Point   *Different playing requirements*

   Scrabble requires a board and letter tiles.

   Volleyball needs a ball and net.

   Scrabble can be played by two people.

   Twelve people are needed for a volleyball game.

   Scrabble can be played anywhere there's room for two people to sit down.

   Volleyball needs a large room and high ceilings or an outdoor playing area.

Point <u>*Different traits and skills involved*</u>

> You have to concentrate mentally to play Scrabble.
>
> You need mental and physical concentration to play volleyball.
>
> It doesn't matter what size you are to play Scrabble.
>
> It helps to be tall to play volleyball.
>
> There's some chance involved in playing Scrabble.
>
> Chance is not a big part of volleyball.

Point <u>*Different images*</u>

> Scrabble players are seen as "eggheads" by the general public.
>
> Star volleyball players are seen as glamorous by the public.
>
> Volleyball players get contracts to endorse athletic shoes.
>
> Scrabble players don't endorse anything, even dictionaries.
>
> Volleyball players are admired for the power of their spike.
>
> Scrabble players are admired for the number of unusual two-letter words they know.

e Decide which method of development you will use to design your essay: one side at a time or point by point. Be consistent in your use of one method or the other in each of your paragraphs.

f Proceed to write the first draft of your essay.

Rewriting

As you review the first draft of your essay, ask yourself these questions:

- Have I made it clear in my opening paragraph what two things I am writing about, and whether I will compare or contrast them?

- Do my supporting points offer three areas in which I will compare or contrast my two subjects?

- Have I consistently used a single method of development—one side at a time or point by point—in each supporting paragraph?

- Have I used transition words to help readers follow my train of thought?

- If one area of comparison or contrast is stronger than the others, am I using emphatic order and saving that area for my final supporting paragraph?

- Have I rounded off my essay with an appropriate concluding paragraph?

As you revise your essay through one or more additional drafts, continue to refer to this list until you can answer "yes" to each question. Then be sure to check the next-to-final draft of the paper for the sentence skills listed on the inside front cover.

■ Writing Assignment 2

Write a paper in which you contrast two attitudes on a controversial subject. You may want to contrast your views with those of someone else, or contrast the way you felt about the subject in the past with the way you feel now. Some subjects you might consider writing about follow:

Legalization of narcotics

Abortion

Men and women serving together in military units

Prayer in public schools

Nuclear power plants

Gay couples adopting children

Fertility methods that allow older women to have children

Welfare reform

The death penalty

Euthanasia

Prostitution

The public's right to know about elected officials' private lives

Prewriting

a To gather information for the point of view that contrasts with your own, you will need to do some research. You'll find useful material if you go to the library and search through article indexes for recent newsmagazines. (If you need help, ask your instructor or the research librarian.) Or interview friends and acquaintances whose attitude on the subject is different from yours.

b To generate ideas for your paper, try the following two-part exercise.

• Part 1: Pretend that a visitor from Mars who has never heard of the topic of your paper has asked you to explain it, as well as why you take the attitude you do toward it. Using the technique of freewriting—not worrying about sentence structure, organization, spelling, repetition, etc.—write an answer for the Martian. Throw in every reason you can think of for your attitude.

• Part 2: Now the Martian asks you to do the same, taking the opposing point of view. Remember that it's up to you to make this interplanetary visitor understand both sides of the issue, so really try to put yourself in the other guy's shoes as you represent the contrasting attitude.

c As you look over the writing on both sides of the issue you've done for the Martian, note the strongest points on both sides. From them, select your three main supporting points. Are there other thoughts in your writing that can be used as supporting details for those points?

d Write your three supporting paragraphs. Decide whether it is more effective to contrast your attitude and the opposing attitude point by point within each paragraph, or by devoting the first half of each paragraph to one side's attitude and then contrasting it with the other's.

e In your concluding paragraph, summarize the contrast between your attitude and the other point of view. Consider closing with a final comment that makes it clear why you stand where you do.

Rewriting

Refer to the guidelines for rewriting provided on page 281.

■ Writing Assignment 3

In this comparison-contrast essay, you will write with a specific purpose and for a specific audience.

Option 1:   Your niece or nephew is finishing high school soon and is thinking about getting a job instead of going to college. You would prefer to see him or her give college a try. Write him or her a letter in which you compare and contrast the advantages and disadvantages of each course of action. Use the one-side-at-a-time method in making your analysis.

Option 2:   Write a letter to your boss in which you compare your abilities with those of the ideal candidate for a position to which you'd like to be promoted. Use the point-by-point method, discussing each desired qualification and then describing how well you measure up to it. Use the requirements of a job you are familiar with, ideally a job you would really like to apply for some day.

■ Writing Assignment 4

Write an essay that contrasts two characters or two points of view in one or more poems, stories, plays, or novels. The work you choose may be assigned by your instructor, or it may require your instructor's approval. For this assignment, your essay may have two supporting paragraphs, with each paragraph representing one side of the contrast. A student model follows.

Warren and Mary

In "Death of the Hired Man," Robert Frost uses a brief incident—the   1
return of Silas, an aging farmhand—to dramatize the differences between a
husband and wife. As Warren and Mary talk about Silas and reveal his story,
the reader learns their story, too. By the end of the poem, Warren and Mary
emerge as contrasting personalities; one is wary and reserved, while the
other is open and giving.

Warren is a kindly man, but his basic decency is tempered by practicality   2
and emotional reserve. Warren is upset with Mary for sheltering Silas, who is
barely useful and sometimes unreliable: "What use he is there's no
depending on." Warren feels that he has already done his duty toward Silas
by hiring him the previous summer and is under no obligation to care for
him now. "Home," says Warren, "is the place where, when you have to go
there/They have to take you in." Warren's home is not Silas's home, so
Warren does not have a legal or moral duty to keep the shiftless old man.
Warren's temperament, in turn, influences his attitude toward Silas's arrival.
Warren hints to Mary—through a condescending smile—that Silas is
somehow playing on her emotions or faking his illness. Warren considers
Silas's supposed purpose in coming to the farm—to ditch the meadow—
nothing but a flimsy excuse for a free meal. The best that Warren can find to
say about Silas is that he does have one practical skill: the ability to build a
good load of hay.

Mary, in contrast, is distinguished by her giving nature and her   3
concentration on the workings of human emotion. In caring for Silas, Mary
sees not his lack of ability or his laziness but the fact that he is "worn out"
and needs help. To Mary, home represents not obligation ("They have to
take you in") but unconditional love: "I should have called it/Something you
somehow haven't to deserve." Mary is observant, not only of outer
appearances but also of the inner person; this is why she thinks not that Silas
is trying to trick them but that he is a desperate man trying to salvage a little
self-respect. She realizes, too, that he will never ditch the meadow, and she
knows that Silas's insecurity prompted his arguments with the college boy
who helped with the haying. Mary is also perceptive enough to see that Silas
could never humble himself before his estranged brother. Mary's attitude is
more sympathetic than Warren's; whereas Warren wonders why Silas and his
brother don't get along. Mary thinks about how Silas "hurt my heart the way
he lay/And rolled his old head on that sharp-edged chairback."

In describing Silas, Warren and Mary describe themselves. We see a   4
basically good man whose spirit has been toughened by a hard life. Warren,
we learn, would have liked to pay Silas a fixed wage but simply couldn't
afford to. Life has taught Warren to be practical and to rein in his emotions.
In contrast, we see a nurturing woman, alert to human feelings, who could
never refuse to care for a lonely, dying man. Warren and Mary are both
decent people. This is the reason why, as Mary instinctively feels, Silas
chooses their home for his final refuge.

14 Definition

In talking with other people, we sometimes offer informal definitions to explain just what we mean by a particular term. Suppose, for example, we say to a friend, "Larry is really an inconsiderate person." We might then explain what we mean by "inconsiderate" by saying, "He borrowed my accounting book 'overnight' but didn't return it for a week. And when I got it back, it was covered with coffee stains." In a written definition, we make clear in a more complete and formal way our own personal understanding of a term. Such a definition typically starts with one meaning of a term. The meaning is then illustrated with a series of details.

In this section, you will be asked to write an essay in which you define and illustrate a term. To prepare for this assignment, first read the student essays and the professional essay that follow and work through the questions that accompany the essays.

Student Essays to Consider

Definition of a Football Fan

What is a football fan? The word "fan" is an abbreviation of "fanatic," meaning "an insane or crazy person." In the case of football fans, the term is appropriate. They behave insanely, they are insane about the past, and they are insanely loyal.

Football fans wear their official team T-shirts and warm-up jackets to the mall, the supermarket, the classroom, and even—if they can get away with it—to work. If the team offers a giveaway item, the fans rush to the stadium to claim the hat or sports bag or water bottle that is being handed out that day. Baseball fans go similarly nuts when their favorite teams give away some attractive freebie. Football fans just plain behave insanely. Even the fact that fans spend the coldest months of the year huddling on icy metal benches in places like Chicago proves it. In addition, football fans decorate their houses with football-related items of every kind. To them, team bumper stickers don't belong only on car bumpers, but also on fireplace mantels and front doors. When they go to a game, which they do as often as possible, they also decorate their bodies. True football fans not only put on their team jackets and grab their pennants but also paint their heads to look like helmets or wear glow-in-the-dark cheeseheads. At the game, these fans devote enormous energy to trying to get a "wave" going.

Football fans are insanely fascinated by the past. They talk about William "Refrigerator" Perry's 1985 Super Bowl touchdown as though it

1

2

3

had happened last week. The passion they show recounting Franco Harris's "Immaculate Reception" makes you wonder if they realize his playoff-winning catch occurred in 1972. They excitedly discuss the sixty-three-yard field goal kicked by Tom Dempsey—a man with no toes on his foot—as though it's news, instead of having happened in 1970. And if you can't manage to get all that excited about such ancient history, they look at you as though you were the insane one.

Last of all, football fans are insanely loyal to the team of their choice, often dangerously so. Should their beloved team lose three in a row, fans may begin to react negatively as a way to hide their broken hearts. They still obsessively watch each game and spend the entire day afterward reading and listening to the postgame commentary in newspapers, on TV sports segments, and on sports radio. Further, this intense loyalty makes fans dangerous. To anyone who dares to say to a loyal fan that another team has better players or coaches, or, God forbid, to anyone wandering near the home cheering section wearing the jacket of the opposing team, physical damage is a real possibility. Bloody noses, black eyes, and broken bones are just some of the injuries inflicted on people cheering the wrong team when fans are around. In 1997, one man suffered a concussion at a game in Philadelphia when Eagles fans beat him up for wearing a jacket with another team's insignia.

From February through August, football fans act like any other human beings. They pay their taxes, take out the garbage, and complain about the high cost of living. But when September rolls around, the colors and radios go on, the record books come off the shelves, and the devotion returns. For the true football fan, another season of insanity has begun.

Student Zombies

Schools divide people into categories. From first grade on up, students are labeled "advanced" or "deprived" or "remedial" or "antisocial." Students pigeonhole their fellow students, too. We've all known the "brain," the "jock," the "dummy," and the "teacher's pet." In most cases, these narrow labels are misleading and inaccurate. But there is one label for a certain type of college student that says it all: "zombie."

Zombies are the living dead. Most of us haven't known a lot of real zombies personally, but we do know how they act. We have horror movies to guide us. The special effects in horror movies are much better these days. Over the years, we've learned from the movies that zombies stalk around graveyards, their eyes glued open by Hollywood makeup artists, bumping like cheap toy robots into living people. Zombie students in college do just about the same thing. They stalk around campus, eyes glazed, staring off into space. When they do manage to wander into a classroom, they sit down mechanically and contemplate the ceiling. Zombie students rarely eat, dance, talk, laugh, or toss Frisbees on campus lawns. Instead, they vanish when class is dismissed and return only when some mysterious zombie signal summons them back into a classroom. The signal may not occur for weeks.

Zombies are controlled by some mysterious force. According to legend, real zombies are corpses that have been brought back to life to do the bidding of a voodoo master. Student zombies, too, seem directed by a strange power. They continue to attend school although they have no apparent desire to do so. They show no interest in college-related activities like tests, grades, papers, and projects. And yet some inner force compels them to wander through the halls of higher education.   3

An awful fate awaits all zombies unless something happens to break the spell they're under. In the movies, zombies are often shot, stabbed, drowned, electrocuted, and run over by large vehicles, all to no avail. Finally the hero or heroine realizes that a counterspell is needed. Once that spell is cast, with the appropriate props of chicken feet, human hair, and bats' eyeballs, the zombie-corpse can return peacefully to its coffin. The only hope for a student zombie to change is for him or her to undergo a similarly traumatic experience. Sometimes the evil spell can be broken by a grade transcript decorated with large red "F's." At other times a professor will succeed through a private, intensive exorcism session. But in other cases zombies blunder around for years until they are gently persuaded by the college administration to head for another institution. Then they enroll in a new college or get a job in the family business.   4

Every college student knows that it's not necessary to see <u>Night of the Living Dead</u> or <u>The Dead Don't Die</u> in order to see zombies in action—or nonaction. Forget the campus film series or the late-late show. Just sit in a classroom and wait. You know what you're looking for—the students who walk in without books or papers and sit in the very last row of seats. The ones with personal stereos plugged into their ears don't count as zombies— that's a whole different category of "student." <u>Day of the Living Dead</u> is showing every day at a college near you.   5

■ Questions

About Unity

1. Which supporting paragraph in "Definition of a Football Fan" has a topic sentence buried within the paragraph, rather than at the paragraph's beginning? (*Write the paragraph number and the opening words of the topic sentence.*)
   Paragraph 2: Football fans just plain . . .

2. What sentence in paragraph 2 of "Definition of a Football Fan" should be omitted in the interest of paragraph unity? (*Write the opening words*)
   Baseball fans go . . .

3. Which sentence in paragraph 2 of "Student Zombies" should be omitted in the interest of paragraph unity? (*Write the opening words.*)

   The special effects . . .

4. What sentence in the final paragraph of "Student Zombies" introduces a new topic and so should be eliminated? (*Write the opening words.*)

   The ones with personal stereos . . .

About Support

5. Which essay develops its definitions through a series of comparisons?

   "Student Zombies"

6. After which sentence in paragraph 4 of "Definition of a Football Fan" is more support needed? (*Write the opening words.*)

   Should their beloved team . . .

7. In the second paragraph of "Definition of a Football Fan," how many examples are given of fans' "insane" behavior? Circle the letter of the answer.

   a. two

   b. four

   (c.) six

About Coherence

8. Which paragraph in "Definition of a Football Fall" begins with a transitional phrase? ____4____

9. Which sentence in paragraph 2 of "Student Zombies" begins with a change-of-direction transitional word? (*Write the opening words.*)

   Instead, they vanish . . .

About the Introduction and Conclusion

10. Which method of introduction is used in the opening paragraph of "Student Zombies"? Circle the letter of the appropriate answer.

    a. Anecdote

    b. Idea that is the opposite of the one to be developed

    c. Quotation

    (d.) Broad, general statement narrowing to a thesis

    e. Questions

Developing a Definition Essay

Development Through Prewriting

In a definition essay, you provide your reader with your personal understanding of a concept or term. In contrast to a very limited dictionary definition, your definition conveys what your understanding and experience have taught you about that concept or term.

As with other essay forms, you should think in terms of supporting your definition (which will serve as your thesis) with two or three paragraphs, each of which has its own topic sentence.

In thinking of possible topics for this essay, you should consider subjects that you are especially qualified to discuss. A topic that you know a good deal about, or a concept that you like to think about, makes the best subject for a definition essay.

Brian, the author of "Definition of a Football Fan," spent a few minutes jotting down a number of possible essay topics, keeping in mind the question, "What do I know a good deal about, or at least have an interest in exploring?" Here is his list of topic ideas. Notice how they reflect Brian's interest in outdoor activities, sports, and history:

Definition of . . .

A person who fishes

A soccer goalie

A reenactor of Civil War battles

People who vacation at Gettysburg

A bodybuilder

A Green Bay Packers fan

A history buff

A Little League coach

After looking over his list, Brian selected "A Green Bay Packers fan" as the topic that interested him most. He thought it would lend itself well to a lighthearted essay that defined the sometimes nutty fans of the Wisconsin football team. After giving it further thought, however, Brian decided to broaden his topic to include all football fans. "I realized I just didn't know enough specifically about Green Bay fans to support an entire essay," he said.

A person who likes to think in visual terms, Brian decided to develop ideas and details about his topic by diagramming his thoughts.

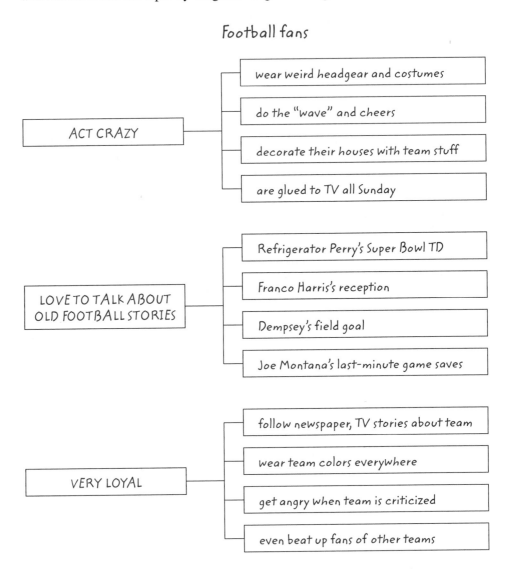

Football fans

ACT CRAZY
- wear weird headgear and costumes
- do the "wave" and cheers
- decorate their houses with team stuff
- are glued to TV all Sunday

LOVE TO TALK ABOUT OLD FOOTBALL STORIES
- Refrigerator Perry's Super Bowl TD
- Franco Harris's reception
- Dempsey's field goal
- Joe Montana's last-minute game saves

VERY LOYAL
- follow newspaper, TV stories about team
- wear team colors everywhere
- get angry when team is criticized
- even beat up fans of other teams

As he looked over his diagram, Brian realized that he could characterize each of his three main topics as a kind of "insanity." He decided on a thesis (he would define football fans as insane) that would indicate his essay's plan of development ("they act insanely, they are insane about the past, and they are insanely loyal").

With that thesis and plan of development in mind, Brian wrote the first draft of his essay.

First Draft

Definition of a Football Fan

Football fans are by definition crazy. They behave insanely, they are insane about the past, and they are insanely loyal.

If their team gives away something free, the fans rush to the stadium to claim the hat or sports bag or water bottle. Football fans just plain behave insanely. Baseball fans go similarly nuts when their favorite teams give away some attractive freebie. But football fans are even worse. Football fans freeze themselves in order to watch their favorite game. In addition, football fans decorate their houses with football-related items of every kind. When they go to a game, which they do as often as possible, the true football fans make themselves look ridiculous by decorating themselves in weird team-related ways. At the game, these fans do the "wave" more than they watch the game.

Football fans love to talk about the past. They talk about William "Refrigerator" Perry's 1985 Super Bowl touchdown as though it had happened last week. They still get all excited about the "Immaculate Reception" of 1972. They talk about Tom Dempsey's field goal as though it's news, instead of having happened in 1970. They think everyone should be as excited as they are about such old stories.

Last of all, football fans are insanely loyal to the team of their choice. Football fans wear their team T-shirts and warm-up jackets everywhere, even to work. Of course if they have to dress up in business clothes they can't do that. Should their beloved team lose three in a row, their fans may begin to criticize their team. But these reactions only hide their broken hearts. They still obsessively watch each game and read all the newspaper stories about it. This intense loyalty makes fans dangerous. To anyone who dares to say to a loyal fan that another team is better, or, God forbid, to anyone wandering near the home cheering section wearing the jacket of the opposing team, physical damage is a real possibility. Incidents of violence in football stadiums have increased in recent years and are a matter of growing concern.

Football fans really act as if they're crazy. They behave insanely, they are crazy about the past, and they're too loyal.

Development Through Revising

The next day, Brian showed his first draft to a study partner from his composition class. She returned it with comments noted in the margins.

Reader's Comments

Definition of a Football Fan

Football fans are by definition crazy. They behave insanely, they are insane about the past, and they are insanely loyal.

Huh? I guess this is about the weather—make it clearer.

Like what? Details here.

If their team gives away a freebie, the fans rush to the stadium to get the hat or whatever. Football fans just plain behave insanely. Baseball fans go similarly nuts when their favorite teams give away some attractive freebie. But football fans are even worse. Football fans freeze themselves in order to watch their favorite game. In addition, football fans decorate their houses with football-related items of every kind. When they go to a game, which they do as often as possible, the true football fans make themselves look ridiculous by decorating themselves in weird team-related ways. At the game, these fans do the "wave" more than they watch the game.

Details needed. How do they decorate themselves?

Football fans love to talk about the past. They talk about William "Refrigerator" Perry's 1985 Super Bowl touchdown as though it had happened last week. They get all excited about the "Immaculate Reception" of 1972. They talk about Tom Dempsey's field goal as though it's news, instead of having happened in 1970. They think everyone should be as excited as they are about such old stories.

I'm not a football fan, so I don't understand these references. Can you briefly explain them?

Shouldn't this be in the first paragraph? It seems to belong to "they act insanely," not "loyalty."

This doesn't support your topic statement, so take it out.

Last of all, football fans are insanely loyal to the team of their choice. Football fans wear their team T-shirts and warm-up jackets everywhere, even to work. Of course if they have to dress up in business clothes they can't do that. Should their beloved team lose three in a row, their fans may begin to criticize their team. But these reactions only hide their broken hearts. They still obsessively watch each game and read all the newspaper stories about it. This intense loyalty makes fans dangerous. To anyone who dares to say to a loyal fan that another team is better, or, God forbid, to anyone wandering near the home cheering section wearing the jacket of the opposing team, physical damage is a real possibility. Incidents of violence in football stadiums have increased in recent years and are a matter of growing concern.

Football fans really act as if they're crazy. They behave insanely, they are crazy about the past, and they're too loyal.

Kind of a boring way to end it. You're just repeating your thesis.

After reading his classmate's comments, Brian went to work on his next draft. As he worked, he read his essay aloud several times and noticed places where his wording sounded awkward or too informal. (Example: "If their team gives away a freebie, the fans rush to the stadium to get the hat or whatever.") A few drafts later, he produced the version of "Definition of a Football Fan" that appears on page 285.

A Professional Essay to Consider

Read the following professional essay. Then answer the questions and read the comments that follow.

Television Addiction

by Marie Winn

The word "addiction" is often used loosely and wryly in conversation. People will refer to themselves as "mystery book addicts" or "cookie addicts." E. B. White writes of his annual surge of interest in gardening, "We are hooked and are making an attempt to kick the habit." Yet nobody really believes that reading mysteries or ordering seeds by catalogue is serious enough to be compared to an addiction to heroin or alcohol. The word "addiction" is here used jokingly to denote a tendency to overindulge in some pleasurable activity.

People often refer to being "hooked on TV." Does this, too, fall into 2
the lighthearted category of eating cookies and other pleasures that people
pursue with unusual intensity, or is there a kind of television viewing that falls
into the more serious category of destructive addiction?

When we think about addiction to drugs or alcohol, we frequently focus 3
on negative aspects, ignoring the pleasures that accompany drinking or
taking drugs. And yet the essence of any serious addiction is a pursuit of
pleasure, a search for a "high" that normal life does not supply. It is only the
inability to function without the addictive substance that is dismaying, the
dependence of the organism upon a certain experience and an increasing
inability to function without it. Thus a person will take two or three drinks at
the end of the day not merely for the pleasure drinking provides, but
also because he "doesn't feel normal" without them.

An addict does not merely pursue a pleasurable experience and need to 4
experience it in order to function normally. He needs to repeat it again and
again. Something about that particular experience makes life without it less
than complete. Other potentially pleasurable experiences are no longer
possible, for under the spell of the addictive experience, his life is peculiarly
distorted. The addict craves an experience, and yet he is never really satisfied.
The organism may be temporarily sated, but soon it begins to crave again.

Finally, a serious addiction is distinguished from a harmless pursuit of 5
pleasure by its distinctly destructive elements. A heroin addict, for instance,
leads a damaged life: his increasing need for heroin in increasing doses
prevents him from working, from maintaining relationships, from developing
in human ways. Similarly, an alcoholic's life is narrowed and dehumanized by
his dependence on alcohol.

Let us consider television viewing in the light of the conditions that 6
define serious addictions.

Not unlike drugs and alcohol, the television experience allows the 7
participant to blot out the real world and enter into a pleasurable and passive
mental state. The worries and anxieties of reality are as effectively deferred
by becoming absorbed in a television program as by going on a "trip"
induced by drugs or alcohol. And just as alcoholics are only inchoately aware
of their addiction, feeling that they control their drinking more than they
really do ("I can cut it out any time I want—I just like to have three or four
drinks before dinner"), people similarly overestimate their control over
watching television. Even as they put off other activities to spend hour after
hour watching television, they feel they could easily resume living in a
different, less passive style. But somehow or other while the television set is
present in their homes, the click doesn't sound. With television pleasures
available, those other experiences seem less attractive, more difficult
somehow.

A heavy viewer (a college English instructor) observes: "I find television 8
almost irresistible. When the set is on, I cannot ignore it. I can't turn it off. I
feel sapped, will-less, enervated. As I reach out to turn off the set, the
strength goes out of my arms. I sit there for hours and hours."

The self-confessed television addict often feels he "ought" to do other 9
things—but the fact that he doesn't read and doesn't plant his garden or sew
or crochet or play games or have conversations means that those activities are
no longer as desirable as television. In a way the heavy viewer's life is as
imbalanced by his television "habit" as a drug addict's or an alcoholic's. He is
living in a holding pattern, as it were, passing up the activities that lead to
growth or development or a sense of accomplishment. This is one reason
people talk about their television viewing so ruefully, so apologetically. They
are aware that it is an unproductive experience, that almost any other
endeavor is more worthwhile by any human measure.

Finally, it is the adverse effect of television viewing on the lives of so many 10
people that defines it as a serious addiction. The television habit distorts the
sense of time. It renders other experiences vague and curiously unreal while
taking on a greater reality for itself. It weakens relationships by reducing and
sometimes eliminating normal opportunities for talking, for communicating.

And yet television does not satisfy, else why would the viewer continue to 11
watch hour after hour, day after day? "The measure of health," writes
Lawrence Kubie, "is flexibility . . . and especially the freedom to cease when
sated." But the television viewer can never be sated with his television
experiences—they do not provide the true nourishment that satiation
requires—and thus he finds that he cannot stop watching.

■ Questions

About Unity

1. Winn's thesis is not presented directly in the essay. See if you can state it in
   your own words.

   Answers will vary. Example: Addiction to TV resembles addiction to alcohol

   or drugs in several ways.

2. Which statement would best serve as a topic sentence for paragraph 4?

   a. Addicts enjoy pleasurable experiences more than nonaddicts.

   b. Addicts feel that their lives are not really complete.

   c. Addicts would give up their addiction if other pleasurable experiences
       were available.

   d. Addicts need to endlessly repeat the experiences on which they are
       dependent.

3. Which statement would best serve as a topic sentence for paragraph 7?

    a. People become television addicts because they have more troubled lives than most other people.

    (b) Television addicts develop a distorted perception of reality and lose self-control.

    c. Few experiences in life are as pleasurable as watching television.

    d. Alcoholics often believe they have more control over their drinking than they really do.

About Support

4. The author defines TV as an addiction by first defining

    a. being hooked on TV.

    (b) serious addiction.

    c. a heavy viewer.

    d. the real world.

5. The topic sentence of paragraph 5 states, "Finally, a serious addiction is distinguished from a harmless pursuit of pleasure by its distinctly destructive elements." What details does the author use to support this point?

    heroin addict's damaged life

    alcoholic's narrowed and dehumanized life

6. Paragraph 8

    (a) supports the idea in paragraph 7 that TV addicts overestimate their control over TV watching.

    b. raises a point not dealt with elsewhere.

    c. supports the idea in paragraph 9 that TV addicts are stuck in a living holding pattern.

About Coherence

7. Which paragraph fully signals the author's switch from discussing addiction in general terms to talking specifically about addiction to television? __*6*__

8. What key transitional word is used twice in the essay? __*Finally*__

About the Introduction and Conclusion

9. Which statement best describes the introductory paragraph of Winn's essay?

   a. It explains the importance of the topic of television addiction.

   b. It tells an anecdote that illustrates the nature of television addiction.

   (c.) It presents a type of "addiction" very different from the one discussed in the essay.

10. Which statement best describes the conclusion of "Television Addiction"?

   a. Winn recommends that the television addict try to "kick the habit."

   (b.) Winn summarizes the points made in the body of the essay.

   c. Winn comments on the damage television does to society at large.

Writing a Definition Essay

■ Writing Assignment 1

Shown below are an introduction, a thesis, and supporting points for an essay that defines the word *maturity*. Using separate paper, plan out and write the supporting paragraphs and a conclusion for the essay.

The Meaning of Maturity

> Being a mature student does not mean being an old-timer. Maturity is not measured by the number of years a person has lived. Instead, the yardstick of maturity is marked by the qualities of self-denial, determination, and dependability.

> Self-denial is an important quality in the mature student. . . .

> Determination is another characteristic of a mature student. . . .

> Although self-denial and determination are both vital, probably the most important measure of maturity is dependability. . . .

Prewriting

a Prepare examples for the three qualities of maturity. For each quality, you should have one extended example that takes up an entire paragraph *or* two or three shorter examples that together form enough material for a paragraph.

b To generate these details, ask yourself questions like these, based on the topic sentence of the first supporting paragraph:

What could I do, or what have I done, that would be an example of self-denial?

What has someone I know ever done that could be described as self-denial?

What kind of behavior on the part of a student could be considered self-denial?

Write down quickly whatever answers occur to you. As when you freewrite, don't worry about grammar, punctuation, or spelling. Instead, concentrate on getting down as many details relating to self-denial as you can think of. Then repeat the questioning and writing process, substituting "determination" and "dependability" for "self-denial."

c Now go through the material you have compiled. If you think of other details as you read, jot them down. Next, decide just what information you will use in each supporting paragraph. List the details in the order in which you will present them.

d Now write the first draft of your paper.

Rewriting

After you have completed the first draft of the paper, set it aside for a while (if possible). When you reread what you have written, prepare for rewriting by asking yourself these questions:

- Have I provided enough details to support each of the three characteristics of maturity?
- Have I eliminated or rewritten any irrelevant material?
- Have I used transition words to help readers follow my train of thought?
- Does my concluding paragraph provide a summary or a final thought or both?

As you revise your essay through one or more additional drafts, continue to refer to this list until you can answer "yes" to each question. Then be sure to check the next-to-final draft of the paper for the sentence skills listed on the inside front cover.

■ Writing Assignment 2

Choose one of the terms below as the subject of a definition essay. Each term refers to a certain kind of person.

Snob	Optimist	Slob
Cheapskate	Pessimist	Tease
Loser	Team player	Practical joker
Good neighbor	Bully	Procrastinator
Busybody	Scapegoat	Loner
Whiner	Religious person	Straight arrow
Con artist	Hypocrite	

Prewriting

a As you devise your opening paragraph, you may want to refer to the dictionary definition of the term. If so, be sure to use only one meaning of the term. (Dictionaries often provide several different meanings for a term.) *Don't* begin your paper with the overused phrase, "According to Webster . . ."

b Remember that the thesis of a definition essay is a version of "What _____ means to me." The thesis presents what *your* experience has made *you* think the term actually means.

c As you plan your supporting paragraphs, think of different parts or qualities of your term. Here, for example, are the three-part divisions of the student essays considered in this chapter:

Football fans are crazy in terms of their behavior, their fascination with the past, and their loyalty.

Student zombies are the "living dead," are controlled by a "mysterious force," and are likely to suffer an "awful fate."

d Support each part of your division with either a series of examples or a single extended example.

e You may find outlining to be the most helpful prewriting strategy for your definition essay. As a guide, write your thesis and three supporting points in the spaces below.

Thesis: _____

Support: 1. _____

           2. _____

           3. _____

Rewriting

Once you have the first draft of your essay completed, review it with these questions in mind:

- Does my thesis statement indicate how I define the term, and does it indicate my plan of development for the essay?
- Does each of my supporting paragraphs have a clear topic sentence?
- Have I supported each of my three topic sentences with one extended example or a series of examples?
- Have I rounded off my essay with an appropriate concluding paragraph?
- Have I proofread my essay, referring to the list of sentence skills on the inside front cover?

■ Writing Assignment 3

Write an essay that defines one of the terms below.

Persistence	Responsibility	Fear
Rebellion	Insecurity	Arrogance
Sense of humor	Assertiveness	Conscience
Escape	Jealousy	Class
Laziness	Practicality	Innocence
Danger	Nostalgia	Freedom
Curiosity	Gentleness	Violence
Common sense	Depression	Shyness
Soul	Obsession	Idealism
Family	Christianity	Spirituality

■ Writing Assignment 4

In this definition essay, you will write with a specific purpose and for a specific audience.

Option 1:   You work in a doctor's office and have been asked to write a brochure that will be placed in the waiting room. The brochure is intended to tell patients what a healthy lifestyle is. Write a definition of *healthy lifestyle* for your readers, using examples wherever appropriate. Your definition might focus on both mental and physical health and might include eating, sleeping, exercise, and recreational habits.

Alternatively, you might decide to take a playful point of view and write a brochure defining an *unhealthy lifestyle*.

Option 2:   Your Spanish class is host to some students from Mexico. The class is preparing a "dictionary of slang" for the visitors. Your job is to write a paragraph in which you define the term *to gross out*.

In your introduction, consider including the nonslang definition of *gross*, which led to the slang usage. To find that definition, consult a dictionary. Your thesis should reflect your understanding of the slang usage of *to gross out*. Each of your supporting paragraphs can be based on an example of how the term is used, or a circumstance in which the term is appropriate.

Alternatively, you may write about any other slang term. If necessary, first get the approval of your instructor.

15 Division and Classification

When you return home from your weekly trip to the supermarket with five bags packed with your purchases, how do you sort them out? You might separate food items from nonfood items (like toothpaste, paper towels, and detergent). Or you might divide and classify the items into groups intended for the freezer compartment, the refrigerator, and the kitchen cupboards. You might even put the items into groups like "to be used tonight," "to be used soon," and "to be used last." Sorting supermarket items in such ways is just one simple example of how we spend a great deal of our time organizing our environment in one manner or another.

In this chapter, you will be asked to write an essay in which you divide or classify a subject according to a single principle. To prepare for this assignment, first read the student essays and the professional essay that follow and work through the questions that accompany the essays.

Student Essays to Consider

Mall People

Just what goes into "having fun"? For many people, "fun" involves getting out of the house, seeing other people, having something interesting to look at, and enjoying a choice of activities, all at a reasonable price. Going out to dinner or to the movies may satisfy some of those desires, but often not all. But an attractive alternative does exist in the form of the free-admission shopping mall. Teenagers, couples on dates, and the nuclear family can all be observed having a good time at the mall.

Teenagers are drawn to the mall to pass time with pals and to see and be seen by other teens. The guys saunter by in sneakers, T-shirts, and blue jeans, complete with a package of cigarettes sticking out of a pocket. The girls stumble along in high-heeled shoes and daring tank tops, with a hairbrush tucked snugly in the rear pocket of their tight-fitting designer jeans. Traveling in a gang that resembles a wolf pack, the teenagers make the shopping mall their hunting ground. Mall managers have obviously made a decision to attract all this teenage activity. The kids' raised voices, loud laughter, and occasional shouted obscenities can be heard from as far as half a mall away. They come to "pick up chicks," to "meet guys," and just to "hang out."

Couples find fun of another sort at shopping malls. The young lovers are easy to spot because they walk hand in hand, stopping to sneak a quick kiss

1

2

3

after every few steps. They first pause at a jewelry store window so that they can gaze at diamond engagement rings and gold wedding bands. Then, they wander into furniture departments in the large mall stores. Finally, they drift away, their arms wrapped around each other's waist.

Mom, Dad, little Jenny, and Fred, Jr., visit the mall on Friday and Saturday evenings for inexpensive recreation. Hearing the music of the antique carousel housed there, Jenny begs to ride her favorite pony with its shining golden mane. Shouting "I'm starving!" Fred, Jr., drags the family toward the food court, where he detects the seductive odor of pizza. Mom walks through a fabric store, running her hand over the soft velvets and slippery silks. Meanwhile, Dad has wandered into an electronics store and is admiring the sound system he'd love to buy someday. The mall provides something special for every member of the family.   4

Sure, some people visit the mall in a brief, businesslike way, just to pick up a specific purchase or two. But many more are shopping for inexpensive recreation. The teenagers, the dating couples, and the nuclear families all find cheap entertainment at the mall.   5

Genuine Draft

The other night, my six-year-old son turned to me and asked for a light beer. My husband and I sat there for a moment, stunned, and then explained to him that beer was only for grown-ups. I suddenly realized how many beer ads appear on television, and how often they appear. To my little boy, it must seem that every American drinks beer after work, or after playing softball, or while watching a football game. Brewers have pounded audiences with all kinds of campaigns to sell beer. There seems to be an ad to appeal to the self-image of every beer drinker.   1

One type of ad attracts people who think of themselves as grown-up kids. Budweiser's animated frogs, squatting on lily pads and croaking "Bud," "Weis," "Er," are a perfect example of this type. The frogs are an example of the wonders of computer animation, which is being increasingly mixed in with real-life action in advertisements. The campaign was an immediate hit with the underage set as well as with adult beer-drinkers. Within weeks, the frogs were as recognizable to children as Tony the Tiger or Big Bird. They became so popular that the new Bud ads were a feverishly anticipated part of the Super Bowl—as much a part of the entertainment as the game itself or the halftime show. These humorous ads suggest that beer is part of a lighthearted approach to life.   2

A second kind of ad is aimed not at wanna-be kids but at macho men, guys who think of themselves as "men's men," doing "guy things" together.   3

One campaign features men who see themselves as victims of their nagging wives. Ads in this series show men howling with laughter about how they've fooled their wives into thinking they're home doing chores (by leaving dummy-stuffed pants lying under leaky sinks or broken furnaces) while they're really out drinking. Beer is a man's drink, the ads seem to say, and women are a nuisance to be gotten around.

European and European-sounding beers such as Löwenbräu and   4
Heineken like to show handsome, wealthy-looking adults enjoying their money and leisure time. A typical scene shows such people enjoying an expensive hobby in a luxurious location. Beer, these ads tell us, is an essential part of the "good life." This type of ad appeals to people who want to see themselves as successful and upper-class.

To a little boy, it may well seem that beer is necessary to every adult's   5
life. After all, we need it to make us laugh, to bond with our friends, and to celebrate our financial success. At least, that's what advertisers tell him—and us.

■ Questions

About Unity

1. In which supporting paragraph in "Genuine Draft" is the topic sentence at the end rather than, as is more appropriate for student essays, at the beginning?
   <u>4</u>

2. Which sentence in paragraph 2 of "Mall People" should be omitted in the interest of paragraph unity? (*Write the opening words.*)

   Mall managers have obviously . . .

3. What sentence in paragraph 2 of "Genuine Draft" should be omitted in the interest of paragraph unity? (*Write the opening words.*)

   These frogs are an example . . .

About Support

4. After which sentence in paragraph 3 of "Mall People" are more supporting details needed? *(Write the opening words.)*

   Then, they wander . . .

5. Which paragraph in "Genuine Draft" lacks sufficient specific details? <u>4</u>

6. Label as *sight*, *touch*, *hearing*, or *smell* all the sensory details in the following sentences taken from "Mall People."

   a. *hearing*
       Hearing the music of the antique carousel housed there, Jenny begs to
       sight
       ride her favorite pony with its shining golden mane.

   b. *hearing*   *sight*
       Shouting "I'm starving!" Fred, Jr., drags the family toward the food court,
       smell
       where he detects the seductive odor of pizza.

   c. *sight*   *touch*
       Mom walks through a fabric store, running her hand over the soft velvets
       touch
       and slippery silks.

About Coherence

7. What are the time transition words used paragraph 3 of "Mall People"?

   _____*first*_____   _____*Then*_____   _____*Finally*_____

8. Which topic sentence in "Genuine Draft" functions as a linking sentence between paragraphs? (Write the opening words.)

   _*A second kind of ad . . .*_____

About the Introduction and Conclusion

9. What kind of introduction is used in "Genuine Draft"? Circle the appropriate letter.

   a. Broad, general statement narrowing to a thesis

   b. Idea that is the opposite of the one to be developed

   c. Quotation

   (d.) Anecdote

   e. Questions

10. What conclusion technique is used in "Mall People"? Circle the appropriate letter.

    (a.) Summary

    b. Prediction or recommendation

    c. Question

Developing a Division-Classification Essay

Development Through Prewriting

Julia, the writer of "Mall People," believed from her observations that "people at malls" would make a good topic for a division-classification essay. But she did not immediately know how she wanted to group those people or what she wanted to say about them. She decided to begin her prewriting by making a list of observations about mall shoppers. Here is what she came up with:

Families with kids

Lots of snacking

Crowds around special displays—automobiles, kiddie rides

Older people walking in mall for exercise

Groups of teenagers

Women getting made over at makeup counter

Dating couples

Blind woman with Seeing Eye dog

Lots of people talking and laughing rather than shopping

Interviewers stopping shoppers to fill out questionnaires

Kids hanging out, meeting each other

As Julia reviewed her list, she concluded that the three largest groups of "mall people" were families with children, groups of teens, and dating couples. She decided to organize her essay around those three groups. To further flesh out her idea, she created a scratch outline that her essay would follow. Here is the scratch outline Julia prepared:

Thesis statement: Mall offers inexpensive fun for several groups.

1   Teens

    a. Roam in packs

    b. Dress alike

    c. Meet new people

2   Dating couples

    a. Act romantic

    b. Window-shop for future home

    c. Have lovers' quarrels

3   Families

    a. Kids' activities

    b. Cheap food

    c. Adults shop

Julia's list and outline prepared her to write the first draft of her essay.

First Draft

Mall People

Malls aren't only places to go shopping. They also offer free or at least cheap fun and activities for lots of people. Teenagers, dating couples, and families all like to visit the mall.

Teenagers love to roam the mall in packs, like wolves. They often dress alike, depending on the latest fashion. They're noisy and sometimes rude, and mall security officers sometimes kick them out of the building. Then they find somewhere else to go, maybe one of the warehouse-sized amusement and video-game arcades that are springing up everywhere. Those places are fun, but they tend to be more expensive than just "hanging out" at the mall. Teens are usually not as interested in shopping at the mall as they are in picking up members of the opposite sex and seeing their friends.

Dating couples also enjoy wandering around the mall. They are easy to spot because they walk along holding hands and sometimes kissing. They stare at diamond rings and wedding bands and shop for furniture together. Sometimes they have spats and one of them stamps off to sulk on a bench for a while.

Little kids and their parents make up a big group of mall-goers. There is something for every member of the family there. There are usually some special displays that interest the kids, and Mom and Dad can always find things they like to window-shop for. Another plus for the family is that there is inexpensive food, like burgers and pizza, available at the mall's food court.

Development Through Revision

After Julia completed her first draft, she put it aside. She knew from previous experience that she was a better critic of her own writing after she took a break from it. The following morning, when Julia read over her first draft, she noticed several places where it could be improved. Here are the observations she put in her writing journal:

- "My first paragraph does present a thesis (malls offer inexpensive entertainment) and it tells how I'm going to develop that thesis (by discussing three groups of people). But it isn't very interesting. I think I could do a better job of drawing readers in by describing what is fun about malls.

- Some of the details in the essay aren't necessary; they don't support my main idea. For instance, the stuff about teens being kicked out of the mall and about dating couples having fights doesn't have anything to do with the entertainment malls provide. I'll eliminate this.

- Some of my statements that do support the main idea need more support. For example, when I say there are "special displays that interest the kids" in paragraph 4, I should give an example of such a display. I should also back up the idea that many teens dress alike.

With these observations in mind, Julia returned to her essay and revised it, producing the version that appears on page 303.

A Professional Essay to Consider

Now read the following professional essay. Then answer the questions and read the comments that follow.

Wait Divisions

by Tom Bodett

I read somewhere that we spend a full third of our lives waiting. I've also read that we spend a third of our lives sleeping, a third working, and a third at our leisure. Now either somebody's lying, or we're spending all our leisure time waiting to go to work or sleep. That can't be true or league softball and Winnebagos never would have caught on.

So where are we doing all of this waiting, and what does it mean to an impatient society like ours? Could this unseen waiting be the source of all our problems? A shrinking economy? The staggering deficit? Declining mental health and moral apathy? Probably not, but let's take a look at some of the more classic "waits" anyway.

The very purest form of waiting is what we'll call the *Watched-Pot Wait*. 3
This type of wait is without a doubt the most annoying of all. Take filling up
the kitchen sink. There is absolutely nothing you can do while this is going on
but keep both eyes glued to the sink until it's full. If you try to cram in some
extracurricular activity, you're asking for it. So you stand there, your hands on
the faucets, and wait. A temporary suspension of duties. During these waits
it's common for your eyes to lapse out of focus. The brain disengages from
the body and wanders around the imagination in search of distraction. It
finds none and springs back into action only when the water runs over the
edge of the counter and onto your socks.

The phrase "a watched pot never boils" comes of this experience. Pots 4
don't care whether they are watched or not; the problem is that nobody has
ever seen a pot actually come to a boil. While people are waiting, their brains
turn off.

Other forms of the Watched-Pot Wait would include waiting for your 5
dryer to quit at the laundromat, waiting for your toast to pop out of the
toaster, or waiting for a decent idea to come to mind at a typewriter. What
they all have in common is that they render the waiter helpless and mindless.

A cousin to the Watched-Pot Wait is the *Forced Wait*. Not for the weak of 6
will, this one requires a bit of discipline. The classic Forced Wait is starting
your car in the winter and letting it slowly idle up to temperature before
engaging the clutch. This is every bit as uninteresting as watching a pot, but
with one big difference. You have a choice. There is nothing keeping you
from racing to work behind a stone-cold engine save the thought of the early
demise of several thousand dollars' worth of equipment you haven't paid for
yet. Thoughts like that will help you get through a Forced Wait.

Properly preparing packaged soup mixes also requires a Forced Wait. 7
Directions are very specific on these mixes. "Bring three cups of water to boil,
add mix, simmer three minutes, remove from heat, let stand five minutes." I
have my doubts that anyone has actually done this. I'm fairly spineless when
it comes to instant soups and usually just boil the bejeezus out of them until
the noodles sink. Some things just aren't worth a Forced Wait.

All in all Forced Waiting requires a lot of a thing called patience, which is 8
a virtue. Once we get into virtues I'm out of my element and can't expound
on the virtues of virtue, or even lie about them. So let's move on to some of
the more far-reaching varieties of waiting.

The *Payday Wait* is certainly a leader in the long-term anticipation field. 9
The problem with waits that last more than a few minutes is that you have to
actually do other things in the meantime. Like go to work. By far the most
aggravating feature of the Payday Wait is that even though you must keep
functioning in the interludes, there is less and less you are able to do as the
big day draws near. For some of us the last few days are best spent alone in a

dark room for fear we'll accidentally do something that costs money. With the Payday Wait comes a certain amount of hope that we'll make it, and faith that everything will be all right once we do.

With the introduction of faith and hope, I've ushered in the most potent   10 wait class of all, the *Lucky-Break Wait*, or the *Wait for One's Ship to Come In*. This type of wait is unusual in that it is for the most part voluntary. Unlike the Forced Wait, which is also voluntary, waiting for your lucky break does not necessarily mean that it will happen.

Turning one's life into a waiting game of these proportions requires gobs   11 of the aforementioned faith and hope, and is strictly for the optimists among us. For these people life is the thing that happens to them while they're waiting for something to happen to them. On the surface it seems as ridiculous as following the directions on soup mixes, but the Lucky-Break Wait performs an outstanding service to those who take it upon themselves to do it. As long as one doesn't come to rely on it, wishing for a few good things to happen never hurt anybody.

In the end it is obvious that we certainly do spend a good deal of our time   12 waiting. The person who said we do it a third of the time may have been going easy on us. It makes a guy wonder how anything at all gets done around here. But things do get done, people grow old, and time boils on whether you watch it or not.

The next time you're standing at the sink waiting for it to fill while   13 cooking soup mix that you'll have to eat until payday or until a large bag of cash falls out of the sky, don't despair. You're probably just as busy as the next guy.

■ Questions

About Unity

1. The thesis of Bodett's essay is not presented directly. See if you can state it in your own words.   *Answers will vary. An example is given.*

    Various kinds of waiting interrupt everyone's life.

2. In paragraph 2, Bodett introduces several possible effects of waiting, then dismisses them with a "probably not." Is it a sign of careless writing that Bodett mentions irrelevant topics and then dismisses them? Or does he intend a particular effect by introducing unnecessary topics? If he does intend an effect, how would you describe it? *Answers will vary. An example is given.*

    This is intentional; it is done for a humorous effect.

About Support

3. Bodett writes of four "classic waits": the Watched-Pot Wait, the Forced Wait, the Payday Wait, and the Lucky-Break Wait. For which two "waits" does he provide several examples?

    Watched-Pot Wait   _Forced Wait_

4. Bodett refers to the first two waits as cousins. How does he differentiate between them?

    "You have a choice" in the Forced Wait.

    _____

5. How does Bodett support his claim that the Forced Wait "requires a bit of discipline"?

    He gives examples: protecting your car by not running it cold, and preparing

    soup properly.

About Coherence

6. Bodett's essay does not follow the strict one-three-one model (introduction, three supporting paragraphs, conclusion) often used in student essays. Instead, its form is a looser one that includes an introduction, four topics for development (the four "waits"), and a conclusion. Indicate in the following outline how the paragraphs of Bodett's essay are broken up:

    Introduction: Paragraph(s) _1–2_

    Topic 1:   Paragraph(s) _3–5_

    Topic 2:   Paragraph(s) _6–8_

    Topic 3:   Paragraph(s) _9_

    Topic 4:   Paragraph(s) _10–11_

    Conclusion: Paragraph(s) _12–13_

7. Which words in the first sentence of paragraph 6 link that sentence to the preceding three paragraphs?

    A cousin to the Watched-Pot Wait is . . .

8. Bodett organizes the waits

    a. from the most harmful to the least harmful.

    (b.) from the shortest waits to the longest.

    c. from the most difficult wait to the easiest one.

    d. in no particular order.

About the Introduction and Conclusion

9. Which method best describes the introduction to "Wait Divisions"?

   a. Quotation

   b. Idea that is the opposite of the one to be developed

   c. Anecdote

   (d.) Broad, general statement narrowing to thesis

10. In what way does the first sentence in paragraph 13 serve as a summary of Bodett's main points? *Wording of answer may vary. An example is given.*

   He uses an image in which all the waits are involved.
   _____

   _____

Writing a Division-Classification Essay

■ Writing Assignment 1

Shown below are an introduction, a thesis, and supporting details for a classification essay on stress in college. Using separate paper, plan out and write the supporting paragraphs and a conclusion for the essay.

College Stress

> Jack's heart pounds as he casts panicky looks around the classroom. He doesn't recognize the professor, he doesn't know any of the students, and he can't even figure out what the subject is. In front of him is a test. At the last minute his roommate awakens him. It's only another anxiety dream. The very fact that dreams like Jack's are common suggests that college is a stressful situation for young people. The causes of this stress can be academic, financial, and personal.

> Academic stress is common. . . .

> In addition to academic stress, the student often feels financial pressure. . . .

> Along with academic and financial worries, the student faces personal pressures. . . .

Prewriting

a To develop some ideas for the division-classification essay in assignment 1, freewrite for five minutes apiece on (1) *academic,* (2) *financial,* and (3) *personal* problems of college students.

b Then add to the material you have written by asking yourself these questions:

What are some examples of academic problems that are stressful for students?

What are some examples of financial problems that students must contend with?

What are some examples of personal problems that create stress in students?

Write down quickly whatever answers occur to you. As with freewriting, do not worry at this stage about writing correct sentences. Instead, concentrate on getting down as much information as you can think of that supports each of the three points.

c Now go through all the material you have accumulated. Perhaps some of the details you have written down may help you think of even better details that would fit. If so, write down these additional details. Then make decisions about the exact information that you will use in each supporting paragraph. List the details in the order in which you will present them (1, 2, 3, and so on).

d Now write out the first draft of your paper.

Rewriting

After you have completed the first draft of the paper (and ideally set it aside for a while), you should prepare yourself to rewrite by asking the following questions:

- Have I provided relevant examples for each of the three kinds of stress?
- Have I provided enough details to support each of the three kinds of stress?
- Have I used transition words to help readers follow my train of thought?
- Have I added a concluding paragraph that rounds out and completes the essay?
- Have I checked the paper carefully for the sentence skills listed on the inside front cover?

As you revise your essay, continue to refer to this list until you can answer "yes" to each question.

■ Writing Assignment 2

Choose one of the following subjects as the basis for a division-classification essay:

Music	Pet owners
Videos	Junk food
TV shows	College courses
Fiction	Dating couples
Comic strips	Shoppers
Vacations	Bosses
Answering-machine messages	Parties
Breakfast foods	Advertisements
Pets	Catalogs
Attitudes toward exercise	

Prewriting

a For a division-classification essay, the prewriting strategy that may be especially helpful is outlining. The success of your essay will depend on your division of your topic into three well-balanced parts. In order to create those three parts, you must use the same rule, or principle, of division for each. Most topics can be divided in several ways according to several principles. For example, the topic "Hit movies" could be divided in the following ways:

Divided by the principle of *film categories:* Action, comedy, romance

Divided by the principle of *intended audience:* Families, dating couples, teens

The topic "My favorite books" could be divided like this:

Divided by the principle of *book categories:* Novels, how-to books, biographies

Divided by the principle of *purpose they serve for me:* Escape, self-improvement, amusement

The topic "Places to eat" could be divided in these ways:

Divided by the principle of *cost:* Cheap, moderate, expensive

Divided by the principle of *type of food:* American, Italian, Chinese

If you look back at the essays that appear earlier in this chapter, you'll see that the topics are divided as follows:

"Mall People" is divided by the principle of *groups of shoppers:* Teens, dating couples, families

"Genuine Draft" is divided by the principle of *beer-drinkers' self-images:* Grown-up kids, men's men, upper-class

"Wait Divisions" is divided by principle of *types of waits:* Watched-Pot Wait, Forced Wait, Payday Wait, Lucky-Break Wait

The important point to remember is to divide your topic consistently, according to a single principle. It would be illogical, for example, to divide the topic "Places to eat" into "American," (type of food served), "Italian" (type of food served), and "Expensive" (cost). In order for the essay to be balanced and consistent, choose one principle of division and stick to it.

b As you consider a topic for your own paper, think of principles of division you might use. Test them out by filling out this outline and answering the question.

Topic: _____

Principle of division: _____

Three-part division of topic:

    1. _____

    2. _____

    3. _____

Have I used the same principle of division for each of the three parts?

When you are confident that you have chosen a topic of interest to you that you can divide into three parts according to one principle, you are ready to begin writing.

c Before writing your first draft, you may want to freewrite on each of the three parts, make lists, or ask and answer questions to generate the supporting details you will need to develop your ideas.

Rewriting

Once you have completed a first draft of your essay, you should review it with these questions in mind:

- Have I included the essay's thesis in my introductory paragraph?
- Does my thesis state my topic and the principle of division I have chosen?
- Is each of the paragraphs in the body of my essay based on one division of my topic?
- Have I backed up statements in my essay with relevant examples or illustrations?
- Have I eliminated irrelevant material that does not support my thesis?
- Have I used transition words within the paragraphs to help readers follow my train of thought?
- Have I used linking sentences between paragraphs to help tie those paragraphs together?
- Have I included a concluding paragraph that provides a sense of completion to the essay?

As you revise your essay, continue to refer to this list until you can answer "yes" to each question.

■ Writing Assignment 3

In this division-classification essay, you will write with a specific purpose and for a specific audience.

Option 1:   Your younger sister or brother has moved to another city and is about to choose a roommate. Write her or him a letter about what to expect from different types of roommates. Label each type of roommate ("The Messy Type," "The Neatnik," "The Loud-Music Lover," etc.) and explain what it would be like to live with each.

Option 2:   Unsure about your career direction, you have gone to a vocational counseling service. To help you select the type of work you are best suited for, a counselor has asked you to write a detailed description of your "ideal job." You will present this description to three other people who are also seeking to choose a career.

To describe your ideal job, divide work life into three or more elements, such as:

Activities done on the job

Skills used on the job

Physical environment

People you work with and under

How the job affects society

In your paper, explain your ideals for each element. Use specific examples where possible to illustrate your points.

16 Argumentation

Do you know someone who enjoys a good argument? Such a person likes to challenge any sweeping statement we might make. For example, when we say something like, "Ms. Lucci doesn't grade fairly," he or she comes back with, "Why do you say that? What are your reasons?"

Our questioner then listens carefully as we state our case, judging if we really do have solid evidence to support our point of view. We realize that saying, "Ms. Lucci just doesn't, that's all," sounds weak and unconvincing, so we try to come up with stronger evidence to back up our statement. Such a questioner may make us feel uncomfortable, but we may also feel grateful to him or her for helping us clarify our opinions.

The ability to put forth sound and compelling arguments is an important skill in everyday life. You can use argumentation to make a point in a class discussion, persuade a friend to lend you money, or talk an employer into giving you a day off. Becoming skilled in clear, logical reasoning can also help you see through faulty arguments that others may make. You'll become a better critic of advertisements, newspaper articles, political speeches, and the other persuasive appeals you see and hear every day.

In this chapter, you will be asked to write an essay in which you defend a position with a series of solid reasons. In a general way, you have done the same thing—making a point and then supporting it—with all the essays in this book. The difference here is that argumentation advances a *controversial* point, a point that at least some of your readers will not be inclined to accept. To prepare for this assignment, first read about five strategies you can use in advancing an argument. Then read the student essays and the professional essay that follow and work through the questions that accompany the essays.

Strategies for Argumentation

Because argumentation assumes controversy, you have to work especially hard to convince readers of the validity of your position. Here are five strategies you can use to help win over readers whose viewpoint may differ from yours.

1 Use Tactful, Courteous Language

In an argumentation essay, you are attempting to persuade readers to accept your viewpoint. It is important, therefore, not to anger them by referring to them or their opinions in rude or belittling terms. Stay away from sweeping statements like "Everybody knows that . . ." or "People with any intelligence agree that . . ." Also, keep the focus on the issue you are discussing, not on the people involved in the debate. Don't write, "*My opponents* say that orphanages cost less than foster care." Instead, write, "*Supporters of orphanages* say that orphanages cost less than foster care." Terms like *my opponents* imply that the argument is between you and anyone who disagrees with you. By contrast, a term such as *supporters of orphanages* suggest that those who don't agree with you are nevertheless reasonable people who are willing to consider differing opinions.

2 Point Out Common Ground

Another way to persuade readers to consider your opinion is to point out common ground that you share. Find points on which people on all sides of the argument can agree. Perhaps you are arguing that there should be an 11 P.M. curfew for juveniles in your town. Before going into detail about your proposal, remind readers who oppose such a curfew that you and they share certain goals: a safer city, a lower crime rate, and fewer gang-related tragedies. Readers will be more receptive to your idea once they have considered the ways in which you and they think alike.

3 Acknowledge Differing Viewpoints

It is a mistake to simply ignore points of view that conflict with yours. Acknowledging other viewpoints strengthens your position in several ways. First, it helps you spot flaws in the opposing position—as well as in your own argument. Second, and equally important, it give the impression that you are a reasonable person, willing to look at an issue from all side. Readers will be more likely to consider your point of view if you indicate a willingness to consider theirs.

At what point in your essay should you acknowledge opposing arguments? The earlier the better—ideally, in the introduction. By quickly establishing that you recognize the other side's position, you get your readers "on board" with you, ready to hear what else you have to say.

One effective technique is to *cite the opposing viewpoint in your thesis statement.* You do this by dividing your thesis into two parts. In the first part, you acknowledge the other side's point of view; in the second, you state your opinion, suggesting that yours is the stronger viewpoint. In the following example, the opposing viewpoint is underlined once; the writer's own position is underlined twice:

<u>Although some students believe that studying a foreign language is a waste of time</u>, <u>two years of foreign-language study should be required of all college graduates.</u>

For another example of a thesis that acknowledges an opposing viewpoint, look at this thesis statement, taken from the essay entitled "Once Over Lightly: Local TV News" (page 323):

<u>While local TV newscasts can provide a valuable community resource</u>, <u>too often such programs provide mere entertainment at the expense of solid news.</u>

Another effective technique is to use one or two sentences (separate from the thesis) in the introduction to acknowledge the alternative position. Such sentences briefly state the "other side's" argument. To see this technique at work, look at the introduction to the essay "Teenager and Jobs" (page 322), noting the sentence "Many people argue that working can be a valuable experience for the young."

A third technique is to *use a paragraph within the body of your essay to summarize opposing opinions in greater detail.* To do this successfully, you must spend some time researching those opposing arguments. A fair, evenhanded summary of the other side's ideas will help convince readers that you have looked at the issue from all angles before deciding where you stand. Imagine, for instance, that you are writing an essay arguing that the manufacture and sale of handguns should be outlawed. You would begin by doing some library research to find information on both sides of the issue, making sure to pay attention to material that argues against your viewpoint. You might also talk with local representatives of the National Rifle Association or other organizations that support gun ownership. Having done your research, you would be in a good position to write a paragraph summarizing the opposing viewpoints. In this paragraph, you might mention that many citizens believe that gun ownership is a right guaranteed by the Constitution and that gun owners fear that outlawing handguns would deprive law-abiding people of protection against gun-toting criminals. Once you had demonstrated that you understood opposing views, you would be in a stronger position to present your own point of view.

4 When Appropriate, Grant the Merits of Differing Viewpoints

Sometimes an opposing argument contains a point whose validity you cannot deny. What should you do then? The strongest strategy is to admit that the point is a good one. You will lose credibility if you argue against something that clearly makes sense. Admit the merit of one aspect of the other argument while making it clear that you still believe your argument to be stronger overall. Suppose that you were arguing against the use of computers in writing classrooms. You might say, "Granted, students who are already accustomed to computers can use them to write papers more quickly and efficiently"—admitting that the other side has a valid point. But you could quickly follow this admission with a statement making your own viewpoint clear: "But for students like me who write and think in longhand, a computer in the classroom is more a hindrance than a help; it would require too great a learning curve to be of any value to me."

5 Rebut Differing Viewpoints

Sometimes it may not be enough simply to acknowledge other points of view and present your own argument. When you are dealing with an issue that your readers feel strongly about, you may need to *rebut* the opposing arguments. To *rebut* means to point out problems with an opposing view, to show where an opponent's argument breaks down.

Imagine that you are writing an essay arguing that your college should use money intended to build a campus health and fitness center to upgrade the library instead. From reading the school paper, you know that supporters of the center say it will help attract new students to the college. You rebut that point by citing a study conducted by the admissions office which shows that most students choose a college because they can afford it and because they like its academic programs and facilities. You also emphasize that many students, already financially strapped, would have trouble paying the proposed fee for using the center.

A rebuttal can take two forms. (1) You can first mention all the points raised by the other side and then present your counterargument to each of those points. (2) You can present the first point raised by the opposition and rebut that point, then move on to the second opposing point and rebut that, and so on.

Student Essays to Consider

Teenagers and Jobs

"The pressure for a teenager to work is great, and not just because   1
of the economic plight in the world today. Much of it is peer pressure to
have a little bit of freedom and independence, and to have their own
spending money. The concern we have is when the part-time work becomes
the primary focus." These are the words of Roxanne Bradshaw, educator
and officer of the National Education Association. Many people argue that
working can be a valuable experience for the young. However, working
more than about fifteen hours a week is harmful to adolescents because
it reduces their involvement with school, encourages a materialistic and
expensive lifestyle, and increases the chance of having problems with drugs
and alcohol.

Schoolwork and the benefits of extracurricular activities tend to go by   2
the wayside when adolescents work long hours. As more and more teens
have filled the numerous part-time jobs offered by fast-food restaurants and
malls, teachers have faced increasing difficulties. They must both keep the
attention of tired pupils and give homework to students who simply don't
have time to do it. In addition, educators have noticed less involvement in
the extracurricular activities that many consider a healthy influence on
young people. School bands and athletic teams are losing players to work,
and sports events are poorly attended by working students. Those teens who
try to do it all—homework, extracurricular activities, and work—may find
themselves exhausted and prone to illness. A recent newspaper story, for
example, described a girl in Pennsylvania who came down with
mononucleosis as a result of aiming for good grades, playing on two school
athletic teams, and working thirty hours a week.

Another drawback of too much work is that it may promote materialism   3
and an unrealistic lifestyle. Some parents claim that working helps teach
adolescents the value of a dollar. Undoubtedly that can be true. It's also
true that some teens work to help out with the family budget or to save for
college. However, surveys have shown that the majority of working teens
use their earnings to buy luxuries—video game systems, CD players and disks,
clothing, even cars. These young people, some of whom earn $400 or more
a month, don't worry about spending wisely—they can just about have it all.
In many cases, experts point out, they are becoming accustomed to a lifestyle
they won't be able to afford several years down the road, when they no
longer have parents paying for car insurance, food, lodging, and so on. At
that point, they'll be hard-pressed to pay for necessities as well as luxuries.

Finally, teenagers who work a lot are more likely than others to get   4
involved with alcohol and drugs. Teens who put in long hours may seek a
quick release from stress, just like the adults who need to drink a couple of
martinis after a hard day at work. Stress is probably greater in our society
today than it has been at any time in the past. Also, teens who have money
are more likely to get involved with drugs.

Teenagers can enjoy the benefits of work while avoiding its drawbacks,   5
simply by limiting their work hours during the school year. As is often the
case, a moderate approach will be the most healthy and rewarding.

Once Over Lightly: Local TV News

Are local television newscasts a reliable source of news? Do they provide   1
in-depth coverage and analysis of important local issues? Unfortunately, all
too often they do not. While local TV newscasts can provide a valuable
community resource, too often such programs provide mere entertainment
at the expense of solid news. In their battle for high ratings, local programs
emphasize news personalities at the expense of stories. Visual appeal has a
higher priority than actual news. And stories and reports are too brief and
shallow.

Local TV newscasters are as much the subject of the news as are the   2
stories they present. Nowhere is this more obvious than in weather reports.
Weatherpersons spend valuable news time joking, drawing cartoons,
chatting about weather fronts as "good guys" and "bad guys," and
dispensing weather trivia such as statistics about relative humidity and
record highs and lows for the date. Reporters, too, draw attention to
themselves. Rather than just getting the story, the reporters are shown
jumping into or getting out of helicopters to get the story. When reporters
interview crime victims or the residents of poor neighborhoods, the camera
angle typically includes them and their reaction as well as their subjects.
When they report on a storm, they stand outside in the storm, their styled
hair blowing, so we can admire how they "brave the elements." Then there
are the anchorpersons, who are chosen as much for their looks as their skills.
They too dilute the news by putting their personalities at center stage.

Often the selection of stories and the way they are presented are based   3
on visual impact rather than news value. If a story is not accompanied by an
interesting film clip, it is not likely to be shown on the local news. The result
is an overemphasis on fires and car crashes and little attention to such
important issues as the economy. A tractor-trailer spill on the highway
slightly injures one person and inconveniences motorists for only an hour.
But because it provides dramatic pictures—the big truck on its side, its load
spilled, emergency personnel running around, lots of flashing lights—it is
given greater emphasis in the local newscast than a rise in local taxes, which
has far more lasting effect on the viewer. "If it bleeds, it leads" is the
unofficial motto of many local news programs. A story that includes pictures
of death and destruction, no matter how meaningless, is preferable on the
local news to a solid, important story without flashy visuals. The mania for
visuals is so strong that local news programs will even slap irrelevant visuals
onto an otherwise strong story. A recent story on falling oil prices, for
example, was accompanied by footage of a working oil well that drew
attention away from the important economic information in the report.

On the average, about half a minute is devoted to a story. Clearly, stories   4
that take less than half a minute are superficial. Even the longest stories,
which can take up several minutes, are not accompanied by meaningful
analysis. Instead, the camera jumps from one location to another, and the
newscaster simplifies and trivializes the issues. For instance, one recent "in-
depth" story about the homeless consisted of a glamorous reporter talking
to a homeless person and asking him what should be done about the
problem. The poor man was in no condition to respond intelligently. The
story then cut to an interview with a city bureaucrat who mechanically
rambled on about the need for more government funding. Is raising taxes
the answer to every social problem? There were also shots of homeless
people sleeping in doorways and on top of heating vents, and there were
interviews with people in the street, all of whom said that something should

be done about the terrible problem of homelessness. There was, in all of this, no real exploration of the issue and no proposed solution. It was also apparent that the homeless were just the issue of the week. After the week's coverage was over, the topic was not mentioned again.

Because of the emphasis on newscasters' personalities and on the visual impact of stories and the short time span for stories, local news shows provide little more than diversion. What viewers need instead is news that has real significance. Rather than being amused and entertained, we need to deal with complex issues and learn uncomfortable truths that will help us become more responsible consumers and citizens.

5

■ Questions

About Unity

1. Which paragraph in "Once Over Lightly" lacks a topic sentence? ___4___

   Write a topic sentence for the paragraph: _Answers may vary; an example is_ _given: Local news is often lacking in depth._

2. What sentence in paragraph 4 of "Once Over Lightly" should be omitted in the interest of paragraph unity? *(Write the opening words)*

   Is raising taxes . . .

3. Which sentence in paragraph 4 of "Teenagers and Jobs" should be omitted in the interest of paragraph unity? *(Write the opening words.)*

   Stress is probably greater . . .

About Support

4. Which sentence in paragraph 4 of "Teenagers and Jobs" needs to be followed by more supporting details? Which sentence in paragraph 2 of "Once Over Lightly" needs to be followed by supporting details? *(Write the opening words of each sentence.)*

   "Teenagers and Jobs": Also, teens who have money . . .

   "Once Over Lightly": They too dilute the news . . .

5. In "Teenagers and Jobs," which supporting paragraph raises an opposing idea and then argues against that idea? ___3___ What transition word is used to signal the author's change of direction? _____However_____

6. In paragraph 2 of "Once Over Lightly," the topic sentence is supported by details about three types of newscasters. What are those three types?

   ___weatherpersons___   ___reporters___   ___anchorpersons___

About Coherence

7. Which two paragraphs of "Teenagers and Jobs" begin with an addition transition, and what are those words?

   ___3: Another___   ___4: Finally___

8. Write the change-of-direction transition and the illustration transition in paragraph 3 of "Once Over Lightly."

   Change of direction: ___But___   *Illustration:* ___for example___

About the Introduction and Conclusion

9. Two methods of introduction are used in "Teenagers and Jobs." Circle the letters of these two methods.

   a. Broad, general statement narrowing to thesis

   (b.) Idea that is the opposite of the one to be developed

   (c.) Quotation

   d. Anecdote

   e. Questions

10. Both essays end with the same type of conclusion. What method do they use?

   a. Summary only

   (b.) Summary and recommendation

   c. Prediction

Developing an Argumentation Essay

Development Through Prewriting

Before choosing a topic for her essay, Anna, the writer of "Teenagers and Jobs,"
asked herself what controversial subject she was particularly well qualified to argue.
She wanted to select something she cared about, something she could "sink her teeth
into." As a person who had been an active member of her high school community—
she had worked on the newspaper, played basketball, and sung in a chorus—Anna
first thought of writing about "student apathy." It had always bothered her to see
few students taking advantage of the opportunities available to them in school. But
as she thought more about individual students she knew and their reasons for not
getting more involved in school and extracurricular activities, she changed her
opinion. "I realized that 'apathy' was not really the problem," she explained. "Many
of them worked so much that they literally didn't have time for school life."

After narrowing her thesis to the idea of "teenagers and work," Anna made a list of what she perceived as the bad points of students' working too much:

No time for sports and other activities

Students leave right after school—can't stay for clubs, practice

Don't have time to attend games, other school functions

Students sleep in class and skip homework

Stress, extra money contribute to drug and alcohol use

Teachers frustrated trying to teach tired students

Ability to buy luxuries makes teens materialistic, unrealistic about lifestyle

Some drop out of school to work full time

Students miss the fun of being young, developing talents and social abilities

Students burned out, even get sick

As she reviewed and revised her list of points, Anna identified three main points to develop in her essay. Those she identified as points 1, 2, and 3. She realized that some of the other items she had jotted down were related ideas that might be used to support her main topics. She marked those with the number of the main idea they supported, in parentheses, like this: (1).

1 No time for real involvement in school and school activities

(1) Students leave right after school—can't stay for clubs, practices

(1) Don't have time to attend games, other school functions

Students sleep in class and skip homework

2 Stress, extra money contribute to drug and alcohol use

(1) Teachers frustrated trying to teach tired students

3 Having extra money makes teens materialistic

(3) Some get so greedy for money they drop out of school to work full-time

Students miss the fun of being young, developing talents and social abilities

Students burn out, even get sick

(2) Hanging around older coworkers can contribute to drug, alcohol use

(3) Buying luxuries gives teens unrealistic idea of standard of living

Referring to this list, Anna wrote the following first draft of her essay.

Teenagers and Jobs

Many people think that working is a valuable experience for young people. But when teenagers have jobs, they are too likely to neglect their schoolwork, become overly materialistic, and get into trouble with drugs and alcohol.

Schoolwork and the benefits of extracurricular activities tend to go by the wayside when adolescents work long hours. As more and more teens have taken jobs, teachers have faced increasing difficulties. They must both keep the attention of tired pupils and give homework to students who simply don't have time to do it. In addition, educators have noticed less involvement in extracurricular activities. School bands and athletic teams are losing players to work, and sports events are poorly attended by working students. Those teens who try to do it all—homework, extracurricular activities, and work—may find themselves exhausted and burned out.

Another drawback of too much work is that it may promote materialism and an unrealistic lifestyle. Most working teens use their earnings to buy luxuries. These young people don't worry about spending wisely—they can just about have it all. They are becoming accustomed to a lifestyle they won't be able to afford several years down the road, when they have to support themselves.

Finally, teenagers who work are more likely than others to get involved with alcohol and drugs. Teens who put in long hours may seek a quick release from stress, just like the adults who need to drink a couple of martinis after a hard day at work. Also, teens who have money are more likely to get involved with drugs.

In short, teens and work just don't mix.

Development Through Revising

Anna's instructor had offered to look over students' first drafts and suggest improvements for revision. Here is the note she wrote at the end of Anna's work:

Anna — Good beginning. While I think your thesis is overstated, it and each of your main topics are on the right track. Here are some points to consider as you write your next draft:

- Many teenagers find working a <u>limited</u> number of hours a week to be a good experience. I think it's a mistake to state flatly that it's <u>always</u> a negative thing for teenagers to have jobs. Think about acknowledging that there can be good points to students' working part-time.

- You do a pretty good job of supporting your first main point ("Schoolwork and the benefits of extracurricular activities tend to go by the wayside when adolescents work long hours") by noting the effect of too much work on scholastic achievement and extracurricular activities. You <u>less</u> effectively support points 2 and 3 ("Another drawback of too much work is that it may promote materialism and an unrealistic lifestyle" and "Finally, teenagers who work are more likely than others to get involved with alcohol and drugs"). <u>Show</u> how teens become too materialistic; don't just state that they do. And what evidence do you have that working teens use drugs and alcohol more than others?

- Throughout the essay, can you come up with evidence beyond your own observations to support the idea that too much working is detrimental to teens? Look into the magazine indexes in the library and on the Internet for studies or stories that might support your thesis.

I'll look forward to seeing your final draft.

After considering her instructor's comments, Anna wrote the version of "Teenagers and Jobs" that appears on page 322.

A Professional Essay to Consider

Read the following professional essay. Then answer the questions and read the comments that follow.

Ban the Things. Ban Them All.

by Molly Ivins

Guns. Everywhere guns. 1

Let me start this discussion by pointing out that I am not anti-gun. I'm 2 pro-knife. Consider the merits of the knife.

In the first place, you have to catch up with someone to stab him. A 3 general substitution of knives for guns would promote physical fitness. We'd turn into a whole nation of great runners. Plus, knives don't ricochet. And people are seldom killed while cleaning their knives.

As a civil libertarian, I of course support the Second Amendment. And I 4 believe it means exactly what it says: "A well-regulated militia being necessary to the security of a free state, the right of the people to keep and bear arms shall not be infringed." Fourteen-year-old boys are not part of a well-regulated militia. Members of wacky religious cults are not part of a well-regulated militia. Permitting unregulated citizens to have guns is destroying the security of this free state.

I am intrigued by the arguments of those who claim to follow the judicial 5 doctrine of original intent. How do they know it as the dearest wish of Thomas Jefferson's heart that teenage drug dealers should cruise the cities of this nation perforating their fellow citizens with assault rifles? Channeling?

There is more hooey spread about the Second Amendment. It says quite 6 clearly that guns are for those who form part of a well-regulated militia, i.e., the armed forces including the National Guard. The reasons for keeping them away from everyone else get clearer by the day.

The comparison most often used is that of the automobile, another lethal 7 object that is regularly used to wreak great carnage. Obviously, this society is full of people who haven't got enough common sense to use an automobile properly. But we haven't outlawed cars yet.

We do, however, license them and their owners, restrict their use to 8 presumably sane and sober adults and keep track of who sells them to whom. At a minimum, we should do the same with guns.

In truth, there is no rational argument for guns in this society. This is no 9 longer a frontier nation in which people hunt their own food. It is a crowded, overwhelmingly urban country in which letting people have access to guns is a continuing disaster. Those who want guns—whether for target shooting, hunting or potting rattlesnakes (get a hoe)—should be subjected to the same restrictions placed on gun owners in England, a nation in which liberty has survived nicely without an armed populace.

The argument that "guns don't kill people" is patent nonsense. Anyone 10 who has ever worked in a cop shop knows how many family arguments end in murder because there was a gun in the house. Did the gun kill someone? No. But if there had been no gun, no one would have died. At least not without a good footrace first. Guns do kill. Unlike cars, that is all they do.

Michael Crichton makes an interesting argument about technology in his 11 thriller *Jurassic Park*. He points out that power without discipline is making this society into wreckage. By the time someone who studies the martial arts becomes a master—literally able to kill with bare hands—that person has also undergone years of training and discipline. But any fool can pick up a gun and kill with it.

"A well-regulated militia" surely implies both long training and long 12 discipline. That is the least, the very least, that should be required of those who are permitted to have guns, because a gun is literally the power to kill. For years, I used to enjoy taunting my gun-nut friends about their psychosexual hangups—always in a spirit of good cheer, you understand. But letting the noisy minority in the National Rifle Association force us to allow this carnage to continue is just plain insane.

I do think gun nuts have a power hangup. I don't know what is missing in their psyches that they need to feel they have the power to kill. But no sane society would allow this to continue. 13

Ban the damn things. Ban them all. 14

You want protection? Get a dog. 15

Questions

About Unity

1. Which of the following statements best represents the implied thesis of the essay?

   a. The author is pro-knife.

   b. The Second Amendment is poorly understood.

   c. Despite arguments to the contrary, people without long training and discipline should not be allowed to have guns.

   d. In his novel *Jurassic Park*, Michael Crichton argues that power without discipline is making society a wreckage.

2. Which statement would best serve as a topic sentence for paragraphs 5 and 6?

   a. Drug dealers should not be allowed to purchase assault rifles.

   b. Ivins is interested in other people's points of view concerning gun ownership.

   c. Thomas Jefferson was opposed to the idea of a "well-regulated militia."

   d. Applying the original intent of the Second Amendment to modern circumstances is not so clear-cut and must be done with common sense.

3. Which sentence in paragraph 9 is the topic sentence of the paragraph?

   a. In truth, there is no rational argument for guns in this society.

   b. This is no longer a frontier nation in which people hunt their own food.

   c. It is a crowded, overwhelmingly urban country in which letting people have access to guns is a continuing disaster.

   d. Those who want guns . . . should be subject to the same restrictions placed on gun owners in England . . . .

About Support

4. Why does Ivins contrast the use of martial arts with the use of guns?

    a. To support the idea that gun owners should be required to study the martial arts

    b. To support the idea that a martial arts master can kill with his bare hands

    (c) To support the idea that power without discipline is dangerous

    d. To support the idea that guns are more practical than the martial arts

5. Which statement best expresses the implied point of paragraph 10?

    a. Guns don't really kill people.

    b. Many family arguments are surprisingly violent.

    (c) Many arguments end in death only because a gun was handy.

    d. Guns and cars are similar.

6. In what ways, according to Ivins, is the knife preferable to the gun? Is Ivins really "pro-knife," or is she making some other point in her discussion of knives versus guns?

    Knives promote physical fitness, don't ricochet, don't kill people cleaning them.

    No, she is not really pro-knife; her point is that guns are even more

    dangerous than knives. Answers may vary.

About Coherence

7. In paragraph 3, Ivins uses three addition signals—one to introduce each of her three reasons for being pro-knife. What are those three signals? (Two are *not* in the list of addition signals on page 81.)

    In the first place   *plus*   *and*

8. In paragraph 7, Ivins acknowledges an opposing point of view when she mentions that automobiles, like guns, "wreak great carnage." In paragraph 8, what sentence includes a "change of direction" signal indicating that Ivins will present her argument against that point of view? Write the first few words of that sentence.

    We do, however, license . . .

About the Introduction and Conclusion

9. Ivins's introduction consists of three very brief paragraphs. Which statement best describes the style of her introduction?

    a.   It presents an anecdote that is related to the topic of unregulated gun ownership.

    b.   It presents a provocative question that grabs the reader's attention.

    (c.) It makes a startling point that at first seems unrelated to the topic.

    d.   It presents a quotation that puts the topic in some sort of historical context.

10. Which of these best describes the conclusion of "Ban the Things"?

    (a.) It makes a blunt recommendation.

    b.   It asks a thought-provoking question.

    c.   It narrates an anecdote about guns.

    d.   It predicts what will happen if guns are not banned.

Writing an Argumentation Essay

■ Writing Assignment 1

Write a paper in which you argue *for* or *against* any one of the three comments below (options 1–3). Support and defend your argument by drawing on your reasoning ability and general experience.

Option 1:   In many ways, television has proved to be one of the worst inventions of modern times. All too often, television is harmful because of the shows it broadcasts and the way it is used in the home.

Option 2   Many of society's worst problems with drugs result from the fact that they are illegal. During Prohibition, Americans discovered that making popular substances unlawful causes more problems than it solves. Like alcohol and tobacco, drugs should be legal in this country.

Option 3   Statistics show that newly licensed teenage boys cause a higher number of serious automobile accidents than any other group. It is evident that many young men are too reckless and impulsive to be good drivers. In order to protect the larger society, the age at which a boy can earn his license should be raised to eighteen.

Prewriting

a Take a few minutes to think about the three options. Which one in particular are you for or against, and *why*?

b On a sheet of paper, make a brief outline of support for your position on one of the options. (Remember, you may choose to argue *against* one of the three comments, as well as for it.) Preparing the outline will give you a chance to think further about your position. And the outline will show whether you have enough support for your position. (If you find that you don't, choose another position and prepare another outline.)

c Next, decide how you will develop each of your three supporting points. Make up brief outlines of the three supporting paragraphs. In addition to preparing brief outlines, you may also want to use other prewriting techniques. You may want to freewrite or ask questions or make up lists.

d Decide in which order you want to present your paragraphs. *Emphatic order* (in which you *end* with your most important reason) is often the most effective way to organize an argument. Your reader is most likely to remember your final reason.

e As you write, think of your audience as a jury that will ultimately believe or disbelieve your argument. Have you presented a convincing case? Do you need more details? If *you* were on the jury, would you be favorably impressed with this argument?

f Proceed to write the first draft of your essay.

Rewriting

After you have completed the first draft of the paper, set it aside for a while (if possible). When you review it, try to do so as critically as you would if it were not your own work. Ask yourself these questions:

- Have I provided persuasive details to support my argument?
- Have I acknowledged the opposing point of view, showing that I am a reasonable person willing to consider other arguments?
- Is my language tactful and courteous? Have I avoided insulting anyone who doesn't agree with me?
- Have I used transition words to help readers follow my train of thought?
- Does my final supporting paragraph include a strong argument for my position?
- Have I provided a concluding paragraph to summarize my argument or add a final persuasive touch?

As you revise your essay through added drafts, continue to refer to this list until you can answer "yes" to each question. Then be sure to check the next-to-final draft of the paper for the sentence skills listed on the inside front cover.

■ Writing Assignment 2

Write a paper in which you argue *for* or *against* any one of the three comments below. Support and defend your argument by drawing on your reasoning ability and general experience.

Option 1 Giving students grades does more harm than good. Schools should replace grades with written evaluations of the student's strengths and weaknesses. These would benefit both students and parents.

Option 2 Jails are overcrowded. Furthermore, jails often function as "schools for crime" in which petty lawbreakers learn to become hardened criminals. Of course, it is necessary to put violent criminals in jail in order to protect others. But society would benefit if nonviolent criminals received punishments other than jail sentences.

Option 3 Physical punishment "works" in the sense that it may stop a child from misbehaving, but adults who frequently spank and hit are also teaching children that violence is a good method of accomplishing a goal. Nonviolent methods are a more effective way of training children.

Prewriting

a As you write your opening paragraph, acknowledge the opposing point of view before stating your thesis. If you have trouble figuring out what the "other side" would argue, completing this exercise will give you practice in acknowledging another way of looking at the question.

In each item, you will see a statement and then a question related to that statement. Write *two* answers to each question. Your first will answer "yes" to the question and briefly explain why. The other will answer "no" to the question, and also state why. The first item is done for you as an example:

1. Smoking has been proved to be bad for health. Should it therefore be made illegal?

    "Yes": *Because smoking has been shown to have so many negative effects on health, the sale of tobacco should be made illegal.*

    "No": *Although smoking has been linked to various health problems, adults should have the right to make their own decision about whether or not to smoke. Smoking should not be made illegal.*

2. Animals feel pain when they are killed for food. Is eating animals therefore immoral?

"Yes": _____

_____

"No": _____

_____

3. Professional boxing often leads to serious injury. Should it be outlawed?

"Yes": _____

_____

"No": _____

_____

4. Some high school students are sexually active. Should birth control devices and information be given out by high schools to their students?

"Yes": _____

_____

"No": _____

_____

b Make a list of the thoughts that support your argument. Don't worry about repetition, spelling, or grammar at this point. Just write down everything that occurs to you.

Once you have written down all the thoughts that occur to you, identify what you see as your strongest points. Select your three main supporting points. Are there other thoughts in your list that can be used as supporting details for those points?

c Write your three supporting paragraphs. Keep in mind that you are writing for an audience of people who, initially, will not all agree with you. It isn't enough to state your opinion. You must show *why* you feel as you do, persuading your reader that your point of view is valid.

d Your concluding paragraph is your final chance to persuade your readers to accept your argument. Consider ending with a prediction of what will happen if your point of view does not prevail. Will an existing situation grow worse? Will a new problem arise?

Rewriting

Follow the suggestions for rewriting provided on page 334.

■ Writing Assignment 3

In this argument essay, you will write with a specific purpose and for a specific audience.

Option 1 You'd like to live in a big city, but your parent or spouse refuses to budge from the suburbs. Write him or her a letter in which you argue the advantages of city life. Since the success of your argument will depend to some degree on how well you overcome the other person's objections to city life, be sure to address those as well. Use specific, colorful examples wherever possible.

Option 2 Find an editorial in your local newspaper that you either strongly agree with or strongly disagree with. Write a letter to the editor responding to that editorial. State why you agree or disagree with the position taken by the paper. Provide several short paragraphs of supporting evidence for your position. Actually send your letter to the newspaper. When you turn in a copy of your letter to your instructor, also turn in the editorial that you are responding to.

■ Writing Assignment 4

Write a paper in which you argue *for* or *against* any one of the three comments below. Support and defend your argument by drawing on your reasoning ability and general experience.

Option 1 Junk food is available in school cafeterias and school vending machines, and the cafeteria menus do not encourage the best of eating habits. But good education should include good examples as well as classwork. Schools should practice what they preach about a healthy diet and stop providing junk food.

Option 2 By the time many students reach high school, they have learned the basics in most subjects. Some still have much to gain from the education that high schools offer, but others might be better off spending the next four years in other ways. For their benefit, high school attendance should be voluntary.

Option 3 Many of today's young people are mainly concerned with prestigious careers, making money, and owning things. It seems we no longer teach the benefits of spending time and money to help the community, the country, or the world. Our country can strengthen these human values and improve the world by requiring young people to spend a year working in some type of community service.

Part Three
Special Skills

17 Taking Essay Exams

Essay exams are perhaps the most common type of writing you will do in school. They include one or more questions to which you must respond in detail, writing your answers in a clear, well-organized manner. Many students have trouble with essay exams because they do not realize there is a sequence to follow that will help them do well on such tests. This section describes five basic steps needed to prepare adequately for an essay test and to take the test. It is assumed, however, that you are already doing two essential things: first, attending class regularly and taking notes on what happens in class; second, reading your textbook and other assignments and taking notes on them. If you are *not* consistently going to class, reading your text, and taking notes in both cases, you are likely to have trouble with essay exams and other tests as well.

To write an effective exam essay, follow these five steps:

Step 1: Anticipate ten probable questions.

Step 2: Prepare and memorize an informal outline answer for each question.

Step 3: Look at the exam carefully and do several things.

Step 4: Prepare a brief, informal outline before writing your essay answer.

Step 5: Write a clear, well-organized essay.

The following pages explain and illustrate these steps.

Step 1: Anticipate Ten Probable Questions

Because exam time is limited, the instructor can give you only several questions to answer. He or she will, reasonably, focus on questions dealing with the most important areas of the subject. You can probably guess most of them.

Go through your class notes with a colored pen and mark off those areas where your instructor has spent a good deal of time. The more time spent on any one area, the better the chance you will get an essay question on it. If the instructor spent a week talking about present-day changes in the traditional family structure, or the importance of the carbon molecule, or the advantages of capitalism, or key early figures in the development of psychology as a science, you can reasonably expect that you will get a question on the emphasized area.

In both your class notes and your textbooks, pay special attention to definitions and examples and to basic lists of items (enumerations). Enumerations in particular are often a key to essay questions. For instance, if your instructor spoke at length about causes of the Great Depression, effects of water pollution, or advantages of capitalism, you should probably expect a question such as "What were the causes of the Great Depression?" or "What are the effects of water pollution?" or "What are the advantages of capitalism?"

If your instructor has given you study guides, look for probable essay questions there. (Some instructors choose essay questions from those listed in a study guide.) Look for clues to essay questions on any short quizzes that you may have been given. Finally, consider very carefully any review that the instructor provides. Always write down such reviews—your instructor has often made up the test or is making it up at the time of the review and is likely to give you valuable hints about it. Take advantage of them! Note also that if the instructor does not offer to provide a review, do not hesitate to *ask* for one in a friendly way. Essay questions are likely to come from areas the instructor may mention.

An Illustration of Step 1

A psychology class was given one day to prepare for an essay exam on stress—a subject that had been covered in class and comprised a chapter in the textbook for the course. One student, Mark, read carefully through his class notes and the textbook chapter. On the basis of the headings, major enumerations, and definitions he noted, he decided that there were five likely essay questions:

1. What are the common sources of stress?
2. What are the types of conflict?
3. What are the defense mechanisms that people use to cope with stress?
4. What effects can stress have on people?
5. What are the characteristics of the well-adjusted person?

Step 2: Prepare and Memorize an Informal Outline Answer for Each Question

Write out each question you have made up and, under it, list the main points that need to be discussed. Put important supporting information in parentheses after each main point. You now have an informal outline that you can memorize.

Pick out a *key word* in each part, and then create a *catchphrase* to help you remember the key words.

Note: If you have spelling problems, make up a list of words you might have to spell in writing your answers. For example, if you are having a psychology test on the principles of learning, you might want to study such terms as *conditioning, reinforcement, Pavlov, reflex, stimulus,* and so on.

An Illustration of Step 2

After identifying the likely questions on the exam, Mark made up an outline answer for each of the questions. For example, here is the outline answer that he made up for the first question:

Common sources of stress:
1. (Pressure) (internal and external)
2. (Anxiety) (sign of internal conflict)
3. (Frustration) (can't reach desired goal)
4. (Conflict) (three types of approach-avoidance)

   P A F C (People are funny creatures.)

Activity

See whether you can complete the following explanation of what Mark has done in preparing for the essay question.

First, Mark wrote down the heading and then numbered the sources of stress under it. Also, in parentheses beside each point he added __an explanation__ _____. Then he circled the four key words, and he wrote down the first _____letter_____ of each word underneath his outline. Mark then used the first letter in each key word to make up a catchphrase that he could easily remember. Finally, he _____tested_____ himself over and over until he could recall all four of the sources of stress that the first letters stood for. He also made sure that he recalled the supporting material that went with each idea.

Step 3: Look at the Exam Carefully and Do Several Things

1 Get an overview of the exam by reading *all* the questions on the test.

2 Note *direction words (compare, illustrate, list,* and so on) for each question. Be sure to write the kind of answer that each question requires. For example, if a question says "illustrate," do not "compare." The list on the opposite page will help clarify the distinctions among various direction words.

3 Budget your time. Write in the margin the number of minutes you should spend for each essay. For example, if you have three essays worth an equal number of points and a one-hour time limit, figure twenty minutes for each one. Make sure you are not left with only a couple of minutes to do a high-point essay.

4 Start with the easiest question. Getting a good answer down on paper will help build up your confidence and momentum. Number your answers plainly so your instructor knows what question you are answering first.

An Illustration of Step 3

When Mark received the exam, the question was, "Describe the four common sources of stress in our lives." Mark circled the direction word *describe,* which meant he should explain in detail each of the four causes of stress. He also jotted a "30" in the margin when the instructor said that students would have a half hour to write the answer.

Activity

Complete the short matching quiz below. It will help you review the meanings of some of the direction words listed on the following page.

1. List ___*b*___
2. Contrast ___*d*___
3. Define ___*e*___
4. Summarize ___*c*___
5. Describe ___*a*___

a. Tell in detail about something.

b. Give a series of points and number them 1, 2, 3, etc.

c. Give a condensed account of the main points.

d. Show differences between two things.

e. Give the normal meaning of a term.

Direction Words

Term	Meaning
Compare	Show similarities between things.
Contrast	Show differences between things.
Criticize	Give the positive and negative points of a subject as well as evidence for those positions.
Define	Give the formal meaning of a term.
Describe	Tell in detail about something.
Diagram	Make a drawing and label it.
Discuss	Give details and, if relevant, the positive and negative points of a subject as well as evidence for those positions.
Enumerate	List points and number them 1, 2, 3, etc.
Evaluate	Give the positive and negative points of a subject as well as your judgment about which outweighs the other and why.
Illustrate	Explain by giving examples.
Interpret	Explain the meaning of something.
Justify	Give reasons for something.
List	Give a series of points and number them 1, 2, 3, etc.
Outline	Give the main points and important secondary points. Put main points at the margin and indent secondary points under the main points. Relationships may also be described with logical symbols, as follows:

1. _____

    a. _____

    b. _____

2. _____

Prove	Show to be true by giving facts or reasons.
Relate	Show connections among things.
State	Give the main points.
Summarize	Give a condensed account of the main points.
Trace	Describe the development or history of a subject.

Step 4: Prepare a Brief, Informal Outline Before Writing Your Essay Answer

Use the margin of the exam or a separate piece of scratch paper to jot down quickly, as they occur to you, the main points you want to discuss in each answer. Then decide in what order you want to present these points in your response. Write 1 in front of the first item, 2 beside the second, and so on. You now have an informal outline to guide you as you answer your essay question.

If there is a question on the exam which is similar to the questions you anticipated and outlined at home, quickly write down the catchphrase that calls back the content of the outline. Below the catchphrase, write the key words represented by each letter in the catchphrase. The key words, in turn, will remind you of the concepts they represent. If you have prepared properly, this step will take only a minute or so, and you will have before you the guide you need to write a focused, supported, organized answer.

An Illustration of Step 4

Mark immediately wrote down his catchphrase, "People are funny creatures." He next jotted down the first letters in his catchphrase and then the key words that went with each letter. He then filled in several key details and was ready to write his essay answer. Here is what his brief outline looked like:

People are funny creatures.
P   Pressure (internal and external)
A   Anxiety (internal conflict)
F   Frustration (prevented from reaching goal)
C   Conflict (approach-avoidance)

Step 5: Write a Clear, Well-Organized Essay

If you have followed steps 1 through 4, you have done all the preliminary work needed to write an effective essay. Now, be sure not to wreck your chance of getting a good grade by writing carelessly. Keep in mind the principles of good writing: unity, support, coherence, and clear, error-free sentences.

First, start your essay with a sentence that clearly states what your answer will be about. Then make sure that everything in your paper relates to your opening statement.

Second, though you must obviously take time limitations into account, provide as much support as possible for each of your main points.

Third, use transitions to guide your reader through your answer. Words such as *first, next, then, however,* and *finally* make it easy to follow your thought.

Last, leave time to proofread your essay for sentence-skills mistakes you may have made while you concentrated on writing your answer. Look for words omitted, miswritten, or misspelled (if it is possible, bring a dictionary with you); look for awkward phrasings or misplaced punctuation marks; and look for whatever else may prevent the reader from understanding your thought. Cross out any mistakes and make your corrections neatly above the errors. If you want to change or add to some point, insert an asterisk at the appropriate spot, put another asterisk at the bottom of the page, and add the corrected material there.

An Illustration of Step 5

Read Mark's answer, reproduced below, and then do the activity that follows.

There are four common sources of stress in our lives. The first one is pressure, which can be internal or external. Internal pressure occurs when a person tries to live up to his or her own goals and standards. This kind of pressure can help (when a person strives to be a better musician, for instance) or hurt (as when someone tries to reach impossible standards of beauty). External pressure occurs when people must compete, deal with rapid change, or cope with outside demands. Another source of stress is anxiety. People who are anxious often don't know why they feel this way. Some psychologists think anxiety comes from some internal conflict, like feeling angry and trying hard to repress this anger. A third source of stress is frustration, which occurs when people are prevented from reaching goals or obtaining certain needs. For example, a woman may do poorly on an important exam because she has a bad cold. She feels angry and frustrated because she could not reach her goal of an A or B grade. The most common source of stress is conflict. Conflict results when a person is faced with two incompatible desires. The person may want both goals (a demanding career and motherhood, for instance). This is called approach/approach. Or a person may want to avoid both choices (avoidance/avoidance). Or a person may be both attracted to and repelled by a desire (as a woman who wants to marry a gambler). This is approach/avoidance.

Activity 1

The following sentences comment on Mark's essay. Fill in the missing word or words in each case.

1. Mark begins with a sentence that clearly states what his paper _is about_

    _____. Always begin with such a clear statement!

2. Notice the _corrections_ that Mark made when writing and proof-reading his paper. He neatly crossed out miswritten or unwanted words, and he used insertion signs (^) to add omitted words.

3. The four signal words that Mark used to guide his readers, and himself,

    through the main points of his answer are _first_,

    Another, _third_, and _most common_.

Activity 2   Answers will vary.

1. Make up five questions you might be expected to answer on an essay exam for a course in a social or physical science (sociology, psychology, biology, or other).

2. For each of the five questions, make up an outline answer comparable to the one on anxiety.

3. Finally, write a full essay answer, in complete sentences, to one of the questions. Your outline will serve as your guide.

Be sure to begin your essay with a statement that makes clear the direction of your answer. An example might be, "The six major defense mechanisms are defined and illustrated below." If you are explaining in detail the different causes of, reasons for, or characteristics of something, you may want to develop each point in a separate paragraph. For example, if you were answering a question in sociology about the primary functions of the family unit, you could start with the statement, "There are three primary functions of the family unit," and go on to develop and describe each function in a separate paragraph.

You will turn in the essay answer to your English instructor, who will evaluate it using the standards for effective writing applied to your other written assignments.

18 Writing a Summary

At some point in a course, your instructor may ask you to write a summary of a book, an article, a TV show, or the like. In a *summary* (also referred to as a *précis* or an *abstract*), you reduce material in an original work to its main points and key supporting details. Unlike an outline, however, a summary does not use symbols such as I, A, 1, 2, etc., to indicate the relations among parts of the original material.

A summary may consist of a single word, a phrase, several sentences, or one or more paragraphs. The length of any summary you prepare will depend on your instructor's expectations and the length of the original work. Most often, you will be asked to write a summary consisting of one or more paragraphs.

Writing a summary brings together a number of important reading, study, and writing skills. To condense the original assigned material, you must preview, read, evaluate, organize, and perhaps outline it. Summarizing, then, can be a real aid to understanding; you must "get inside" the material and realize fully what is being said before you can reduce its meaning to a few words.

How to Summarize an Article

To write a summary of an article, follow the steps described below. If the assigned material is a TV show or film, adapt the suggestions accordingly.

1 Take a few minutes to preview the work. You can preview an article in a magazine by taking a quick look at the following:

   a *Title.* A title often summarizes what an article is about. Think about the title for a minute, and about how it may condense the meaning of the article.

   b *Subtitle.* A subtitle, if given, is a short summary appearing under or next to the title. For example, in a *Newsweek* article entitled "Growing Old, Feeling Young," the following caption appeared: "Not only are Americans living longer, they are staying active longer—and their worst enemy is not nature, but the myths and prejudices about growing old." In short, the subtitle, the caption, or any other words in large print under or next to the title often provide a quick insight into the meaning of an article.

   c *First and last several paragraphs.* In the first several paragraphs, the author may introduce you to the subject and state the purpose of the article. In the last several paragraphs, the writer may present conclusions or a summary. The previews or summaries can give you a quick overview of what the entire article is about.

d *Other items.* Note any heads or subheads that appear in the article. They often provide clues to the article's main points and give an immediate sense of what each section is about. Look carefully at any pictures, charts, or diagrams that accompany the article. Page space in a magazine or journal is limited, and such visual aids are generally used only when they help illustrate important points in the article. Note any words or phrases set off in *italic type* or **boldface print;** such words have probably been emphasized because they deal with important points in the article.

2 Read the article for all you can understand the first time through. Do not slow down or turn back. Check or otherwise mark main points and key supporting details. Pay special attention to all the items noted in the preview. Also, look for definitions, examples, and enumerations (lists of items), as they often indicate key ideas. You can also identify important points by turning any heads into questions and reading to find the answers to the questions.

3 Go back and reread more carefully the areas you have identified as most important. Also, focus on other key points you may have missed in your first reading.

4 Take notes on the material. Concentrate on getting down the main ideas and the key supporting points.

5 Prepare the first draft of your summary, keeping these points in mind:

   a Identify at the start of the summary the title and author of the work. Include in parentheses the date of publication. For example, "In 'Beyond the Gender Myths' (*Time,* October 19, 1998), Margot Hornblower states . . ."

   b Do not write an overly detailed summary. Remember that the purpose of a summary is to reduce the original work to its main points and essential supporting details.

   c Express the main points and key supporting details in your own words. Do not imitate the style of the original work.

   d Quote from the material only to illustrate key points. Also, limit your quotations. A one-paragraph summary should not contain more than one or two quoted sentences.

   e Preserve the balance and proportion of the original work. If the original devoted 70 percent of its space to one idea and only 30 percent to another, your summary should reflect that emphasis.

   f Revise your first draft, paying attention to the principles of effective writing (*unity, support, coherence,* and *clear, error-free sentences*) explained in Part One.

   g Write the final draft of the paper.

A Model Summary of an Article

Here is a model summary of a magazine article.

> In "Beyond the Gender Myths" (<u>Time</u>, October 19, 1998), Margot Hornblower reports on a growing interest in the educational needs of girls and boys. In the early 1990s, researchers found that the education system shortchanged and harmed girls. Various creative solutions included Take Our Daughters to Work Day, which encourages girls to consider varied careers. Teachers also devised programs to help girls progress in math and science, stereotypical male fields. Another approach has been segregated schools and classrooms for girls only. In reaction to the programs for girls, parents and researchers are saying that solutions must also be found for special problems boys face, such as restlessness in class. Despite the gender-specific agendas, writes Hornblower, a recent report found that "what helps girls is what helps boys: smaller classes, a demanding curriculum, and encouragement." Another researcher found that successful math and science teachers shared certain techniques: allowing no disrespect, using a variety of instruction methods, and dividing their attention equally among students. Educational advocates agree that stereotyping should be ended for both genders. Then, writes Hornblower, "teachers can concentrate on paying more nuanced attention to our children as individuals."

Activity 1

Write an essay-length summary of the following article. Include a short introductory paragraph that states the thesis of the article. Then summarize in your three supporting paragraphs the three important areas in which study skills can be useful. Your conclusion might be a single sentence restating the thesis.

Power Learning

Jill had not done as well in high school as she had hoped. Since college involved even more work, it was no surprise that she didn't do better there. 1

The reason for her so-so performance was not a lack of effort. She attended most of her classes and read her textbooks. And she never missed handing in any assignment, even though it often meant staying up late the night before homework was due. Still, she just got by in her classes. Before long, she came to the conclusion that she simply couldn't do any better. 2

Then one day, one of her instructors said something to make her think otherwise. "You can probably build some sort of house by banging a few boards together," he said. "But if you want a sturdy home, you'll have to use the right techniques and tools. Building carefully takes work, but it gets 3 better results. The same can be said of your education. There are no short-cuts, but there are some proven study skills that can really help. If you don't use them, you may end up with a pretty flimsy education."

Jill signed up for a study-skills course and found out a crucial fact—that 4
learning how to learn is the key to success in school. There are certain depend-able skills that have made the difference between disappointment and success for generations of students. These techniques won't free you from work, but they will make your work far more productive. They include three important areas: time control, classroom note-taking, and textbook study.

Time Control

Success in college depends on time control. *Time control* means that you 5
deliberately organize and plan your time, instead of letting it drift by. Planning means that you should never be faced with a night-before-the-test "cram" session or an overdue term paper.

There are three steps involved in time control. *First,* you should prepare 6
a large monthly calendar. Buy a calendar with a large white block around each date, or make one yourself. At the beginning of the college semester, circle important dates on this calendar. Circle the days on which tests are scheduled; circle the days when papers are due. This calendar can also be used to schedule study plans. At the beginning of the week, you can jot down your plans for each day. An alternative method would be to make plans for each day the night before. On Tuesday night, for example, you might write down "Read Chapter 5 in psychology" in the Wednesday block. Hang this calendar where you will see it every day—your kitchen, bedroom, even your bathroom!

The *second step* in time control is to have a weekly study schedule for the 7
semester—a chart that covers all the days of the week and all the waking hours in each day. Below is part of one student's schedule:

Time	Mon.	Tues.	Wed.	Thurs.	Fri.	Sat.	Sun.
6:00 A.M.							
7:00	B	B	B	B	B		
8:00	Math	STUDY	Math	STUDY	Math		
9:00	STUDY	Biology	STUDY	Biology	STUDY	Job	
10:00	Psychology	↓	Psychology	↓	Psychology		
11:00	STUDY	English		English			
12:00	L		L	↓	L	↓	

On your own schedule, mark in all the fixed hours in each day—hours for meals, classes, job (if any), and travel time. Next, mark in time blocks that you can *realistically* use for study each day. Depending on the number of courses you are taking and the demands of the courses, you may want to block off five, ten, or even twenty or more hours of study time a week. Keep in mind that you should not block off time that you do not truly intend to use for study. Otherwise, your schedule will be a meaningless gimmick. Also, remember that you should allow time for "rest and relaxation." You will be happiest, and able to accomplish the most, when you have time for both work and play.

The *third step* in time control is to make a daily or weekly "to do" list. 8 This may be the most valuable time control method you ever use. On this list, you write down the things you need to do for the following day or the following week. If you choose to write a weekly list, do it on Sunday night. If you choose to write a daily list, do it the night before. Here is part of one student's daily list:

To Do   Tuesday
 *1.   Review biology notes before class
 *2.   Proofread English paper due today
  3.   See Dick about game on Friday
 *4.   Gas for car
  5.   Read next chapter of psychology text

You may use a three- by five-inch note pad or a small spiral-bound notebook for this list. Carry the list around with you during the day. Always concentrate on doing the most important items first. To make the best use of your time, mark high-priority items with an asterisk and give them precedence over low-priority items. For instance, you may find yourself wondering what to do after dinner on Thursday evening. Among the items on your list are "Clean inside of car" and "Review chapter for math quiz." It is obviously more important for you to review your notes at this point; you can clean out the car some other time. As you complete items on your "to do" list, cross them out. Do not worry about unfinished items. They can be rescheduled. You will still be accomplishing a great deal and making more effective use of your time.

Classroom Note-Taking

One of the most important single things you can do to perform well in 9
a college course is to take effective class notes. The following hints should
help you become a better note-taker.

First, attend class faithfully. Your alternatives—reading the text, reading 10
someone else's notes, or both—cannot substitute for the class experience
of hearing ideas in person as someone presents them to you. Also, in class
lectures and discussions, your instructor typically presents and develops the
main ideas and facts of the course—the ones you will be expected to know
on exams.

Another valuable hint is to make use of abbreviations while taking notes. 11
Using abbreviations saves time when you are trying to get down a great deal
of information. Abbreviate terms that recur frequently in a lecture and put
a key to your abbreviations at the top of your notes. For example, in sociology
class, *eth* could stand for *ethnocentrism;* in a psychology class, STM could
stand for *short-term memory.* (When a lecture is over, you may want to go
back and write out the terms you have abbreviated.) Also, use e for *example; def* for *definition; info* for *information;* + for *and;* and so on. If you use
the same abbreviations all the time, you will soon develop a kind of personal
shorthand that makes taking notes much easier.

A third hint for taking notes is to be on the lookout for signals of 12
importance. Write down whatever your instructor puts on the board. If he
or she takes the time to put material on the board, it is probably important,
and the chances are good that it will come up later on exams. Always write
down definitions and enumerations. Enumerations are lists of items. They are
signaled in such ways as: "The four steps in the process are . . ."; "There were
three reasons for . . ."; "The two effects were . . ."; "Five characteristics of
. . ."; and so on. In your notes, always number such enumerations (1, 2, 3, etc.).
They will help you understand relationships among ideas and organize the
material of the lecture. Watch for emphasis words—words your instructor
may use to indicate that something is important. Examples of such words are
"This is an important reason . . ."; "A point that will keep coming up later
. . ."; "The chief cause was . . ."; "The basic idea here is . . ."; and so on. Always
write down the important statements announced by these and other emphasis words. Finally, if your instructor repeats a point, you can assume that it is
important. You might put an R for *repeated* in the margin, so that later you
will know that your instructor stressed it.

Next, be sure to write down the instructor's examples and mark them 13
with an e. The examples help you understand abstract points. If you do not
write them down, you are likely to forget them later, when they are needed
to help make sense of an idea.

Also, be sure to write down the connections between ideas. Too many 14
students merely copy terms the instructor puts on the board. They forget that,
as time passes, the details that serve as connecting bridges between ideas
quickly fade. You should, then, write down the relationships and connections
in class. That way you'll have them to help tie together your notes later on.

Review your notes as soon as possible after class. You must make them 15
as clear as possible while they are fresh in your mind. A day later may be too
late, because forgetting sets in very quickly. Make sure that punctuation is
clear, that all words are readable and correctly spelled, and that unfinished
sentences are completed (or at least marked off so that you can check your
notes with another student's). Add clarifying or connecting comments
wherever necessary. Make sure that important ideas are clearly marked.
Improve the organization if necessary, so that you can see at a glance main
points and relationships among them.

Finally, try in general to get down a written record of each class. You must 16
do this because forgetting begins almost immediately. Studies have shown
that within two weeks you are likely to have forgotten 80 percent or more
of what you have heard. And in four weeks you are lucky if 5 percent remains!
This is so crucial that it bears repeating: To guard against the relentlessness
of forgetting, it is absolutely essential that you write down what you hear in
class. Later you can concentrate on working to understand fully and to
remember the ideas that have been presented in class. And then, the more
complete your notes are, the more you are likely to learn.

Textbook Study

In many college courses, success means being able to read and study a 17
textbook skillfully. For many students, unfortunately, textbooks are heavy
going. After an hour or two of study, the textbook material is as formless and
as hard to understand as ever. But there is a way to attack even the most
difficult textbook and make sense of it. Use a sequence in which you preview
a chapter, mark it, take notes on it, and then study the notes.

Previewing

Previewing a selection is an important first step to understanding. Taking 18
the time to preview a section or chapter can give you a bird's-eye view of the
way the material is organized. You will have a sense of where you are beginning, what you will cover, and where you will end.

There are several steps in previewing a selection. First, study the title. The 19
title is the shortest possible summary of a selection and will often tell you the
limits of the material you will cover. For example, the title "FDR and the
Supreme Court" tells you to expect a discussion of President Roosevelt's deal-
ings with the Court. You know that you will probably not encounter any

material dealing with FDR's foreign policies or personal life. Next, quickly read over the first and last paragraphs of the selection; these may contain important introductions to, and summaries of, the main ideas. Then briefly examine the headings and subheadings in the selection. Together, the headings and subheadings are a mini-outline of what you are reading. Headings are often main ideas or important concepts in capsule form; subheadings are breakdowns of ideas within main areas. Finally, read the first sentence of some paragraphs, look for words set off in **boldface** or *italics,* and look at pictures or diagrams. After you have previewed a selection in this way, you should have a good general sense of the material to be read.

Marking

You should mark a textbook selection at the same time that you read it 20 through carefully. Use a felt-tip highlighter to shade material that seems important, or use a ballpoint pen and put symbols in the margin next to the material: stars, checks, or NB (*nota bene,* Latin for "note well"). What to mark is not as mysterious as some students believe. You should try to find main ideas by looking for clues: definitions and examples, enumerations, and emphasis words.

1   *Definitions and examples:* Definitions are often among the most impor- 21 tant ideas in a selection. They are particularly significant in introductory courses in almost any subject area, where much of your learning involves mastering the specialized vocabulary of that subject. In a sense, you are learning the "language" of psychology or business or whatever the subject might be.

Most definitions are abstract, and so they usually are followed by one 22 or more examples to help clarify their meaning. Always mark off definitions and at least one example that makes a definition clear to you. In a psychology text, for example, we are told that "rationalization is an attempt to reduce anxiety by deciding that you have not really been frustrated." Several examples follow, among them: "A young man, frustrated because he was rejected when he asked for a date, convinces himself that the girl is not very attractive or interesting."

2   *Enumerations:* Enumerations are lists of items (causes, reasons, types, and 23 so on) that are numbered 1, 2, 3, . . . or that could easily be numbered. They are often signaled by addition words. Many of the paragraphs in this book, for instance, use words like *First of all, Another, In addition,* and *Finally* to signal items in a series. Other textbooks also use this very common and effective organizational method.

3   *Emphasis words:* Emphasis words tell you that an idea is important. 24 Common emphasis words include phrases such as *a major event, a key feature, the chief factor, important to note, above all,* and *most of all.* Here is an example: "The most significant contemporary use of marketing is its application to nonbusiness areas, such as political parties."

Note-Taking

Next, you should take notes. Go through the chapter a second time, 25 rereading the most important parts. Try to write down the main ideas in a simple outline form. For example, in taking notes on a psychology selection, you might write down the heading "Defense Mechanisms." Below the heading you would define them, number and describe each kind, and give an example of each.

Defense Mechanisms
a. Definition: unconscious attempts to reduce anxiety
b. Kinds:
   (1) Rationalization: An attempt to reduce anxiety by deciding that you have not really be frustrated.
      Example: A man turned down for a date decides that the woman was not worth going out with anyway.
   (2) Projection: Projecting onto other people motives or thoughts of one's own.
      Example: A wife who wants to have an affair accuses her husband of having one.

Studying Notes

To study your notes, use the method of repeated self-testing. For 26 example, look at the heading "Defense Mechanisms" and say to yourself, "What are the kinds of defense mechanisms?" When you can recite them, then say to yourself, "What is rationalization?" "What is an example of rationalization?" Then ask yourself, "What is projection?" "What is an example of projection?" After you learn each section, review it, and then go on to the next section.

Do not simply read your notes; keep looking away and seeing if you can 27 recite them to yourself. This self-testing is the key to effective learning.

Summary: Textbook Study

In summary, remember this sequence for dealing with a textbook: 28 preview, mark, take notes, study the notes. Approaching a textbook in this methodical way will give you very positive results. You will no longer feel bogged down in a swamp of words, unable to figure out what you are supposed to know. Instead, you will understand exactly what you have to do, and how to go about doing it.

Take a minute now to evaluate your own study habits. Do you practice 29 many of the above skills in order to take effective classroom notes, control your time, and learn from your textbooks? If not, perhaps you should. The skills are not magic, but they are too valuable to ignore. Use them carefully and consistently, and they will make academic success possible for you. Try them, and you won't need convincing.

Activity 2

Write an essay-length summary of a broadcast of the CBS television show *Sixty Minutes*. In your first sentence, include the date of the show. For example, "The December 7, 1999, broadcast of CBS's *Sixty Minutes* dealt with three subjects most people would find of interest. The first segment of the show centered on . . . ; the second segment examined . . . ; the final segment discussed . . . ." Be sure to use parallel form in describing the three segments of the show. Then summarize each segment in the three supporting paragraphs that follow.

Activity 3

Write an essay-length summary of a cover story of interest to you in a recent issue of *Time, Newsweek,* or *U.S. News and World Report.*

How to Summarize a Book

To write a summary of a book, first preview the book by briefly looking at:

1 *Title.* A title is often the shortest possible summary of what a book is about. Think about the title and how it may summarize the whole book.

2 *Table of contents.* The contents will tell you the number of chapters in the book and the subject of each chapter. Use the contents to get a general sense of how the book is organized. You should also note the number of pages in each chapter. If thirty pages are devoted to one episode or idea and an average of fifteen pages to other episodes or ideas, you should probably give more space in your summary to the contents of the longer chapter .

3 *Preface.* Here you will probably find out why the author wrote the book. Also, the preface may summarize the main ideas developed in the book and may describe briefly how the book is organized.

4 *First and last chapters.* In these chapters, the author may preview or review important ideas and themes developed in the book.

5 *Other items.* Note how the author has used headings and subheadings to organize information in the book. Check the opening and closing paragraphs of each chapter to see if they contain introduction or summaries. Look quickly at charts, diagrams, and pictures in the book, since they are probably there to illustrate key points. Note any special features (index, glossary, appendixes) that may appear at the end of the book.

Next, adapt steps 2 through 5 for summarizing an article on pages 349–350.

Activity

Write an essay-length summary of a book you have read.

19 Writing a Report

Each semester, you will probably be asked by at least one instructor to read a book or an article and write a paper recording your response to the material. In these reports or reaction papers, your instructor will most likely expect you to do two things: *summarize the material* and *detail your reaction to it.* The following pages explain both parts of a report.

Part 1 of a Report: A Summary of the Work

To develop the first part of a report, do the following. (An example follows, on page 361.)

1 Identify the author and title of the work and include in parentheses the publisher and publication date. With magazines, give the date of publication.

2 Write an informative summary of the material. Condense the content of the work by highlighting its main points and key supporting points. (See pages 349–358 for a complete discussion of summarizing techniques.) Use direct quotations from the work to illustrate important ideas.

   Do *not* discuss in great detail any single aspect of the work while neglecting to mention other equally important points. Summarize the material so that the reader gets a general sense of *all* key aspects of the original work. Also, keep the summary objective and factual. Do not include in the first part of the paper your personal reaction to the work; your subjective impression will form the basis of the second part of the paper.

Part 2 of a Report: Your Reaction to the Work

To develop the second part of a report, do the following:

1 Focus on any or all of the questions that follow. (Check with your instructors to see if they want you to emphasize specific points.)

   a How is the assigned work related to ideas and concerns discussed in the course? For example, what points made in the course textbook, class discussions, or lectures are treated more fully in the work?

b How is the work related to problems in our present-day world?

c How is the work related to your life, experiences, feelings, and ideas? For instance, what emotions did it arouse in you? Did it increase your understanding of an issue or change your perspective?

2 Evaluate the merit of the work: the importance of its points; its accuracy, completeness, and organization; and so on. You should also indicate here whether you would recommend the work to others, and why.

Points to Keep in Mind When Writing a Report

Here are some important matters to consider as you prepare a report.

1 Apply the four basic standards of effective writing (unity, support, coherence, and clear, error-free sentences).

a Make sure each major paragraph presents and then develops a single main point. For example, in the model report that follows, a paragraph summarizes the book, and the three paragraphs that follow detail three separate reactions that the student writer had. The student then closes the report with a short concluding paragraph.

b Support with specific reasons and details any general points or attitudes you express. Statements such as "I agreed with many ideas in this article" and "I found the book very interesting" are meaningless without specific evidence that shows why you feel as you do. Look at the model report to see how the main point or topic sentence of each paragraph is developed by specific supporting evidence.

c Organize the material in the paper. Follow the basic *plan of organization* already described: an introduction, a summary consisting of one or more paragraphs, a reaction consisting of two or more paragraphs, and a conclusion. Use *transitions* to connect the parts of the paper.

d Proofread the paper for grammar, mechanics, punctuation, and word use.

2 Document quotations from all works by placing the page number in parentheses after the quoted material (see the model report). You may use quotations in the summary and reaction parts of the paper, but do not rely too much on them. Use them only to emphasize key ideas.

A Model Report

Here is a report written by a student in an introductory sociology source. Look at the paper closely to see how it follows the guidelines for report writing described in this chapter.

A Report on <u>I Know Why the Caged Bird Sings</u>

Introductory paragraph

In <u>I Know Why the Caged Bird Sings</u> (New York: Bantam Books, 1971), Maya Angelou tells the story of her earliest years. Angelou, a dancer, poet, and television producer as well as a writer, has continued her life story in three more volumes of autobiography. <u>I Know Why the Caged Bird Sings</u> is the start of Mayo Angelou's story; in this book, she writes with crystal clarity about the pains and joys of being black in America.   1

PART 1: SUMMARY Topic sentence for summary paragraph

<u>I Know Why the Caged Bird Sings</u> covers Maya Angelou's life from age three to age sixteen. We first meet her as a gawky little girl in a white woman's cut-down lavender silk dress. She has forgotten the poem she had memorized for the Easter service, and all she can do is rush out of the church. At this point, Angelou is living in Stamps, Arkansas, with her grandmother and uncle. The town is heavily segregated: "People in Stamps used to say that the whites in our town were so prejudiced that a Negro couldn't buy vanilla ice cream" (40). Yet Angelou has some good things in her life: her adored older brother Bailey, her success in school, and her pride in her grandmother's quiet strength and importance in the black community. There is laughter, too, as when the preacher is interrupted in midsermon by an overly enthusiastic woman shouting, "Preach it, I say preach it!" The woman, in a frenzied rush of excitement, hits the preacher with her purse, making his false teeth fly out of his mouth and land at Angelou's feet. Shortly after this incident, Angelou and her brother are taken by her father to live in California with their mother. Here, at age eight, she is raped by her mother's boyfriend, who is mysteriously murdered after receiving only a suspended sentence for his crime. She returns, silent and withdrawn, to Stamps, where the gloom is broken when a friend of her mother introduces her to the magic of great books. Later, at age thirteen, Angelou returns to California. She learns how to dance. She runs away after a violent family fight and lives for a month in a junkyard. She becomes the first black female to get a job on the San Francisco streetcars. She graduates from high school eight months pregnant. And she survives.   2

PART 2: REACTION Topic sentence for first reaction paragraph

I was impressed with the vividness of Maya Angelou's writing style. For example, she describes the lazy dullness of her life in Stamps: "Weekdays revolved in a sameness wheel. They turned into themselves so steadily and inevitably that each seemed to be the original of yesterday's rough draft" (93). She also knows how to bring a scene to life, as when she describes her eighth-grade graduation. For months, she has been looking forward to this   3 event, knowing she will be honored for her academic successes. She is even happy with her appearance: her hair has become pretty, and her yellow dress is a miracle of hand-sewing. But the ceremony is spoiled when the speaker—a white man—implies that the only success available to blacks is in athletics. Angelou remembers: "The man's dead words fell like bricks around the auditorium and too many settled in my belly. . . . The proud graduating class of 1940 had dropped their heads" (152). Later, Angelou uses a crystal-clear image to describe her father's mistress sewing: "She worked the thread through the flowered cloth as if she were sewing the torn ends of her life together" (208). With such vivid details and figures of speech, Maya Angelou re-creates her life for her readers.

Topic sentence for second reaction paragraph → I also reacted strongly to the descriptions of injustices suffered by blacks two generations ago. I was as horrified as the seven-year-old Maya when some "powhitetrash" girls torment her dignified grandmother, calling her "Annie" and mimicking her mannerisms. In another incident. Mrs. Cullinan, Angelou's white employer, decides that Marguerite (Angelou's real name) is too difficult to pronounce and so renames her Mary. This loss of her name—a "hellish horror" (91)—is another humiliation suffered at white hands, and Angelou leaves Mrs. Cullinan's employ soon afterward. Later, Angelou encounters overt discrimination when a white dentist tells her grandmother, "Annie, my policy is I'd rather stick my hand in a dog's mouth than in a nigger's" (160)—and only slightly less obvious prejudice when the streetcar company refuses to accept her application for a conductor's job. We see Angelou over and over as the victim of a white society.   4

Topic sentence for third reaction paragraph → Although I was saddened to read about the injustices, I rejoiced in Angelou's triumphs. Angelou is thrilled when she hears the radio broadcast of Joe Louis's victory over Primo Carnera: "A Black boy. Some Black mother's son. He was the strongest man in the world" (114). She weeps with pride when the class valedictorian leads her and her fellow eighth-graders in singing the Negro National Anthem. And there are personal victories, too. One of these comes after her father has gotten drunk in a small Mexican town. Though she has never driven before, she manages to get her father into the car and drives fifty miles through the night as he lies intoxicated in the backseat. Finally, she rejoices in the birth of her son: "He was beautiful and mine. Totally mine. No one had bought him for me" (245). Angelou shows us, through these examples, that she is proud of her race—and of herself.   5

Concluding paragraph → I Know Why the Caged Bird Sings is a remarkable book. Angelou could have been just another casualty of race prejudice. Yet by using her intelligence, sensitivity, and determination, she succeeds in spite of the odds against her. And by writing with such power, she makes us share her defeats and joys. She also teaches us a vital lesson: with strength and persistence, we can all escape our cages—and sing our songs.   6

Activity 1

Read a magazine article that interests you. Then write a report on the article. Include an introduction, a one-paragraph summary, a reaction (consisting of one or more paragraphs), and a brief conclusion. You may, if you like, quote briefly from the article. Be sure to enclose the words that you take from the article in quotation marks and put the page number in parentheses at the end of the quoted material.

Activity 2

Read a book suggested by your instructor. Then write a report on the book. Include an introduction, a one-paragraph summary, a reaction consisting of one or more paragraphs, and a brief conclusion. Make sure that each major paragraph in your report develops a single main point. You may quote some sentences from the book, but they should be only a small part of your report. When you quote material, follow the directions in Activity 1 above.

20 Writing a Résumé and Job Application Letter

When applying for a job through the mail, you should ordinarily send (1) a résumé and (2) a letter of application.

Résumé

A résumé is a summary of your personal background and your qualifications for a job. It helps your potential employer see at a glance whether you are suited for a job opening. A sample job résumé follows.

ERIC KURLAND
27 Hawkins Road
Clarksboro, New Jersey 08020
609-723-2166

Professional objective	A challenging position in the computer technology field.
Education	1996 to present: Rowan University, Glassboro, New Jersey 08028
	Degree: B.S. (in June)
Major courses:	Introduction to Computer Science I and II Data Structures and Algorithms I and II Programming Languages Programming in Pascal Assembly Language Operating Systems I and II

<u>Related courses</u>:	Introduction to Discrete Mathematics I and II Calculus I and II Logic Entrepreneurship and Small Business Management Business Law Organizational Behavior
<u>Special school project</u>	As part of a class project, I chaired a study group which advised a local business about the advantages of installing a computerized payroll system. We projected comparative cost figures, developed a time-sharing purchase plan, and prepared a budget. The fifteen-page report received the highest grade in the class.
<u>Work experience</u>	1997 to present: As a salesperson at Radio Shack, I am involved in sales, inventory control, repairs, and customer relations. I have designed a computer program that our store uses to demonstrate the multimedia aspects of a personal computer. This program, written in Visual Basic, demonstrates ways the Compaq Presario 5062 can be used in the home and small businesses. 1994–1997: My temporary jobs included word processing secretary, theater usher, and child care aide.
<u>Skills</u>	I am experienced in the following computer languages: C++, Visual Basic, Pascal, and COBOL. I have sales experience, am good with figures, am detail-oriented, relate easily to people, have initiative, and am dependable.
<u>References</u>	My references are available on request from Rowan University Placement Office, Glassboro, New Jersey 08028.

Points to Note about the Résumé

1 Your résumé, along with your letter of application, is your introduction to a potential employer. First impressions count, so *make the résumé neat!*

   a Type the résumé on good-quality letter (8½ by 11 inches) paper. If possible, prepare your résumé on a computer; if you don't have access to a computer, you can use a résumé service listed in the yellow pages of the telephone directory.

b   Proofread *very carefully* for sentence-skills and spelling mistakes. A potential employer may regard such mistakes as signs of carelessness in your character. You might even want to get someone else to proofread the résumé for you. If you are using word-processing software, see if it has a "spell-check" feature.

c   Be brief and to the point: use only one page if possible.

d   Use a format like that of the model résumé (see also the variations described ahead). Balance your résumé on the page so that you have roughly the same margin on all sides.

e   Note that you should start with your most recent education or employment and work backward in time.

2   Your résumé should point up strengths, not weaknesses. Don't include "Special Training" if you have had none. Don't refer to your grade point average if it's a low C.

On the other hand, include a main heading like "Extracurricular Activities" if the activities or awards seem relevant. For example, if Eric Kurland had been a member of the Management Club or vice president of the Computer Club in high school or college, he should have mentioned those facts.

If you have no work experience related to the job for which you're applying, then list the jobs you have had. Any job that shows a period of responsible employment may favorably impress a potential employer.

3   You can list the names of your references directly on the résumé. Be sure to get the permission of people you cite before listing their names.

You can also give the address of a placement office file that holds references, as shown on the model résumé.

Or you can simply say that you will provide references on request.

Job Application Letter

The purpose of the letter of application that goes with your résumé is to introduce yourself briefly and to try to make an employer interested in you. You should include only the high points of the information about yourself given in the résumé.

Following is the letter of application that Eric Kurland sent with his résumé.

27 Hawkins Road
Clarksboro, New Jersey 08020
May 13, 1999

Mr. George C. Arline
Personnel Manager, Indesco Associates
301 Sharptown Road
White Plains, New York 10019

Dear Mr. Arline:

   I would like to be considered as a candidate for the assistant computer programmer position advertised in the <u>Philadelphia Inquirer</u> on April 28, 1999.

   I am currently finishing my degree in Computer Science at Rowan University. I have taken every required computer course offered at Rowan and have a solid background in the following computer languages: C++, Visual Basic, Pascal, and COBOL. In addition to my computer background, I have supplemented my education with business and mathematics courses.

   My knowledge of computers and the business field goes beyond my formal classroom education. For the past two years I have worked part time at Radio Shack, where I have gained experience in sales and inventory control. Also, on my own initiative, I designed a demonstration program for the Compaq Presario 5062 and developed promotional fliers about the program.

   In short, I believe I have the up-to-date computer background and professional drive needed to contribute to your organization. I have enclosed a copy of my résumé to give you further details about my experience. Sometime next week, I'll plan to give you a call to see whether I can come in for an interview at your convenience. I look forward to speaking with you then.

                              Sincerely,

                              Eric Kurland
                              Eric Kurland

Points to Note about the Job Application Letter

1   Your letter should do the following:

    a   In the first paragraph, state that you are an applicant for a job and identify the source through which you learned about the job.

        Here is how Eric Kurland's letter might have opened if his source had been the college placement office. "I learned through the placement office at Rowan University of the assistant computer programmer position at your company. I would like to be considered as a candidate for the job."

        Sometimes an ad will list only a box number (such as Y 172) to reply to. Your inside address should then be:

Y 172
Philadelphia Inquirer
Philadelphia, Pennsylvania 19101

Dear Sir or Madam:

    b   In the second paragraph, state briefly your qualifications for the job and refer the reader to your résumé.

    c   In the last paragraph, state your willingness to come for an interview. If you can be available for an interview only at certain times, indicate this.

2   As with your résumé, neatness is crucial. Follow the same hints for the letter that you did for the résumé.

    a   Type the letter on good paper.

    b   Proofread *very carefully* for sentence-skills mistakes and spelling mistakes. Use the checklist of sentence skills on the inside front cover.

    c   Be brief and to the point: use no more than one page.

    d   Use a format like the model letter. Keep roughly the same margin on all sides.

    e   Use punctuation and spelling in the model letter as a guide. For example:

        (1)   Skip two spaces between the inside address and the salutation ("Dear Mr. Arline").

        (2)   Use a colon after the salutation.

        (3)   Sign your name at the bottom, in addition to typing it.

Activity

Clip a job listing from a newspaper or copy a job description posted in your school placement office. The job should be one that you feel you are qualified for or that you would one day like to have.

Write a résumé and a letter of application for the job. Use the models already considered as guides.

Use the checklist of the four bases on the inside front cover as a guide in your writing.

21 Using the Library and the Internet

This chapter provides the basic information you need to use your college library and the Internet with confidence. You will learn that for most research topics there are two basic steps you should take:

1 Find books on your topic.
2 Find articles on your topic.

You will learn, too, that while the library is the traditional way of doing such research, a home computer with an online service and Internet access now enables you to thoroughly investigate any topic.

Using the Library

Most students seem to know that libraries provide study space, typing facilities, and copying machines. They are also aware of a library's reading area, which contains recent copies of magazines and newspapers. But the true heart of a library consists of the following: a *main desk,* a *book file, book stacks,* and a *periodicals file.* Each of these will be discussed in the pages that follow.

Main Desk

The main desk is usually located in a central spot. Check with the main desk to see if there is a brochure that describes the layout and services of the library. You might also ask if the library staff provides tours of the library. If not, explore your library to find each of the areas in the activity below.

Activity

Make up a floor plan of your college library. Label the main desk, card file, book stacks, magazine file, and magazine storage area.

Book File

The book file will be your starting point for almost any research project. The book file is a list of all the books in the library. It may be an actual card catalog: a file of cards alphabetically arranged in drawers. More likely, the book file is computerized and can be accessed on computer terminals located at different spots in the library.

Finding a Book: Author, Title, and Subject

Whether you use an actual file of cards or a computer terminal, it is important for you to know that there are three ways to look up a book. You can look it up according to *author, title,* or *subject.* For example, suppose you wanted to see if the library had the book *A Tribe Apart*, by Patricia Hersch. You could check for the book in any of three ways:

1 You could go to the *author* section of the book file and look it up there under *H.* An author is always listed under his or her last name.

2 You could go to the *title* section of the book file and look it up there under *T.* Note that you always look up a book under the first word in the title, excluding the words *A, An,* or *The.*

3 If you know the subject that the book deals with—in this case the subject is "teenagers"—you could go to the *subject* section of the book file and look it up under *T.*

Here is the author entry in a computerized card catalog for Hersch's book *A Tribe Apart*:

AUTHOR:	Hersch, Patricia
TITLE:	A Tribe Apart
PUBLISHER:	Ballantine, 1998
SUBJECTS:	1. Teenagers.

Call Number	Location	Status
HQ796/H43	Gibbsboro	Available

Note that in addition to giving you the publisher (Ballantine) and year of publication (1998), the entry also tells you the *call number*—where to find the book in the library. If the computerized card catalog is part of a network of libraries, you may also learn at what branch or location the book is available. If the book is not at your library, you can probably arrange for an interlibrary loan.

Using Subject Headings to Research a Topic

Generally, if you are looking for a particular book, it is easier to use the *author* or *title* section of the card catalog. On the other hand, if you are researching a topic, then the *subject* section is where you should look.

The subject section performs three valuable functions:

- It will give you a list of books on a given topic.
- It will often provide related topics that might have information on your subject.
- It will suggest to you more limited topics, helping you narrow your general topic.

Chances are you will be asked to do a research paper of about five to fifteen pages. You do not want to choose a topic so broad that it could be covered only by an entire book or more. Instead, you want to come up with a limited topic that can be adequately supported in a relatively short paper. As you search the subject section, take advantage of ideas that it might offer on how you can narrow your topic.

Activity

Part A:
Answer the following questions about the card catalog.

1. Is your library's book card catalog an actual file of cards in drawers, or is it computerized? _Answers will vary._
2. Which section of the book file will help you research and limit a topic? _subject section_

Part B:

Use your library's card catalog to answer the following questions.

1. What is the title of one book by Toni Morrison?

   Answers will vary. Example: _Beloved_

2. What is the title of one book by George Will?

   Answers will vary. Example: _Men at Work_

3. Who is the author of _The Decline and Fall of the Roman Empire?_ (Remember to look up the title under _Decline_, not _The._)

   Edward Gibbon

4. Who is the author of _What Color Is Your Parachute?_

   Richard Nelson Belles

5. List two books and their authors dealing with the subject of adoption:
   Answers will vary. Examples:
   a. _Being Adopted: The Lifelong Search for Self_

      David M. Brodzinsky et al.

   b. _Raising Adopted Children_

      Lois Ruskai Melina

6. Look up a book titled _Silent Spring_ or _The Lives of a Cell_ and give the following information:
   Answers for:

		Lives of a Cell:	_Silent Spring:_
a.	Author	Lewis Thomas	Rachel Carson
b.	Publisher	Viking	Houghton Mifflin
c.	Date of publication	1974	1994
d.	Call number	574.01 Tho	632.95 Car
e.	Subject headings:	Biology—Philosophy	Pesticides-En

7. Look up a book written by Deborah Tannen or Russell Baker and give the following information:
   Answers will vary:

		Example for Russell Baker:	for Deborah Tannen:
a.	Title	_Growing Up_	_You Just Don't Understand_
b.	Publisher	Congdon and Weed/St. Martin's	Ballantine/Random House
c.	Date of publication	1982	1990
d.	Call number	B Bak	302 Tan
e.	Subject headings:	Journalists-US-Biography	Conversation

   Note: Dewey Decimal call numbers are shown.

Book Stacks

The book stacks are the library shelves where books are arranged according to their call numbers. The call number, as distinctive as a social security number, always appears on a call file for any book. It is also printed on the spine of every book in the library.

If your library has open stacks (ones that you are permitted to enter), here is how to find a book. Suppose you are looking for *A Tribe Apart,* which has the call number HQ796/H43 in the Library of Congress system. (Libraries using the Dewey decimal system have call letters made up entirely of numbers rather than letters and numbers. However, you use the same basic method to locate a book.) First, you go to the section of the stacks that holds the *H*'s. When you locate the *H*'s, you look for the *HQ*'s. After that, you look for *HQ796*. Finally, you look for *HQ796/H43*, and you have the book.

If your library has closed stacks (ones you are not permitted to enter), you will have to write down the title, author, and call number on a slip of paper. (Such slips of paper will be available near the card catalog or computer terminals.) You'll then give the slip to a library staff person, who will locate the book and bring it to you.

Activity

Use the book stacks to answer one of the following set of questions. Choose the questions that relate to the system of classifying books used by your library.

Option 1: Library of Congress System (letters and numbers)

1. Books in the E184.6–E185.9 area deal with:

   a. Benjamin Franklin
   b. American Indians
   c. American presidents
   d. African Americans

2. Books in the HM–HN65 area deal with:

   a. sociology
   b. history
   c. economics
   d. psychology

3. Books in the M1–M220 area deal with:

   a. painting
   b. sculpture
   c. music
   d. architecture

Option 2: Dewey Decimal System (numbers):

1. Books in the 200–299 area deal with:
   a. language   (c.) religion
   b. philosophy   d. sports
2. Books in the 370–372 area deal with:
   a. education   (c.) the military
   b. death   d. waste disposal
3. Books in the 613 area deal with:
   a. wildflowers   c. drugs
   (b.) health   d. the solar system

Periodicals File

The first step in researching a topic is to check for relevant books; the second step is to locate relevant periodicals. *Periodicals* (from the word *periodic*, which means "at regular periods") are magazines, journals, and newspapers. The periodicals file often contains recent or very specialized information about a subject, which may not be available in a book.

Just as you use the book file to find books on your subject, so you use the periodicals file to find articles on your subject in magazines and other publications. Following are three files that are widely used in libraries.

Readers' Guide to Periodical Literature

The old-fashioned way to do research is to use the familiar green volumes of the *Readers' Guide*, found in just about every library. They list articles published in more than one hundred popular magazines, such as *Newsweek, Health, People, Ebony, Redbook,* and *Popular Science.* Articles appear alphabetically under both subject and author. For example, if you wanted to learn the titles of articles published on the subject of child abuse within a certain time span, you would look under the heading "Child abuse."

At the top of the follwing page is a typical entry from the *Guide.*

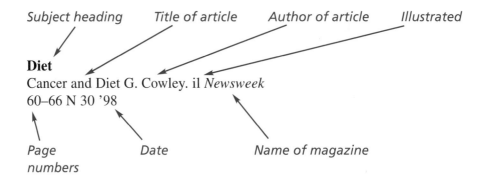

Subject heading   Title of article   Author of article   Illustrated

Diet
Cancer and Diet G. Cowley. il *Newsweek*
60–66 N 30 '98

Page
numbers   Date   Name of magazine

Note the sequence in which information is given about the article:

1 Subject heading.
2 Title of the article. In some cases, there will be bracketed words [ ] after the title that help make clear just what the article is about.
3 Author (if it is a signed article). The author's first name is always abbreviated.
4 Whether the article has a bibliography (*bibl*) or is illustrated with pictures (*il*). Other abbreviations sometimes used are shown in the front of the *Readers' Guide.*
5 Name of the magazine. A short title like *Newsweek* is not abbreviated, but longer titles are. For example, the magazine *Popular Science* is abbreviated *Pop Sci.* Refer to the list of magazines in the front of the index to identify abbreviations.
6 Page numbers on which the article appears.
7 Date when the article appeared. Dates are abbreviated: for example, *Mr* stands for *March*, *Ag* for *August*, *O* for *October*. Other abbreviations are shown in the front of the *Guide.*

The *Readers' Guide* is published in monthly supplements. At the end of a year, a volume is published covering the entire year. You will see in your library large green volumes that say, for instance, *Readers' Guide 1996* or *Readers' Guide 1998.* You will also see the small monthly supplements for the current year.

The drawback of the *Readers' Guide* is that it gives you only a list of articles; you must then go to your library's periodicals storage area to see if the library actually has copies of the magazines that contain those articles. If you're lucky and it does, you must take the time right then to read and take notes on the articles or to makes copies of them.

The *Readers' Guide* is also available in a much more useful form on a CD-ROM (compact disk, read-only memory) player. Using a computer terminal that accesses the compact disks, you can quickly search for articles on a given subject. You do this by typing into a box a key word or phrase that will enable the computer to search for articles on your subject.

Magazine Index Plus

This CD-ROM computerized file lists articles published over the last several years in about four hundred general-interest magazines. Once again, by sitting at a computer terminal and typing in a key word or words for your subject, you can rapidly locate relevant articles.

Ebscohost

Many libraries now provide an online computer search service such as *InfoTrac, Dialog,* or *Ebscohost.* Sitting at a terminal and using Ebscohost, for instance, you will be able to use key words to quickly search many hundreds of periodicals for articles on your subject. When you find relevant articles, you can either print them off using a library printer (libraries may charge you about ten cents a page) or E-mail those articles to your home computer and run them off on your own printer. Obviously, if an online resource is available, that is is the way you should conduct your research.

Activity 1

At this point in the chapter, you now know the two basic steps in researching a topic in the library. What are the steps?

1. Find books on your topic.
    _____

2. Find articles on your topic.
    _____

Activity 2

1. Look up a recent article on nursing home costs using your library's periodicals file and fill in the following information: Answers will vary.

    a. Name of the index you used _____

    b. Article title _____

    c. Author (if given) _____

    d. Name of magazine _____

    e. Pages _____   f. Date _____

2. Look up a recent article on organ donation using your library's periodicals file and fill in the following information: Answers will vary.

    a. Name of the index you used _____

    b. Article title _____

    c. Author (if given) _____

    d. Name of magazine _____

    e. Pages _____   f. Date _____

A Note on Specialized Indexes

Through either CD-ROM disks or online databases, your library will make available to you a number of specialized indexes. Examples include *Social Sciences Index, Business Periodicals Index, Education Index, Health Index,* and *National Newspaper Index.* Your instructors may expect you to consult one or more of these indexes to obtain more specialized and professional information on a given subject.

Using the Internet

The Internet is dramatic proof of the computer revolution that has occurred in our lives. It is a giant network that connects computers at tens of thousands of educational, scientific, government, and commercial agencies around the world. Existing within the Internet is the World Wide Web, a global information system which got its name because countless individual websites contain links to other sites, forming a kind of web.

To use the Internet, you need a personal computer with a *modem*—a device that sends or receives electronic data over a telephone line for no more than the cost of a local telephone call. You also need to subscribe to an online service such as America Online. If you have an online service as well as a printer for your computer, you can do a good deal of your research for a paper at home. As with the library, you should proceed by searching for books and articles on your topic.

Find Books on Your Topic

To find books on your topic, go online and type in the address of one of the large online booksellers:

Barnes and Noble Books at *www.barnesandnoble.com*
Amazon Books at *www.amazon.com*

In most cases, you may not have to type the *www.* (for *World Wide Web*); the search program you are using will provide it for you. (Note, by the way, that *.com* in the two addresses above is simply an abbreviation for *commercial*. Other common abbreviations are *.edu*, which ends the address of educational institutions; *.org,* for nonprofit organizations; *.gov*, for government agencies; and *.net*, for Internet service providers.)

Use the "Browse Subjects" Box

Use the "Browse Subjects" box on the opening page of either site to locate categories where you might find books on your general subject. For example, if your assignment was to report on personal obstacles faced by an American president, you would notice that one of the subject listings is "Biography." If you then clicked on "Biography," you would get several subcategories, one of which is "Presidents." When you click on that, you would get a list of recent books on American presidents. You could then click on each title for information about each book, including reviewers' comments. All this browsing and searching could be done very quickly and would help you decide on a specific president as your topic.

Use the "Key Words" Box

If your assignment is, for example, a paper on some aspect of adoption, type in the key word "adoption" in the key word search box provided on the opening page. You'll then get a list of books on that subject. Just looking at the list may help you narrow your subject and decide on a specific topic you might want to develop. For instance, one student typed in "adoption" as her key word and got back a list of six hundred books on the subject of adoption. Just looking at part of the list helped her realize that she wanted to write on some aspect of international adoption. She typed "international adoption" and got back a list of nineteen titles. After looking at information about those books, she was able to decide on a limited topic for her paper.

Visit Other Sites

Even if your search at Barnes and Noble is helpful, you may want to visit Amazon or another large online bookseller as well. It's easy to visit this other "store" quickly, and chances are that you'll get additional information and ideas about a given subject. As you become skillful at visiting sites and using subject headings as well as key words and phrases, you'll find that you can quickly access an enormous amount of information, discovering and narrowing your research topic as you proceed.

A Few Points to Note

Remember that at any time, you can use your printer to quickly print out information presented on the screen. The student planning a paper on adoption could, for example, print out a list of the nineteen books on international adoption, along with sheets of information about individual books. You could then go to your library knowing just what books you want to borrow. Indeed, in some cases you can even visit your library online to find out in advance whether it has in its holdings the books you want. Also, if you have time and money and some of the books are in paperback, you may want to purchase them from the online bookstore, which typically ships books in two or three days.

Find Articles on Your Topic

There are many online sources that will help you find articles on your subject. Following are descriptions of three of them.

The Electric Library: A Resource for Magazines and Newspaper Articles

As its name implies, The Electric Library is an online research resource; it's available at *www.elibrary.com*. Chances are you may get a free thirty-day trial subscription, or you'll be able to enroll on a monthly basis at a limited cost. The Electric Library contains millions of newspaper and magazine articles as well as many thousands of book chapters and television and radio transcripts. By typing in key words, you'll get long lists of articles that may relate to your subject. When you then click on a given title, the full text of the article appears. If it fits your needs, you can print it out right away on your printer. *There has never been an easier way to research a full range of magazine and newspaper articles.*

AOL NetFind: A Search Engine

A *search engine* is a tool that combs through the vast amount of information on the Web for sites or articles that match your research needs. You activate a search engine by typing in a key word or phrase that tells the engine what to look for. It then provides you with a list of "hits," or links, to websites where your key word is found. Like most search engines, it also provides a brief description of each site. Well-known search engines include AltaVista, at *www.altavista.digital.com*; Lycos, at *www.lycos.com*; and WebCrawler, at *www.webcrawler.com*. If you are a subscriber to America Online, you might find it convenient to use a search engine called AOL NetFind.

For example, the student planning a paper on adoption first typed the word "adoption" into the NetFind search box, and within seconds she got back a list of 138,807 matches! She realized she needed to narrow her search, so she typed "adoption and international" and got back 4,300 matches. Each match or entry includes a *link* to another site. Typically, a link shows up as an underlined word or phrase that is different in color from the type elsewhere on the page. When you click on a link, you are automatically transported to that related site.

Very often your challenge with searches will be getting too much information rather than too little. Most search engines include a *help* feature that will provide you with suggestions on ways to limit your search.

Yahoo! and My Virtual Reference Desk: Search Directories

Yahoo! is one of the most popular and user-friendly search resources to use on the Web; its address is *www.yahoo.com*. While Yahoo also provides a search engine, it may be even more valuable to you as a *search directory*, for it organizes websites by categories.

If, for instance, you felt you wanted to do a research paper on some aspect of health, you could click on the category "Health" on the opening page (also called the *home page*) of Yahoo! Doing so would bring up almost fifty subcategories, including "Alternative Medicine," "Environmental Health," "Long Term Care," "Traditional Medicine," and "Women's Health." Let's say you wanted to explore possible topics in the area of alternative medicine. Simply click on that item, and you get a list of almost forty subgroupings, including "Biofeedback," "Herbs," and "Therapeutic Touch." In other words, Yahoo! can help you discover a limited topic that you might want to research.

My Virtual Reference Desk, available at *www.refdesk.com*, is another search directory you may want to consult. It gives you access to daily newspapers from around the world and online versions of current issues of many popular magazines. It also provides an impressive variety of reference tools as well as online links to several hundred search engines.

Practice in Using the Library and the Internet

Activity

Use your library or the Internet to research a subject that interests you. Select one of the following areas, or (with your teacher's permission) an area of your own choice:

Assisted suicide	Computer use and carpal tunnel syndrome
Interracial adoptions	Noise control
Ritalin and children	Animals nearing extinction
Sexual harassment	Animal rights movement
State lotteries	Antigay violence
Greenhouse effect	Drug treatment programs for adolescents
Nursing home costs	Fertility drugs
Pro-choice movement today	Witchcraft today
Pro-life movement today	New treatments for AIDS
Health insurance reform	Mind-body medicine
Pollution of drinking water	Origins of Kwanzaa
Problems of retirement	Hazardous substances in the home
Cremation	Airbags
Capital punishment	Gambling and youth
Prenatal care	Nongraded schools
Acid rain	Forecasting earthquakes
New aid for the handicapped	Ethical aspects of hunting
New remedies for allergies	Ethics of cloning
Censorship on the Internet	Recent consumer frauds
New prison reforms	Stress reduction in the workplace
Drug treatment programs	Sex on television
Sudden infant death syndrome	Everyday addictions
New treatments for insomnia	Toxic waste disposal
Organ donation	Self-help groups
Child abuse	Telephone crimes
Voucher system in schools	Date rape
Food poisoning (salmonella)	Heroes for today

Alzheimer's disease	Steroids
Holistic healing	Surrogate mothers
Best job prospects today	Vegetarianism

Research the topic first through the subject section of a library book file or an online bookstore. Then research the topic through a library periodicals file or an online source. On a separate sheet of paper, provide the following information.
Answers will vary.

1. Topic

2. Three books that either cover the topic directly or at least in some way touch on the topic. Include:

    Author
    Title
    Place of publication
    Publisher
    Date of publication

3. Three articles on the topic published in 1995 or later. Include:

    Title of article
    Author (if given)
    Title of magazine
    Date
    Page(s) (if given)

4. Finally, include a paragraph describing just how you went about researching your topic. In addition, include a photocopy or printout of one of the three articles.

22 Writing a Research Paper

The process of writing a research paper can be divided into six steps:

1 Select a topic that you can readily research.
2 Limit your topic and make the purpose of your paper clear.
3 Gather information on your limited topic.
4 Plan your paper and take notes on your limited topic.
5 Write the paper.
6 Use an acceptable format and method of documentation.

This chapter explains and illustrates each of these steps and then provides a model research paper.

Step 1: Select a Topic That You Can Readily Research

Researching at a Local Library

First of all, go to the *subjects* section of your library book file (as described on page 372) and see whether there are several books on your general topic. For example, if you initially choose the broad topic "parenting," try to find at least three books on being a parent. Make sure that the books are actually available on the library shelves.

Next, go to the *periodicals* file in your library (see pages 375–378) to see if there are a fair number of magazine, newspaper, or journal articles on your subject. For instance, when Sonya Philips, author of the model research paper "Successful Families," visited her local library, she found a CD-ROM index called *Magazine Index Plus,* which indexes all the articles published over a three- to four-year period in over four hundred popular magazines. When Sonya typed in the search term "parenting," *Magazine Index Plus* came back with hundreds of "hits"—titles, locations, and brief descriptions of articles about parenting. The index also marked those articles that were in magazines available in Sonya's library.

Researching on the Internet

If you have access to the Internet on a home or library computer, you can use it to determine if resources are available for your topic.

The first step is to go to the *subjects* section of a large online bookseller to find relevant books. (Don't worry—you don't have to buy the books; you're just browsing for information.) As mentioned in Chapter 21, two of the largest online booksellers are Barnes and Noble and Amazon Books.

"I checked out both Barnes and Noble and Amazon as I began my research," said Sonya Philips. "When I went to their websites, I saw that I could search for books by subject, and I knew that I was in business. All I had to do was click on a box titled 'Browse Subjects.'

"Barnes and Noble has a category called 'Parenting and Families,' and when I clicked on that, I got a bunch of subcategories, including one for 'Teenagers.' I clicked on 'Teenagers' and that brought up a list of hundreds of books! I went through the list, and when I got to a book that sounded promising, I just clicked on that title and up like magic came reviews of the book—and sometimes a table of contents and a summary as well! All this information helped me decide on the dozen or so books I eventually picked out that seemed relevant to my paper. I then went to my local library and found five of those titles on the shelves. Another title was a recent paperback, so I went to a nearby bookstore and bought it." (If you find relevant books in your online search that your local library does not own, ask your research librarian if he or she can obtain them from another library through an interlibrary loan program.)

Next, determine if magazine or newspaper articles on your topic are available online. You can go about this in several ways. Your Internet service provider (such as America Online) has a built-in "engine" that allows you to search the Internet for any topic you like. When you type in a key word or key words related to your topic, you'll get back a listing of sources, or "hits," on the Internet. Sonya relates her experience searching the Internet in this way:

"First I typed in the word 'parenting' in the key word box," she said. "I got more than a hundred thousand hits! So I tried more specific search terms. I tried 'parenting and teenagers,' 'parenting and television,' 'parenting and adolescents.' Those search terms worked better, and I found some useful sites—like 'The Television Project,' which is an online resource that doesn't exist anywhere else—but I was still getting lots of stuff I couldn't use, such as sites that were selling products, or parents' discussion groups, and so on.

"So I asked my instructor how to look just for magazine or newspaper articles. She suggested I go directly to the sites of some popular publications. I went to three sites (*Newsweek*, at *newsweek.com*; *Time*, at *time.com*; and *USA Today,* at *usatoday.com*). I was able to search each one for recent articles about parenting, and it was clear there was plenty of material that related to my topic."

However you choose to do your research, the outcome is the same: If both books and articles are available, pursue your topic. Otherwise, you may have to choose another topic. You cannot write a paper on a topic for which research materials are not readily available.

Step 2: Limit Your Topic and Make the Purpose of Your Paper Clear

A research paper should *thoroughly* develop a *limited* topic. The paper should be narrow and deep rather than broad and shallow. Therefore, as you read through books and articles, look for ways to limit your general topic.

For instance, as Sonya read through materials on the general topic "parenting," she chose to limit her topic to the particular problems of parents raising children in today's culture. Furthermore, she decided to limit it even more by focusing on what successful parents do to deal with those challenges. To take some other examples, the general topic "drug abuse" might be narrowed to successful drug treatment programs for adolescents. After doing some reading on the worldwide problem of overpopulation, you might decide to limit your paper to the birth-control policies enforced by the Chinese government. The broad subject "death" could be reduced to euthanasia or the unfair pricing practices in some funeral homes. "Divorce" might be limited to its most damaging effects on the children of divorced parents; "stress in everyday life" could be narrowed to methods of reducing stress in the workplace.

The subject headings in the book file and the magazine file will give you helpful ideas about how to limit your subject. For example, under the subject heading "Parenting" in the book file were several related headings, such as "moral and ethical considerations of parenting" and "stepparenting." In addition, there was a list of seventy-eight books, including several titles that suggested limited directions for research: parents and discipline, parenting and adolescent girls, how parents can protect their kids from violence, parents' questions about teenagers' development. Under the subject heading "Parenting" in the magazine file at the same library were subheadings and titles of many articles which suggested additional limited topics that a research paper might explore: how parents can limit the impact of TV on kids, keeping the lines of communication open between parents and teenagers, how much influence parents can have on kids, secrets to raising a successful teen. The point is that *subject headings and related headings, as well as book and article titles, may be of great help to you in narrowing your topic.* Take advantage of them.

Do not expect to limit your topic and make your purpose clear all at once. You may have to do quite a bit of reading as you work out the limited focus of your paper. Note that many research papers have one of two general purposes. Your purpose might be to make and defend a point of some kind. (For example, your purpose in a paper might be to provide evidence that elected officials should be limited to serving a single term in office.) Or, depending on the course and the instructor, your purpose might simply be to present information about a particular subject. (For instance, you might be asked to write a paper describing the most recent scientific findings about the effect of diet on heart disease.)

Step 3: Gather Information on Your Limited Topic

After you have a good sense of your limited topic, you can begin gathering relevant information. A helpful way to proceed is to sign out the books that you need from your library. In addition, make copies of all relevant articles from magazines, newspapers, or journals. If your library has an online periodicals database, you may be able to print those articles right out.

In other words, take the steps needed to get all your key source materials together in one place. You can then sit and work on these materials in a quiet, unhurried way in your home or some other place of study.

Step 4: Plan Your Paper and Take Notes on Your Limited Topic

Preparing a Scratch Outline

As you carefully read through the material you have gathered, think constantly about the specific content and organization of your paper. Begin making decisions about exactly what information you will present and how you will arrange it. Prepare a scratch outline for your paper that shows both its thesis and the areas of support for the thesis. It may help to try to plan at least three areas of support.

Thesis: _____

Support: (1) _____

(2) _____

(3) _____

Following, for example, is the brief outline that Sonya Philips prepared for her paper on successful parenting.

> Thesis: There are things parents can do to overcome the negative influences hurting their families.
>
> Support: (1) Create quality time with families
>
>   (2) Increase families' sense of community
>
>   (3) Minimize the impact of media and technology

Note-Taking

With a tentative outline in mind, you can begin taking notes on the information that you expect to include in your paper. Write your notes on four- by six-inch or five- by eight-inch cards or on sheets of loose-leaf paper. The notes you take should be in the form of *direct quotations, summaries in your own words,* or both. (At times you may also *paraphrase*—use an equal number of your own words in place of someone else's words. Since most research involves condensing information, you will summarize much more than you will paraphrase.)

A *direct quotation* must be written *exactly* as it appears in the original work. But as long as you don't change the meaning, you may omit words from a quotation if they are not relevant to your point. To show such an omission, use three spaced periods (known as *ellipses*) in place of the deleted words:

Original passage	We cannot guarantee that bad things will happen, but we can argue that good things are not happening. It is the contention of this report that increasing numbers of young people are left to their own devices at a critical time in their development.
Direct quotation with ellipses	"We cannot guarantee that bad things will happen, but we can argue that good things are not happening [. . .]. [I]ncreasing numbers of young people are left to their own devices at a critical time in their development. "

(Note that there are four dots in the above example, with the first dot indicating the period at the end of the sentence. The capital letter in brackets shows that the word was capitalized by the student but did not begin the sentence in the original source.)

In a *summary,* you condense the original material by expressing it in your own words. Summaries may be written as lists, as brief paragraphs, or both. Following is one of Sonya Phillips's summary note cards:

> *Movie content*
>
> *Study conducted in 1996 showed that of PG-13 movies, 91 percent had crude language, 89 percent had obscene language, 45 percent had actual or suggested sex. Worrisome because most parents assume PG-13 movies are OK for their kids.*
>
> *Medved and Medved, 62*

Keep in mind the following points about your research notes:

- Write on only one side of each card or sheet of paper.
- Write only one kind of information, from one source, on any one card or sheet. For example, the sample card above has information on only one idea (movie content) from one source (Medved and Medved).
- At the top of each card or sheet, write a heading that summarizes its content. This will help you organize the different kinds of information that you gather.
- Identify the source and page number at the bottom.

Whether you quote or summarize, be sure to record the exact source and page from which you take each piece of information. In a research paper, you must document all information that is not common knowledge or a matter of historical record. For example, the birth and death dates of Dr. Martin Luther King, Jr., are established facts and do not need documenting. On the other hand, the average number of hours worked annually today compared with the 1980s is a specialized fact that should be documented. As you read several sources on a subject, you will develop a sense of what authors regard as generally shared or common information and what is more specialized information that must be documented.

If you do not document specialized information or ideas that are not your own, you will be stealing (the formal term is *plagiarizing*—using someone else's work as your own work). A good deal of the material in research writing, it can usually be assumed, will need to be documented.

Step 5: Write the Paper

After you have finished your reading and note-taking, you should have a fairly clear idea of the plan of your paper. Make a *final outline* and use it as a guide to write your first full draft. If your instructor requires an outline as part of your paper, you should prepare either a *topic outline*, which contains your thesis plus supporting words and phrases; or a *sentence outline,* which consists of complete sentences. In the model paper shown on pages 395–405, a topic outline appears on page 396. You will note that roman numerals are used for first-level headings, capital letters for second-level headings, and arabic numbers for third-level headings.

In an *introduction,* include a thesis statement expressing the purpose of your paper and indicate the plan of development that you will follow. The section on writing introductions for an essay (pages 87–90) is also appropriate for the introductory section of the research paper. Notice that the model research paper uses a two-paragraph introduction (page 397).

As you move from introduction to *main body* to *conclusion*, strive for unity, support, and coherence so that your paper will be clear and effective. Repeatedly ask, "Does each of my supporting paragraphs develop the thesis of my paper?" Use the checklist on the inside front cover of this book to make sure that your paper touches all four bases of effective writing.

Step 6: Use an Acceptable Format and Method of Documentation

Format

The model paper shows an acceptable format for a research paper. Be sure to note carefully the comments and directions that are set in small print in the margins of each page.

Documentation of Sources

You must tell the reader the sources (books, articles, and so on) of the borrowed material in your paper. Whether you quote directly or summarize ideas in your own words, you must acknowledge your sources. In the past, you may have used footnotes and a bibliography to cite your sources. Here you will learn a simplified and widely accepted documentation style used by the Modern Language Association.

Citations Within a Paper: When citing a source, you must mention the author's name and the relevant page number. The author's name may be given either in the sentence you are writing or in parentheses following the sentence. Here are two examples:

> In <u>The Way We Really Are</u>, Stephanie Coontz writes, "Right up through the 1940s, ties of work, friendship, neighborhood, ethnicity, extended kin, and voluntary organizations were as important a source of identity for most Americans, and sometimes a <u>more</u> important source of obligation, than marriage and the nuclear family" (37).

> "Some . . . are looking for a way to reclaim family closeness in an increasingly fast-paced society. . . . Still others worry about unsavory influences in school—drugs, alcohol, sex, violence" (Kantrowitz and Wingert 66).

There are several points to note about citations within the paper:

- When the author's name is provided in parentheses, only the last name is given.
- There is no punctuation between the author's name and the page number.
- The parenthetical citation is placed after the borrowed material but before the period at the end of the sentence.
- If you are using more than one work by the same author, include a shortened version of the title within the parenthetical citation. For example, suppose you were using two books by Stephanie Coontz, and you included a second quotation from her book *The Way We Really Are*. Your citation within the text would be:

> (Coontz, <u>Really Are</u>, 39).

Note that commas separate the author's last name and the page number from the abbreviated title.

Citations at the End of a Paper: Your paper should end with a list of "Works Cited" which includes all the sources actually used in the paper. (Don't list any other sources, no matter how many you have read.) Look at the "Works Cited" page in the model research paper (page 405) and note the following points:

- The list is organized alphabetically according to the authors' last names. Entries are not numbered.
- Entries are double-spaced, with no extra space between entries.

- After the first line of each entry, there is a half-inch indentation for each additional line in the entry.
- Use the abbreviation *qtd. in* when citing a quotation from another source. For example, a quotation from Edward Wolff on page 2 of the paper is from a book not by Wolff but by Sylvia Ann Hewlett and Cornel West. The citation is therefore handled as follows:

> . . . The economist Edward Wolff explains the loss of time:
> Over a thirty-year time span, parental time has declined 13 percent. The time parents have available for their children has been squeezed by the rapid shift of mothers into the paid labor force, by escalating divorce rates and the subsequent abandonment of children by their fathers, and by an increase in the number of hours required on the job. The average worker is now at work 163 hours a year more than in 1969, which adds up to an extra month of work annually (qtd. in Hewlett and West 48).

Model Entries for a List of "Works Cited": Model entries of "Works Cited" are given below. Use these entries as a guide when you prepare your own list.

Book by One Author

Goodwin, Doris Kearns. <u>No Ordinary Time</u>. New York: Simon and Schuster, 1994.

Note that the author's last name is written first.

Two or More Entries by the Same Author

- - -. <u>Wait Till Next Year</u>. New York: Simon and Schuster, 1997.

If you cite two or more entries by the same author (in the example above, a second book by Doris Kearns Goodwin is cited), do not repeat the author's name. Instead, begin the line with three hyphens followed by a period. Then give the remaining information as usual. Arrange works by the same author alphabetically by title. The words *A, An,* and *The* are ignored in alphabetizing by title.

Book by Two or More Authors

Simon, David, and Edward Burns. <u>The Corner</u>. New York: Broadway Books, 1997.

For a book with two or more authors, give all the authors' names but reverse only the first name.

Magazine Article

Cowley, Geoffrey. "Cancer and Diet." <u>Newsweek</u> 30 Nov. 1998: 60-66.

Write the date of the issue as follows: day, month (abbreviated in most cases to three letters), and year. The final number or numbers refer to the page or pages of the issue on which the article appears.

Newspaper Article	Chavez, Linda. "Father Passes on Lessons of Poverty." <u>Philadelphia Inquirer</u> 25 Nov. 1998: A18.

The final letter and number refer to section A, page 18.

Editorial	"Confronting an Unfair Census." Editorial. <u>New York Times</u> 30 Nov. 1998: A24.

List an editorial as you would any signed or unsigned article, but indicate the nature of the piece by adding *Editorial* after the article's title.

Selection in an Edited Collection	McClane, Kenneth A. "A Death in the Family." <u>Bearing Witness</u>. Ed. Henry Louis Gates, Jr. New York: Pantheon, 1991: 96–102.
Revised or Later Edition	Myers, David G. <u>Social Psychology</u>. 6th ed. New York: McGraw-Hill, 1999.

The abbreviations *Rev. ed., 2nd ed., 3rd ed.,* and so on, are placed right after the title.

Chapter or Section in a Book by One Author	Schor, Juliet B. "The Visible Lifestyle: American Symbols of Status." <u>The Overspent American</u>. New York: Basic Books, 1998. 43-64.
Pamphlet	<u>1998 Heart and Stroke Facts</u>. New York: American Heart Association, 1998.
Television Program	"Smoke Screen." Narr. Lesley Stahl. Prod. Rome Hartman. <u>60 Minutes</u>. CBS. 11 Nov. 1998.
Film	<u>American History X</u>. Dir. Tony Kaye. New Line Cinema, 1998.
Sound Recording	Diamond, Neil. "Yesterday's Songs." <u>In My Lifetime</u>. Sony Music,1996.
Videocassette	"Cedric's Journey." Narr. Ted Koppel. <u>Nightline</u>. ABC. WABC, New York. 24 June 1998. Videocassette. ABC/FDCH, 1998.
Personal Interview	McClintock, Ann. Personal interview. 20 July 1999.

Online
Source in a
Reference
Database

"Organ Transplants." <u>Britannica Online</u>. Vers. 98.10.1. Nov. 1998.
    Encyclopaedia Britannica. 1 Dec. 1998. <http://www.eb.com:180/
    cgi-bin/g?DocF-macro/5006/37/3.html>

The first date refers to when the material was electronically published, updated, or posted; the second date refers to when the student researcher accessed the source.

Online
Article

Woodward, Kenneth L. "Sex, Sin, and Salvation." <u>Newsweek Online</u> 2 Nov.
    1998. 6 Nov. 1998 <http://www.newsweek.com/nw-srv/issue/18_986/
    printed/us/na/na0318_1.htm>.

The first date refers to the issue of the publication in which the article appeared; the second date refers to the day when the student researcher accessed the source.

Activity

On a separate sheet of paper, convert the information in each of the following references into the correct form for a list of "Works Cited." Use the appropriate model above as a guide.

1. A book by Larry Zuckerman called *The Potato* and published in Boston by Faber and Faber in 1998.
2. An article by Nancy Gibbs titled "The Age of Ritalin" on pages 86–96 of the November 30, 1998, issue of *Time*.
3. An article by Andrea Stone titled "Today's Military Tougher on Families" on pages 1A–2A of the November 27, 1998, issue of *USA Today*.
4. A book by Diane E. Papalia and Sally W. Olds titled *Human Development* and published in a seventh edition by McGraw-Hill in New York in 1999.
5. An article by Christopher Hitchens titled "Goodbye to All That" on pages 37–47 of the November 1998 issue of *Harper's*.

1. Zuckerman, Larry. <u>The Potato</u>. Boston: Faber and Faber, 1998.
2. Gibbs, Nancy. "The Age of Ritalin." <u>Time</u>. 30 Nov. 1998: 86–96.
3. Stone, Andrea. "Today's Military Tougher on Families." <u>USA Today</u>. 27 Nov. 1998: 1A–2A.
4. Papalia, Diane E., and Sally W. Olds. <u>Human Development</u>. 7th ed. New York: McGraw-Hill, 1999.
5. Hitchens, Christopher. "Goodbye to All That." <u>Harper's</u>. Nov. 1998: 37–47.

Model Paper

Model Title Page

The title should begin about one-third of the way down the page. Center the title. Double-space between lines of the title and your name. Also center and double-space the instructor's name and the date.

> Although a title page and outline are not strictly required, your instructor may ask you to provide them.
>
>
> Successful Families:
>
> Fighting for Their Kids
>
> by
>
> Sonya Philips
>
> English 101
>
> Professor Lessig
>
> 5 May 1999

Model First Page with a Top Heading

For a paper without a title page or outline, use a top heading on the first page.

1 inch

½ inch

Philips 1

Double-space between lines. Leave a one-inch margin on all sides.

> Sonya Philips
> Professor Lessig
> English 101
> 5 May 1999
>
> Successful Families: Fighting for Their Kids
>
> It's a terrible time to be a teenager, or even a teenager's parent. That message is everywhere. The TV, the magazines, and the newspapers are all full of frightening stories about teenagers and families. They say that America's families are falling apart, that kids don't care about anything, and that parents have trouble doing anything. . . .

Model
Outline
Page

After the
title page,
number all
pages in
upper-
right
corner, a
half-inch
from the
top. Place
your name
before the
page
number.
Use small
Roman
numerals
on outline
pages. Use
arabic
numbers
on pages
following
the
outline.

The word
Outline
(without
underlining
or
quotation
marks) is
centered
one inch
from the
top.
Double-
space
between
lines.
Leave a
one-inch
margin on
all sides.

Philips i

Outline

Thesis: Although these are difficult times to be raising teenagers, successful families are finding ways to cope with the challenges.

I.   Meeting the challenge of spending quality time together

    A. Barriers to spending quality time

        1. Increased working hours

        2. Rising divorce rates

        3. Women in workforce

    B. Danger of lack of quality time

    C. Ways found to spend time together

        1. Working less and scaling back lifestyle

        2. Home schooling

II. Meeting the challenge of creating sense of community

    A. Lack of traditional community ties

    B. Ways found to create sense of community

        1. Intentional communities

        2. Religious ties

III. Meeting the challenge of limiting the negative impact of media and technology

    A. Negative impact of media and technology

        1. Creation of environment without protection

        2. Flood of uncontrolled, inappropriate information

    B. Ways of controlling media and technology

        1. Banning TV

        2. Using technology in beneficial ways

Double-space between lines of the text. Leave a one-inch margin all the way around the page. Your name and the page number should be typed one-half inch from the top of the page.

Common knowledge is not documented.

This typical citation gives the author's last name and the relevant page number. "Works Cited" provides full information about the source.

Thesis, followed by plan of development.

Philips 1

Successful Families: Fighting for Their Kids

It's a terrible time to be a teenager, or even a teenager's parent. That message is everywhere. Television, magazines, and newspapers are all full of frightening stories about teenagers and families. They say that America's families are falling apart, that kids don't care about anything, and that parents have trouble doing anything about it. Bookstores are full of scary-sounding titles like these: Teenage Wasteland, Cold New World, A Tribe Apart, and The Scapegoat Generation: America's War on Adolescents. These books describe teenage problems that include apathy, violence, suicide, sexual abuse, depression, loss of values, poor mental health, crime, gang involvement, and drug and alcohol addiction.

Naturally, caring parents are worried by all this. Their worry showed in a national poll in which nine out of ten people said it was harder to raise kids to be "good people" today than it was twenty years ago (Donahue D1). But just as most popular TV shows don't give a realistic view of American teens, these frightening books and statistics do not provide a complete picture of what's going on in families today. The fact is that not all teens and families are lost and without values. While they struggle with problems in our culture like everyone else, successful families are doing what they've always done: finding ways to protect and nurture their children. They are fighting the battle for their families in three ways: by fighting against the loss of quality family time, by fighting against the loss of community, and by fighting against the influence of the media and technology.

Source is identified by name and area of expertise.

Direct quotations of five typed lines or more are indented ten spaces from the left margin. Quotation marks are not used.

The abbre-viation *qtd.* means *quoted.* No comma is used between the authors' names and the page number.

When citing a work in general, not part of a work, it is best to include the author's name in the text instead of using a parenthetical citation. No page number is needed, as the citation refers to the findings of the study overall.

Philips 2

It's true that these days, parents face more challenges than ever before when it comes to finding quality time to spend with their children. The economist Edward Wolff explains the loss of time:

> Over a thirty-year time span, parental time has declined 13 percent. The time parents have available for their children has been squeezed by the rapid shift of mothers into the paid labor force, by escalating divorce rates and the subsequent abandonment of children by their fathers, and by an increase in the number of hours required on the job. The average worker is now at work 163 hours a year more than in 1969, which adds up to an extra month of work annually. (Qtd. in Hewlett and West 48)

As a result, more children are at home alone than ever before. And this situation does leave children vulnerable to getting into trouble. Richardson and others, in their study of five thousand eighth-graders in California, found that children who were home alone after school were twice as likely to experiment with drugs and alcohol as children who had a parent (or another adult) home in the after-school hours.

But creative parents still come up with ways to be there for their kids. For some, it's been a matter of cutting back on working hours and living more simply. For example, in her book <u>The Shelter of Each Other</u>, Mary Pipher tells the story of a couple with three-year-old twin boys. Edwardo worked sixty-hour weeks at a factory. Sabrina supervised

Philips 3

checkers at a K-Mart, cared for the boys, and tried to watch over her mother, who had cancer. Money was tight, especially since day care was expensive and the parents felt they had to keep the twins stylishly dressed and supplied with new toys. The parents were stressed over money problems, their lack of time together, and especially having so little time with their boys. It bothered them that the twins had begun to cry when their parents picked them up at day care, as if they'd rather stay with the day care workers. Finally, Sabrina and Edwardo made a difficult decision. Sabrina quit her job, and the couple invited her mother (whose illness was in remission) to live with them. With three adults pooling their resources, Sabrina and Edwardo found that they could manage without Sabrina's salary. The family no longer ate out, and they gave up their cable TV. Their sons loved having their grandmother in the house. Sabrina was able to begin doing relaxed, fun projects with the boys. They planted a garden and built a sandbox together. Sabrina observed, "I learned I could get off the merry-go-round" (195). Other parents have "gotten off the merry-go-round" by working at home, even if it means less money than they had previously. "[H]eading home is a real possibility for those parents who can master the new home-office technology [. . .] . If enough people can manage to do this, the neighborhoods might once again come alive for workers and their children" (Louv 285).

Only the page number is needed, as the author has already been named in the text.

The capital letter in brackets shows that the word was capitalized by the student but did not begin the sentence in the original source.

The spaced periods (ellipses) in brackets show that material from the original source has been omitted.

Author and page number, with no comma.

Some parents even home-school their children as a way to be sure they have plenty of time together. Home schooling used to be thought of as a choice made only by very religious people or back-to-nature radicals. Now, teaching children at home is much less unusual. It's estimated that as many as 1.5 million American children are being home-schooled. Harvard even has an admissions officer whose job it is to review applications from home-schooled kids. Parents who home-school have different reasons, but, according to a cover story in Newsweek, "Some [. . .]are looking for a way to reclaim family closeness in an increasingly fast-paced society [. . .]. Still others worry about unsavory influences in school—drugs, alcohol, sex, violence" (Kantrowitz and Wingert 66). Home schooling is no guarantee that a child will resist those temptations, but some families do believe it's a great way to promote family closeness. One fifteen-year-old, home-schooled since kindergarten, explained why he liked the way he'd been raised and educated. He ended by saying, "Another way I'm different is that I love my family. One guy asked me if I'd been brainwashed. I think it's spooky that liking my family is considered crazy" (Pipher 103).

Many parents can't quit their jobs or teach their children at home. But some parents find a second way to nurture their children, through building community ties. They help their children develop a healthy sense of belonging by creating links with positive, constructive people and activities. In the past, community wasn't so hard to find. In The Way

Philips 5

We Really Are, Stephanie Coontz writes, "Right up through the 1940s, ties of work, friendship, neighborhood, ethnicity, extended kin, and voluntary organizations were as important a source of identity for most Americans, and sometimes a more important source of obligation, than marriage and the nuclear family" (37). Even when today's parents were teenagers, neighborhoods were places where kids felt a sense of belonging and responsibility. But today "parents [. . .] mourn the disappearance of neighborhoods where a web of relatives and friends kept a close eye on everyone's kids. And they worry their own children grow up isolated, knowing more about the cast of Friends than the people in surrounding homes" (USA Today).

One way that some families are trying to build old-fashioned community is through "intentional community" or "cohousing." Begun in Denmark in 1972, the cohousing movement is modeled after the traditional village. It brings together a number of families who live in separate houses but share some common space. For instance, families might share central meeting rooms, dining areas, gardens, day care, workshops, or office space. They might own tools and lawn mowers together, rather than each household having its own. The point is that they treat their neighbors as extended family, not as strangers. "Creating a cohousing neighborhood can be as simple as taking down the fences between existing homes, or as complex as designing and constructing a new development from scratch," writes Wendy Priesnitz

Bracketed ellipses show where the student has omitted material from the original source. The quoted material is not capitalized because the student has blended it into a sentence with an introductory phrase.

Philips 6

Citation for an online source. No page number is given because the online document does not provide one.

in the online magazine <u>Natural Life</u>. More than five hundred such communities now exist in North America (Forsey).

Other families turn to religion as a source of community. Michael Medved and Diane Medved, authors of <u>Saving Childhood</u>, are raising their family in a religious Jewish home. Their children attend Jewish schools, go to synagogue, and follow religious customs. They frequently visit, eat, play with, and are cared for by neighboring Jewish families. The Medveds believe their family is stronger because of their belief "in planting roots—in your home, in your family, in your community. That involves making a commitment, making an investment both physically and emotionally, in your surroundings" (200). Other religious traditions offer families a similar sense of community, purpose, and belonging. Marcus and Tracy Glover are members of the Nation of Islam. They credit the Nation with making their marriage and family strong and breaking a three-generation cycle of single motherhood (Hewlett and West 201-202).

Cited material extends from one page to another, so both page numbers are given.

A third way that families are fighting to protect their children is by controlling the impact of the media and technology. Hewlett and West and Pipher use similar words to describe this impact. As they describe growing up today, Hewlett and West write about children living "without a skin" (xiii), and Pipher writes about "houses without walls" (12). These authors mean that today—unlike in the old days, when children were protected from the outside world while they were in their

Philips 7

homes—the home offers little protection. Even in their own living rooms, all children have to do is to turn on a TV, radio, or computer to be hit with a flood of violence, sick humor, and often weird sexuality. Children are growing up watching programs like <u>The Jerry Springer Show</u>, which has featured twisted topics such as a mother stealing her twelve-year-old's boyfriend, people who advocate associating with people only of their own race, and men who pass as women. Sadly, many parents seem to have given up even trying to protect their growing kids against garbage like this. They are like the mother quoted in <u>USA Today</u> as saying, "How can I fight five hundred channels on TV?"

Fortunately, some parents are still insisting on control over the information and entertainment that comes into their homes. Some subscribe to "The Television Project," an online educational organization that helps parents "understand how television affects their families and community and proposes alternatives that foster positive emotional, cognitive and spiritual development within families and communities." Others ban TV entirely from their homes. More try to find a way to use TV and other electronics as useful tools, but not allow them to dominate their homes. One family in Nebraska, the Millers, who home-school their children, described to Mary Pipher their attitude toward TV. They hadn't owned a TV for years, but they bought one so that they could watch the Olympics. The set is now stored in a closet unless a program is on that the family agrees is worthwhile. Some programs the Millers have

enjoyed together include the World Cup soccer games, the TV drama
Sarah Plain and Tall, and an educational TV course in sign language.
Pipher was impressed by the Miller children, and she thought their
limited exposure to TV was one reason why. In her words:

> Calm, happy children and relaxed, confident parents are so rare
> today. Probably most notable were the long attention spans of
> the children and their willingness to sit and listen to the grown-
> ups talk. The family had a manageable amount of information
> to deal with. They weren't stressed by more information than
> they could assimilate. The kids weren't overstimulated and edgy.
> Nor were they sexualized in the way most kids now are. (107)

The
conclusion
provides a
summary
and
restates
the thesis.

Pipher's words describe children raised by parents who won't give in
to the idea that their children are lost. Such parents structure ways to be
present in the home, build family ties to a community, and control the
impact of the media and technology in their homes. Through their
efforts, they succeed in raising nurtured, grounded, successful children.
Such parents acknowledge the challenges of raising kids in today's
America, but they are up to the job.

Works cited should be double-spaced. Titles of books, magazines, and the like should be underline.

Include the date you accessed a Web source—in this case, March 29, 1999.

Several of these sources—Forsey, Priesnitz, and The Television Project— are online. By going online and typing the letters after *www.* in each citation, you can access any of the sources. For example, you could type *life.ca/nl/62 /cohousing* to call up the article by Wendy Priesnitz on cohousing.

Philips 9

Works Cited

Coontz, Stephanie. <u>The Way We Really Are</u>. New York: Basic Books, 1997.

Donahue, Deirdre. "Struggling to Raise Good Kids in Toxic Times." <u>USA Today</u> 1 Oct. 1998: D1+

Forsey, Helen. "Intentional Communities." <u>Natural Life</u>; July/Aug. 1995. 29 Mar. 1999 <http://www.life.ca/nl/44/commun.html>.

Hewlett, Sylvia Ann, and Cornel West. <u>The War Against Parents</u>. Boston: Houghton Mifflin, 1998.

Kantrowitz, Barbara, and Pat Wingert. "Learning at Home: Does It Pass the Test?" <u>Newsweek</u> 5 Oct. 1998: 64-70.

Louv, Richard. <u>Childhood's Future</u>. Boston: Houghton Mifflin, 1990.

Medved, Michael, and Diane Medved. <u>Saving Childhood</u>. New York: HarperCollins, 1998.

Pipher, Mary. <u>The Shelter of Each Other</u>. New York: G. P. Putnam, 1996.

Priesnitz, Wendy. "Cohousing—A Sustainable Housing Solution." <u>Natural Life</u>; July/Aug. 1998. 30 Mar. 1999 <http://www.life.ca/nl/62/cohousing.html>.

Richardson, J. L., et al. "Substance Abuse Among Eighth-Grade Students Who Take Care of Themselves After School." <u>Pediatrics</u> 84 (1989): 556-566.

<u>The Television Project Home Page</u>. The Television Project. Apr. 6 1999 <http://www.tvp.org>.

Part Four

Handbook of Sentence Skills

23 Subjects and Verbs

The basic building blocks of English sentences are subjects and verbs. Understanding them is an important first step toward mastering a number of sentence skills.

Every sentence has a subject and a verb. Who or what the sentence speaks about is called the *subject*; what the sentence says about the subject is called the *verb*. In the following sentences, the subject is underlined once and the verb twice.

The <u>boy</u> <u>cried</u>.
That <u>fish</u> <u>smells</u>.
Many <u>people</u> <u>applied</u> for the job.
The <u>show</u> <u>is</u> a documentary.

A Simple Way to Find a Subject

To find a subject, ask *who* or *what* the sentence is about. As shown below, your answer is the subject.

Who is the first sentence about? The <u>boy</u>
What is the second sentence about? That <u>fish</u>
Who is the third sentence about? Many <u>people</u>
What is the fourth sentence about? The <u>show</u>

A Simple Way to Find a Verb

To find a verb, ask what the sentence *says about* the subject. As shown below, your answer is the verb.

What does the first sentence *say about* the boy? He <u>cried</u>.
What does the second sentence *say about* the fish? It <u>smells</u>.

What does the third sentence *say about* the people? They <u>applied</u>.

What does the fourth sentence *say about* the show? It <u>is</u> a documentary.

A second way to find the verb is to put *I, you, he, she, it,* or *they* in front of the word you think is a verb. If the result makes sense, you have a verb. For example, you could put *he* in front of *cried* in the first sentence above, with the result, *he cried,* making sense. Therefore, you know that *cried* is a verb. You could use the same test with the other three verbs as well.

Finally, it helps to remember that most verbs show action. In the sentences already considered, the three action verbs are *cried, smells,* and *applied.* Certain other verbs, known as *linking verbs,* do not show action. They do, however, give information about the subject. In "The show is a documentary," the linking verb *is* joins the subject (*show*) with a word that identifies or describes it (*documentary*). Other common linking verbs include *am, are, was, were, feel, appear, look, become,* and *seem.*

Activity

In each of the following sentences, draw one line under the subject and two lines under the verb.

1. The ripening <u>tomatoes</u> <u>glistened</u> on the sunny windowsill.
2. <u>Acupuncture</u> <u>reduces</u> the pain of my headaches.
3. <u>Elena</u> <u>twisted</u> a strand of hair around her fingers.
4. My <u>brother</u> <u>built</u> his bookshelves from cinder blocks and planks of wood.
5. A <u>jackrabbit</u> <u>bounds</u> up to fifteen feet in one leap.
6. The singer's diamond <u>earrings</u> <u>sparkled</u> in the spotlight.
7. My <u>roommate</u> <u>dries</u> her nylons over the lampshade in her bedroom.
8. On St. Patrick's Day, our neighborhood <u>tavern</u> <u>serves</u> green beer.
9. My six-year-old <u>brother</u> <u>survives</u> on a diet of peanut butter and jelly.
10. During my parents' divorce, <u>I</u> <u>felt</u> like a rag doll being torn between two people.

More about Subjects and Verbs

1 A sentence may have more than one verb, more than one subject, or several subjects and verbs.

The <u>engine</u> <u>coughed</u> and <u>sputtered</u>.

Broken <u>glass</u> and empty <u>cans</u> <u>littered</u> the parking lot.

<u>Joyce</u>, <u>Brenda</u>, and <u>Robert</u> <u>met</u> after class and <u>headed</u> downtown.

2   The subject of the sentence never appears within a prepositional phrase. A *prepositional phrase* is simply a group of words that begins with a preposition. Following is a list of common prepositions.

about	before	by	inside	over
above	behind	during	into	through
across	below	except	like	to
among	beneath	for	of	toward
around	beside	from	off	under
at	between	in	on, onto	with

Crossing out prepositional phrases will help you find the subject or subjects of a sentence.

A <u>stream</u> ~~of cold air~~ <u>seeps</u> in ~~through the space below the door~~.

<u>Specks</u> ~~of dust~~ <u>dance</u> gently ~~in a ray of sunlight~~.

The <u>people</u> ~~in the apartment above ours~~ <u>fight</u> loudly.

The murky <u>waters</u> ~~of the polluted lake~~ <u>spilled</u> ~~over the dam~~.

The amber <u>lights</u> ~~on its sides~~ <u>outlined</u> the tractor-trailer ~~in the hazy dusk~~.

3   Many verbs consist of more than one word. (The extra verbs are called *auxiliary*, or *helping*, verbs.) Here, for example, are some of the many forms of the verb *work*.

work	worked	should work
works	were working	will be working
does work	have worked	can work
is working	had worked	could be working
are working	had been working	must have worked

4 Words like *not, just, never, only,* and *always* are not part of the verb, although they may appear within the verb.

Ruby has never liked cold weather.
Our boss will not be singing with the choir this year.
The intersection has not always been this dangerous.

5 No verb preceded by *to* is ever the verb of a sentence.

At night, my son likes to read under the covers.
Evelyn decided to separate from her husband.

6 No *-ing* word by itself is ever the verb of a sentence. (It may be part of the verb, but it must have a helping verb in front of it.)

They going on a trip this weekend.
(not a sentence, because the verb is not complete)
They are going on a trip this weekend. (a sentence)

Activity

Draw a single line under subjects and a double line under verbs. Cross out prepositional phrases as necessary to find the subjects.

1. A thick layer of dust covers the top of our refrigerator.
2. In June, sagging Christmas decorations were still hanging in the windows of the abandoned house.
3. The people in the all-night coffee shop seemed weary and lost.
4. Every plant in the dim room bent toward the small window.
5. A glaring headline about the conviction of a local congressman attracted my attention.
6. Two of the biggest stores in the mall are going out of business.
7. The modem's tiny red lights suddenly started to flicker.
8. A neighbor of mine does all her work at home and E-mails it to her office.
9. The jar of peppercorns tumbled from the spice shelf and shattered on the floor.
10. The scar in the hollow of Brian's throat is the result of an emergency operation to clear his windpipe.

Review Test

Draw a single line under subjects and a double line under verbs. Cross out prepositional phrases as necessary to find the subjects.

1. With one graceful motion, the shortstop fielded the grounder and threw to first base.

2. Like human mothers, sheep and goat mothers develop close bonds with their babies.

3. Before class, Antonietta and Jorge rushed to the coffee machine in the hall.

4. I shifted uncomfortably on the lumpy mattress before falling into a restless sleep.

5. Waiting in the long ticket line, Matt shifted his weight from one foot to the other.

6. Ancient Egyptians were branding cattle more than four thousand years ago.

7. Lilacs and honeysuckle perfume our yard on summer nights.

8. The driver abruptly halted her Jeep and backed up toward a narrow parking place.

9. During the American Revolution, some brides rejected white wedding gowns and wore red as a symbol of rebellion.

10. The little girl's frantic family called a psychic to locate the child.

24 Fragments

Every sentence must have a subject and a verb and must express a complete thought. A word group that lacks a subject or a verb and does not express a complete thought is a *fragment*. Following are the most common types of fragments that people write:

1 Dependent-word fragments
2 *-ing* and *to* fragments
3 Added-detail fragments
4 Missing-subject fragments

Once you understand what specific kinds of fragments you might write, you should be able to eliminate them from your writing. The following pages explain all four types.

Dependent-Word Fragments

Some word groups that begin with a dependent word are fragments. Following is a list of common dependent words. Whenever you start a sentence with one of these words, you must be careful that a fragment does not result.

Dependent Words		
after	if, even if	when, whenever
although, though	in order that	where, wherever
as	since	whether
because	that, so that	which, whichever
before	unless	while
even though	until	who
how	what, whatever	whose

In the example below, the word group beginning with the dependent word *after* is a fragment:

After I cashed my paycheck. I treated myself to dinner.

A *dependent statement*—one starting with a dependent word like *after*—cannot stand alone. It depends on another statement to complete the thought. *After I cashed my paycheck* is a dependent statement. It leaves us hanging. We expect to find out, in the same sentence, *what happened after* the writer cashed the check. When a writer does not follow through and complete a thought, a fragment results.

To correct the fragment, simply follow through and complete the thought:

After I cashed my paycheck, I treated myself to dinner.

Remember, then, that *dependent statements by themselves are fragments.* They must be attached to a statement that makes sense standing alone.

Here are two other examples of dependent-word fragments.

I won't leave the house. Until I hear from you.

Rick finally picked up the socks. That he had thrown on the floor days ago.

Until I hear from you is a fragment; it does not make sense standing by itself. We want to know in the same statement *what cannot happen* until I hear from you. The writer must complete the thought. Likewise, *That he had thrown on the floor days ago* is not in itself a complete thought. We want to know in the same statement what *that* refers to.

How to Correct a Dependent-Word Fragment

In most cases you can correct a dependent-word fragment by attaching it to the sentence that comes after it or the sentence that comes before it:

After I cashed my paycheck, I treated myself to dinner.
(The fragment has been attached to the sentence that comes after it.)

I won't leave the house until I hear from you.
(The fragment has been attached to the sentence that comes before it.)

Rick finally picked up the socks that he had thrown on the floor days ago.
(The fragment has been attached to the sentence that comes before it.)

Another way of correcting a dependent-word fragment is simply to eliminate the dependent word by rewriting the sentence.

I cashed my paycheck and then treated myself to dinner.

I will wait to hear from you.

He had thrown them on the floor days ago.

Notes

a   Use a comma if a dependent word group comes at the *beginning* of a sentence (see also page 569):

After I cashed my paycheck, I treated myself to dinner.

However, do not generally use a comma if the dependent word group comes at the *end* of a sentence.

I won't leave the house until I hear from you.

Rick finally picked up the socks that he had thrown on the floor days ago.

b   Sometimes the dependent words *who, that, which,* or *where* appear not at the very start but *near* the start of a word group. A fragment often results:

I drove slowly past the old brick house. The place where I grew up.

The place where I grew up is not in itself a complete thought. We want to know in the same statement *where was the place* the writer grew up. The fragment can be corrected by attaching it to the sentence that comes before it:

I drove slowly past the old brick house, the place where I grew up.

Activity 1

Turn each of the following dependent word groups into a sentence by adding a complete thought. Use a comma after the dependent word group if a dependent word starts the sentence. Note the examples.

Examples   Although I felt miserable
            Although I felt miserable, I tried to smile for the photographer.

            The man who found my wallet
            The man who found my wallet returned it the next day.

Answers will vary. Examples are shown.
1. If I don't get a raise soon

    If I don't get a raise soon, I'll quit.

    _____

2. Because it was raining

    Because it was raining, we canceled the picnic.

    _____

3. When I heard the news

    When I heard the news, I cried.

    _____

4. Because I couldn't find the car keys

    Because I couldn't find the car keys, I had to walk.

    _____

5. The restaurant that we tried

    The restaurant that we tried was disappointing.

    _____

Activity 2

Underline the dependent-word fragment in each item. Then rewrite the items, correcting each fragment by attaching it to the sentence that comes before or the sentence that comes after it—whichever sounds more natural. Use a comma after the dependent word group if it starts the sentence.

1. <u>Whenever I spray deodorant.</u> My cat arches her back. She thinks she is hearing a hissing enemy.

    . . . deodorant, my cat . . .

    _____

2. My father, a salesman, was on the road all week. We had a great time playing football in the house. <u>Until he came home for the weekend.</u>

    . . . house until he . . .

    _____

3. <u>If Kim takes too long saying good-bye to her boyfriend.</u> Her father will start flicking the porch light. Then he will come out with a flashlight.

    . . . boyfriend, her father . . .

    _____

4. Scientists are studying mummified remains. <u>That are thousands of years old</u>. Most of the people were killed by parasites.

    . . . remains that are thousands . . . _____

    _____

5. <u>Before I turn on the microwave oven</u>. I have to turn off the overhead light in the kitchen. Otherwise the fuse blows.

    . . . oven, I have to . . . _____

    _____

-ing and *to* Fragments

When an *-ing* word appears at or near the start of a word group, a fragment may result. Such fragments often lack a subject and part of the verb. In the items below, underline the word groups that contain *-ing* words. Each is a fragment.

1. Ellen walked all over the neighborhood yesterday. <u>Trying to find her dog Bo</u>. Several people claimed they had seen him only hours before.

2. We sat back to watch the movie. <u>Not expecting anything special</u>. To our surprise, we clapped, cheered, and cried for the next two hours.

3. I telephoned the balloon store. <u>It being the day before our wedding anniversary</u>. I knew my wife would be surprised to receive a dozen heart-shaped balloons.

People sometimes write *-ing* fragments because they think that the subject of one sentence will work for the next word group as well. Thus, in item 1 the writer thinks that the subject *Ellen* in the opening sentence will also serve as the subject for *Trying to find her dog Bo*. But the subject must actually be in the same sentence.

How to Correct *-ing* Fragments

1 Attach the fragment to the sentence that comes before it or the sentence that comes after it, whichever makes sense. Item 1 could read: "Ellen walked all over the neighborhood yesterday trying to find her dog Bo."

2 Add a subject and change the *-ing* verb part to the correct form of the verb. Item 2 could read: "We didn't expect anything special."

3 Change *being* to the correct form of the verb *be (am, are, is, was, were)*. Item 3 could read: "It was the day before our wedding anniversary."

How to Correct *to* Fragments

When *to* appears at or near the start of a word group, a fragment sometimes results:

> At the Chinese restaurant, Tim used chopsticks. To impress his date. He spent one hour eating a small bowl of rice.

The second word group is a fragment and can be corrected by adding it to the preceding sentence:

> At the Chinese restaurant, Tim used chopsticks to impress his date.

Activity 1

Underline the *-ing* fragment in each of the following items. Then correct the item by using the method described in parentheses.

Example   <u>Stepping hard on the accelerator.</u> Stan tried to beat the truck to the intersection. He lost by a hood.
(Add the fragment to the sentence that comes after it.)
Stepping hard on the accelerator, Stan tried to beat the truck to the intersection.

1. Marble-sized hailstones fell from the sky. <u>Flattening the young plants in the cornfield.</u> A year's work was lost in an hour.
(Add the fragment to the preceding sentence.)
. . . sky, flattening . . .

2. Fire trucks raced wildly through the town, their sirens blaring. <u>Coming to a stop at my house.</u> I was only burning a pile of leaves.
(Correct the fragment by adding the subject *they* and changing *coming* to the proper form of the verb, *came*.)
. . . blaring. They came to a stop at my house. . . .

3. My phone doesn't ring. Instead, a light on it blinks. <u>The reason for this being that I am partially deaf.</u>
(Correct the fragment by changing *being* to the proper form of the verb, *is*.)
The reason for this is that I am . . .

Activity 2

Underline the *-ing* or *to* fragment in each item. Then rewrite each item, correcting the fragment by using one of the three methods described above.

1. <u>Looking at the worm on the table.</u> Shelby groaned. She knew she wouldn't like what the biology teacher said next.

   . . . table, Shelby groaned. . . .

   _____

2. I put a box of baking soda in the freezer. <u>To get rid of the musty smell.</u> However, my ice cubes still taste like old socks.

   . . . freezer to get rid of the musty smell. . . .

   _____

3. <u>Staring at the clock on the far wall.</u> I nervously began my speech. I was afraid to look at any of the people in the room.

   . . . wall, I nervously began my speech. . . .

   _____

4. Jerome sat quietly at his desk. <u>Fantasizing about the upcoming weekend.</u> He might meet the girl of his dreams at Saturday night's party.

   . . . desk, fantasizing about . . .

   _____

5. <u>To get to the bus station from here.</u> You have to walk two blocks out of your way. The sidewalk is torn up because of construction work.

   . . . from here, you have to . . .

   _____

Added-Detail Fragments

Added-detail fragments lack a subject and a verb. They often begin with one of the following words:

also	especially	except	for example	like	including	such as

Underline the one added-detail fragment in each of the following items:

1. Before a race, I eat starchy foods. <u>Such as bread and spaghetti</u>. The carbohydrates provide quick energy.
2. Bob is taking a night course in auto mechanics. <u>Also, one in plumbing</u>. He wants to save money on household repairs.
3. My son keeps several pets in his room. <u>Including hamsters and mice</u>.

People often write added-detail fragments for much the same reason they write -*ing* fragments. They think the subject and verb in one sentence will serve for the next word group. But the subject and verb must be in *each* word group.

How to Correct Added-Detail Fragments

1 Attach the fragment to the complete thought that precedes it. Item 1 could read: "Before a race, I eat starchy foods such as bread and spaghetti."

2 Add a subject and a verb to the fragment to make it a complete sentence. Item 2 could read: "Bob is taking a night course in auto mechanics. Also, he is taking one in plumbing."

3 Insert the fragment within the preceding sentence. Item 3 could read: "My son keeps several pets, including hamsters and mice, in his room."

Activity 1

Underline the fragment in each of the following items. Then make it a sentence by rewriting it, using the method described in parentheses.

Example   My mother likes watching daytime television shows. <u>Especially old movies and soap operas</u>. She says that daytime television is less violent. (Add the fragment to the preceding sentence.)

My mother likes watching daytime television shows, especially old

movies and soap operas.

1. Luis works evenings in a video store. He enjoys the fringe benefits. <u>For example, seeing the new movies first</u>. (Correct the fragment by adding the subject and verb *he sees*.)

    . . . For example, he sees the new movies first.

2. Bob's fingernails are ragged from years of working as a mechanic. And his fingertips are always black. <u>Like ink pads.</u>
    (Attach the fragment to the preceding sentence.)

    . . . black, like ink pads.

    _____

3. Electronic devices keep getting smaller. <u>Such as video cameras and cell phones.</u> Some are so tiny they look like toys.
    (Correct the fragment by inserting it in the preceding sentence.)

    Electronic devices, such as video cameras and cell phones, keep getting

    smaller. Some are . . .

Activity 2

Underline the added-detail fragment in each item. Then rewrite to correct the fragment. Use one of the three methods described above.

Methods of correction may vary.

1. Left-handed students face problems. <u>For example, right-handed desks.</u> Spiral notebooks can also be uncomfortable to use.

    . . . problems. For example, they must sit at right-handed desks. . . .

    _____

2. Mrs. Fields always wears her lucky clothes to bingo. <u>Such as a blouse printed with four-leaf clovers.</u> She also carries a rhinestone horseshoe.

    . . . clothes, such as a blouse printed with four-leaf clovers, to bingo. . . .

    _____

3. Hundreds of moths were swarming around the stadium lights. <u>Like large flecks of snow.</u> However, I knew they couldn't be snow—it was eighty degrees outside.

    . . . lights like large flecks of snow. . . .

    _____

4. Trevor buys and sells paper collectors' items. <u>For instance, comic books and movie posters.</u> He sets up a display at local flea markets and carnivals.

    . . . items. For instance, he buys and sells comic books and movie posters. . . .

    _____

5. I wonder now why I had to learn certain subjects. <u>Such as geometry.</u> No one has ever asked me about the hypotenuse of a triangle.

    . . .subjects, such as geometry. No one . . .

    _____

Missing-Subject Fragments

In each item below, underline the word group in which the subject is missing:

1. Alicia loved getting wedding presents. <u>But hated writing thank-you notes.</u>
2. Mickey has orange soda and potato chips for breakfast. <u>Then eats more junk food, like root beer and cookies, for lunch.</u>

How to Correct Missing-Subject Fragments

1 Attach the fragment to the preceding sentence. Item 1 could read: "Alicia loved getting wedding presents but hated writing thank-you notes."

2 Add a subject (which can often be a pronoun standing for the subject in the preceding sentence). Item 2 could read: "Then he eats more junk food, like root beer and cookies, for lunch."

Activity

Underline the missing-subject fragment in each item. Then rewrite that part of the item needed to correct the fragment. Use one of the two methods of correction described above.

Methods of correction may vary.

1. Every other day, Kara runs two miles. <u>Then does fifty sit-ups.</u> She hasn't lost weight, but she looks trimmer and more muscular.

   . . . miles. Then she does . . .

2. I like all kinds of fresh pizza. <u>But refuse to eat frozen pizza.</u> The sauce is always dried out, and the crust tastes like leather.

   . . . pizza. But I refuse . . .

3. Many people are allergic to seafood. They break out in hives when they eat it. <u>And can even have trouble breathing.</u>

   . . . they eat it, and they can even . . .

4.   To distract me, the dentist tugged at a corner of my mouth. <u>Then jabbed a</u>
     <u>needle into my gums and injected a painkiller.</u> I hardly felt it.
          . . . mouth. Then he jabbed a needle . . .

     _____

5.   Last semester, I took six courses. <u>And worked part-time in a discount</u>
     <u>drugstore.</u> Now that the term is all over, I don't know how I did it.
          . . . courses and worked . . .

     _____

A Review: How to Check for Sentence Fragments

1   Read your paper aloud from the *last* sentence to the *first*. You will
    be better able to see and hear whether each word group you read is a
    complete thought.

2   If you think a word group may be a fragment, ask yourself: Does this
    contain a subject and a verb and express a complete thought?

3   More specifically, be on the lookout for the most common fragments:

    • Dependent-word fragments (starting with words like *after, because,
       since, when,* and *before*)

    • *-ing* and *to* fragments *(-ing* and *to* at or near the start of a word
       group)

    • Added-detail fragments (starting with words like *for example, such
       as, also,* and *especially*)

    • Missing-subject fragments (a verb is present but not the subject)

Review Test 1

Each word group in the following student paragraph is numbered. In the space provided, write C if a word group is a complete sentence; write F if it is a fragment. You will find eight fragments in the paragraph.

C	1.	[1]I'm starting to think that there is no safe place left. [2]To ride a bicycle.
F	2.	[3]When I try to ride on the highway, in order to go to school. [4]I feel like a
F	3.	rabbit being pursued by predators. [5]Drivers whip past me at high speeds.
C	4.	[6]And try to see how close they can get to my bike without actually killing
C	5.	me. [7]When they pull onto the shoulder of the road or make a right turn.
F	6.	[8]Drivers completely ignore my vehicle. [9]On city streets, I feel more like a
F	7.	cockroach than a rabbit. [10]Drivers in the city despise bicycles. [11]Regardless
C	8.	of an approaching bike rider. [12]Street-side car doors will unexpectedly
C	9.	open. [13]Frustrated drivers who are stuck in traffic will make nasty
C	10.	comments. [14]Or shout out obscene propositions. [15]Even pedestrians in
F	11.	the city show their disregard for me. [16]While jaywalking across the street.
C	12.	[17]The pedestrian will treat me, a law-abiding bicyclist, to a withering look
C	13.	of disdain. [18]Pedestrians may even cross my path deliberately. [19]As if to
F	14.	prove their higher position in the pecking order of the city streets. [20]Today,
C	15.	bicycling can be hazardous to the rider's health.
F	16.	
C	17.	
C	18.	
F	19.	
C	20.	

Now (on separate paper) correct the fragments you have found. Attach the fragments to sentences that come before or after them or make whatever other change is needed to turn each fragment into a sentence.
Answers will vary for this part of the test.

■ Review Test 2

Underline the two fragments in each item below. Then make whatever changes are needed to turn the fragments into sentences.

Example   Sharon was going to charge her new suit. But then decided to pay cash
instead. She remembered her New Year's resolution. To cut down on her
use of credit cards.

1. We both began to tire. As we passed the halfway mark in the race. But whenever I'd hear Reggie's footsteps behind me, I would pump my legs faster.

2. I have a few phobias. Such as fear of heights and fear of dogs. My nightmare is to be trapped in a hot-air balloon. With three German shepherds.

3. Punching all the buttons on his radio in sequence, Phil kept looking for a good song. He was in the mood to cruise down the highway. And sing at the top of his voice.

4. My children joke that we celebrate "Hanumas." With our Jewish neighbors. We share Hanukkah and Christmas activities, Including making potato pancakes at their house and decorating our tree.

5. I noticed two cartons of cigarettes. Sticking up out of my neighbor's trash bag. I realized he had made up his mind. To give up smoking for the fifth time this year.

6. I've decided to leave home. And rent an apartment. By being away from home and on my own, I will get along better with my parents.

7. The alley behind our house was flat. Except for a wide groove in the center. We used to sail paper boats down the groove. Whenever it rained hard enough to create a "river" there.

8. Don passed the computer school's aptitude test. Which qualifies him for nine months of training. Don kidded that anyone could be accepted. If he or she had $4,000.

- **Review Test 3**

Turn each of the following word groups into a complete sentence.

Examples   With trembling hands
With trembling hands, I headed for the front of the classroom.

As the race wore on
Some runners dropped out as the race wore on.

Answers will vary; examples are given.

1. After the storm passed
   . . . passed, the sun came out.

2. Such as fresh fruits and vegetables
   I hate any food that's good for me, such as fresh fruit and vegetables.

3. During the mystery movie
   . . . movie, I fell asleep.

4. Unless I study harder
   . . . harder, I'll flunk out.

5. Enrique, who works at his uncle's restaurant
   . . . restaurant, is hoping to become a chef.

6. Knocking over the table
   A strong wind suddenly came up, knocking over the table.

7. To get to class on time
   . . . on time, Jeannie ran all the way.

8. Hurrying to get dressed
   . . . dressed, Dana put his shoes on the wrong feet.

9. Up in the attic
   . . . attic is an old violin.

10. Losing my temper
    temper, I yelled at the kids.

25 Run-Ons

What Are Run-Ons?

A *run-on* is two complete thoughts that are run together with no adequate sign given to mark the break between them.*

Some run-ons have no punctuation at all to mark the break between the thoughts. Such run-ons are known as *fused sentences:* they are fused, or joined together, as if they were only one thought.

Fused Sentences

Mario told everyone in the room to be quiet his favorite show was on.

My blow-drier shorted out I showed up for work with Harpo Marx hair.

In other run-ons, known as *comma splices,* a comma is used to connect, or "splice" together, the two complete thoughts. However, a comma alone is *not enough* to connect two complete thoughts. Some stronger connection than a comma alone is needed.

Comma Splices

Mario told everyone in the room to be quiet, his favorite show was on.

My blow-drier shorted out, I showed up for work with Harpo Marx hair.

Comma splices are the most common kind of run-on. Students sense that some kind of connection is needed between two thoughts, and so they often put a comma at the dividing point. But the comma alone is *not sufficient.* A stronger, clearer mark is needed between the two complete thoughts.

---

*Notes:

1. Some instructors regard all run-ons as fused sentences. A run-on or fused sentence is one kind of error, and a comma splice is another kind of error. The bottom line is that you do not want either fused sentences or comma splices in your writing.

2. Some instructors refer to each complete thought in a run-on as an *independent clause.* A *clause* is simply a group of words having a subject and a verb. A clause may be *independent* (expressing a complete thought and able to stand alone) or *dependent* (not expressing a complete thought and not able to stand alone). Using this terminology, we'd say that a run-on is two independent clauses run together with no adequate sign given to mark the break between them.

A Warning—Words That Can Lead to Run-Ons:

People often write run-ons when the second complete thought begins with one of the following words:

I	we	there	now
you	they	this	then
he, she, it	that	next	

Whenever you use one of these words in writing a paper, remember to be on the alert for run-ons.

How to Correct Run-Ons

Here are three common methods of correcting a run-on:

1 Use a period and a capital letter to break the two complete thoughts into separate sentences:

Mario told everyone in the room to be quiet. His favorite show was on.
My blow-drier shorted out. I showed up for work with Harpo Marx hair.

2 Use a comma plus a joining word (*and, but, for, or, nor, so, yet*) to connect the two complete thoughts:

Mario told everyone in the room to be quiet, for his favorite show was on.
My blow-drier shorted out, and I showed up for work with Harpo Marx hair.

3 Use a semicolon to connect the two complete thoughts:

Mario told everyone in the room to be quiet; his favorite show was on.
My blow-drier shorted out; I showed up for work with Harpo Marx hair.

A fourth method of correcting a run-on is to use *subordination.* The following activities will give you practice in the first three methods. Subordination is described fully on page 116, in the section of the book that deals with sentence variety.

Method 1: Period and a Capital Letter

One way of correcting a run-on is to use a period and a capital letter between the two complete thoughts. Use this method especially if the thoughts are not closely related or if another method would make the sentence too long.

Activity

In each of the following run-ons, locate the point at which one complete thought ends and another begins. Each is a *fused sentence*—that is, each consists of two sentences fused, or joined together, with no punctuation at all between them. Reading each sentence aloud will help you "hear" where a major break or split between the thoughts occurs. At such a point, your voice will probably drop and pause.

Correct the run-on by putting a period at the end of the first thought and a capital letter at the start of the next thought.

Example   Bev's clock radio doesn't work anymore. She spilled a glass of soda
on it.

1. The men at the door claimed to have paving material left over from another
   job. They wanted to pave our driveway for a "bargain price."

2. Linh, a paralegal who speaks Vietnamese, helps other people from her country
   write wills. She assists others by going with them when they have to appear
   in court.

3. Vicky has her own unique style of dressing. She wore a man's tuxedo with a
   red bow tie to her cousin's wedding.

4. In the summer, ants are attracted to water. They will often enter a house through
   the dishwasher.

5. Humans have managed to adapt to any environment. They can survive in Arctic
   wastes, tropical jungles, and barren deserts.

6. A five-year-old child knows over six thousand words. He or she has also
   learned more than one thousand rules of grammar.

7. I rummaged around the crowded drawer looking for a pair of scissors. $\overset{T}{\cancel{t}}$hen it suddenly stabbed me in the finger.

8. Squirrels like to jump from trees onto our roof. $\overset{T}{\cancel{t}}$heir footsteps sound like ghosts running around our attic.

9. Today I didn't make good time driving to work. $\overset{E}{\cancel{e}}$very traffic light along the way was red.

10. Since I signed up for premium movie channels on cable, I've taped more than forty movies. I'll never have time to watch them all.

Method 2: Comma and a Joining Word

Another way of correcting a run-on is to use a comma plus a joining word to connect the two complete thoughts. Joining words (also called *conjunctions*) include *and, but, for, or, nor, so,* and *yet.* Here is what the four most common joining words mean:

and   in addition

Teresa works full time for an accounting firm, and she takes evening classes.

(*And* means *in addition:* Teresa works full time for an accounting firm; *in addition,* she takes evening classes.)

but   however, on the other hand

I turned to the want ads, but I knew my dream job wouldn't be listed.

(*But* means *however:* I turned to the want ads; *however,* I knew my dream job wouldn't be listed.)

for   because

Lizards become sluggish at night, for they need the sun's warmth to maintain an active body temperature.

(*For* means *because*: Lizards become sluggish at night *because* they need the sun's warmth to maintain an active body temperature.)

so   as a result, therefore

> The canoe touched bottom, so Dave pushed it toward deeper water.

(*So* means *as a result:* The canoe touched bottom; *as a result*, Dave pushed it toward deeper water.)

Activity 1

Insert the joining word (*and, but, for, so*) that logically connects the two thoughts in each sentence.

1. Napoleon may have been a brave general, ____*but*____ he was afraid of cats.

2. The large dog was growling at me, ____*and*____ there were white bubbles of foam around his mouth.

3. The library had just closed, ____*so*____ I couldn't get any of the reserved books.

4. He checked on the new baby every five minutes, ____*for*____ he was afraid that something would happen to her.

5. Kate thought the milk was fresh, ____*but*____ it broke up into little sour flakes in her coffee.

6. Elephants have no thumbs, ____*so*____ baby elephants suck their trunks.

7. Lonnie heard a noise and looked out the window, ____*but*____ the only thing there was his reflection.

8. Although I like most creatures, I am not fond of snakes, ____*and*____ I like spiders even less.

9. My sister wants to exercise more and use her car less, ____*so*____ she walks to the grocery store.

10. A young woman in our neighborhood recently tried to kill herself, ____*and (or so)*____ her friends are afraid that she will try it again.

Activity 2

Add a complete and closely related thought to go with each of the following statements. Use a comma plus the indicated joining word when you write the second thought.

Example   for   I decided to leave school an hour early, ____*for I had a pounding*____

____*headache.*____

Answers will vary; examples are given.

but   1.   The corner store is convenient __, but it's not very clean.__

for   2.   Leo attended night class __, for he had a daytime job.__

and   3.   Aisha studied for an hour before dinner __, and after dinner she went to the__ library.

so   4.   Paul can't retrieve his E-mail __, so he feels very frustrated.__

but   5.   I needed a haircut __, but I decided to wait another week.__

Activity 3

Correct each run-on with either (1) a period and a capital letter or (2) a comma and a logical joining word. Do not use the same method of correction for every sentence.

Some of the run-ons are fused sentences (there is no punctuation between the two complete thoughts), and some are comma splices (there is only a comma between the two complete thoughts). One sentence is correct.

Example   There was a strange odor in the house_so_ Burt called the gas company immediately.

Answers may vary; examples are shown.

1.   Luis got a can of soda from the refrigerator_and_ then he walked outside to sit on the porch steps.

2.   Cockroaches adapt to any environment_T_hey have even been found living inside nuclear reactors.

3.   My dog was panting from the heat_,so_ I decided to wet him down with the garden hose.

4.   Our science class is working on a weather project with students from Russia_W_e communicate by computer almost every day.

5.   The best-selling items in the zoo gift shop are the stuffed pandas and the polar-bear T-shirts_T_he profits from these items help support the real animals in the zoo.

6. The bristles of the paintbrushes were very stiff,~*but*~ soaking them in turpentine made them soft again.

7. Tri Lee borrows cassettes from the library to listen to on the way to work~*S*~ some are music, and some are recordings of best-selling books.

8. Last week, Rita's two boys chased the baby-sitter out of the house,~*so*~ now the girl won't come back.

9. We knew a power failure had occurred, for all the clocks in the building were forty-seven minutes slow. *Correct*

10. I volunteered to run the "Meals on Wheels" service in our city.~*W*~ we deliver hot meals to sick or housebound people.

Method 3: Semicolon

A third method of correcting a run-on is to use a semicolon to mark the break between two thoughts. A *semicolon* (;) looks like a period above a comma and is sometimes called a *strong comma*. A semicolon signals more of a pause than a comma alone but not quite the full pause of a period. When it is used to correct run-ons, the semicolon can be used alone or with a transitional word.

Semicolon Alone: Here are some earlier sentences that were connected with a comma plus a joining word. Now they are connected by a semicolon alone. Notice that the semicolon alone—unlike the comma alone—can be used to connect the two complete thoughts in each sentence:

Lonnie heard a noise and looked out the window; the only thing there was his reflection.

He checked on the new baby every five minutes; he was afraid something would happen to her.

Lizards become sluggish at night; they need the sun's warmth to maintain an active body temperature.

The large dog was growling at me; there were white bubbles of foam around his mouth.

We knew a power failure had occurred; all the clocks in the building were forty-seven minutes slow.

Using semicolons can add to sentence variety. For some people, however, the semicolon is a confusing punctuation mark. Keep in mind that if you are not comfortable using it, you can and should use one of the the first two methods of correcting run-ons.

Activity

Insert a semicolon where the break occurs between the two complete thoughts in each of the following sentences.

Example   The plumber gave me an estimate of $60; I decided to repair the faucet myself.

1. The children stared at the artichokes on their plates; they didn't know how to eat the strange vegetable.
2. I changed that lightbulb just last week; now it's blown again.
3. The Great Wall of China is immense; it's the only man-made structure visible from the Moon.
4. Elaine woke up at 3 A.M. to the smell of sizzling bacon; her husband was having another insomnia attack.
5. Jamie curled up under the covers; she tried to get warm by grasping her icy feet with her chilly hands.
6. Three single mothers rent one house; they share bills and help each other out.
7. Ice had formed on the inside edge of our window; Joey scratched a J in it with his finger.
8. Charles peered into the microscope; he saw only his own eyelashes.
9. A man in a bear suit walked slowly down the street; the children stopped their play to stare at him.
10. I angrily punched a hole in the wall with my fist; later I covered the hole with a picture.

Semicolon with a Transitional Word: A semicolon can be used with a transitional word and a comma to join two complete thoughts. Here are some examples:

Larry believes in being prepared for emergencies; therefore, he stockpiles canned goods in his basement.

I tried to cash my paycheck; however, I had forgotten to bring identification.

Athletic shoes must fit perfectly; otherwise, wearers may injure their feet or ankles.

A short nap at the end of the day relaxes me; in addition, it gives me the energy to spend the evening on my homework.

Some zoo animals have not learned how to be good parents; as a result, baby animals are sometimes brought up in zoo nurseries and even in private homes.

People use seventeen muscles when they smile; on the other hand, they use forty-three muscles when they frown.

Following is a list of common transitional words (also known as *adverbial conjunctions*), with brief meanings.

Transitional Word	Meaning
however	but
nevertheless	however
on the other hand	however
instead	as a substitute
meanwhile	in the intervening time
otherwise	under other conditions
indeed	in fact
in addition	also, and
also	in addition
moreover	in addition
furthermore	in addition
as a result	thus, therefore
thus	as a result
consequently	as a result
therefore	as a result

Activity

For each sentence, choose a logical transitional word from the box above, and write it in the space provided. Use a semicolon *before* the connector and a comma *after* it.

Example   I dread going to parties; *however,* my husband loves meeting new people.

Some answers may vary.

1. Jackie suffers from migraine headaches *; therefore* her doctor has advised her to avoid caffeine and alcohol.

2. Ray's apartment is always neat and clean *; on the other hand,* the interior of his car looks like the aftermath of a tornado.

3. I try to attend all my math classes *; otherwise* I'll get too far behind to pass the weekly quizzes.

4. B. J. was singing Fiona Apple tunes in the shower *; meanwhile* his toast was burning in the kitchen.

5. The reporter was tough and experienced *; however,* even he was stunned by the tragic events.

A Note on Subordination

A fourth method of joining related thoughts is to use subordination. *Subordination* is a way of showing that one thought in a sentence is not as important as another thought. (Subordination is explained in full on page 116.) Below are three earlier sentences, recast so that one idea is subordinated to (made less important than) the other idea. In each case, the subordinate (or less important) thought is underlined. Note that each subordinate clause begins with a dependent word.

Because the library had just closed, I couldn't get any of the reserved books.

When the canoe touched bottom, Dave pushed the craft toward deeper water.

I didn't make good time driving to work today because every traffic light was red.

A Review: How to Check for Run-Ons

1 To see if a sentence is a run-on, read it aloud and listen for a break marking two complete thoughts. Your voice will probably drop and pause at the break.

2 To check an entire paper, read it aloud from the *last* sentence to the *first*. Doing so will help you hear and see each complete thought.

3 Be on the lookout for words that can lead to run-on sentences:

I	he, she, it	they	this	then	now
you	we	there	that	next	

4 Correct run-ons by using one of the following methods:

Period and a capital letter

Comma and a joining word (*and, but, for, or, nor, so, yet*)

Semicolon, alone or with a transitional word

Subordination

■ Review Test 1

Correct each run-on with either (1) a period and a capital letter or (2) a comma (if needed) and the joining word *and, but, for,* or *so.* Do not use the same method of correction for every sentence.

Some of the run-ons are fused sentences (there is no punctuation between the two complete thoughts), and some are comma splices (there is only a comma between the two complete thoughts). One sentence is correct.

Some answers may vary.

1. Our boss expects us to work four hours without a break, *but* he wanders off to a vending machine at least once an hour.

2. The children in the next car were making faces at other drivers. *W*hen I made a face back, they giggled and sank out of sight.

3. Chuck bent over and lifted the heavy tray. *T*hen he heard an ominous crack in his back.

4. The branches of the tree were bare *, and* they made a dark feathery pattern against the orange-pink sunset.

5. In the grimy bakery window, cobwebs were in every corner, *and* ‸a rat was crawling over a birthday cake.

6. Our class wanted to do something for the earthquake victims, *so* ‸we sent a donation to the Red Cross.

7. My ex-husband hit me just once in our marriage. *F* ~~f~~ive minutes later I was packed and walking out the door.

8. Aunt Jeanne thought a warm dry climate would improve her health *, so* ‸she moved to Arizona.

9. The average American teenager spends thirty-eight hours a week on schoolwork. *T* ~~t~~he average Japanese teenager spends about sixty.

10. We stocked our backpacks with high-calorie candy bars, and we also brought bags of dried apricots and peaches. *Correct*

■ Review Test 2

Correct each run-on by using (1) a period and a capital letter, (2) a comma and a joining word, or (3) a semicolon. Do not use one method exclusively.
Answers may vary.

1. The magazine had lain in the damp mailbox for two days; its pages were blurry and swollen.

2. With a groan, Margo pried off her high heels, *and* ‸then she plunged her swollen feet into a bucket of baking soda and hot water.

3. At 2 A.M. the last customer left the diner, *and* ‸a busboy began stacking chairs on the tables for the night.

4. Hypnosis has nothing to do with the occult. *I* ~~i~~t is merely a state of deep relaxation.

5. Many young adults today live at home with their parents *, for* ‸this allows them to save money.

6. I waited for the clanking train to clear the intersection *, but* ‸rusty boxcars just kept rolling slowly along the rails.

7. Early in life, Thomas Edison suffered with deafness,$\overset{so}{\wedge}$ he taught his wife-to-be Morse code while he was courting her.

8. Originally, horses were too small to carry riders very far$\overset{, so}{\wedge}$ larger horses had to be bred for use in warfare.

9. The words *month, silver, purple,* and *orange* have something in common$\underset{\wedge}{\overset{N}{\not{\text{no}}}}$ other English words rhyme with them.

10. The broken soda machine dispensed a cup or soda,$\overset{but}{\wedge}$ it would not provide both at the same time.

■ Review Test 3

Locate and correct the five run-ons in the passage that follows.
Corrections may vary.

My worst experience of the week was going home for lunch, rather than eating at work. My children didn't know I was coming,$\overset{so}{\wedge}$ they had used most of the bread. All I had to make a sandwich

with were two thin, crumpled pieces of crust. I sat there eating my tattered sandwich and trying

to relax,$\overset{but}{\wedge}$ then the telephone rang. It was for my daughter, who was in the bathroom$\overset{;}{\wedge}$ she called

down to me that I should get the person's name and number. As soon as I sat down again, someone

knocked on the door$\overset{I}{\wedge}$ It was a neatly dressed couple with bright eyes who wanted to talk with

me about a higher power in life. I politely got rid of them and went back to finish lunch. I thought

I would relax over my coffee$\overset{, but}{\wedge}$ I had to break up a fight between my two young sons about which

television channel to watch. As a last bit of frustration, my daughter came downstairs and asked

me to drive her over to a friend's house before I went back to work.

■ Review Test 4

On separate paper, write quickly for five minutes about what you did this past weekend. Don't worry about spelling, punctuation, finding exact words, or organizing your thoughts. Just focus on writing as many words as you can without stopping.

After you have finished, go back and correct any run-ons in your writing.

26 Regular and Irregular Verbs

Regular Verbs

A Brief Review of Regular Verbs

Every verb has four principal parts: *present, past, past participle,* and *present participle.* These parts can be used to build all the verb *tenses*—the times shown by verbs.

Most verbs in English are regular. The past and past participles of a regular verb are formed by adding *-d* or *-ed* to the present. The *past participle* is the form of the verb used with the helping verbs *have, has,* or *had* (or some form of *be* with passive verbs). The *present participle* is formed by adding *-ing* to the present.

Here are the principal parts of some regular verbs:

Present	Past	Past Participle	Present Participle
shout	shouted	shouted	shouting
prepare	prepared	prepared	preparing
surprise	surprised	surprised	surprising
tease	teased	teased	teasing
frighten	frightened	frightened	frightening

Nonstandard Forms of Regular Verbs

Many people have grown up in communities where nonstandard forms of regular verbs are used in everyday speech. Instead of saying, for example, "That girl *looks* tired," a person using a community dialect might say, "That girl *look* tired." Instead of saying, "Yesterday I *fixed* the car," a person using a community dialect might say, "Yesterday I *fix* the car." Community dialects have richness and power but are a drawback in college and in the world of work, where regular English verb forms must be used.

The following chart compares the nonstandard and the regular verb forms of the verb *work.*

Nonstandard Verb Form (Do not use in your writing)		Regular Verb Form (Use for clear communication)	
Present tense			
I works	we works	I work	we work
you works	you works	you work	you work
he, she, it work	they works	he, she, it works	they work
Past tense			
I work	we work	I worked	we worked
you work	you work	you worked	you worked
he, she, it work	they work	he, she, it worked	they worked

To avoid nonstandard usage, memorize the forms shown above for the regular verb *work*. Then use the activities that follow to help make the inclusion of verb endings a writing habit.

Present Tense Endings: The verb ending *-s* or *-es* is needed with a regular verb in the present tense when the subject is *he, she, it,* or any *one person or thing.*

He reads every night.

She watches television every night.

It appears they have little in common.

Activity

Some verbs in the sentences that follow need *-s* or *-es* endings. Cross out each nonstandard verb form and write the standard form in the space provided.

wakes	1.	My radio ~~wake~~ me up every morning with soft music.
clowns	2.	Lyle always ~~clown~~ around at the start of the class.
watches	3.	My wife ~~watch~~ our baby in the morning, and I take over afternoons.
wants	4.	Brenda ~~want~~ to go to nursing school next year.
works	5.	My brain ~~work~~ much better at night than it does in early morning.

Past Tense Endings: The verb ending -*d* or -*ed* is needed with a regular verb in the past tense.

This morning I completed my research paper.
The recovering hospital patient walked slowly down the corridor.
Some students hissed when the new assignment was given out.

Activity

Some verbs in the sentences that follow need -*d* or -*ed* endings. Cross out each nonstandard verb form and write the standard form in the space provided.

caved	1.	One of my teeth ~~cave~~ in when I bit on the hard pretzel.
complained	2.	The accident victim ~~complain~~ of dizziness right before passing out.
realized	3.	We ~~realize~~ a package was missing when we got back from shopping.
burned	4.	I ~~burn~~ a hole in my shirt while ironing it.
edged	5.	The driver ~~edge~~ her car into the intersection while the light was still red.

Irregular Verbs

Irregular verbs have irregular forms in past tense and past participle. For example, the past tense of the irregular verb *choose* is *chose*; its part participle is *chosen*.

Almost everyone has some degree of trouble with irregular verbs. When you are unsure about the form of a verb, you can check the list of irregular verbs below and on the following pages. (The present participle is not shown on this list because it is formed simply by adding -*ing* to the base form of the verb.) Or you can check a dictionary, which gives the principal parts of irregular verbs.

A List of Irregular Verbs

Present	Past	Past Participle
arise	arose	arisen
awake	awoke *or* awaked	awoken *or* awaked
be (am, are, is)	was (were)	been
become	became	become
begin	began	begun
bend	bent	bent
bite	bit	bitten

Present	Past	Past Participle
blow	blew	blown
break	broke	broken
bring	brought	brought
build	built	built
burst	burst	burst
buy	bought	bought
catch	caught	caught
choose	chose	chosen
come	came	come
cost	cost	cost
cut	cut	cut
do (does)	did	done
draw	drew	drawn
drink	drank	drunk
drive	drove	driven
eat	ate	eaten
fall	fell	fallen
feed	fed	fed
feel	felt	felt
fight	fought	fought
find	found	found
fly	flew	flown
freeze	froze	frozen
get	got	got *or* gotten
give	gave	given
go (goes)	went	gone
grow	grew	grown
have (has)	had	had
hear	heard	heard
hide	hid	hidden
hold	held	held
hurt	hurt	hurt
keep	kept	kept
know	knew	known
lay	laid	laid
lead	led	led
leave	left	left
lend	lent	lent

Present	Past	Past Participle
let	let	let
lie	lay	lain
light	lit	lit
lose	lost	lost
make	made	made
meet	met	met
pay	paid	paid
ride	rode	ridden
ring	rang	rung
run	ran	run
say	said	said
see	saw	seen
sell	sold	sold
send	sent	sent
shake	shook	shaken
shrink	shrank	shrunk
shut	shut	shut
sing	sang	sung
sit	sat	sat
sleep	slept	slept
speak	spoke	spoken
spend	spent	spent
stand	stood	stood
steal	stole	stolen
stick	stuck	stuck
sting	stung	stung
swear	swore	sworn
swim	swam	swum
take	took	taken
teach	taught	taught
tear	tore	torn
tell	told	told
think	thought	thought
wake	woke *or* waked	woke *or* waked
wear	wore	worn
win	won	won
write	wrote	written

Activity

Cross out the incorrect verb form in each of the following sentences. Then write the correct form of the verb in the space provided.

___flown___   Example   After it had ~~flew~~ into the picture window, the dazed bird huddled on the ground.

___chosen___   1. As graduation neared, Michelle worried about the practicality of the major she'd ~~chose~~.

___began___   2. Before we could find seats, the theater darkened and the opening credits ~~begun~~ to roll.

___drank___   3. To be polite, I ~~drunk~~ the slightly sour wine that my grandfather poured from his carefully hoarded supply.

___broke___   4. With a thunderous crack, the telephone pole ~~breaked~~ in half from the impact of the speeding car.

___shrank___   5. The inexperienced nurse ~~shrunk~~ from touching the patient's raw, burned skin.

___rang___   6. After a day on the noisy construction site, Sam's ears ~~rung~~ for hours with a steady hum.

___forgotten___   7. Sheila had ~~forgot~~ to write her social security number on the test form, so the computer rejected her answer sheet.

___gone___   8. If I had ~~went~~ to work ten minutes earlier, I would have avoided being caught in the gigantic traffic snarl.

___thrown___   9. After the bicycle hit a patch of soft sand, the rider was ~~throwed~~ into the thorny bushes along the roadside.

___blew___   10. Prehistoric people ~~blowed~~ paint over their outstretched hands to stencil their handprints on cave walls.

Nonstandard Forms of Three Common Irregular Verbs

People who use nonstandard forms of regular verbs also tend to use nonstandard forms of three common irregular verbs: *be, have,* and *do.* Instead of saying, for example, "My neighbors *are* nice people," a person using a nonstandard form might say, "My neighbors *be* nice people." Instead of saying, "She doesn't agree," they might say, "She *don't* agree." Instead of saying, "We have tickets," they might say, "We *has* tickets."

The following charts compare the nonstandard and the standard forms of *be, have,* and *do.*

Be

Community Dialect (Do not use in your writing)		Standard English (Use for clear communication)	
Present tense			
I be (*or* is)	we be	I am	we are
you be	you be	you are	you are
he, she, it be	they be	he, she, it is	they are
Past tense			
I were	we was	I was	we were
you was	you was	you were	you were
he, she, it were	they was	he, she, it was	they were

Have

Community Dialect (Do not use in your writing)		Standard English (Use for clear communication)	
Present tense			
I has	we has	I have	we have
you has	you has	you have	you have
he, she, it have	they has	he, she, it has	they have
Past tense			
I has	we has	I had	we had
you has	you has	you had	you had
he, she, it have	they has	he, she, it had	they had

Do

Community Dialect		Standard English	
(Do not use in you writing)		(Use for clear communication)	
Present tense			
I does	we do	I do	we do
you does	you does	you do	you do
he, she, it do	they does	he, she, it does	they do
Past tense			
I done	we done	I did	we did
you done	you done	you did	you did
he, she, it done	they done	he, she, it did	they did

Note: Many people have trouble with one negative form of *do*. They will say, for example, "He don't agree" instead of "He doesn't agree," or they will say "The door don't work" instead of "The door doesn't work." Be careful to avoid the common mistake of using *don't* instead of *doesn't*.

Activity

Cross out the nonstandard verb form in each sentence. Then write the standard form of *be, have,* or *do* in the space provided.

is	1. My cat, Tugger, be the toughest animal I know.
has	2. He have survived many close calls.
was	3. Three years ago, he were caught inside a car's engine.
had	4. He have one ear torn off and lost the sight in one eye.
were	5. We was surprised that he lived through the accident.
was	6. Within weeks, though, he were back to normal.
were	7. Then, last year, we was worried that we would lose Tugger.
were	8. Lumps that was growing on his back turned out to be cancer.
did	9. But the vet done an operation that saved Tugger's life.
does	10. By now, we know that Tugger really do have nine lives.

■ **Review Test 1**

Cross out the incorrect verb form in each sentence. Then write the correct form in the space provided.

walked   1. The health inspectors ~~walk~~ into the kitchen as the cook was picking up a hamburger off the floor.

stolen   2. The thieves would have ~~stole~~ my stereo, but I had had it engraved with a special identification number.

chose   3. At the Chinese restaurant, Hollis ~~choose~~ his food by the number.

torn   4. He had ~~tore~~ his girl friend's picture into little pieces and tossed them out the window.

have   5. Because I ~~has~~ asthma, I carry an inhaler to use when I lose my breath.

don't   6. Baked potatoes ~~doesn't~~ have as many calories as I thought.

began   7. The grizzly bear, with the dart dangling from its side, ~~begun~~ to feel the effects of the powerful tranquilizer.

checked   8. Yesterday I ~~check~~ my bank balance and saw my money was getting low.

have   9. Many childhood diseases ~~has~~ almost vanished in the United States.

stuck   10. Nancy ~~sticked~~ notes on the refrigerator with fruit-shaped magnets.

■ **Review Test 2**

Write short sentences that use the form requested for the following verbs.

Example   Past of *grow*   *I grew my own tomatoes last year.*

Answers will vary; examples are given.

1. Past of *know*   *I knew I could pass the course, and I did.*

2. Present of *take*   *To get to work, Luz takes two buses and a subway.*

3. Past participle of *give*   *Mom has always given me good advice.*

4. Past participle of *write*   *Have you ever written a narrative essay?*

5. Past of *do*   *As a schoolchild, I never did my homework until the last minute.*

6. Past of *talk*   *They talked for an hour before finally hanging up.*

7. Present of *begin*   *An opera usually begins with an overture.*

8. Past of *go*   *After work, Todd went shopping.*

9. Past participle of *see*   *I have not seen my cousin for years.*

10. Present of *drive*   *My kids drive me crazy sometimes.*

27 Subject-Verb Agreement

A verb must agree with its subject in number. A *singular subject* (one person or thing) takes a singular verb. A *plural subject* (more than one person or thing) takes a plural verb. Mistakes in subject-verb agreement are sometimes made in the following situations:

1 When words come between the subject and the verb
2 When a verb comes before the subject
3 With compound subjects
4 With indefinite pronouns

Each of these situations is explained in this chapter.

Words Between Subject and Verb

Words that come between the subject and the verb do not change subject-verb agreement. In the sentence

The crinkly lines *around Joan's mouth* give her a friendly look.

the subject (*lines*) is plural and so the verb (*give*) is plural. The words that come between the subject and the verb are a prepositional phrase: *around Joan's mouth.* They do not affect subject-verb agreement. (A list of prepositions can be found on page 411.)

To help find the subject of certain sentences, you should cross out prepositional phrases.

The lumpy salt in the shakers needs to be changed.

An old chair with broken legs has sat in our basement for years.

Activity

Underline the subject and lightly cross out any words that come between the subject and the verb. Then double-underline the verb in parentheses that you believe is correct.

1. Some members ~~of the parents' association~~ (want, <u>wants</u>) to ban certain books from the school library.

2. Chung's trench coat, ~~with its big lapels and shoulder flaps~~, (make, <u>makes</u>) him feel like a tough private eye.

3. Misconceptions ~~about apes like the gorilla~~ (has, <u>have</u>) turned a relatively peaceful animal into a terrifying monster.

4. The rising cost ~~of necessities like food and shelter~~ (force, <u>forces</u>) many elderly people to live in poverty.

5. In my opinion, a few slices ~~of pepperoni pizza~~ (<u>make</u>, makes) a great evening.

Verb Before Subject

A verb agrees with its subject even when the verb comes *before* the subject. Words that may precede the subject include *there, here,* and, in questions, *who, which, what,* and *where.*

Here are some examples of sentences in which the verb appears before the subject:

> There are wild dogs in our neighborhood.
> In the distance was a billow of black smoke.
> Here is the newspaper.
> Where are the children's coats?

If you are unsure about the subject, ask *who* or *what* of the verb. With the first example above, you might ask, "*What* are in our neighborhood?" The answer, *wild dogs,* is the subject.

Activity

Write the correct form of each verb in the space provided.

(is, are)   1. There ___are___ dozens of frenzied shoppers waiting for the store to open.

(is, are)   2. Here ___are___ the notes from yesterday's anthropology lecture.

(do, does)   3. When ___do___ we take our break?

(was, were)   4. There ___were___ scraps of yellowing paper stuck between the pages of the cookbook.

(was, were)   5. At the very bottom of the grocery list ___was___ an item that meant a trip all the way back to aisle one.

Compound Subjects

A *compound subject* is two subjects separated by a joining word, such as *and*. Subjects joined by *and* generally take a plural verb.

A patchwork quilt and a sleeping bag cover my bed in the winter.
Clark and Lois are a contented couple.

When subjects are joined by *either . . . or, neither . . . nor, not only . . . but also,* the verb agrees with the subject closer to the verb.

Neither the negotiator nor the union leaders want the strike to continue.

The nearer subject, *leaders,* is plural, and so the verb is plural.

Activity

Write the correct form of the verb in the space provided.

(sit, sits)

1. A crusty baking pan and a greasy plate __sit__ on the countertop.

(cover, covers)

2. Spidery cracks and a layer of dust __cover__ the ivory keys on the old piano.

(know, knows)

3. Not only the assistant manager but also the secretaries __know__ that the company is folding.

(was, were)

4. In eighteenth-century France, makeup and high heels __were__ worn by men.

(smell, smells)

5. Either the trash can or those socks __smell__ horrible.

Indefinite Pronouns

The following words, known as *indefinite pronouns,* always take singular verbs:

(-one words)	(-body words)	(-thing words)	
one	nobody	nothing	each
anyone	anybody	anything	either
everyone	everybody	everything	neither
someone	somebody	something	

Note: *Both* always takes a plural verb.

Activity

Write the correct form of the verb in the space provided.

(suit, suits)   1.   Neither of those hairstyles __suits__ the shape of your face.

(mention, mentions)   2.   Somebody without much sensitivity always __mentions__ my birthmark.

(is, are)   3.   Both of the puppies __are__ cute in their own ways.

(enter, enters)   4.   Everyone __enters__ the college kite-flying contest in the spring.

(fall, falls)   5.   One of these earrings constantly __falls__ off my ear.

■ Review Test 1

In the space provided, write the correct form of the verb shown in the margin.

(is, are)   1.   Some wheelchair-bound patients, as a result of a successful experiment, __are__ using trained monkeys as helpers.

(was, were)   2.   Each of their children __was__ given a name picked at random from a page of the Bible.

(seem, seems)   3.   Many of the headlines in the *National Enquirer* __seem__ hard to believe.

(is, are)   4.   Envelopes, file folders, and a telephone book __are__ jammed into Lupe's kitchen drawers.

(contains,   5. Neither of the main dishes at tonight's dinner <u>contains</u> any meat.
contain)

(damage,   6. The use of metal chains and studded tires <u>damages</u> roadways by chipping
damages)   away at the paved surface.

(was, were)   7. Next to the cash register <u>was</u> a can for donations to the animal
                 protection society.

(makes,   8. A metal grab bar bolted onto the tiles <u>makes</u> it easier for elderly people
make)   to get in and out of the bathtub.

(cleans,   9. In exchange for a reduced rent, Karla and James <u>clean</u> the dentist's office
clean)   beneath their second-floor apartment.

(is, are)   10. One of the hospital's delivery rooms <u>is</u> furnished with bright carpets
                 and curtains to resemble a room at home.

■ Review Test 2

Cross out the incorrect verb form in each sentence. In addition, underline the subject or subjects that go with the verb. Then write the correct form of the verb in the space provided.

<u>are</u>   1. Why ~~is~~ <u>Martha</u> and her <u>mother</u> digging a hole in their garden so late
                       at night?

<u>looks</u>   2. <u>Neither</u> of my children ~~look~~ like me.

<u>were</u>   3. Three <u>goats</u>, a potbellied <u>pig</u>, and a <u>duck</u> ~~was~~ among the entrants in the pet
                       parade.

<u>look</u>   4. The little <u>balls</u> all over my pink sweater ~~looks~~ like woolen goose bumps.

<u>are</u>   5. Here ~~is~~ the low-calorie <u>cola</u> and the double-chocolate <u>cake</u> you ordered.

<u>interferes</u>   6. The <u>odor</u> of those perfumed ads ~~interfere~~ with my enjoyment of a magazine.

<u>is</u>   7. <u>One</u> of my roommates ~~are~~ always leaving wet towels on the bathroom floor.

<u>are</u>   8. A tiny piece of <u>gum</u> and some <u>tape</u> ~~is~~ holding my old glasses together.

<u>begins</u>   9. A <u>man</u> in his forties often ~~begin~~ to think about making a contribution to the
                       world and not just about himself.

<u>has</u>   10. <u>Each</u> of the child's thirty-four stuffed animals ~~have~~ a name and an entire life
                       history.

■ **Review Test 3**

Complete each of the following sentences using *is, are, was, were, have,* or *has.*
Then underline the subject.

Example   For me, <u>popcorn</u> at the movies *is like coffee at breakfast.*
Answers will vary.

1.   The <u>magazines</u> under my roommate's bed *are collecting dust.*

2.   The <u>car</u> with the purple fenders *is Ken's.*

3.   My <u>boss</u> and her <u>secretary</u> *were both out sick today.*

4.   <u>Neither</u> of the football players *was able to score.*

5.   Here *are the <u>sneakers</u> you were looking for.*

28 Additional Information about Verbs

The purpose of this chapter is to provide additional information about verbs. Some people will find the grammatical terms here a helpful reminder of what they've learned earlier, in school, about verbs. For them, the terms will increase their understanding of how verbs function in English. Other people may welcome more detailed information about terms used elsewhere in the text. In either case, remember that the most common mistakes people make when writing verbs have been treated in previous sections of the book.

Verb Tense

Verbs tell us the time of an action. The time that a verb shows is usually called *tense*. The most common tenses are the simple present, past, and future. In addition, there are nine other tenses that enable us to express more specific ideas about time than we could with the simple tenses alone. Following are the twelve verb tenses and examples of each tense. Read them over to increase your sense of the many different ways of expressing time in English.

Tenses	*Examples*
Present	I *work*.
	Tony *works*.
Past	Ellen *worked* on her car.
Future	You *will work* on a new project next week.
Present perfect	He *has worked* on his term paper for a month.
	The *have worked* out a compromise.
Past perfect	The nurse *had worked* two straight shifts.
Future perfect	Next Monday, I *will have worked* here exactly two years.
Present progressive	I *am working* on my speech for the debate.
	You *are working* too hard.
	The tape recorder *is* not *working* properly.

Tenses	Examples
Past progressive	He *was working* in the basement. The contestants *were working* on their talent routines.
Future progressive	My son *will be working* in our store this summer.
Present perfect progressive	Sarah *has been working* late this week.
Past perfect progressive	Until recently, I *had been working* nights.
Future perfect progressive	My mother *will have been working* as a nurse for forty-five years by the time she retires.

Activity

Answers will vary.

On separate paper, write twelve sentences using the twelve verb tenses.

Helping Verbs

There are three common verbs that can either stand alone or combine with (and "help") other verbs. Here are the verbs and their forms:

> be (am, are, is, was, were, being, been)
> have (has, having, had)
> do (does, did)

Here are examples of the helping verbs:

Used Alone	Used as Helping Verbs
I *was* angry.	I *was growing* angry.
Sue *has* the key.	Sue *has forgotten* the key.
He *did* well in the test.	He *did fail* the previous test.

There are nine helping verbs (traditionally known as *modals,* or *modal auxiliaries*) that are always used in combination with other verbs. Here are the nine verbs and a sentence example of each:

can	I *can see* the rainbow.
could	I *could* not *find* a seat.
may	The game *may be postponed.*
might	Cindy *might resent* your advice.
shall	I *shall see* you tomorrow.
should	He *should get* his car serviced.
will	Tony *will want* to see you.
would	They *would* not *understand.*
must	You *must visit* us again.

Note from the examples that these verbs have only one form. They do not, for instance, add an *-s* when used with *he, she, it,* or any one person or thing.

Activity

Answers will vary.
On separate paper, write nine sentences using the nine helping verbs.

Verbals

Verbals are words formed from verbs. Verbals, like verbs, often express action. They can add variety to your sentences and vigor to your writing style. The three kinds of verbals are *infinitives, participles,* and *gerunds.*

Infinitive

An infinitive is *to* plus the base form of the verb.

I love *to dance.*
Lina hopes *to write* for a newspaper.
I asked the children *to clean* the kitchen.

Participle

A participle is a verb form used as an adjective (a descriptive word). The present participle ends in -*ing*. The part participle ends in -*ed* or has an irregular ending.

Peering into the cracked mirror, the *crying* woman wiped her eyes.

The *astounded* man stared at his *winning* lottery ticket.

Swinging a sharp ax, Omar split the *rotted* beam.

Gerund

A gerund is the -*ing* form of a verb used as a noun.

Swimming is the perfect exercise.

Eating junk food is my diet downfall.

Through *doodling*, people express their inner feelings.

Activity

Answers will vary.

On separate paper, write three sentences using infinitives, three sentences using participles, and three sentences using gerunds.

29 Pronoun Agreement and Reference

Nouns name persons, places, or things. *Pronouns* are words that take the place of nouns. In fact, the word *pronoun* means "for a noun." Pronouns are shortcuts that keep you from unnecessarily repeating words in writing. Here are some examples of pronouns:

> Eddie left *his* camera on the bus.
> (*His* is a pronoun that takes the place of *Eddie's*.)
>
> Elena drank the coffee even though *it* was cold. (*It* replaces *coffee*.)
>
> As I turned the newspaper's damp pages, *they* disintegrated in my hands.
> (*They* is a pronoun that takes the place of *pages*.)

This chapter presents rules that will help you avoid two common mistakes people make with pronouns. The rules are:

1 A pronoun must agree in number with the word or words it replaces.

2 A pronoun must refer clearly to the word it replaces.

Pronoun Agreement

A pronoun must agree in number with the word or words it replaces. If the word a pronoun refers to is singular, the pronoun must be singular; if that word is plural, the pronoun must be plural. (Note that the word a pronoun refers to is known as the *antecedent*.)

> Marie showed me (her) antique wedding band.
>
> Students enrolled in the art class must provide (their) own supplies.

In the first example, the pronoun *her* refers to the singular word *Marie;* in the second example, the pronoun *their* refers to the plural word *Students.*

Activity

Write the appropriate pronoun (*their, they, them, it*) in the blank space in each of the following sentences.

Example   I opened the wet umbrella and put ___*it*___ in the bathtub to dry.

1. Kate and Bruce left for the movies earlier than usual, because ___*they*___ knew the theater would be packed.

2. The clothes were still damp, but I decided to fold ___*them*___ anyway.

3. Young adults often face a difficult transition period when ___*they*___ leave home for the first time.

4. Paul's grandparents renewed ___*their*___ marriage vows at a huge fiftieth wedding anniversary celebration.

5. The car's steering wheel began to pull to one side, and then ___*it*___ started to shimmy.

Indefinite Pronouns

The following words are always singular.

(*-one* words)	(*-body* words)	
one	nobody	each
anyone	anybody	either
everyone	everybody	neither
someone	somebody	

If a pronoun in a sentence refers to one of these singular words (also known as *indefinite pronouns*), the pronoun should be singular.

Somebody left her shoulder bag on the back of a chair.

One of the busboys just called and said he would be an hour late.

Everyone in the club must pay his dues next week.

Each circled pronoun is singular because it refers to an indefinite pronoun.

Note: There are two important points to remember about indefinite pronouns:

1 In the last example, if everyone in the club was a woman, the pronoun would be *her*. If the club had women and men, the pronoun would be *his or her:*

Everyone in the club must pay his or her dues next week.

Some writers follow the traditional practice of using *his* to refer to both women and men. Some now use *his or her* to avoid an implied sexual bias. To avoid using *his* or the somewhat awkward *his or her,* a sentence can often be rewritten in the plural:

Club members must pay their dues next week.

2 In informal spoken English, *plural* pronouns are often used with the indefinite pronouns. Many people would probably not say:

Everybody has his or her own opinion about the election.

Instead, they would be likely to say:

Everybody has their own opinion about the election.

Here are other examples:

Everyone in the choir must buy their robes.
Everybody in the line has their ticket ready.
No one in the class remembered to bring their books.

In such cases, the indefinite pronouns are clearly plural in meaning, and using them helps people avoid the awkward *his or her.* In time, the plural pronoun may be accepted in formal speech or writing. Until then, however, you should use the grammatically correct singular form in your writing.

Activity

Underline the correct pronoun.

1. Neither of the potential buyers had really made up (her, their) mind.
2. Not one of the new cashiers knows what (he, they) should be doing.
3. Each of these computers has (its, their) drawbacks.
4. Anyone trying to reduce (his or her, their) salt intake should avoid canned and processed foods.
5. If anybody calls when I'm out, tell (him, them) I'll return in an hour.

Pronoun Reference

A sentence may be confusing and unclear if a pronoun appears to refer to more than one word or does not refer to any specific word. Look at this sentence:

Miriam was annoyed when they failed her car for a faulty turn signal.

Who failed her car? There is no specific word that *they* refers to. Be clear:

Miriam was annoyed when the inspectors failed her car for a faulty turn signal.

Here are sentences with other faulty pronoun references. Read the explanations of why they are faulty and look carefully at how they are corrected.

Faulty	*Clear*
Peter told Alan that his wife was unhappy.	Peter told Alan, "My wife is unhappy."
(Whose wife is unhappy: Peter's or Alan's? Be clear.)	
Kia is really a shy person, but she keeps it hidden.	Kia is really a shy person, but she keeps her shyness hidden.
(There is no specific word that *it* refers to. It would not make sense to say, "Kia keeps shy hidden.")	
Marsha attributed her success to her husband's support, which was generous.	Generously, Marsha attributed her success to her husband's support.
(Does *which* mean that Marsha's action was generous or that her husband's support was generous?)	*Or:* Marsha attributed her success to her husband's generous support.

Activity

Rewrite each of the following sentences to make clear the vague pronoun reference. Add, change, or omit words an necessary.

Example   Susan's mother wondered if she was tall enough to be a model.

Susan's mother wondered if Susan was tall enough to be a model.

Answers may vary.

1. Dad spent all morning bird-watching but didn't see a single one.

    . . . a single bird.

2. At that fast-food restaurant, they give you free glasses with your soft drinks.

The waiters at that fast-food restaurant give you . . .

3. Ruth told Annette that her bouts of depression were becoming serious.

Ruth told Annette, "My bouts of depression are becoming serious."

4. Dipping her spoon into the pot of simmering spaghetti sauce, Helen felt it slip out of her hand.

. . . felt the spoon slip out of her hand.

5. Pete visited the tutoring center because they can help him with his economics course.

. . . center because its staff can help . . .

■ Review Test 1

Underline the correct word in parentheses.

1. Each of the little girls may choose one prize for (<u>her</u>, their) own.
2. I asked at the body shop how quickly (they, <u>the shop employees</u>) could fix my car.
3. The coaches told each member of the football team that (<u>his</u>, their) position was the most important in the game.
4. Darlene tried to take notes during the class, but she didn't really understand (it, <u>the subject</u>).
5. When someone has a cold, (they, <u>he or she</u>) should take extra vitamin C and drink a lot of fluids.

■ Review Test 2

Cross out the pronoun error in each of the following sentences and write the correction in the space provided at the left. Then circle the letter that correctly describes the type of error that was made.

Examples

Anyone without a ticket will lose ~~their~~ place in the line.

his (or her)   *Mistake in:*   a. pronoun reference   ⓑ pronoun agreement

When Ellen takes her daughter Kim to the park, ~~she~~ enjoys herself.

Ellen (or Kim)   *Mistake in:*   ⓐ pronoun reference   b. pronoun agreement _his (or her)_ 1. Could someone volunteer ~~their~~ services to clean up after the party?

Mistake in: a. pronoun reference (b.) pronoun agreement

the players 2. The referee watched the basketball game closely to make sure ~~they~~ didn't commit any fouls.

Mistake in: (a.) pronoun reference b. pronoun agreement

they 3. If job-hunters want to make a good impression at an interview, ~~he~~ should be sure to arrive on time.

Mistake in: a. pronoun reference (b.) pronoun agreement

her 4. Neither of those girls appreciates ~~their~~ parents' sacrifices.

Mistake in: a. pronoun reference (b.) pronoun agreement

the owners 5. There wasn't much to do on Friday nights after ~~they~~ closed the only movie theater in town.

Mistake in: (a.) pronoun reference b. pronoun agreement

30 Pronoun Types

This chapter describes some common types of pronouns: subject and object pronouns, possessive pronouns, and demonstrative pronouns.

Subject and Object Pronouns

Most pronouns change their form depending on what place they occupy in a sentence. In the box that follows is a list of subject and object pronouns.

Subject Pronouns	Object Pronouns
I	me
you	you (no change)
he	him
she	her
it	it (no change)
we	us
they	them

Subject Pronouns

Subject pronouns are subjects of verbs.

> *He* is wearing an artificial arm. (*He* is the subject of the verb *is wearing*.)
>
> *They* are moving into our old apartment. (*They* is the subject of the verb *are moving*.)
>
> *We* students should have a say in the decision. (*We* is the subject of the verb *should have*.)

Several rules for using subject pronouns—and several kinds of mistakes people sometimes make with subject pronouns—are explained on the following page.

Rule 1:   Use a subject pronoun in spots where you have a compound subject (more than one subject).

Incorrect	Correct
My brother and *me* are Bruce Springsteen fanatics.	My brother and *I* are Bruce Springsteen fanatics.
Him and *me* know the lyrics to all of Bruce's songs.	*He* and *I* know the lyrics to all of Bruce's songs.

Hint for Rule 1:   If you are not sure what pronoun to use, try each pronoun by itself in the sentence. The correct pronoun will be the one that sounds right. For example, "Him knows the lyrics to all of Bruce's songs" does not sound right; "He knows the lyrics to all of Bruce's songs" does.

Rule 2:   Use a subject pronoun after forms of the verb *be*. Forms of *be* include *am, are, is, was, were, has been, have been,* and others.

It was *I* who left the light on.

It may be *they* in that car.

It is *he*.

The sentences above may sound strange and stilted to you because they are seldom used in conversation. When we speak with one another, forms such as "It was me," "It may be them," and "It is him" are widely accepted. In formal writing, however, the grammatically correct forms are still preferred.

Hint for Rule 2:   You can avoid having to use a subject pronoun after *be* by simply rewording a sentence. Here is how the preceding examples could be reworded:

I was the one who left the light on.

They may be in that car.

He is here.

Rule 3:   Use subject pronouns after *than* or *as*. The subject pronoun is used because a verb is understood after the pronoun.

You play better than I (play). (The verb *play* is understood after *I*.)

Jenny is as bored as I (am). (The verb *am* is understood after *I*.)

We don't need the money as much as they (do). (The verb *do* is understood after *they*.)

Hint for Rule 3:   Avoid mistakes by mentally adding the "missing" verb at the end of the sentence.

Object Pronouns

Object pronouns (*me, him, her, us, them*) are the objects of verbs or prepositions. (*Prepositions* are connecting words like *for, at, about, to, before, by, with,* and *of.* See also page 411.)

Tony helped me.   (*Me* is the object of the verb *helped.*)

We took *them* to the college.   (*Them* is the object of the verb *took.*)

Leave the children with *us.*   (*Us* is the object of the preposition *with.*)

I got in line behind *him.*   (*Him* is the object of the preposition *behind.*)

People are sometimes uncertain about what pronoun to use when two objects follow the verb.

Incorrect	*Correct*
I gave a gift to Ray and *she.*	I gave a gift to Ray and *her.*
She came to the movie with Bobbie and *I.*	She came to the movie with Bobbie and *me.*

Hint: If you are not sure what pronoun to use, try each pronoun by itself in the sentence. The correct pronoun will be the one that sounds right. For example, "I gave a gift to she" does not sound right; "I gave a gift to her" does.

Activity

Underline the correct subject or object pronoun in each of the following sentences. Then show whether your answer is a subject or object pronoun by circling the S or O in the margin. The first one is done for you as an example.

S   Ⓞ   1.   The sweater Mom knitted for Victor and (I, <u>me</u>) are too small.

Ⓢ   O   2.   The umpire and (<u>he</u>, him) started to argue.

Ⓢ   O   3.   No one has a quicker temper than (<u>she</u>, her).

Ⓢ   O   4.   Your grades prove that you worked harder than (<u>they</u>, them).

Ⓢ   O   5.   (<u>We</u>, Us) runners train indoors when the weather turns cold.

Ⓢ   O   6.   (<u>She</u>, Her) and Betty never put the cap back on the toothpaste.

Ⓢ O   7. Chris and (he, him) are the most energetic kids in the first grade.

S Ⓞ   8. Arguing over clothes is a favorite pastime for my sister and (I, me).

S Ⓞ   9. The rest of (they, them) will be arriving in about ten minutes.

S Ⓞ   10. The head of the ticket committee asked Melba and (I, me) to help with sales.

Possessive Pronouns

Here is a list of possessive pronouns:

my, mine	our, ours
your, yours	your, yours
his	their, theirs
her, hers	
its	

Possessive pronouns show ownership or possession.

Clyde revved up *his* motorcycle and blasted off.
The keys are *mine*.

Note: A possessive pronoun *never* uses an apostrophe. (See also page 501.)

Incorrect	*Correct*
That coat is *hers'*.	That coat is *hers*.
The card table is *theirs'*.	The card table is *theirs*.

Activity

Cross out the incorrect pronoun form in each of the sentences below. Write the correct form in the space at the left.

Example ___hers___   Those gloves are ~~hers'~~.

___its___   1.   I discovered that my car had somehow lost ~~its'~~ rear license plate.

___theirs___   2.   Are those seats ~~theirs'~~?

hers 3. I knew that sweater was ~~hers'~~ when I saw the monogram.

ours 4. The dog in that cage is ~~our's~~.

yours 5. These books are ~~yours'~~ if you want them.

Demonstrative Pronouns

Demonstrative pronouns point to or single out a person or thing. There are four demonstrative pronouns:

this	these
that	those

Generally speaking, *this* and *these* refer to things close at hand; *that* and *those* refer to things farther away. The four pronouns are commonly used in the role of demonstrative adjectives as well.

Is anyone using *this* spoon?

I am going to throw away *these* magazines.

I just bought *that* white Volvo at the curb.

Pick up *those* toys in the corner.

Note: Do not use *them, this here, that there, these here,* or *those there* to point out. Use only *this, that, these,* or *those.*

Activity

Cross out the incorrect form of the demonstrative pronoun and write the correct form in the space provided.

Example   _Those_   ~~Them~~ tires look worn.

This 1. ~~This here~~ map is out of date.

those 2. Leave ~~them~~ keys out on the coffee table.

those 3. I've seen ~~them~~ girls somewhere before.

that 4. Jack entered ~~that there~~ dog in an obedience contest.

those 5. Where are ~~them~~ new knives?

■ **Review Test**

Underline the correct word in the parentheses.

1. If the contract negotiations are left up to (they, <u>them</u>), we'll have to accept the results.
2. (Them, <u>Those</u>) student crafts projects have won several awards.
3. Our grandmother told David and (I, <u>me</u>) to leave our muddy shoes outside on the porch.
4. The judge decided that the fault was (theirs', <u>theirs</u>) and ordered them to pay the damages.
5. I gave the money to (she, <u>her</u>) and asked her to put it in the bank's night deposit slot.
6. The black-masked raccoon stared at Rudy and (I, <u>me</u>) for an instant and then ran away.
7. When we saw the smashed window, Lynn and (<u>I</u>, me) didn't know whether to enter the house.
8. (This here, <u>This</u>) is my cousin Manuel.
9. This coat can't be (<u>hers</u>, her's); it's too small.
10. Because we weren't wearing shoes, Tara and (<u>I</u>, me) had a hard time walking on the sharp gravel.

31 Adjectives and Adverbs

Adjectives

What Are Adjectives?

Adjectives describe nouns (names of persons, places, or things) or pronouns.

Yoko is a *wise* woman. (The adjective *wise* describes the noun *woman.*)

She is also *funny.* (The adjective *funny* describes the pronoun *she.*)

I'll carry the *heavy* bag of groceries. (The adjective *heavy* describes the noun *bag.*)

It is *torn.* (The adjective *torn* describes the pronoun *it.*)

Adjectives usually come before the word they describe (as in *wise* woman and *heavy* bag). But they also come after forms of the verb *be* (*is, are, was, were,* and so on). They also follow verbs such as *look, appear, seem, become, sound, taste,* and *smell.*

That road is *slippery.* (The adjective *slippery* describes the road.)

The dogs are *noisy.* (The adjective *noisy* describes the dogs.)

Those customers were *impatient.* (The adjective *impatient* describes the customers.)

Your room looks *neat.* (The adjective *neat* describes the room.)

Using Adjectives to Compare

For all one-syllable adjectives and some two-syllable adjectives, add *-er* when comparing two things and *-est* when comparing three or more things.

Phil's beard is *longer* than mine, but Lee's is the *longest.*

Meg may be the *quieter* of the two sisters; but that's not saying much, since they're the *loudest* girls in school.

For some two-syllable adjectives and all longer adjectives, use *more* when comparing two things and *most* when comparing three or more things.

> Liza Minnelli is *more famous* than her sister; but their mother, Judy Garland, is still the *most famous* member of the family.

> The red letters on the sign are *more noticeable* than the black ones, but the Day-Glo letters are the *most noticeable.*

You can usually tell when to use *more* and *most* by the sound of a word. For example, you can probably tell by its sound that "carefuller" would be too awkward to say and that *more careful* is thus correct. But there are many words for which both *-er* or *-est* and *more* or *most* are equally correct. For instance, either "a more fair rule" or "a fairer rule" is correct.

To form negative comparisons, use *less* and *least.*

> During my first dance class, I felt *less graceful* than an injured elephant.

> When the teacher came to our house to complain to my parents, I offered her the *least* comfortable chair in the room.

Points to Remember about Comparing

Point 1:   Use only one form of comparison at a time. That is, do not use both an *-er* ending and *more* or both an *-est* ending and *most:*

Incorrect	Correct
My mother's suitcase is always *more heavier* than my father's.	My mother's suitcase is always *heavier* than my father's.
Rosemary's Baby is still the *most frighteningest* movie I've ever seen.	*Rosemary's Baby* is still the *most frightening* movie I've ever seen.

Point 2:   Learn the irregular forms of the words shown below.

	Comparative (for comparing two things)	*Superlative (for comparing three or more things)*
bad	worse	worst
good, well	better	best
little (in amount)	less	least
much, many	more	most

Do not use both *more* and an irregular comparative or *most* and an irregular superlative.

Incorrect	*Correct*
It is *more better* to give than to receive.	It is *better* to give than to receive.
Last night I got the *most worst* snack attack I ever had.	Last night I got the *worst* snack attack I ever had.

Activity

Add to each sentence the correct form of the word in the margin.

bad   Examples   The ___worst___ job I ever had was baby-sitting for spoiled four-year-old twins.

wonderful   The ___most wonderful___ day of my life was when my child was born.

good   1. The ___best___ chocolate cake I ever ate had bananas in it.

young   2. Aunt Sonja is the ___youngest___ of the three sisters.

bad   3. A rain that freezes is ___worse___ than a snowstorm.

unusual   4. That's the ___most unusual___ home I've ever seen—it's shaped like a teapot.

little   5. Being painfully shy has made Leon the ___least___ friendly person I know.

Adverbs

What Are Adverbs?

Adverbs describe verbs, adjectives, or other adverbs. They usually end in *-ly*.

The father *gently* hugged the sick child. (The adverb *gently* describes the verb *hugged*.)

Newborns are *totally* innocent. (The adverb *totally* describes the adjective *innocent*.)

The lecturer spoke so *terribly* fast that I had trouble taking notes. (The adverb *terribly* describes the adverb *fast*.)

A Common Mistake with Adverbs and Adjectives

People often mistakenly use an adjective instead of an adverb after a verb.

Incorrect	*Correct*
Sam needs a haircut *bad*.	Sam needs a haircut *badly*.
I laugh too *loud* when I'm embarrassed.	I laugh too *loudly* when I'm embarrassed.
You might have won the race if you hadn't run so *slow* at the beginning.	You might have won the race if you hadn't run so *slowly* at the beginning.

Activity

Underline the adjective or adverb needed. (Remember that adjectives describe nouns, and adverbs describe verbs and other adverbs.)

1. As Mac danced, his earring bounced (rapid, <u>rapidly</u>).
2. A drop of (<u>thick</u>, thickly) pea soup dripped down his chin.
3. I hiccuped (continuous, <u>continuously</u>) for fifteen minutes.
4. The detective opened the door (careful, <u>carefully</u>).
5. All she heard when she answered the phone was (<u>heavy</u>, heavily) breathing.

Well and *Good*

Two words that are often confused are *well* and *good*. *Good* is an adjective; it describes nouns. *Well* is usually an adverb; it describes verbs. But *well* (rather than *good*) is used as an adjective when referring to health.

Activity

Write *well* or *good* in each of the sentences that follow.

1. If you girls do a _____*good*_____ job of cleaning the garage, I'll take you for some ice cream.
2. If I organize the office records too _____*well*_____, my bosses may not need me anymore.
3. After eating a pound of peanuts, I didn't feel too _____*well*_____.
4. When Ernie got AIDS, he discovered who his _____*good*_____ friends really were.
5. Just because brothers and sisters fight when they're young doesn't mean they won't get along _____*well*_____ as adults.

■ Review Test 1

Underline the correct word in parentheses.

1. The waitress poured (littler, <u>less</u>) coffee into my cup than yours.
2. Humid air seems to make Sid's asthma (more worse, <u>worse</u>).
3. The movie is so interesting that the three hours pass (quick, <u>quickly</u>).
4. The talented boy sang as (confident, <u>confidently</u>) as a seasoned performer.
5. Our band played so (good, <u>well</u>) that a local firm hired us for its annual dinner.
6. Tri Lee is always (<u>truthful</u>, truthfully), even when it might be better to tell a white lie.
7. The driver stopped the bus (sudden, <u>suddenly</u>) and yelled, "Everybody out!"
8. Shirt and pants in one color make you look (more thin, <u>thinner</u>) than ones in contrasting colors.
9. Your intentions may have been (<u>good</u>, well), but I'd prefer that you ask before arranging a blind date for me.
10. Our cat likes to sit in the (<u>warmest</u>, most warm) spot in any room—by a fireplace, on a windowsill in the sunshine, or on my lap.

■ Review Test 2

Write a sentence that uses each of the following adjectives and adverbs correctly.
Answers will vary; examples are shown.

1. careless _It's embarassing to make a careless mistake._
2. angrily _"Get out!" the shop owner shouted angrily to the panhandler._
3. well _If a thing is worth doing, it's worth doing well._
4. most relaxing _A lullaby is one of the most relaxing kinds of music._
5. best _My husband is also my best friend._

32 Misplaced Modifiers

Misplaced modifiers are words that, because of awkward placement, do not describe what the writer intended them to describe. Misplaced modifiers often confuse the meaning of a sentence. To avoid them, place words as close as possible to what they describe.

Misplaced Words	*Correctly Placed Words*
George couldn't drive to work in his small sports car *with a broken leg.* (The sports car had a broken leg?)	With a broken leg, George couldn't drive to work in his small sports car. (The words describing George are now placed next to *George.*)
The toaster was sold to us by a charming salesman with a *money-back guarantee.* (The salesman had a money-back guarantee?)	The toaster with a money-back guarantee was sold to us by a charming salesman. (The words describing the toaster are now placed next to it.)
He *nearly* brushed his teeth for twenty minutes every night. (He came close to brushing his teeth but in fact did not brush them at all?)	He brushed his teeth for nearly twenty minutes every night. (The meaning—that he brushed his teeth for a long time—is now clear.)

Activity

Underline the misplaced word or words in each sentence. Then rewrite the sentence, placing related words together and thereby making the meaning clear.

Examples   Frozen shrimp lay in the steel pans that were melting rapidly.

> *Frozen shrimp that were melting rapidly lay in the steel pans.*

The speaker discussed the problem of crowded prisons at the college.

> *At the college, the speaker discussed the problem of crowded*
> *prisons.*

1. The patient talked about his childhood on the psychiatrist's couch.

   The patient on the psychiatrist's couch talked . . .

2. The crowd watched the tennis players with swiveling heads.

   With swiveling heads, the crowd watched . . .

3. Vonnie put four hamburger patties on the counter <u>which she was cooking for dinner.</u>

   . . . patties, which she was cooking for dinner, on . . .

4. Steve carefully hung the new suit that he would wear to his first job interview <u>in the bedroom closet.</u>

   . . . hung in the bedroom closet the new suit that he . . .

5. Anne ripped the shirt on a car door <u>that she made in sewing class.</u>

   . . . shirt that she made in sewing class on a car door.

6. The latest Tom Hanks movie has <u>almost</u> opened in 2,200 theaters across the country.

   . . . has opened in almost 2,220 theaters . . .

7. The newscaster spoke softly into a microphone <u>wearing a bulletproof vest.</u>

   Wearing a bulletproof vest, the newscaster spoke . . .

8. The tenants left town in a dilapidated old car <u>owing two months' rent.</u>

   Owing two months' rent, the tenants left town . . .

9. The woman picked up a heavy frying pan <u>with arthritis.</u>

   The woman with arthritis picked up a heavy frying pan.

10. I discovered an unusual plant <u>in the greenhouse</u> that oozed a milky juice.

    In the greenhouse, I discovered . . .

■ **Review Test 1**

Write MM for *misplaced modifier* or C for *correct* in the space provided for each sentence.

MM	1. I nearly napped for twenty minutes during the biology lecture.
C	2. I napped for nearly twenty minutes during the biology lecture.
C	3. Ron paused as the girl he had been following stopped at a shop window.
MM	4. Ron paused as the girl stopped at a shop window he had been following.
MM	5. Marta dropped out of school after taking ten courses on Friday.
C	6. On Friday, Marta dropped out of school after taking ten courses.
C	7. Under his shirt, the player wore a good luck charm which resembled a tiny elephant.
MM	8. The player wore a good luck charm under his shirt which resembled a tiny elephant.

_____MM_____   9. I ordered a new telephone from the mail-order catalog shaped like a cartoon character.

_____C_____   10. I ordered from the mail-order catalog a new telephone shaped like a cartoon character.

■ Review Test 2

Make the changes needed to correct the misplaced modifier in each sentence.

1. Henry Wadsworth Longfellow wrote that rainbows are the flowers that have died and gone to heaven in a poem.

   In a poem, Henry Wadsworth Longfellow wrote that . . .

   _____

2. I almost filled an entire notebook with biology lab drawings.

   I filled almost an entire notebook . . .

   _____

3. The apprentice watched the carpenter expertly fit the door with envious eyes.

   With envious eyes, the apprentice watched . . .

   _____

4. The photographer pointed the camera at the shy deer equipped with a special night-vision scope.

   . . . pointed at the shy deer the camera . . .

   or: . . . scope at the shy deer.

5. The people on the bus stared at the ceiling or read newspapers with tired faces.

   The people with tired faces on the bus stared . . .

   Or: With tired faces, the people . . .

33 Dangling Modifiers

A modifier that opens a sentence must be followed immediately by the word it is meant to describe. Otherwise, the modifier is said to be dangling, and the sentence takes on an unintended meaning. For example, in the sentence

> While reading the newspaper, my dog sat with me on the front steps.

the unintended meaning is that the *dog* was reading the paper. What the writer meant, of course, was that *he* (or *she*), the writer, was reading the paper. The writer should have said,

> While reading the newspaper, *I* sat with my dog on the front steps.

The dangling modifier could also be corrected by placing the subject within the opening word group:

> While *I* was reading the newspaper, my dog sat with me on the front steps.

Here are other sentences with dangling modifiers. Read the explanations of why they are dangling and look carefully at the ways they are corrected.

Dangling	Correct
Shaving in front of the steamy mirror, the razor nicked Ed's chin. (*Who* was shaving in front of the mirror? The answer is not *razor* but *Ed*. The subject Ed must be added.)	Shaving in front of the steamy mirror, *Ed* nicked his chin with the razor. *Or:* When *Ed* was shaving in front of the steamy mirror, he nicked his chin with the razor.
While turning over the bacon, hot grease splashed my arm. (*Who* is turning over the bacon? The answer is not *hot grease,* as it unintentionally seems to be, but *I*. The subject *I* must be added.)	While *I* was turning over the bacon, hot grease splashed my arm. *Or:* While turning over the bacon, *I* was splashed by hot grease.
Taking the exam, the room was so stuffy that Keisha almost fainted. (*Who* took the exam? The answer is not *the room* but *Keisha*. The subject *Keisha* must follow the modifier.)	Taking the exam, *Keisha* found the room so stuffy that she almost fainted. *Or:* When *Keisha* took the exam, the room was so stuffy that she almost fainted.

Dangling	*Correct*
To impress the interviewer, punctuality is essential.	To impress the interviewer, *you* must be punctual.
(*Who* is to impress the interviewer? The answer is not *punctuality* but *you*. The subject *you* must be added.)	*Or:* For *you* to impress the interviewer, punctuality is essential.

The examples above make clear two ways of correcting a dangling modifier. Decide on a logical subject and do one of the following:

1 Place the subject *within* the opening word group:

When *Ed* was shaving in front of the steamy mirror, he nicked his chin.

Note: In some cases an appropriate subordinating word such as *when* must be added, and the verb may have to be changed slightly as well.

2 Place the subject right *after* the opening word group:

Shaving in front of the steamy mirror, *Ed* nicked his chin.

Activity

Ask *Who?* of the opening words in each sentence. The subject that answers the question should be nearby in the sentence. If it is not, provide the logical subject by using either method of correction described above.

Example   While pitching his tent, a snake bit Tony on the ankle.

While Tony was pitching his tent, a snake bit him on the ankle.

Or: _While pitching his tent, Tony was bitten on the ankle by a snake._

Answers may vary.

1. Dancing on their hind legs, the audience cheered wildly as the elephants paraded by.

   The audience cheered wildly as the elephants, dancing on their hind legs,

   paraded by.

2. Last seen wearing dark glasses and a blond wig, the police spokesperson said the suspect was still being sought.

   The police spokesman said the suspect, last seen wearing dark glasses and

   a blond wig, was . . .

3. Pouring out the cereal, a coupon fell into my bowl of milk.

As I poured out the cereal, a coupon fell . . .

4. Escorted by dozens of police motorcycles, I knew the limousine carried some-one important.

Because it was escorted by dozens of police motorcycles, I knew the

limousine . . .

5. Tired and exasperated, the fight we had was inevitable.

We were tired and exasperated, so the fight we had . . .

6. Packed tightly in a tiny can, Fran had difficulty removing the anchovies.

. . . removing the anchovies, which were packed tightly . . .

7. Kicked carelessly under the bed, Raquel finally found her sneakers.

Raquel finally found her sneakers, which were kicked carelessly under

the bed.

8. Working at the Xerox machine, the morning dragged on.

As I worked at the Xerox machine, the morning . . .

9. Sitting at a sidewalk café, all sorts of interesting people passed by.

As we sat at a sidewalk café, all sorts . . .

10. Though somewhat warped, Uncle Zeke played his records from the forties.

Though they were somewhat warped, Uncle Zeke played his records from the

forties.

■ Review Test 1

Write DM for *dangling modifier* or C for *correct* in the space provided for each sentence.

DM 1. While riding the bicycle, a vicious-looking German shepherd snapped at Tim's ankles.

C 2. While Tim was riding the bicycle, a vicious-looking German shepherd snapped at his ankles.

_C_   3. Afraid to look his father in the eye, Howard kept his head bowed.

_DM_   4. Afraid to look his father in the eye, Howard's head remained bowed.

_DM_   5. Boring and silly, I turned the TV show off.

_C_   6. I turned off the boring and silly TV show.

_C_   7. Munching leaves from a tall tree, the giraffe fascinated the children.

_DM_   8. Munching leaves from a tall tree, the children were fascinated by the giraffe.

_DM_   9. At the age of twelve, several colleges had already accepted the boy genius.

_C_   10. At the age of twelve, the boy genius had already been accepted by several colleges.

■ Review Test 2

Make the changes needed to correct the dangling modifier in each sentence.
Answers may vary; examples are shown.

1. Not having had much sleep, my concentration during class was weak.

   Since I had not had much sleep, my concentration . . .

   _____

2. Joined at the hip, a team of surgeons successfully separated the Siamese twins.

   . . . separated the Siamese twins, who were joined at the hip.

   _____

3. Wading in the shallow surf, a baby shark brushed past my leg.

   As I was wading in the shallow surf, a baby . . .

   _____

4. While being restrained by federal marshals, the judge sentenced the kidnapper.

   The judge sentenced the kidnapper, who was being restrained . . .

   _____

5. In a sentimental frame of mind, the music brought tears to Beth's eyes.

   Beth was in a sentimental frame of mind, so the music brought tears to

   her eyes.

■ **Review Test 3**

Complete the following sentences. In each case, a logical subject should follow the opening words.

Example   Looking through the door's peephole, *I couldn't see who rang the doorbell.*

Answers will vary; examples are shown.

1. Noticing the light turn yellow, *Barry slowed the car down.*

2. Being fragile, *the vase broke when I set it down too hard.*

3. While washing the car, *the kids got soaking wet.*

4. Although very expensive, *the coat did not wear well.*

5. Driving by the cemetery, *Terry had gloomy thoughts of death.*

34 Manuscript Form

When you hand in a paper for any course, it will probably be judged first by its format. It is important, then, to make the paper look attractive, neat, and easy to read. Here is a checklist you should use when preparing a paper for an instructor:

_____ • Is the paper full-sized, 8½ by 11 inches?

_____ • Are there wide margins (1 to 1½ inches) all around the paper? In particular, have you been careful not to crowd the right-hand or bottom margin?

_____ • If the paper is handwritten, have you:

Used a blue or black pen?

Been careful not to overlap letters or to make decorative loops on letters?

Made all your letters distinct, with special attention to *a, e, i, o,* and *u* —five letters that people sometimes write illegibly?

Kept all your capital letters clearly distinct from small letters?

_____ • Have you centered the title of your paper on the first line of page 1? Have you been careful *not* to put quotation marks around the title and *not* to underline it? Have you capitalized all the words in the title except for short connecting words like *of, for, the, and, in,* and *to?*

_____ • Have you skipped a line between the title and the first line of your paper?

_____ • Have you indented the first line of each paragraph about five spaces (half an inch) from the left-hand margin?

_____ • Have you made commas, periods, and other punctuation marks firm and clear? If typing, have you left a double space after a period?

_____ • If you have broken any words at the end of a line, have you been careful to break only between syllables?

_____ • Have you put your name, the date, and other information at the end of the paper (or wherever your instructor has specified)?

Also ask yourself these important questions about the title and the first sentence of your paper:

_____   • Is your title made up of several words that tell what the paper is about? (The title should be just several words, *not* a complete sentence.)

_____   • Does the first sentence of your paper stand independent of the title? (The reader should *not* have to use the words in the title to make sense of the opening sentence.)

Activity

Use the checklist to locate the seven mistakes in format in the following lines from a student paper. Explain the mistakes in the spaces provided. One mistake is described for you as an example.

	"Being alone"
	This is something that I simply cannot tolerate, and I will predi-
	ctably go to great lengths to prevent it. For example, if I know that

1. Hyphenate only between syllables (predict-ably, not predi-ctably).

2. Right-hand margin should not be crowded.

3. Title should not be in quotation marks.

4. In title, the word "Alone" should be capitalized.

5. A line should be skipped below the title.

6. Paragraph indent is needed.

7. The first sentence should stand independent of the title. (Here, the meaning of "This" depends on the title.)

35 Capital Letters

Main Uses of Capital Letters

Capital letters are used with:

1 First word in a sentence or direct quotation
2 Names of persons and the word *I*
3 Names of particular places
4 Names of days of the week, months, and holidays
5 Names of commercial products
6 Titles of books, magazines, newspapers, articles, stories, poems, films, television shows, songs, papers that you write, and the like
7 Names of companies, associations, unions, clubs, religious and political groups, and other organizations

Each use is illustrated in this chapter.

First Word in a Sentence or Direct Quotation

The corner grocery was robbed last night.

The alien said, "Take me to your leader."

"If you feel lonely," said Teri, "call me. I'll be over in no time."

Note: In the third example above, *If* and *I'll* are capitalized because they start new sentences. But *call* is not capitalized, because it is part of the first sentence.

Names of Persons and the Word *I*

Last night, I saw a hilarious movie starring Stan Laurel and Oliver Hardy.

Names of Particular Places

Although Bill dropped out of Port Charles High School, he eventually earned his degree and got a job with Atlas Realty Company.

But: Use small letters if the specific name of a place is not given.

Although Bill dropped out of high school, he eventually earned his degree and got a job with a real estate company.

Names of Days of the Week, Months, and Holidays

On the last Friday afternoon in May, the day before Memorial Day, my boss is having a barbecue for all the employees.

But: Use small letters for the seasons—summer, fall, winter, spring.

Most people feel more energetic in the spring and fall.

Names of Commercial Products

My little sister knows all the words to the jingles for Oscar Mayer hot dogs, Diet Pepsi, Meow Mix cat food, and McDonald's hamburgers.

But: Use small letters for the *type* of product (hot dogs, cat food, hamburgers, and so on).

Titles of Books, Magazines, Newspapers, Articles, Stories, Poems, Films, Television Shows, Songs, Papers That You Write, and the Like

We read the book *Hiroshima*, by John Hersey, for our history class.

In the doctor's waiting room, I watched *All My Children*, read an article in *Reader's Digest*, and leafed through the *Miami Herald*.

Names of Companies, Associations, Unions, Clubs, Religious and Political Groups, and Other Organizations

Joe Naples is a Roman Catholic, but his wife is a Methodist.

The Hilldale Square Dancers' Club has won many competitions.

Brian, a member of Bricklayers Local 431 and the Knights of Columbus, works for Ace Construction.

Activity

Underline the words that need capitals in the following sentences. Then write the capitalized form of each word in the space provided. The number of spaces tells you how many corrections to make in each case.

Example   In our biology class, each student must do a report on an article in the magazine *scientific american*.   *Scientific   American*

1. Leon's collection of <u>beatles</u> souvenirs includes a pair of tickets from their last concert in <u>candlestick park</u> in San Francisco.

   Beatles   Candlestick   Park

2. Yumi read in *natural health* magazine that <u>abraham lincoln</u> suffered from severe depression.

   Natural   Health   Abraham   Lincoln

3. When <u>i</u> have a cold, I use <u>vick's</u> ointment and chew <u>listerine</u> lozenges.

   I   Vick's   Listerine

4. Since no man volunteered for the job, the <u>boy scouts</u> in <u>springfield, illinois</u>, have a woman troop leader.

   Boy   Scouts   Springfield   Illinois

5. A nature trail for the blind in <u>cape cod, massachusetts</u>, has signs written in Braille which encourage visitors to smell and touch the plants.

   Cape   Cod   Massachusetts

6. Some of the most popular items at a restaurant called <u>big river</u> are <u>chilean</u> sea bass and <u>atlantic</u> clam chowder.

   Big   River   Chilean   Atlantic

7. My father is a confirmed Dallas <u>cowboys</u> fan, though he lives in <u>boston</u>.

   Cowboys   Boston

8. Martha bought a <u>diet pepsi</u> to wash down her <u>hostess twinkie</u>.

   Diet   Pepsi   Hostess   Twinkie

9. Vince listened to a Billy Joel album called *The Stranger* while Donna read an article in *glamour* entitled "What Do <u>men</u> Really <u>want</u>?"

     Glamour   *Men*   *Want*

10. After having her baby, <u>joan</u> received a card from one of her friends that read, "<u>congratulations</u>, we all knew you had it in you."

     Joan   *Congratulations*

Other Uses of Capital Letters

Capital letters are also used with:

1   Names that show family relationships
2   Titles of persons when used with their names
3   Specific school courses
4   Languages
5   Geographic locations
6   Historical periods and events
7   Races, nations, and nationalities
8   Opening and closing of a letter

Each use is illustrated on the pages that follow.

Names That Show Family Relationships

All his life, Father has been addicted to gadgets.

I browsed through Grandmother's collection of old photographs.

Aunt Florence and Uncle Bill bought a mobile home.

But: Do not capitalize words like *mother, father, grandmother, grandfather, uncle, aunt,* and so on when they are preceded by a possessive word (such as *my, your, his, her, our, their*).

All his life, my father has been addicted to gadgets.

I browsed through my grandmother's collection of old photographs.

My aunt and uncle bought a mobile home.

Titles of Persons When Used with Their Names

> I contributed to Senator McGrath's campaign fund.
>
> Is Dr. Gregory on vacation?
>
> Professor Adams announced that there would be no tests in the course.

But: Use small letters when titles appear by themselves, without specific names.

> I contributed to my senator's campaign fund.
>
> Is the doctor on vacation?
>
> The professor announced that there would be no tests in the course.

Specific School Courses

> The college offers evening sections of Introductory Psychology I, Abnormal Psychology, Psychology and Statistics, and Educational Psychology.

But: Use small letters for general subject areas.

> The college offers evening sections of many psychology courses.

Languages

> My grandfather's Polish accent makes his English difficult to understand.

Geographic Locations

> He grew up in the Midwest but moved to the South to look for a better job.

But: Use small letters in directions.

> Head west for five blocks and then turn south on State Street.

Historical Periods and Events

> During the Middle Ages, the Black Death killed over one-quarter of Europe's population.

Races, Nations, and Nationalities

The questionnaire asked if the head of our household was Caucasian, African American, Asian, or Native American.

Tanya has lived on army bases in Germany, Italy, and Spain.

Denise's beautiful features reflect her Chinese and Mexican parentage.

Opening and Closing of a Letter

Dear Sir:	Sincerely yours,
Dear Ms. Henderson:	Truly yours,

Note: Capitalize only the first word in a closing.

Activity

Underline the words that need capitals in the following sentences. Then write the capitalized forms of the words in the spaces provided. The number of spaces tells you how many corrections to make in each case.

1. During <u>world war</u> II, many <u>americans</u> were afraid that the <u>japanese</u> would invade California.

   <u>World</u>   <u>War</u>   <u>Americans</u>   <u>Japanese</u>

2. On their job site in <u>korea</u>, the <u>french</u>, <u>swiss</u>, and <u>chinese</u> coworkers used English to communicate.

   <u>Korea</u>   <u>French</u>   <u>Swiss</u>   <u>Chinese</u>

3. When <u>uncle harvey</u> got the bill from his doctor, he called the American Medical Association to complain.

   <u>Uncle</u>   <u>Harvey</u>

4. Dr. Freeling of the business department is offering a new course called <u>introduction</u> to <u>word processing</u>.

   <u>Introduction</u>   <u>Word</u>   <u>Processing</u>

5. The new restaurant featuring <u>vietnamese</u> cuisine has just opened on the south side of the city.

   <u>Vietnamese</u>

Unnecessary Use of Capitals

Activity

Many errors in capitalization are caused by using capitals where they are not needed. Underline the incorrectly capitalized letters in the following sentences, and write the correct forms in the spaces provided. The number of spaces tells you how many corrections to make in each sentence.

1. George Washington's <u>F</u>orces starved at Valley Forge because Pennsylvania <u>F</u>armers preferred to sell food to the British for cash.

   _____forces_____   _____farmers_____

2. For her fortieth birthday, my <u>A</u>unt bought herself a red LeSabre <u>C</u>onvertible.

   _____aunt_____   _____convertible_____

3. The country cheered in the summer of 1998 when Mark McGwire of the St. Louis Cardinals <u>B</u>aseball <u>T</u>eam broke the single-season <u>H</u>ome <u>R</u>un record set by Roger Maris.

   _____baseball_____   _____team_____   _____home_____   _____run_____

4. In his <u>B</u>ook titled *Offbeat Museums,* Saul Rubin tells about various <u>U</u>nusual <u>M</u>useums, such as, <u>B</u>elieve it or not, the Kansas Barbed Wire Museum.

   _____book_____   _____unusual_____   _____museums_____   _____believe_____

5. Einstein's theory of relativity, which he developed when he was only twenty-six, led to the invention of the <u>E</u>lectron <u>M</u>icroscope, <u>T</u>elevision, and the <u>A</u>tomic bomb.

   _____election_____   _____microscope_____   _____television_____   _____atomic_____

■ Review Test 1

Add capitals where needed in the following sentences.

Example   In an injured tone, Mary demanded, "<u>w</u>[W]hy wasn't <u>u</u>[U]ncle Lou invited to the party?"

1. To keep warm, a homeless old man sits on a steam vent near <u>h</u>[H]ampton <u>p</u>[P]ark on <u>t</u>[T]enth <u>s</u>[S]treet.

2. Silent movie stars of the twenties, like <u>c</u>[C]harlie <u>c</u>[C]haplin and <u>g</u>[G]loria <u>s</u>[S]wanson, earned more than a million tax-free dollars a year.

3. Insects living in ᴹmammoth ᶜcave in ᴷkentucky include blind crickets, spiders, and flies.

4. When Bill Clinton was a boy in ᴬarkansas, he was photographed shaking hands with ᴾpresident John F. Kennedy.

5. In an old movie, an attractive young lady invites ᴳgroucho ᴹmarx to join her.

6. "ᵂwhy?" asks ᴳgroucho. "ᴬare you coming apart?"

7. I was halfway to the ᵂwash & ᴰdry ᵀLaundromat on ᴱelm ˢstreet when ᴵi realized that my box of ᵀtide was still home on the kitchen counter.

8. Although I know that ᴹmother loves holidays, even I was surprised when she announced a party in ᶠfebruary to celebrate ᴳgroundhog ᴰday.

9. *Rolling ˢstone* magazine features an article about plans to remake the Alfred Hitchcock classic *ᵀthe ᴮbirds* and a review of a new ᵀtori ᴬamos album.

10. Celebrities have earned big money by endorsing products, including ᴾpolaroid ᵀcameras, ᵀtrident gum, and ᴶjell-O pudding.

■ Review Test 2

On separate paper, write:

1. Seven sentences demonstrating the seven main uses of capital letters.
2. Eight sentences demonstrating the eight other uses of capital letters.

Answers will vary.

36 Numbers and Abbreviations

Numbers

Here are three helpful rules for using numbers.

Rule 1:   Spell out numbers that take no more than two words. Otherwise, use the numbers themselves.

> In Jody's kitchen is her collection of seventy-two cookbooks.
> Jody has a file of 350 recipes.
>
> It will take about two weeks to fix the computer database.
> Since a number of people use the database, the company will lose over 150 workdays.
>
> Only twelve students have signed up for the field trip.
> Nearly 250 students came to the lecture.

Rule 2:   Be consistent when you use a series of numbers. If some numbers in a sentence or paragraph require more than two words, then use numbers for the others, too.

> After the storm, maintenance workers unclogged 46 drains, removed 123 broken tree limbs, and rescued 3 kittens who were stuck in a drainpipe.

Rule 3:   Use numbers to show dates, times, addresses, percentages, and parts of a book.

> The burglary was committed on October 30, 1995, but not discovered until January 2, 1996.
>
> Before I went to bed, I set my alarm for 6:45 A.M. (*But*: Spell out numbers before *o'clock*. For example: I didn't get out of bed until seven o'clock.)
>
> The library is located at 45 West 52d Street.
>
> When you take the skin off a piece of chicken, you remove about 40 percent of the fat.
>
> The name of the murderer is revealed in Chapter 8 on page 236.

Activity

Cross out the mistakes in numbers and write the corrections in the spaces provided.

1. The Puerto Rican Pride Parade will begin at ~~three-thirty~~ in front of the newspaper office at ~~one-oh-six~~ South ~~Forty-Second~~ Street.

       3:30   106   42nd
   _____   _____   _____

2. It took ~~4~~ hours to proofread all ~~75~~ pages of the manuscript.

       four   seventy-five
   _____   _____

3. We expect to have ~~fifty~~ percent of the work completed by March ~~tenth~~.

       50   10
   _____   _____

Abbreviations

Using abbreviations can save you time when you take notes. In formal writing, however, you should avoid most abbreviations. Listed below are some of the few abbreviations that are considered acceptable in compositions. Note that a period is used after most abbreviations.

1 Mr., Mrs., Ms., Jr., Sr., Dr. when used with proper names:

Mrs. Johnson   Dr. Garcia   Howard Kelley, Jr.

2 Time references:

A.M. or a.m.   P.M. or p.m.   B.C., A.D.

3 Initials in a person's name:

J. Edgar Hoover   John F. Kennedy   Michael J. Fox

4 Organizations, technical words, and company names known primarily by their initials:

IBM   UNICEF   ABC   IRS   NBA   AIDS

Activity

Cross out the words that should not be abbreviated, and correct them in the spaces provided.

1. Between mid-~~Nov.~~ and the beginning of ~~Jan.~~, I typically gain about five ~~lbs.~~
   <u> November </u>   <u> January </u>   <u> pounds </u>

2. I had such a bad headache this ~~aftern.~~ that I called my ~~doc.~~ for an ~~appt.~~
   <u> afternoon </u>   <u> doctor </u>   <u> appointment </u>

3. I stopped at the ~~p.o.~~ at about twenty ~~min.~~ past ten and bought five ~~dol.~~ worth of stamps.
   <u> post </u>   <u> office </u>   <u> minutes </u>   <u> dollars </u>

■ Review Test

Cross out the mistakes in numbers and abbreviations, and correct them in the spaces provided.

1. Sanjay was shocked when he transferred from a small ~~h.s.~~ to one with over ~~5,000~~ students.
   <u> high </u>   <u> school </u>   <u> five </u>   <u> thousand </u>

2. Grandpa lived to be ninety-nine despite smoking ~~3~~ packs of ~~cigs.~~ every day.
   <u> three </u>   <u> cigarettes </u>

3. Although the ~~2~~ girls are twins, they have different birthdays: one was born just before midnight on ~~Feb. twenty-fifth~~ and the other a few minutes later, after midnight.
   <u> two </u>   <u> February </u>   <u> 25 </u>

4. In their first week of ~~Span.~~ class, students learned to count from ~~1~~ to twenty-one and studied Chapter ~~One~~ in their textbook.
   <u> Spanish </u>   <u> one </u>   <u> 1 </u>

5. When I cleaned out the junk drawer in the ~~kitch.~~, I found twelve rubber bands, thirty-seven paper clips, and ~~3~~ used-up batteries.
   <u> kitchen </u>   <u> three </u>

37 Apostrophe

The two main uses of the apostrophe are:

1 To show the omission of one or more letters in a contraction
2 To show ownership or possession

Each use is explained in this chapter.

Apostrophe in Contractions

A *contraction* is formed when two words are combined to make one word. An apostrophe is used to show where letters are omitted in forming the contraction. Here are two contractions:

>   have + not = haven't (the *o* in *not* has been omitted)
>   I + will = I'll (the *wi* in *will* has been omitted)

Following are some other common contractions:

I + am = I'm	it + is = it's
I + have = I've	it + has = it's
I + had = I'd	is + not = isn't
who + is = who's	could + not = couldn't
do + not = don't	I + would = I'd
did + not = didn't	they + are = they're

Note: Will + not has an unusual contraction: won't.

Activity

Write the contractions for the words in parentheses. One is done for you.

1. (Are not) _____Aren't_____ the reserve books in the library kept at the circulation desk?

2. If (they are) __they're__ coming over, (I had) __I'd__ better cook more hot dogs.

3. (I am) __I'm__ the kind of student (who is) __who's__ extremely nervous before tests.

4. (We are) __We're__ hoping to find out (who is) __who's__ responsible for this error; (it is) __it's__ important to us to keep our customers happy.

5. I (can not) __can't__ remember if (there is) __there's__ gas in the car or not.

Note: Even though contractions are common in everyday speech and in written dialogue, it is often best to avoid them in formal writing.

Apostrophe to Show Ownership or Possession

To show ownership or possession, we can use such words as *belongs to, possessed by, owned by,* or (most commonly) *of.*

> the umbrella *that belongs to* Mark
>
> the tape recorder *owned by* the school
>
> the gentleness *of* my father

But the apostrophe plus *s* (if the word does not end in *s*) is often the quickest and easiest way to show possession. Thus we can say:

> Mark's umbrella
>
> the school's tape recorder
>
> my father's gentleness

Points to Remember

1 The *'s* goes with the owner or possessor (in the examples given, *Mark, the school, my father*). What follows is the person or thing possessed (in the examples given, *the umbrella, the tape recorder, gentleness*).

2 There should always be a break between the word and *'s*.

Mark's   not   Marks

Yes   No

3 An apostrophe plus *s* is used to show possession even with a singular word that already ends in *s*: for example, Doris's purse (the purse belonging to Doris).

Activity 1

Rewrite the *italicized* part of each of the sentences below, using *'s* to show possession. Remember that the *'s* goes with the owner or possessor.

Example   *The wing of the bluejay* was broken.

The bluejay's wing was broken.

1. *The annoying voice of the comedian* irritated me, so I changed the TV channel.

   The comedian's annoying voice

2. *The performance of the quarterback* is inconsistent.

   The quarterback's performance

3. *The thin hand belonging to the old woman* felt as dry as parchment.

   The old woman's thin hand

4. *In the window of the jewelry store* is a sign reading "Ears Pierced While You Wait."

   In the jewelry store's window

5. A fly flew into *the mouth of the TV weatherperson.*

   the TV weatherperson's mouth

6. *The new denim shirt belonging to Lamont* was as scratchy as sandpaper.

   Lamont's new denim shirt

7. *The hair belonging to Rachel* is usually not green—she colored it for Halloween.

   Rachel's hair

8. *The bowl of cereal belonging to Dennis* refused to snap, crackle, or pop.

   Dennis's bowl of cereal

9. *The Honda owned by Donna* was crammed with boxes and furniture.

   Donna's Honda

10. *The previous tenant of the apartment* had painted all the walls bright green.

    The apartment's previous tenant

Activity 2

Add '*s* to each of the following words to make it the possessor or owner of something. Then write sentences using the words. The first one is done for you.
Sentences will vary; examples are given.

1. rock star __rock star's__

   The rock star's limousine pulled up to the curb.

2. Felipe _____Felipe's_____

   Felipe's name is the Spanish version of Philip.

3. pilot _____pilot's_____

   The pilot's last message was, "We're losing altitude!"

4. neighbor _____neighbor's_____

   Our neighbor's yard is filled with flowers.

5. school _____school's_____

   The school's enrollment is about five hundred students.

6. gunslinger _____gunslinger's_____

   The gunslinger's moll is a favorite character in crime movies.

Apostrophe versus Possessive Pronouns

Do not use an apostrophe with possessive pronouns. They already show ownership. Possessive pronouns include *his, hers, its, yours, ours,* and *theirs.*

Incorrect	Correct
The sun warped his' albums.	The sun warped his albums.
The restored Model T is theirs'.	The restored Model T is theirs.
The decision is yours'.	The decision is yours.
The plaid suitcase is ours'.	The plaid suitcase is ours.
The lion charged its' prey.	The lion charged its prey.

Apostrophe versus Simple Plurals

When you want to make a word plural, just add an *s* at the end of the word. Do not add an apostrophe. For example, the plural of the word *movie* is *movies*, not *movie's* or *movies'*.

Look at this sentence:

Tim coveted his roommate's collection of cassette tapes and compact disks.

The words *tapes* and *disks* are simple plurals, meaning more than one tape, more than one disk. The plural is shown by adding *s* only. On the other hand, the *'s* after *roommate* shows possession—that the roommate owns the tapes and disks.

Activity

Insert an apostrophe where needed to show possession in the following sentences. Write *plural* above words where the *s* ending simply means more than one thing.

Example   Arlene's tinted contact lenses protect her eyes from glare.

1. Harry grasped his wife's arm as she stood on in-line skates for the first time.

2. Vonette's decision to study computer science is based on predictions of good opportunities for women in that field.

3. The fire's extreme heat had melted the telephones in the office and welded the metal chairs into a twisted heap.

4. At the doctor's request, Lyndon pulled up his shirt and revealed the zipper-like scars from his operation.

5. Of all the people's names in all the world's countries, the most common is Muhammad.

6. At the end of the day, Hal's shirt and pants smelled like gasoline, and his fingernails were rimmed with grease.

7. The children's shouts of delight grew louder as the clown added eggs, lightbulbs, and a bowling ball to the items he was juggling.

8. Tina's camping handbook suggests that we bring water purification tablets and nylon ropes.

9. Carmen's leaky pen had stained her fingers a deep blue. *plural*

10. The rattlesnake's head has a sensitive pit below the eyes, capable of detecting the body heat of warm-blooded prey. *plural*

Apostrophe with Plurals Ending in *-s*

Plurals that end in *-s* show possession simply by adding the apostrophe, rather than an apostrophe plus *s*.

the Thompsons' porch
the players' victory
her parents' motor home
the Rolling Stones' last album
the soldiers' hats

Activity

Add an apostrophe where needed.

1. Several campers' tents collapsed during the storm.

2. The Murrays' phone bills are often over $100 a month.

3. Many buildings' steep steps make it difficult for wheelchair users to gain access.

4. The twins' habit of dressing alike was started by their mother when they were children.

5. At the crowded intersection, several young men rushed out to wash the cars' windshields.

■ Review Test

In each sentence, underline the two words that need apostrophes. Then write the words correctly in the spaces provided.

<u>sofa's</u>   1. The sagging <u>sofas</u> stuffing was coming out in several places, and one of
<u>chair's</u>   the <u>chairs</u> legs was broken.

<u>barn's</u>   2. A shaky rope ladder led from the <u>barns</u> wooden floor to the <u>haylofts</u>
<u>hayloft's</u>   dusty shadows.

book's	3. The paperback <u>books</u> glaring purple and orange cover was designed to attract a hurrying <u>customers</u> eye.
customer's	
Phil's	4. <u>Phils</u> essay was due in a matter of hours, but he suffered a <u>writers</u> block that emptied his brain.
writer's	
boss's	5. While he waited in his <u>bosss</u> office, <u>Charlies</u> nervous fingers shredded a Styrofoam coffee cup into a pile of jagged white flakes.
Charlie's	
couldn't	6. Gregory <u>couldnt</u> remember whether he had left his wallet in his <u>cars</u> glove compartment or at home.
car's	
parents'	7. Members of the <u>parents</u> association constructed a maze made of old tires for the <u>childrens</u> playground.
children's	
cat's	8. The <u>cats</u> great green eyes grew even wider as the curious <u>dogs</u> sniffing nose came too close to her.
dog's	
sun's	9. The <u>suns</u> rays beat down until the <u>streets</u> blacktopped surface softened with the heat.
street's	
river's	10. The <u>rivers</u> swirling floodwaters lapped against the <u>Thompsons</u> porch.
Thompsons'	

38 Quotation Marks

The two main uses of quotation marks are:

1 To set off the exact words of a speaker or writer

2 To set off the titles of short works

Each use is explained here.

Quotation Marks to Set Off the Words of a Speaker or Writer

Use quotation marks to show the exact words of a speaker or writer.

"I feel as though I've been here before," Angie murmured to her husband.
(Quotation marks set off the exact words that Angie spoke to her husband.)

Ben Franklin once wrote, "To lengthen thy life, lessen thy meals."
(Quotation marks set off the exact words that Ben Franklin wrote.)

"Did you know," said the nutrition expert, "that it's healthier to be ten pounds overweight?"
(Two pairs of quotation marks are used to enclose the nutrition expert's exact words.)

The biology professor said, "Ants are a lot like human beings. They farm their own food and raise smaller insects as livestock. And, like humans, ants send armies to war."
(Note that the end quotation marks do not come until the end of the biology professor's speech. Place quotation marks before the first quoted word and after the last quoted word. As long as no interruption occurs in the speech, do not use quotation marks for each new sentence.)

Punctuation Hint: In the four examples above, notice that a comma sets off the quoted part from the rest of the sentence. Also, observe that commas and periods at the end of a quotation always go *inside* quotation marks.

Complete the following statements, which explain how capital letters, commas, and periods are used in quotations. Refer to the four examples as guides.

1. Every quotation begins with a _____capital_____ letter.
2. When a quotation is split (as in the sentence about the nutrition expert), the second part does not begin with a capital letter unless it is a _____new_____ sentence.
3. _____Commas_____ are used to separate the quoted part of a sentence from the rest of the sentence.
4. Commas and periods that come at the end of a quotation go _____inside_____ the quotation marks.

The answers are *capital, new, Commas,* and *inside.*

Activity 1

Place quotation marks around the exact words of a speaker or writer in the sentences that follow.

1. Several people have been credited with saying, "The more I see of people, the more I like dogs."
2. Beatrice asked, "Do you give a discount to senior citizens?"
3. "This hamburger is raw!" cried Leon.
4. The bumper sticker on the rear of the battered old car read, "Don't laugh—it's paid for."
5. "I know why Robin Hood robbed only the rich," said the comedian. "The poor don't have any money."
6. "These records," proclaimed the television announcer, "are not sold in any store."
7. "When chefs go to great lengths," the woman at the diet center said, "I go to great widths."
8. "If you accept an invitation to dinner," said the Duchess of Windsor, "you have a moral obligation to be amusing."
9. On a tombstone in a Maryland cemetery are the words, "Here lies an atheist, all dressed up and no place to go."
10. The columnist advised, "Be nice to people on your way up because you'll meet them on your way down."

Activity 2

Answers will vary; examples are shown.

1. Write a sentence in which you quote a favorite expression of someone you know. In the same sentence, identify the person's relationship to you.

   Example   *My grandfather loves to say, "It can't be as bad as all that."*

   _____

   _____

   _____

   _____

2. Write a quotation that contains the words *Pablo asked Teresa.* Write a second quotation that includes the words *Teresa replied.*

   "What time is it?" Pablo asked Teresa.

   "How should I know?" Teresa replied.

   _____

   _____

   _____

   _____

   _____

3. Quote an interesting sentence or two from a book or magazine. In the same sentence, identify the title and author of the work.

   Example   *In The Dilbert Desk Calendar by Scott Adams, the cartoon*

   character Dilbert says, "I can please only one person per day.

   Today isn't your day, and tomorrow isn't looking good either."

   _____

   _____

   _____

   _____

   _____

   _____

Indirect Quotations

An indirect quotation is a rewording of someone else's comments rather than a word-for-word direct quotation. The word *that* often signals an indirect quotation.

Direct Quotation	Indirect Quotation
The nurse said, "Some babies cannot tolerate cows' milk."	The nurse said that some babies cannot tolerate cows' milk.
(The nurse's exact spoken words are given, so quotation marks are used.)	(We learn the nurse's words indirectly, so no quotation marks are used.)
Vicky's note to Dan read, "I'll be home by 7:30."	Vicky left a note for Dan saying that she would be home by 7:30.
(The exact words that Vicky wrote in the note are given, so quotation marks are used.)	(We learn Vicky's words indirectly, so no quotation marks are used.)

Activity

Rewrite the following sentences, changing words as necessary to convert the sentences into direct quotations. The first one has been done for you as an example.

1. Teddy asked Margie if she wanted to see his spider collection.

   Teddy asked Margie, "Do you want to see my spider collection?"

   _____

2. Sonya said that her uncle looks just like a large basset hound.

   Sonya said, "My uncle looks just like a large basset hound."

   _____

3. Angelo said that he wanted a box of the extra-crispy chicken.

   Angelo said, "I want a box of the extra-crispy chicken."

   _____

4. My boss told me that I could make mistakes as long as I didn't repeat them.

   My boss told me, "You can make mistakes as long as you don't repeat

   them."

5. The instructor announced that Thursday's test had been canceled.

   The instructor announced, "Thursday's test has been canceled."

   _____

Quotation Marks to Set Off Titles of Short Works

Titles of short works are usually set off by quotation marks, while titles of long works are underlined. Use quotation marks to set off titles of such short works as articles in books, newspapers, or magazines; chapters in a book; short stories; poems; and songs. But you should underline titles of books, newspapers, magazines, plays, movies, record albums, and television shows. Following are some examples.

Quotation Marks	Underlines
the essay "On Self-Respect"	in the book <u>Slouching Towards Bethlehem</u>
the article "The Problem of Acid Rain"	in the newspaper <u>The New York Times</u>
the article "Living with Inflation"	in the magazine <u>Newsweek</u>
the chapter "Chinese Religion"	in the book <u>Paths of Faith</u>
the story "Hands"	in the book <u>Winesburg, Ohio</u>
the poem "When I Have Fears"	in the book <u>Complete Poems of John Keats</u>
the song "Ziggy Stardust"	in the album <u>Changes</u>
	the television show <u>Sixty Minutes</u>
	the movie <u>High Noon</u>

Note: In printed works, including papers that are prepared on a word processor, italic type—slanted type that looks *like this*—is used instead of underlining.

Activity

Use quotation marks or underlines as needed.

1. In her short story "A Sea Worry," Maxine Hong Kingston describes a group of teenage surfers and a mother who tries to understand them.

2. I bought the <u>National Enquirer</u> to read an article entitled "Painful Beauty Secrets of the Stars."

3. We read the chapter "Pulling Up Roots" in Gail Sheehy's book <u>Passages</u>.

4. Jamila used an article titled "Winter Blues" from <u>Time</u> magazine in her research paper about seasonal depression.

5. The movie Casablanca, which starred Humphrey Bogart, was originally cast with Ronald Reagan in the leading role.

6. My favorite old TV show was Thriller, a horror series hosted by Boris Karloff, the man who starred in the 1931 movie Frankenstein.

7. When the Beatles' movie A Hard Day's Night was first shown, fans screamed so much that no one could hear the songs or the dialogue.

8. On my father's wall is a framed front page of The New York Times of February 25, 1940—the day he was born.

9. The sociology test will cover the first two chapters: "Culture and Diversity" and "Social Stratification."

10. An article in Consumer Reports called "Which Cereal for Breakfast?" claims that children can learn to like low-sugar cereals like Cheerios and Wheaties.

Other Uses of Quotation Marks

Quotation marks are also used as follows:

1 To set off special words or phrases from the rest of a sentence:

> In grade school, we were taught a little jingle about the spelling rule "*i* before *e*."
> What is the difference between "it's" and "its"?
> (In this book, *italics* are often used instead of quotation marks to set off words.)

2 To mark off a quotation within a quotation:

> The physics professor said, "For class on Friday, do the problems at the end of the chapter titled 'Work and Energy.'"
> Brendan remarked, "Did you know that Humphrey Bogart never actually said, 'Play it again, Sam' in the movie *Casablanca*?"

Note: A quotation within a quotation is indicated by *single* quotation marks, as shown above.

■ Review Test 1

Insert quotation marks where needed in the sentences that follow.

1. The psychology class read a short story called "Silent Snow, Secret Snow," about a young boy who creates his own fantasy world.

2. While filming the movie *Vertigo*, the actress Kim Novak was agonizing over how to play a particular scene until the director, Alfred Hitchcock, reminded her, "Kim, it's only a movie!"

3. "I'm against grade school students' using pocket calculators," said Fred. "I spent three years learning long division, and so should they."

4. The composer George Gershwin wrote many hundreds of hit songs, including classics like "Summertime" and "Somebody Loves Me."

5. When I gagged while taking a foul-tasting medicine, my wife said, "Put an ice cube on your tongue first, and then you won't taste it."

6. I looked twice at the newspaper headline that read, "Man in River Had Drinking Problem."

7. To learn more about the stock market for his business class, Jared began reading the column by Pablo Galarza in *Money* magazine called "MarketRap."

8. When a guest at the wedding was asked what he was giving the couple, he replied, "About six months."

9. Theodore Roosevelt, a pioneer in conservation, once said, "When I hear of the destruction of a species, I feel as if all the works of some great writer had perished."

10. "If you're ever in trouble," said the police officer, "you'll have a better chance of attracting aid if you shout 'Fire' instead of 'Help.'"

■ Review Test 2

Go through the comics section of a newspaper to find a comic strip that amuses you. Be sure to choose a strip where two or more characters are speaking to each other. Write a full description that will enable people who have not read the comic strip to visualize it clearly and appreciate its humor. Describe the setting and action in each panel, and enclose the words of the speakers in quotation marks.

Answers will vary.

39 Comma

Six Main Uses of the Comma

Commas are used mainly as follows:

1 To separate items in a series
2 To set off introductory material
3 On both sides of words that interrupt the flow of thought in a sentence
4 Between two complete thoughts connected by *and, but, for, or, nor, so, yet*
5 To set off a direct quotation from the rest of a sentence
6 For certain everyday material

You may find it helpful to remember that the comma often marks a slight pause or break in a sentence. Read aloud the sentence examples given for each rule, and listen for the minor pauses or breaks that are signaled by commas.

1 Comma Between Items in a Series

Use commas to separate items in a series.

> The street vendor sold watches, necklaces, and earrings.
> The pitcher adjusted his cap, pawed the ground, and peered over his shoulder.
> The exercise instructor told us to inhale, exhale, and relax.
> Joe peered into the hot, still-smoking engine.

Notes

a The final comma in a series is optional, but it is often used.
b A comma is used between two descriptive words in a series only if *and* inserted between the words sounds natural. You could say:

Joe peered into the hot *and* still-smoking engine.

But notice in the following sentence that the descriptive words do not sound natural when *and* is inserted between them. In such cases, no comma is used.

Tony wore a pale green tuxedo. (A pale *and* green tuxedo does not sound right, so no comma is used.)

Activity

Place commas between items in a series.

1. The old kitchen cabinets were littered with dead insects, crumbs, and dust balls.
2. Rudy stretched out on the swaying hammock, popped open a frosty can of soda, and balanced it carefully on his stomach.
3. The children splashed through the warm, deep, swirling rainwater that flooded the street.
4. The police officer's warm brown eyes, relaxed manner, and pleasant smile made him easy to talk to.
5. The musty, shadowy cellar with the crumbling cement floor was our favorite playground.

2 Comma after Introductory Material

Use a comma to set off introductory material.

Just in time, Sherry slid a plastic tray under the overwatered philodendron.

Muttering under his breath, Ken reviewed the terms he had memorized.

In a wolf pack, the dominant male holds his tail higher than the other pack members.

Although he had been first in the checkout line, Deion let an elderly woman go ahead of him.

After the fire, we slogged through the ashes of the burned-out house.

Note: If the introductory material is brief, the comma is sometimes omitted. In the activities here, you should include the comma.

Activity

Place commas after introductory material.

1. As Patty struggled with the stuck window gusts of cold rain blew in her face.
2. His heart pounding wildly Jesse opened the letter that would tell him whether or not he had been accepted at college.
3. Along the once-pretty river people had dumped old tires and loads of household trash.
4. When the band hadn't taken the stage forty-five minutes after the concert was supposed to begin the audience members started shouting and stamping their feet.
5. Setting down a smudged glass of murky water the waitress tossed Dennis a greasy menu and asked if he'd care to order.

3 Comma Around Words Interrupting the Flow of Thought

Use a comma on both sides of words or phrases that interrupt the flow of thought in a sentence.

> The vinyl car seat, sticky from the heat, clung to my skin.
>
> Marty's personal computer, which his wife got him as a birthday gift, occupies all of his spare time.
>
> The hallway, dingy and dark, was illuminated by a bare bulb hanging from a wire.

Usually, by reading a sentence aloud, you can "hear" words that interrupt the flow of thought. In cases where you are not sure if certain words are interrupters, remove them from the sentence. If it still makes sense without the words, you know that the words are interrupters and that the information they give is nonessential. *Such nonessential or extra information is set off with commas.*

In the sentence

> Sue Dodd, who goes to aerobics class with me, was in a serious car accident.

the words *who goes to aerobics class with me* are extra information not needed to identify the subject of the sentence, *Sue Dodd.* Commas go around such nonessential information. On the other hand, in the sentence

> The woman who goes to aerobics class with me was in a serious accident.

the words *who goes to aerobics class with me* supply essential information—
information needed for us to identify the woman being spoken of. If the words
were removed from the sentence, we would no longer know exactly who was in
the accident: "The woman was in a serious accident." Here is another example:

> *Watership Down*, a novel by Richard Adams, is the most thrilling adventure
> story I've ever read.

Here the words *a novel by Richard Adams* could be left out, and we would still
know the basic meaning of the sentence. Commas are placed around such
nonessential material. But in the sentence

> Richard Adams's novel *Watership Down* is the most thrilling adventure story
> I've ever read.

the title of the novel is essential. Without it the sentence would read, "Richard
Adams's novel is the most thrilling adventure story I've ever read." We would not
know which of Richard Adams's novels was so thrilling. Commas are not used
around the title because it provides essential information.

Most of the time you will be able to "hear" words that interrupt the flow of
thought in a sentence and will not have to think about whether the words are essential or nonessential.

Activity

Use commas to set off interrupting words.

1. A slight breeze hot and damp ruffled the bedroom curtains.
2. The defrosting chickens loosely wrapped in plastic left a pool on the counter.
3. Lenny's wallet which he kept in his front pants pocket was linked to his belt
   with a metal chain.
4. Mr. Delgado who is an avid Yankees fan remembers the grand days of Mickey
   Mantle and Yogi Berra.
5. The fleet of tall ships a majestic sight made its way into the harbor.

4 Comma Between Complete Thoughts

Use a comma between two complete thoughts connected by *and, but, for, or, nor,
so, yet.*

> Sam closed all the windows, but the predicted thunderstorm never arrived.
> I like wearing comfortable clothing, so I buy oversized shirts and sweaters.

Peggy doesn't envy the skinny models in magazines, for she is happy with her own well-rounded body.

Notes

a The comma is optional when the complete thoughts are short.

The ferris wheel started and Wilson closed his eyes.

Many people left but the band played on.

I made a wrong turn so I doubled back.

b Be careful not to use a comma to separate two verbs that belong to one subject. The comma is used only in sentences made up of two complete thoughts (two subjects and two verbs). In the sentence

The doctor stared over his bifocals and lectured me about smoking.

there is only one subject (*doctor*) and a double verb (*stared* and *lectured*). No comma is needed. Likewise, the sentence

Dean switched the lamp on and off and then tapped it with his fingers.

has only one subject (*Dean*) and a double verb (*switched* and *tapped*); therefore, no comma is needed.

Activity

Place a comma before a joining word that connects two complete thoughts (two subjects and two verbs). Remember, do *not* place a comma within a sentence that has only one subject and a double verb. (Some items may be correct as given.)

1. The television sitcom was interrupted for a special news bulletin, and I poked my head out of the kitchen to listen to the announcement.
2. The puppy was beaten by its former owner and cringes at the sound of a loud voice. *Correct*
3. The eccentric woman brought all her own clips and rollers to the beauty parlor, for she was afraid to use the ones there.
4. The tuna sandwich in my lunch is crushed, and the cream-filled cupcake is plastered to the bottom of the bag.
5. The landlord promised repeatedly to come and fix the leaking shower, but three months later he hasn't done a thing.

6. Ruth was tired of summer reruns, so she visited the town library to pick up some interesting books.

7. You can spend hours driving all over town to look for a particular type of camera, or you can telephone a few stores to find it quickly.

8. Many people strolled among the exhibits at the comic book collectors' convention and stopped to look at a rare first edition of *Superman.* Correct

9. Our neighborhood crime patrol escorts elderly people to the local bank and installs free dead-bolt locks on their apartment doors. Correct

10. Brendan tapped the small geraniums out of their pots and carefully planted them on his grandfather's grave. Correct

5 Comma with Direct Quotations

Use a comma to set off a direct quotation from the rest of a sentence.

The carnival barker cried, "Step right up and win a prize!"

"Now is the time to yield to temptation," my horoscope read.

"I'm sorry," said the restaurant hostess. "You'll have to wait."

"For my first writing assignment," said Scott, "I have to turn in a five-hundred-word description of a stone."

Note: Commas and periods at the end of a quotation go inside quotation marks. See also page 505.

Activity

Use commas to set off direct quotations from the rest of the sentence.

1. The coach announced, "In order to measure your lung capacity, you're going to attempt to blow up a plastic bag with one breath."

2. "A grapefruit," said the comedian, "is a lemon that had a chance and took advantage of it."

3. My father asked, "Did you know that the family moving next door has thirteen children?"

4. "Speak louder," a man in the back row said to the guest speaker. "I paid five dollars to hear you talk, not whisper."

5. The zookeeper explained to the visitors, "We can't tell the sex of a giant tortoise for almost ten years after its birth."

6 Comma with Everyday Material

Use a comma with certain everyday material.

Persons Spoken To	If you're the last to leave, Paul, please switch off the lights. Fred, I think we're on the wrong road. Did you see the playoff game, Lisa?
Dates	June 30, 2003, is the day I make the last payment on my car.
Addresses	I buy discount children's clothing from Isaacs Baby Wear Factory, Box 900, Chicago, Illinois 60614.

Note: No comma is used before a zip code.

Openings and Closings of Letters	Dear Santa, Sincerely yours, Dear Roberto, Truly yours,

Note: In formal letters, a colon is used after the opening:
Dear Sir: *or* Dear Madam: *or* Dear Allan: *or* Dear Ms. Mohr:

Numbers	The insurance agent sold me a $50,000 term life insurance policy.

Activity

Place commas where needed.

1. Would you mind George if we borrowed your picnic cooler this weekend?
2. The enchiladas served at Los Amigos 5607 Pacific Boulevard are the best in town.
3. An estimated 875000 African American men participated in the Million Man March on Washington on October 16 1995.
4. The mileage chart shows Elaine that we'll have to drive 1231 miles to get to Sarasota Florida.
5. The coupon refund address is 2120 Industrial Highway Great Plains Minnesota 55455.

■ Review Test 1

Insert commas where needed. In the space provided below each sentence, summarize briefly the rule that explains the comma or commas used.
Wording of rules may vary.

1. "Kleenex tissues," said the history professor, "were first used as gas mask filters in World War I."

   comma with direct quotation
   _____

2. Dee ordered a sundae with three scoops of vanilla ice cream, miniature marshmallows, and raspberry sauce.

   comma with items in a series
   _____

3. While waiting to enter the movie theater, we studied the faces of the people just leaving to see if they had liked the show.

   comma after introductory material
   _____

4. I had left my wallet on the store counter, but the clerk called me at home to say that it was safe.

   comma between two complete thoughts
   _____

5. The demonstrators protesting nuclear arms carried signs reading, "Humans have never invented a weapon that they haven't used."

   comma to set off a direct quotation
   _____

6. Large cactus plants, which now sell for very high prices, are being stolen from national parks and protected desert areas.

   comma with words interrupting the flow of thought
   _____

7. At the age of twenty-one, Tiger Woods won the 1997 Masters Tournament with the highest margin of victory in the golfing tournament's history.

   comma after introductory material
   _____

8. The talk show guest, a former child star, said that one director threatened to shoot her dog if she didn't cry on cue.

   comma with words interrupting the flow of thought
   _____

9. Tom watched nervously as the dentist assembled drills, mirrors, clamps, picks, and cylinders of cotton on a tray next to the reclining chair.

   comma with items in a series
   _____

10. Cats and dogs, like most animals, love the taste of salt and will lick humans' hands to get it.

    comma with words interrupting the flow of thought
    _____

■ Review Test 2

Insert commas where needed. Mark the one sentence that is correct with a C.

1. Before leaving for the gym, Nikki added extra socks and a tube of shampoo to the gear in her duffel bag.
2. My father said, "Golf isn't for me. I can't afford to buy lots of expensive sticks so that I can lose lots of expensive white balls."
3. Clogged with soggy birds' nests, the chimney had allowed dangerous gases to accumulate in our house.
4. Oscar took a time-exposure photo of the busy highway, so the cars' taillights appeared in the developed print as winding red ribbons.
5. The graduating students, sweltering in their hot black gowns, fanned their faces with commencement programs.
6. After her tragic death in Paris, France, more than two billion people worldwide watched the televised funeral of Princess Diana of England on September 6, 1997.
7. In November 1998, thousands of people died in Honduras because of the mud slides, flooding, and high winds brought by Hurricane Mitch.
8. "When I was little," said Ernie, "my brother told me it was illegal to kill praying mantises. I still don't know if that's true or not."
9. A huge side of beef, its red flesh marbled with streaks of creamy fat, hung from a razor-sharp steel hook.
10. A line of dancing numerals on *Sesame Street* kicked across the screen like a chorus line. *C*

■ Review Test 3

In the following passage, there are ten missing commas. Add the commas where needed. The types of mistakes to look for are shown in the box below.

> 2 commas missing between items in a series
> 1 comma missing after introductory material
> 4 commas missing around interrupting words
> 2 commas missing between complete thoughts
> 1 comma missing with a direct quotation

When I was about ten years old, I developed several schemes to avoid eating liver, a food I despise. My first scheme involved my little brother. Timmy, too young to realize what a horrible food liver is, always ate every bit of his portion. On liver nights, I used to sit next to Tim and slide my slab of meat onto his plate when my parents weren't paying attention. This strategy worked until, older and wiser, Tim decided to reject his liver along with the rest of us. Another liver-disposal method I used was hiding the meat right on the plate. I'd cut the liver into tiny squares half the size of postage stamps, and then I would carefully hide the pieces. I'd put them inside the skin of my baked potato, beneath some mashed peas, or under a crumpled paper napkin. This strategy worked perfectly only if my mother didn't look too closely as she scraped the dishes. Once she said to me, "Do you know you left a lot of liver on your plate?" My best liver trick was to hide the disgusting stuff on a three-inch-wide wooden ledge that ran under our dining-room table. I'd put little pieces of liver on the ledge when Mom wasn't looking; I would sneak the dried-up scraps into the garbage early the next day. Our dog would sometimes smell the liver, try to get at it, and bang his head noisily against the bottom of the table. These strategies seemed like a lot of work, but I never hesitated to take whatever steps I could. Anything was better than eating a piece of meat that tasted like old socks soaked in mud.

■ Review Test 4

On separate paper, write six sentences, one illustrating each of the six main comma rules.

Answers will vary.

40 Other Punctuation Marks

Colon (:)

Use the colon at the end of a complete statement to introduce a list, a long quotation, or an explanation.

1 A list:

The store will close at noon on the following dates: November 26, December 24, and December 31.

2 A quotation:

In his book *Life Lines,* Forrest Church maintains that people should cry more: "Life is difficult. Some people pretend that it is not, that we should be able to breeze through. Yet hardly a week passes in which most of us don't have something worth crying about."

3 An explanation:

Here's a temporary solution to a dripping faucet: tie a string to it, and let the drops slide down the string to the sink.

Activity

Place colons where needed in the sentences below:

1. Bring these items to registration:a ballpoint pen, your student ID card, and a check made out to the college.
2. The road was closed because of an emergency:an enormous tree had fallen and blocked both lanes.
3. Willa Cather, the American author, had an insightful comment about plots : "There are only two or three human stories, and they go on repeating themselves as fiercely as if they had never happened before."

Semicolon (;)

The main use of the semicolon is to mark a break between two complete thoughts, as explained on pages 434–437. Another use is to mark off items in a series when the items themselves contain commas. Here are some examples:

> Maya's children are named Melantha, which means "black flower"; Yonina, which means "dove"; and Cynthia, which means "moon goddess."

> My parents' favorite albums are *Rubber Soul*, by the Beatles; *Songs in the Key of Life,* by Stevie Wonder; and *Bridge over Troubled Water,* by Simon and Garfunkel.

Activity

Place semicolons where needed in the sentences below.

1. Strange things happen at very low temperatures;a rose will shatter like glass.
2. My sister had a profitable summer: by mowing lawns, she earned $125;by washing cars, $85;and by walking the neighbors' dogs, $110.
3. The children who starred in the play were Kari Rosoff, nine years old;Flora Junco, twelve years old;and Ezra Johnson, three years old.

Dash (—)

A dash signals a pause longer than a comma but not as complete as a period. Use a dash to set off words for dramatic effect:

> I was so exhausted that I fell asleep within seconds—standing up.

> He had many good qualities—sincerity, honesty, and thoughtfulness—yet he had few friends.

> The pardon from the governor finally arrived—too late.

Notes

a A dash is formed on a keyboard by striking the hyphen twice (- -). In hand-writing, a dash is as long as two letters would be.

b Be careful not to overuse dashes.

Activity

Place dashes where needed in the following sentences.

1. The victim's leg—broken in three places—lay twisted at an odd angle on the pavement.
2. The wallet was found in a trash can—minus the cash.
3. After nine days of hiking in the wilderness, sleeping under the stars, and communing with nature, I could think of only one thing—a hot shower.

Parentheses ( )

Parentheses are used to set off extra or incidental information from the rest of a sentence:

> In 1913, the tax on an annual income of $4,000 (a comfortable wage at that time) was one penny.
>
> Arthur C. Clarke, author of science fiction books (including *2001: A Space Odyssey*), was inspired as a young man by the magazine *Astounding Stories*.

Note: Do not use parentheses too often in your writing.

Activity

Add parentheses where needed.

1. Though the original *Star Trek* series originally ran for only three seasons (1965–1968), it can still be seen on many stations around the country.
2. Whenever Jack has too much to drink (even one drink is sometimes too much), he gets loud and abusive.
3. When I opened the textbook, I discovered that many pages (mostly in the first chapter) were completely blank.

Hyphen (-)

1 Use a hyphen with two or more words that act as a single unit describing a noun.

> The light-footed burglar silently slipped open the sliding glass door.
> While being interviewed on the late-night talk show, the quarterback announced his intention to retire.
> With a needle, Rich punctured the fluid-filled blister on his toe.

2 Use a hyphen to divide a word at the end of a line of writing or typing. When you need to divide a word at the end of a line, divide it between syllables. Use your dictionary to be sure of correct syllable divisions.

> Selena's first year at college was a time filled with numerous new pressures and responsibilities.

Notes

a Do not divide words of one syllable.

b Do not divide a word if you can avoid dividing it.

Activity

Place hyphens where needed.

1. The blood-red moon hanging low on the horizon made a picture-perfect atmosphere for Halloween night.
2. My father, who grew up in a poverty-stricken household, remembers putting cardboard in his shoes when the soles wore out.
3. The well-written article in *Newsweek* described the nerve-racking experiences of a journalist who infiltrated the mob.

■ Review Test

At the appropriate spot, place the punctuation mark shown in the margin.

—
1. A bad case of flu, a burglary, the death of an uncle it was not what you would call a pleasant week.

( )
2. My grandfather who will be ninety in May says that hard work and a glass of wine every day are the secrets of a long life.

:
3. Mark Twain offered this advice to writers: "The difference between the right word and the nearly right word is the difference between lightning and the lightning bug."

-
4. The passengers in the glass-bottomed boat stared at the colorful fish in the water below.

( )
5. Ellen's birthday December 27 falls so close to Christmas that she gets only one set of presents.

;
6. The dog-show winners included Freckles, a springer spaniel; King Leo, a German shepherd; and Big Guy, a miniature schnauzer.

—
7. I feel I have two chances of winning the lottery slim and none.

-
8. Cold hearted stepmothers are a fixture in many famous fairy tales.

;
9. Some people need absolute quiet in order to study; they can't concentrate with the soft sounds of a radio, air conditioner, or television in the background.

:
10. A critic reviewing a bad play wrote, "I saw the play under the worst possible circumstances: the curtain was up."

41 Spelling Improvement

Poor spelling often results from bad habits developed in the early school years. With work, such habits can be corrected. If you can write your name without misspelling it, there is no reason why you cannot do the same with almost any word in the English language. Following are steps you can take to improve your spelling.

Step 1: Use the Dictionary

Get into the habit of using the dictionary. When you write a paper, allow yourself time to look up the spelling of all those words you are unsure about. Do not overlook the value of this step just because it is such a simple one. By using the dictionary, you can probably make yourself a 95 percent better speller.

Step 2: Keep a Personal Spelling List

Keep a list of words you misspell and study the words regularly. Write the list on the back page of a frequently used notebook or on a separate sheet of paper titled "Personal Spelling List."

To master the words on your personal spelling list, do the following:

1 Write down any hint that will help you remember the spelling of a word. For example, you might want to note that *occasion* is spelled with two *c*'s, or that *all right* is two words, not one word.

2 Study a word by looking at it, saying it, and spelling it. You may also want to write out the word one or more times, or "air write" it with your finger in large, exaggerated motions.

3 When you have trouble spelling a long word, try to break the word into syllables and see whether you can spell the syllables. For example, *inadvertent* can be spelled easily if you can hear and spell in turn its four syllables: *in ad ver tent*. The word *consternation* can be spelled easily if you hear and spell its four syllables in turn: *con ster na tion*. Remember, then: Try to see, hear, and spell long words in terms of their syllables.

4 Keep in mind that review and repeated self-testing are keys to effective learning. When you are learning a series of words, go back after studying each new word and review all the preceding ones.

Step 3: Master Commonly Confused Words

Master the meanings and spellings of the commonly confused words on pages 532–540. Your instructor may assign twenty words for you to study at a time and give you a series of quizzes until you have mastered the words.

Step 4: Learn Key Words in Major Subjects

Make up and master lists of words central to the vocabulary of your major subjects. For example, a list of key words in business might include *economics, management, resources, scarcity, capitalism, decentralization, productivity, enterprise,* and so on; in psychology, *behavior, investigation, experimentation, frustration, cognition, stimulus, response, organism,* and so on. Set aside a specific portion of your various course notebooks to be used only for such lists, and study them using the methods described above for learning words.

Step 5: Study a Basic Word List

Following is a list of 250 English words that are often misspelled. Study their spellings. Your instructor may assign 25 or 50 words for you to study at a time and give you a series of quizzes until you have mastered the entire list.

250 Basic
Words

absence	comfortable	harass
ache	committed	height
achieve	completely	hospital
acknowledge	conceit	hundred
advice	conscience	husband
aisle	conscious	imitation
all right	conversation	incredible
already	cruelty	independent
amateur	50 daughter	instant
answer	deceit	instead
anxious	definite	intelligence
appearance	deposit	interest
appetite	dictionary	interfere
attempt	disastrous	interrupt
attendance	disease	irresistible
autumn	distance	January
awful	doctor	kindergarten
bachelor	doubt	100 leisure
balance	efficient	library
bargain	eighth	lightning
basically	either	likely
beautiful	emphasize	livelihood
believe	entrance	loneliness
beneficial	environment	loose
25 bottom	exaggerate	magazine
breathe	examine	making
brilliant	existence	maintain
bureau	familiar	marriage
business	fascinate	material
cafeteria	February	mathematics
calendar	financial	medicine
candidate	foreign	minute
category	forty	mortgage
ceiling	75 friend	muscle
cemetery	furniture	naturally
chief	government	necessary
choose	grammar	neither
cigarette	grieve	nickel
citizen	guidance	niece
college	hammer	ninety
column	handkerchief	noise

	obedience		relieve		tournament
125	obstacle		religion		toward
	occasion		representative		transferred
	occur		resistance		trousers
	occurrence		restaurant		truly
	omission		rhythm		twelfth
	opinion		ridiculous		unanimous
	opportunity		right		until
	optimist	175	safety		unusual
	ounce		said		usage
	outrageous		salary		used
	pageant		scarcely		usual
	pamphlet		scholastic		usually
	people		science		vacuum
	perform		scissors		valuable
	persistent		secretary		variety
	physically		seize	225	vegetable
	picnic		separate		vengeance
	plausible		sergeant		view
	pleasant		several		villain
	policeman		severely		vision
	possible		shriek		visitor
	precede		siege		voice
	prefer		similar		Washington
	preference		sincerely		wear
	prejudice		sophomore		weather
150	prescription		straight		Wednesday
	probably		succeed		weight
	psychology		suppress		weird
	pursue		telephone		welcome
	quantity		temperature		whether
	quarter		tenant		which
	quiet		tendency		woman
	quiz	200	tenth		women
	raise		than		won't
	really		theater		writing
	recede		though		written
	receive		thousand		wrong
	recognize		through		yesterday
	recommend		tomorrow		yolk
	reference		tongue		your
	region		tonight	250	you're
	reign				

Step 6: Use Electronic Aids

There are several electronic aids that can help your spelling. First, most *electronic typewriters* can be set to beep automatically when you misspell a word. They include built-in dictionaries that will then give you the correct spelling. Second, *electronic spell-checks* are pocket-size devices that look much like the pocket calculators you may use in math class. Electronic spellers can be found in almost any electronics store. The checker includes a tiny keyboard. You type out the word the way you think it is spelled, and the checker quickly provides you with the correct spelling of related words. Finally, *a computer with a spell-checker* as part of its word processing program will identify incorrect words and suggest correct spellings. If you know how to write on the computer, you will have little trouble learning how to use the spell-check feature.

42 Commonly Confused Words

Homonyms

Some words are commonly confused because they have the same sounds but different meanings and spellings; such words are known as *homonyms*. Following are a number of homonyms. Complete the activity for each set of words, and check off and study the words that give you trouble.

all ready   completely prepared
already   previously; before

> It was *already* four o'clock by the time I thought about lunch.
>
> My report was *all ready*, but the class was canceled.

Fill in the blanks: Tyrone was ___all ready___ to sign up for the course when he discovered that it had ___already___ closed.

brake   stop
break   come apart

> The mechanic advised me to add *brake* fluid to my car.
>
> During a commercial *break*, Marie lay on the floor and did fifty sit-ups.

Fill in the blanks: Tim, a poor driver, would always ___brake___ at the last minute and would usually ___break___ the speed limit as well.

course   part of a meal; a school subject; direction
coarse   rough

> At the movies, I tried to decide on a *course* of action that would put an end to the *coarse* language of the man behind me.

Fill in the blanks: Over the ___course___ of time, jagged, ___coarse___ rocks will be polished to smoothness by the pounding waves.

hear   perceive with the ear
here   in this place

> I can *hear* the performers so well from *here* that I don't want to change my seat.

Fill in the blanks: The chairperson explained that the meeting was held _____here_____ in the auditorium to enable everyone to _____hear_____ the debate.

hole   an empty spot
whole   entire

> A *hole* in the crumbling brick mortar made a convenient home for the small bird and its *whole* family.

Fill in the blanks: The _____hole_____ in Dave's argument wouldn't exist if he put his _____whole_____ concentration into his thinking.

its   belonging to it
it's   shortened form for "it is" or "it has"

> The tall giraffe lowered *its* head (the head belonging to the giraffe) to the level of the car window and peered in at us.
> *It's* (it is) too late to sign up for the theater trip to New York.

Fill in the blanks: I decided not to take the course because _____it's_____ too easy; _____its_____ content offers no challenge whatever.

knew   past form of *know*
new   not old

> No one *knew* our *new* phone number, but the obscene calls continued.

Fill in the blanks: Even people who _____knew_____ Charlie well didn't recognize him with his _____new_____ beard.

know   to understand
no   a negative

By the time students complete that course, they *know* two computer languages and have *no* trouble writing their own programs.

Fill in the blanks: Dogs and cats usually _____*know*_____ by the tone of the speaker's voice when they are being told " _____*no*_____ ."

passed   went by; succeeded in; handed to
past   a time before the present; by, as in "I drove past the house"

As Yvonne *passed* exit six on the interstate, she knew she had gone *past* the correct turnoff.

Fill in the blanks: Lewis asked for a meeting with his boss to learn why he had been _____*passed*_____ over for promotion twice in the _____*past*_____ year.

peace   calm
piece   a part

The best *piece* of advice she ever received was to maintain her own inner *peace*.

Fill in the blanks: Upon hearing that _____*piece*_____ of music, my angry mood was gradually replaced by one of _____*peace*_____ .

plain   simple
plane   aircraft

The *plain* box contained a very expensive model *plane* kit.

Fill in the blanks: After unsuccessfully trying to overcome her fear, Sally finally admitted the _____*plain*_____ truth; she was terrified of flying in a _____*plane*_____ .

principal   main; a person in charge of a school
principle   a law or standard

> If the *principal* ingredient in this stew is octopus, I'll abandon my *principle* of trying everything at least once.

Fill in the blanks: Our _____principal_____ insists that all students adhere to every school _____principle_____ regarding dress, tardiness, and smoking.

right   correct; opposite of "left"
write   what you do in English

> Without the *right* amount of advance planning, it is difficult to *write* a good research paper.

Fill in the blanks: Connie wanted to send for the records offered on TV, but she could not _____write_____ fast enough to get all the _____right_____ information down before the commercial ended.

than   (thăn)   used in comparisons
then   (thĕn)   at that time

> I made more money *then,* but I've never been happier *than* I am now.

Fill in the blanks: When I was in high school, I wanted a racy two-seater convertible more _____than_____ anything else; but _____then_____ my friends pointed out that only one person would be able to ride with me.

their   belonging to them
there   at that place; a neutral word used with verbs like *is, are, was, were, have,* and *had*
they're   shortened form of "they are"

> The tenants *there* are complaining because *they're* being cheated by *their* landlord.

Fill in the blanks: The tomatoes I planted _____there_____ in the back of the garden are finally ripening, but _____their_____ bright red color will attract hungry raccoons, and I fear _____they're_____ going to be eaten.

threw   past form of *throw*
through   from one side to the other; finished

> As the inexperienced pizza maker *threw* the pie into the air, he punched a hole *through* its thin crust.

Fill in the blanks: As the president moved slowly ____through____ the cheering crowd, the Secret Service agent suddenly ____threw____ himself at a man waving a small metal object.

to   verb part, as in *to smile;* toward, as in "I'm going *to* heaven"
too   overly, as in "The pizza was *too* hot"; also, as in "The coffee was hot, *too.*"
two   the number 2

> I ran *to* the car *to* roll up the windows. (The first *to* means "toward"; the second *to* is a verb part that goes with *roll.*)
>
> That amusement park is *too* far away; I hear that it's expensive, *too.* (The first *too* means "overly"; the second *too* means "also.")
>
> The *two* players (2 players) jumped up to tap the basketball away.

Fill in the blanks: The ____two____ of them have been dating for a year, but lately they seem ____to____ be arguing ____too____ often to pretend nothing is wrong.

wear   to have on
where   in what place

> *Where* I will *wear* a purple feather boa is not the point; I just want to buy it.

Fill in the blanks: ____Where____ were we going the night I refused to ____wear____ a tie?

weather   atmospheric conditions
whether   if it happens that; in case; if

> Although meteorologists are *weather* specialists, even they can't predict *whether* a hurricane will change course.

Fill in the blanks: The gloomy _____weather_____ report in the paper this morning ended all discussion of _____whether_____ to pack a picnic lunch for later.

whose   belonging to whom
who's   shortened form for "who is" and "who has"

> "*Who's* the patient *whose* filling fell out?" the dentist's assistance asked.

Fill in the blanks: _____Who's_____ the salesperson _____whose_____ customers are always complaining about his high-pressure tactics?

your   belonging to you
you're   shortened form of "you are"

> *You're* making a fool of yourself; *your* Elvis imitation isn't funny.

Fill in the blanks: If _____you're_____ having trouble filling out _____your_____ tax return, why don't you call the IRS's toll-free hot line?

Other Words Frequently Confused

Not all frequently confused words are homonyms. Here is a list of other words that people often confuse. Complete the activities for each set of words, and check off and study the words that give you trouble.

a   Both *a* and *an* are used before other words to mean, approximately, "one."
an

Generally you should use *an* before words starting with a vowel (*a, e, i, o, u*):

an orange   an umbrella   an indication   an ape   an effort

Generally you should use *a* before words starting with a consonant (all other letters):

a genius   a movie   a speech   a study   a typewriter

Fill in the blanks: The morning after the party, I had _____*a*_____ pounding headache and _____*an*_____ upset stomach.

accept (ăk sĕpt′)   to receive; agree to
except (ĕk sĕpt′)   excluding; but

It was easy to *accept* the book's plot, *except* for one unlikely coincidence at the very end.

Fill in the blanks: Ved would _____*accept*_____ the position, _____*except*_____ that it would add twenty minutes to his daily commute.

advice (ăd vīs′)   noun meaning "an opinion"
advise (ăd vīz′)   verb meaning "to counsel, to give advice"

I have learned not to take my sister's *advice* on straightening out my life.
A counselor can *advise* you about the courses you'll need next year.

Fill in the blanks: Karen is so troubled about losing her job that I will _____*advise*_____ her to seek the _____*advice*_____ of a professional counselor.

affect (uh fĕkt′)   verb meaning "to influence"
effect (ĭ fĕkt′)   verb meaning "to cause something"; noun meaning "result"

The bad weather will definitely *affect* the outcome of the election.
If we can *effect* a change in George's attitude, he may do better in his courses.
One *effect* of the strike will be dwindling supplies in the supermarkets.

Fill in the blanks: Scientists have studied the _____*effect*_____ of large quantities of saccharine on lab animals but have yet to learn how similar amounts _____*affect*_____ human beings.

among implies three or more
between implies only two

After the team of surgeons consulted *among* themselves, they decided that the bullet was lodged *between* two of the patient's ribs.

Fill in the blanks: _____Between_____ halves, one enthusiastic fan stood up _____among_____ his equally fanatic friends and took off his coat and shirt.

beside along the side of
besides in addition to

Besides doing daily inventories, I have to stand *beside* the cashier whenever the store gets crowded.

Fill in the blanks: _____Besides_____ those books on the table, I plan to use these magazines stacked _____beside_____ me while doing my research paper.

fewer used with things that can be counted
less refers to amount, value, or degree

I've taken *fewer* classes this semester, so I hope to have *less* trouble finding time to study.

Fill in the blanks: This beer advertises that it has _____fewer_____ calories and is _____less_____ filling.

former refers to the first of two items named
latter refers to the second of two items named

Sue yelled at her sons, Greg and John, when she got home; the *former* had left the refrigerator open and the *latter* had left wet towels all over the bathroom.

Fill in the blanks: Eddy collects coupons and parking tickets: the _____former_____ save him money and the _____latter_____ are going to cost him a great deal of money some day.

learn   to gain knowledge
teach   to give knowledge

I can't *learn* a new skill unless someone with lots of patience *teaches* me.

Fill in the blanks: Because she is quick to _____*learn*_____ new things, Mandy has offered to _____*teach*_____ me how to play the latest video games.

loose   (lo͞os)   not fastened; not tight-fitting
lose   (lo͞oz)   to misplace; fail to win

In this strong wind, the house may *lose* some of its *loose* roof shingles.

Fill in the blanks: A _____*loose*_____ wire in the television set was causing us to _____*lose*_____ the picture.

quiet   (kwī′ĭt)   peaceful
quite   (kwīt)   entirely; really; rather

Jennifer seems *quiet* and demure, but she has *quite* a temper at times.

Fill in the blanks: Most people think the library is _____*quite*_____ a good place to study, but I find the extreme _____*quiet*_____ distracting.

Activity

These sentences check your understanding of *its, it's; there, their, they're; to, too, two;* and *your, you're.* Underline the two incorrect spellings in each sentence. Then spell the words correctly in the spaces provided.

_____*It's*_____

_____*your*_____

1. "Its not a very good idea," yelled Alexandra's boss, "to tell you're customer that the striped dress she plans to buy makes her look like a pregnant tiger."

_____*Your*_____

_____*it's*_____

2. You're long skirt got stuck in the car door, and now its sweeping the highway.

_____*you're*_____

_____*there*_____

3. When your young, their is a tendency to confuse a crush with true love.

two	4. After <u>too</u> hours of typing, Lin was <u>to</u> tired to type any longer.
too	
its	5. It is unusual for a restaurant to lose <u>it's</u> license, but this one had more mice
its	in <u>its'</u> kitchen than cooks.
to	6. The vampires bought a knife sharpener in order <u>too</u> sharpen <u>there</u> teeth.
their	
You're	7. <u>Your</u> sometimes surprised by who <u>you're</u> friends turn out to be in difficult
your	times.
too	8. When the children get <u>to</u> quiet, Clare knows <u>their</u> getting into trouble.
they're	
Their	9. <u>There</u> friendship developed into love as the years passed, and now, in
they're	midlife, <u>their</u> newlyweds.
two	10. There is no reason to panic if you get a bad grade or <u>too</u>. <u>Its</u> well known that
It's	many successful people were not great students.

■ Review Test 1

Underline the correct word in the parentheses. Rather than guessing, look back at the explanations of the words when necessary.

1. I (<u>know</u>, no) that several of the tenants have decided (<u>to</u>, too, two) take (<u>their</u>, there, they're) case to court.
2. (Whose, <u>Who's</u>) the author of that book about the (affects, <u>effects</u>) of eating (to, <u>too</u>, two) much protein?
3. In our supermarket is a counter (<u>where</u>, wear) (<u>your</u>, you're) welcome to sit down and have free coffee and doughnuts.
4. (Its, <u>It's</u>) possible to (loose, <u>lose</u>) friends by constantly giving out unwanted (<u>advice</u>, advise).
5. For a long time, I couldn't (<u>accept</u>, except) the fact that my husband wanted a divorce; (<u>then</u>, than) I decided to stop being angry and get on with life.
6. I spent the (hole, <u>whole</u>) day browsing (threw, <u>through</u>) the chapters in my business textbook, but I didn't really study them.
7. The newly appointed (<u>principal</u>, principle) is (<u>quite</u>, quiet) familiar with the problems (hear, <u>here</u>) at our school.
8. I found that our cat had (all ready, <u>already</u>) had her kittens (<u>among</u>, between) the weeds (<u>beside</u>, besides) the porch.

9. I (advice, <u>advise</u>) you not to take children to that movie; the special (affects, <u>effects</u>) are (to, <u>too</u>, two) frightening.

10. It seems that nobody will ever be able to (learn, <u>teach</u>) Mario to take (<u>fewer</u>, less) chances with his car.

■ Review Test 2

On separate paper, write short sentences using the ten words shown below.
Answers will vary.

1. accept
2. its
3. you're
4. too
5. then
6. principal
7. their
8. passed
9. fewer
10. who's

43 Effective Word Choice

Choose your words carefully when you write. Always take the time to think about your word choices rather than simply use the first word that comes to mind. You want to develop the habit of selecting words that are precise and appropriate for your purpose. One way you can show sensitivity to language is by avoiding slang, clichés, and pretentious words.

Slang

We often use slang expressions when we talk because they are so vivid and colorful. However, slang is usually out of place in formal writing. Here are some examples of slang:

Someone *ripped off* Ken's new Adidas running shoes from his locker.

After the game, we *stuffed our faces* at the diner.

I finally told my parents to *get off my case.*

The movie really *grossed me out.*

Slang expressions have a number of drawbacks. They go out of date quickly, they become tiresome if used excessively in writing, and they may communicate clearly to some readers but not to others. Also, the use of slang can be an evasion of the specific details that are often needed to make one's meaning clear in writing. For example, in "The movie really grossed me out," the writer has not provided the specific details about the movie necessary for us to clearly understand the statement. Was it acting, special effects, or violent scenes that the writer found so disgusting? In general, then, you should avoid slang in your writing. If you are in doubt about whether an expression is slang, it may help to check a recently published hardbound dictionary.

Activity

Rewrite the following sentences, replacing the italicized slang words with more formal ones.

Example   When we told the neighbors to *can the noise,* they *freaked out.*

When we told the neighbors to be quiet, they got upset.

Answers may vary.

1. I didn't realize how *messed up* Joey was until he stole some money from his parents and *split* for a month.

    . . . troubled . . . left

    _____

    _____

2. After a hard day, I like to *veg out* in front of the *idiot box.*

    . . . relax . . . television set.

    _____

    _____

3. Theo was so *wiped out* after his workout at the gym that he couldn't *get it together* to defrost a frozen dinner.

    . . . tired . . . find the energy . . .

    _____

    _____

4. When Rick tried to *put the move on* Lola at the school party, she told him to *shove off.*

    . . . flirt with . . . leave.

    _____

    _____

5. My father claims that most *grease monkeys* are *rip-off artists.*

    . . . mechanics . . . dishonest.

    _____

    _____

Clichés

A *cliché* is an expression that has been worn out through constant use. Some typical clichés are:

short but sweet	last but not least
drop in the bucket	work like a dog
had a hard time of it	all work and no play
word to the wise	it goes without saying
it dawned on me	at a loss for words
sigh of relief	taking a big chance
too little, too late	took a turn for the worse
singing the blues	easier said than done
in the nick of time	on top of the world
too close for comfort	time and time again
saw the light	make ends meet

Clichés are common in speech but make your writing seem tired and stale. Also, they are often an evasion of the specific details that you must work to provide in your writing. You should, then, avoid clichés and try to express your meaning in fresh, original ways.

Activity 1

Underline the cliché in each of the following sentences. Then substitute specific, fresh words for the trite expression.

Example   My boyfriend has stuck with me through thick and thin.

through good times and bad

Rewritten passages may vary.
1. As the only girl in an otherwise all-boy family, I got away with murder.

    . . . was spoiled. (or: . . . could do anything I wanted.)

2. When I realized I'd lost my textbook, I knew I was up the creek without a paddle.

    . . . in serious trouble.

3. My suggestion is just a shot in the dark, but it's better than nothing.
   ...just a guess ...

4. Janice got more than she bargained for when she offered to help Larry with his math homework.
   ... more work than she expected ...

5. Bob is pushing his luck by driving a car with bald tires.
   ... taking a risk ...

6. On a hot, sticky midsummer day, iced tea or any frosty drink really hits the spot.
   ... is really refreshing (or: is really satisfying)

7. Nadia thanks her lucky stars that she was born with brains, beauty, and humility.
   ... is grateful ...

8. Anything that involves mathematical ability has always been right up my alley.
   ... easy for me. (or: I've always done well at anything that ...)

9. Your chance of buying a good used car from that dealer is one in a million.
   ... slim.

10. Even when we are up to our eyeballs in work, our boss wonders if we have enough to do.
    ... overloaded with work ... (or: ... very busy ...; or: ... overworked ...)

Activity 2

Write a short paragraph describing the kind of day you had. Try to put as many clichés as possible into it. For example, "I got up at the crack of dawn, ready to take on the world. I grabbed a bite to eat. . . ." By making yourself aware of clichés in this way, you should lessen the chance that they will appear in your writing.
Answers will vary.

Pretentious Words

Some people feel that they can improve their writing by using fancy, elevated words rather than simple, natural words. They use artificial, stilted language that more often obscures their meaning than communicates it clearly. Here are some unnatural-sounding sentences:

It was a splendid opportunity to get some slumber.

We relished the delicious repast.

The officer apprehended the intoxicated operator of the vehicle.

This establishment sells women's apparel and children's garments.

The same thoughts can be expressed more clearly and effectively by using plain, natural language, as below:

It was a good chance to get some sleep.

We enjoyed the delicious meal.

The officer arrested the car's drunken driver.

This store sells women's and children's clothes.

Here is a list of some other inflated words, and simpler words that could replace them.

Inflated Words	Simpler Words
subsequent to	after
finalize	finish
transmit	send
facilitate	help
component	part
initiate	begin
delineate	describe
manifested	shown
to endeavor	to try

Activity

Cross out the artificial words in each sentence. Then substitute clear, simple language for the artificial words.

Example   The ~~conflagration~~ was ~~initiated~~ by an arsonist.

The fire was started by an arsonist.

Rewritten versions may vary.

1. Rico and his brother do not ~~interrelate in a harmonious manner~~.

   ... get along well.

2. The meaning of the movie's ~~conclusion~~ eluded ~~my comprehension~~.

   I didn't understand the end of the movie.

3. The ~~departmental conference~~ will ~~commence~~ promptly at two o'clock.

   ... department meeting will begin ...

4. A man dressed in odd ~~attire~~ ~~accosted~~ me on the street.

   ... clothing stopped ...

5. When my ~~writing implement malfunctioned~~, I asked the professor for another.

   ... pen (or pencil) broke ...

■ Review Test

Certain words are italicized in the following sentences. In the space provided at the left, identify the words as slang (S), a cliché (C), or pretentious words (PW). Then replace the words with more effective diction.

Rewritten versions may differ.

<u>C</u>   1. Losing weight is *easier said than done* for someone who loves sweets.

   ... difficult ... (or: not easy)

<u>PW</u>   2. After dinner, we washed the *culinary utensils* and wrapped the *excess* food.

   ... dishes ... leftover

<u>C</u>   3. Bruce is so stubborn that talking to him is like *talking to a brick wall*.

   useless (or: hopeless; or: futile)

<u>S</u>   4. Michelle spent the summer *watching the tube* and *catching rays*.

   ... watching television and sunbathing.

<u>S</u>   5. The fans, *all fired up* after the game, *peeled out* of the parking lot and honked their horns.

   ... excited (or: elated) ... drove quickly ...

<u>C</u>   6. The stew I made contained *everything but the kitchen sink*.

   ... many ingredients.

<u>S</u>   7. That *guy* isn't really a criminal; he's just gotten a *bum rap*.

   ... man ... an unjust sentence (or: unfair treatment)

PW

8. A company cannot *implement changes and attain growth* without *input from its personnel.*

   . . . change and grow . . . feedback from its workers.

C

9. I failed the test, and to *add insult to injury,* I got a low grade on my paper.

   . . . and to make matters worse, . . .

PW

10. I *perused* several *periodicals* while I waited for the doctor.

   . . . read . . . magazines . . .

44 Editing Tests

The twelve editing tests in this chapter will give you practice in revising for sentence-skills mistakes. Remember that if you don't edit carefully, you run the risk of sabotaging much of the work you have put into a paper. If readers see too many surface flaws, they may assume that you don't place much value on what you have to say, and they may not give your ideas a fair hearing. Revising to eliminate sentence-skills errors is a basic part of clear, effective writing.

In five of the tests, the spots where errors occur have been underlined; your job is to identify and correct each error. In the rest of the tests, you must locate as well as identify and correct the errors.

Editing Hints

Here are hints that can help you edit the next-to-final draft of a paper for sentence-skills mistakes:

1 Have at hand two essential tools: a good dictionary and a handbook (you can use Chapter 5 and Part Four of this book).

2 Use a sheet of paper to cover your essay so that you will expose only one sentence at a time. Look for errors in grammar, spelling, and typing. It may help to read each sentence out loud. If a sentence does not read clearly and smoothly, chances are something is wrong.

3 Pay special attention to the kinds of errors you yourself tend to make. For example, if you tend to write run-ons or fragments, be especially on the lookout for those errors.

4 Proofreading symbols that may be of particular help are the following:

■ Editing Test 1

In the spaces at the bottom, write the numbers of the ten word groups that contain fragments or run-ons. Then, in the spaces between the lines, edit by making the necessary corrections. One is done for you as an example.

¹I remember my childhood as being generally happy and can recall experiencing some of the most carefree times of my life. ²But I can also remember, even more vividly, other moments, ³When I was deeply frightened. ⁴As a child, I was truly terrified of the dark and of getting lost. ⁵These fears were very real/they caused me some extremely uncomfortable moments.

⁶Maybe it was the strange way things looked and sounded in my familiar room at night, ⁷That scared me so much. ⁸The streetlight outside or passing car lights would create shadows in my room. ⁹As a result, clothes hung over a chair taking on the shape of an unknown beast. ¹⁰Out of the corner of my eye, I saw curtains move when there was no breeze. ¹¹A tiny creak in the floor would sound a hundred times louder than in daylight, my imagination would take over, ¹²Creating burglars and monsters on the prowl. ¹³Because darkness always made me feel so helpless, ¹⁴I would lie there motionless so that the "enemy" would not discover me.

¹⁵Another of my childhood fears was that I would get lost, ¹⁶Especially on the way home from school. ¹⁷After school, all the buses lined up along the curb, I was terrified that I'd get on the wrong one. ¹⁸Scanning the bus windows for the faces of my friends, ¹⁹I'd also look to make sure that the bus driver was the same one I had in the morning.

1. __3__   3. __7__   5. __11__   7. __13__   9. __17__

2. __5__   4. __9__   6. __12__   8. __16__   10. __18__

■ Editing Test 2

Identify the five mistakes in essay format in the student paper that follows. From the box below, choose the letters that describe the five mistakes and write those letters in the spaces provided. Then correct each mistake.

a. Title should not be underlined.
b. Title should not be set off in quotation marks.
c. There should not be a period at the end of a title.
d. All major words in a title should be capitalized.
e. Title should be a phrase, not a complete sentence.
f. First line of a paper should stand independent of the title.
g. One line should be skipped between title and first line of the paper.
h. First line of a paragraph should be indented.
i. Right-hand margin should not be crowded.
j. Hyphenation should occur only between syllables.

	"eating in fast-food restaurants"
	Doing so doesn't have to be terrible for your health. Although I
	often stop at Wendy's or Burger King, I find ways to make healthful
	choices there. For one thing, I order sandwiches that are as plain
	as possible. A broiled hamburger or fish sandwich isn't so bad for
	you, as long as it isn't covered with melted cheese, fatty sauces,
	bacon, or other "extras" that pile on the fat and calories. Another
	health-conscious choice is to skip deep-fat-fried potatoes loaded
	with salt and heavy with cholesterol; instead, I'll order a plain baked
	potato from Wendy's and add just a bit of butter and salt for taste.
	In addition, I take advantage of healthy items on menus. For
	example, most fast-food places now offer green salads and low-fat
	chicken choices. And finally, I order a sensible beverage—ice water
	or a diet soda—instead of soda or a milk shake.

1. _b_   2. _d_   3. _f_   4. _g_   5. _h_

■ Editing Test 3

Identify the ten sentence-skills mistakes at the underlined spots in the student paper that follows. From the box below, choose the letter that describes each mistake and write that letter in the space provided. (The same kind of mistake may appear more than once.) Then, in the spaces between the lines, edit and correct each mistake.

a. fragment	d. dangling modifier
b. run-on	e. missing comma
c. inconsistent verb tense	f. spelling mistake

Corrections may vary.

I had a strange experience last <u>winter, I</u> was shopping for Christmas presents when I came to
winter. I

a small clothing shop. I was going to pass it by. <u>Until I saw a beautiful purple robe on a mannequin</u>
by, until ² *;*

<u>in the window.</u> <u>Stopping to look at it,</u> the mannequin seemed to wink at me. I was really <u>startled, I</u>
³ *When I stopped to look at it,* ⁴

looked around to see if anyone else was watching. Shaking my <u>head I</u> stepped closer to the window.
head, ⁵

Then I really began to question my <u>sanity, it</u> looked as if the mannequin moved <u>it's</u> legs. My face
sanity. It ⁶ *its* ⁷

must have shown alarm because the mannequin then <u>smiles.</u> <u>And even waved her arm.</u> I sighed with
smiled and ⁸ ⁹

<u>relief, it</u> was a human model after all.
relief. It ¹⁰

1. _b_   3. _d_   5. _e_   7. _f_   9. _a_

2. _a_   4. _b_   6. _b_   8. _c_   10. _b_

■ Editing Test 4

Identify the ten sentence-skills mistakes at the underlined spots in the student paper that follows. From the box below, choose the letter that describes each mistake and write that letter in the space provided. (The same kind of mistake may appear more than once.) Then, in the spaces between the lines, edit and correct each mistake.

a. run-on

b. mistake in subject-verb agreement

c. faulty parallelism

d. missing quotation marks

e. wordiness

f. slang

g. missing comma

Corrections may vary.

I think
<u>It is this writer's opinion that</u> smokers should quit smoking for the sake of those who are
  1

are
around them. Perhaps the most helpless creatures that suffer from being near a smoker <u>is</u> unborn
                                                                                         2
babies. One
<u>babies, one</u> study suggests that the risk of having an undersized baby is doubled if pregnant women
  3

are exposed to cigarette smoke for about two hours a day. Pregnant women should refrain from

            should avoid   *at risk.*
smoking and <u>to avoid</u> smoke-filled rooms. Spouses of smokers are also <u>in big trouble</u>. They are more
            4   5

                                                      to develop
likely than spouses of nonsmokers to die of heart disease and <u>the development of</u> fatal cancers. Office
                                                                6

workers are a final group that can be harmed by a smoke-filled environment. The U.S. Surgeon

           said,   *coworkers." While*
General has <u>said</u> "Workers who smoke are a health risk to their <u>coworkers. While</u> <s>it is undoubtedly</s> ℓ
           7   8   9
                                              themselves, they
<s>true that</s> ⌐ one can argue that smokers have the right to hurt <u>themselves they</u> do not have the right
                                                                     10

to hurt others. Smokers should abandon their deadly habit for the health of others at home and

at work.

1. __e__   3. __a__   5. __f__   7. __g__   9. __e__
2. __b__   4. __c__   6. __c__   8. __d__   10. __a__

Editing Test 5

Identify the ten sentence-skills mistakes at the underlined spots in the student paper that follows. From the box below, choose the letter that describes each mistake and write that letter in the space provided. (The same kind of mistake may appear more than once.) Then, in the spaces between the lines, edit and correct each mistake.

a. fragment	e. dangling modifier
b. run-on	f. missing comma
c. mistake in subject-verb agreement	g. wordiness
d. misplaced modifier	h. slang

Corrections may vary.

society, but
The United States will never be a drug-free society but we could eliminate many of our drug-
1
If drugs were legal, they
related problems by legalizing drugs. ~~Drugs~~ would be sold by companies and not criminals, ~~if they~~
2
business, freeing
~~were legal.~~ The drug trade would then take place like any business freeing the police and courts to
3
price, so
devote their time to other problems. Lawful drugs would be sold at a fair price, no one would need to
4
we would deprive   of one of
steal in order to buy them. By legalizing drugs, organized crime ~~would lose one of~~ its major sources
5
We
of revenue. ~~It goes without saying that we~~ would, instead, create important tax revenues for the
6
were
government. Finally, if drugs was sold through legal outlets, we could reduce drug problems among
7
age, just
our young people. It would be illegal to sell drugs to people under a certain age. Just as is the case
8
be so high,
now with alcohol. And because the profits on drugs would no longer be out of sight, there would be
9
little incentive for drug pushers to sell to young people. Decriminalizing drugs, in short, could be a
solution to
solution. To many of the problems that result from the illegal drug trade.
10

1. __f__   3. __f__   5. __e__   7. __c__   9. __h__

2. __d__   4. __b__   6. __g__   8. __a__   10. __a__

■ Editing Test 6

Identify the ten sentence-skills mistakes at the underlined spots in the student paper that follows. From the box below, choose the letter that describes each mistake and write that letter in the space provided. (The same kind of mistake may appear more than once.) Then, in the spaces between the lines, edit and correct each mistake.

a. fragment	e. mistake with quotation marks
b. run-on	f. mistake in pronoun point of
c. mistake in subject-verb agreement	view
	g. spelling error
d. mistake in verb tense	h. missing comma

Corrections may vary.

uninterrupted

One reason that I enjoy the commute to school is that the drive gives me <u>uninterupted</u> time to

1

are

myself. The classes and socializing at college <u>is</u> great, and so is the time I spend with my family, but

2

me

sometimes all this togetherness keeps <u>you</u> from being able to think. In fact, I look forward to the time

3

alone, for

I have <u>alone, it</u> gives me a chance to plan what I'll accomplish in the day ahead. For example, one

4

announced

Tuesday afternoon my history professor <u>announces</u> that a rough outline for our semester report was

5

Fortunately,　　　　　　　　　　　*reading, and*

due that Friday. <u>Fortunatly,</u> I had already done some <u>reading and</u> I had checked my proposed topic

6　　　　　　　　　　　　　　　7

with her the week before. <u>Therefore, on the way home in the car that evening</u>⌢I planned the entire

8

history report in my mind. Then all I had to do when I got home was quickly jot it down before I

morning, she

forgot it. <u>When I handed the professor the outline at 8:30 Wednesday morning.</u> She asked me ⌢"if I had

9　　　　　　　　　　　　　　　　　　　　　　　　　　10

stayed up all night working on it⌢" She was amazed when I told her that I owed it all to commuting.

1. _g_　3. _f_　5. _d_　7. _h_　9. _a_

2. _c_　4. _b_　6. _g_　8. _a_　10. _e_

■ Editing Test 7

Identify the ten sentence-skills mistakes at the underlined spots in the student paper that follows. From the box below, choose the letter that describes each mistake and write that letter in the space provided. (The same kind of mistake may appear more than once.) Then, in the spaces between the lines, edit and correct each mistake.

---

a. fragment	f. dangling modifier
b. run-on	g. homonym mistake
c. mistake in subject-verb agreement	h. missing apostrophe
d. missing comma	i. cliché
e. missing capital letter	

Corrections may vary.

                              all, the

Cars can destroy your ego. First of <u>all the</u> kind of car you drive can make you feel like a second-
                                     1

                                                   clunker, you'll

class citizen. <u>If you can't afford a new, expensive car and are forced to drive an old clunker. You'll be</u>
                                        2

                                                           don't

the object of pitying stares and nasty sneers. Drivers of newer-model cars just <u>doesn't</u> appreciate it
                                                   3

                          Buick

when a '68 <u>buick</u> with terminal body rust lurches into the next parking slot. You may even find that
                  4

                          their

drivers go out of <u>there</u> way not to park near you. Breakdowns, too, can damage your self-respect. You
                       5

                                        foreman, but   *inferior*   *you're*

may be an assistant bank manager or a job <u>foreman, you'll</u> still feel <u>like two cents</u> when <u>your</u> sitting
                                           6   7   8

                                                              car's

on the side of the road. As the other cars whiz past, you'll stare helplessly at your <u>cars</u> open hood or
                                                          9

steaming radiator. In cases like this, you may even be turned into that lowest of creatures, the
                                   As you shuffle

pedestrian. <u>Shuffling humbly along the highway to the nearest pay phone,</u> your car has delivered
                                             10

another staggering blow to your self-esteem.

1. *d*   3. *c*   5. *g*   7. *i*   9. *h*

2. *a*   4. *e*   6. *b*   8. *g*   10. *f*

■ Editing Test 8

See if you can locate the ten sentence-skills mistakes in the following passage. The mistakes are listed in the box below. As you locate each mistake, write the number of the word group in the space provided. Then, in the space between the lines, edit and correct each mistake.

1 fragment ___2___	1 missing comma after
1 run-on ___9___	introductory material ___7___
1 mistake in verb tense ___12___	2 missing quotation marks
1 nonparallel structure ___3___	___5___ ___6___
1 dangling modifier ___5___	1 missing apostrophe ___7___
1 mistake in pronoun point of	
view ___13___	

Corrections may vary.

technology, beginning
[1]The greatest of my everyday fears is technology. [2]Beginning when I couldn't master bike

riding and extending to the present day. [3]Fear kept me from learning to operate a jigsaw, start an
                                use   *When*
outboard motor, or even using a simple tape recorder. [4]I almost didn't learn to drive a car. [5]At age
I was
sixteen, Dad lifted the hood of our Chevy and said, "All right, you're going to start learning to drive.

[6]Now, this is the distributor. . ."[7]When my eyes glazed over, he shouted, "Well, I'm not going to bother
        you're
if youre not interested!" [8]Fortunately, the friend who later taught me to drive skipped what goes on
                                                                camera. I
under the hood. [9]My most recent frustration is the 35 mm camera, I would love to take professional-
        pictures, but
quality pictures. [10]But all the numbers and dials and meters confuse me. [11]As a result, my unused
                                                                gave
camera is hidden away on a shelf in my closet. [12]Just last week, my sister gives me a beautiful digital

watch for my birthday. [13]I may have to put it on the shelf with the camera—the alarm keeps going
        I
off, and you can't figure out how to stop it.

■ Editing Test 9

See if you can locate the ten sentence-skills mistakes in the following passage. The mistakes are listed in the box below. As you locate each mistake, write the number of the word group in the space provided. Then, in the space between the lines, edit and correct each mistake.

1 fragment ___7___	1 mistake in subject-verb
1 run-on ___10___	agreement ___13___
1 missing comma around an	2 missing quotation marks
interrupter ___13___	___3___ ___3___
2 apostrophe mistakes ___2___	1 dangling modifier ___1___
___10___	1 nonparallel structure ___12___

Corrections may vary.

¹I was six years old when, one day, my dog was struck by a car while getting ready for school. *I was*

²My mother and I heard the terrifying sound of squealing brake's. *brakes.* ³In a low voice, she said," Oh, my

God—Rusty." ⁴I remember trailing her out the door and seeing a car filled with teenagers and a

spreading pool of bright blood on our cobblestoned street. ⁵To me, it seemed only a matter of seconds

until a police car pulled up. ⁶The officer glanced at the crumpled dog under the car. *car and* ⁷And drew his

gun. ⁸My mother shouted "No!" ⁹She crawled halfway under the car and took the dog, like a sack of

flour, out from under the wheels. *blood. She* ¹⁰Her housedress was splashed with blood, she cradled the limp

dog in her arms and ordered the officers to drive her to the vets office. *vet's* ¹¹It was only then that she

remembered me, I think. ¹²She patted my head, was telling me to walk up to school, and reassured *told*

me that Rusty would be all right. ¹³The rest of the story including Rusty's slow recovery and few *story,*

more years of life, are fuzzy and vague now. *is* ¹⁴But the sights and sounds of those few moments are

as vivid to me now as they were twenty-five years ago.

■ Editing Test 10

See if you can locate the ten sentence-skills mistakes in the following passage. The mistakes are listed in the box below. As you locate each mistake, write the number of the word group in the space provided. Then, in the space between the lines, edit and correct each mistake.

2 fragments _9_ _12_	2 apostrophe mistakes _1_ _2_	
1 run-on _1_	3 missing commas _2_ _3_ _5_	
1 mistake in subject-verb agreement _6_		
1 nonparallel structure _6_		

Corrections may vary.

                                                          sex, but
[1]Most products have little or nothing to do with sex a person would never know that by looking
                                                          example,
at ads'. [2]A television ad for a headache remedy, for example shows the product being useful because
            woman's
it ends a womans throbbing head pain just in time for sex. [3]Now she will not say "Not tonight,
                                                                                    say,

Honey." [4]Another ad features a detergent that helps a single woman meet a man in a laundry room.
                                                appeal,
[5]When it comes to products that do relate to sex appeal advertisers often present more obvious
                                                                          makes
sexuality. [6]A recent magazine ad for women's clothing, for instance, make no reference to the quality
or comfort of
~~of or how comfortable are~~ the company's clothes. [7]Instead, the ad features a picture of a woman

wearing a low-cut sleeveless T-shirt and a very short skirt. [8]Her eyes are partially covered by semi-
            hair and
wild hair. [9]And stare seductively at the reader. [10]A recent television ad for perfume goes even further.
                                                            woman who is sexily
[11]In this ad, a boy not older than twelve reaches out to a beautiful woman. [12]Sexily dressed in a dark

room filled with sensuous music. [13]With such ads, it is no wonder that young people seem

preoccupied with sex.

■ Editing Test 11

See if you can locate the ten sentence-skills mistakes in the following passage. The mistakes are listed in the box below. As you locate each mistake, write the number of the word group in the space provided. Then, in the space between the lines, edit and correct each mistake.

---

1 fragment ___6___	2 missing apostrophes ___5___
1 run-on ___9___	___9___
1 mistake in subject-verb	1 nonparallel structure ___2___
agreement ___8___	1 dangling modifier ___3___
2 missing commas after	1 mistake in pronoun point
introductory material	of view ___10___
___7___ ___9___	

Corrections may vary.

[1]Being a waitress is an often underrated job. [2]A waitress needs the tact of a diplomat, she must

the organization of   *She serves*
be as organized as a business executive, and the ability of an acrobat. [3]Serving as the link between

                              ;
customers and kitchen, the most demanding diners must be satisfied, and the often-temperamental

kitchen help must be kept tamed. [4]Both groups tend to blame the waitress whenever anything goes

                                                                                                                    kitchen's
wrong. [5]Somehow, she is held responsible by the customer for any delay (even if it's the kitchens

                                                                          dessert, while
fault), for an overcooked steak, or for an unavailable dessert. [6]While the kitchen automatically

                                                                                        addition,
blames her for the diners who change their orders or return those burned steaks. [7]In addition she

must simultaneously keep straight who ordered what at each table, who is yelling for the check, and

whether the new arrivals want cocktails or not. [8]She must be sure empty tables are cleared, everyone

                                                                                                is
has refills of coffee, and no one is scowling because a request for more rolls are going unheard.

[9]Finally˰ the waitress must travel a hazardous route between the busy kitchen and the crowded dining

        ;   *diner's*   *she*
room, she has to dodge a diners leg in the aisle or a swinging kitchen door. [10]And you must do this

while balancing a tray heaped with steaming platters. [11]The hardest task of the waitress, though, is

trying to maintain a decent imitation of a smile on her face—most of the time.

■ Editing Test 12

See if you can locate the ten sentence-skills mistakes in the following passage. The mistakes are listed in the box below. As you locate each mistake, write the number of the word group in the space provided. Then, in the space between the lines, edit and correct each mistake.

2 fragments _6_ _16_	2 missing capital letters _2_
1 run-on _10_	_2_
2 irregular verbs _2_	1 mistake in pronoun point of
_9_	view _4_
1 misplaced modifier _12_	1 subject pronoun mistake
	_7_

Corrections may vary.

¹The thirtieth anniversary party of my uncle and aunt was the worst family gathering I've ever

attended. ²On a hot saturday morning in july, Mom and I drove out into the country to Uncle Ted's
(Saturday)   (July)   (drove)

house. ³It had already rained heavily, and the only place left to park was in a muddy field. ⁴Then, you
(we)

could not believe the crowd. ⁵There must have been two hundred people in Uncle Ted's small yard,

including his five daughters with their husbands and children, all the other relatives, all the neighbors,

and the entire congregation of their church. ⁶Since the ground was soaked and light rain was falling.
(falling,)

⁷Mom and me went under the big rented canopy with everybody else. ⁸We couldn't move between
(I)

the tables, and the humidity fogged my glasses. ⁹After wiping my glasses, I seen that there was a lot
(saw)

of food. ¹⁰It was mainly cold chicken and potato and macaroni salads, I ate a lot just because there
(;)

was nothing else to do. ¹¹We were surprised that Uncle Ted and his wife were doing all the work

themselves. ¹²They ran back and forth with trays of food and gathered trash into plastic bags .
(Staggering with exhaustion, they)   *(,)*

~~staggering with exhaustion.~~ ¹³It didn't seem like much of a way to celebrate. ¹⁴Mom was upset that

she didn't get to speak with them. ¹⁵When we left, I was hot, sticky, and sick to my stomach from

overeating. ¹⁶But quickly pushed our car out of the mud and got us on the road. ¹⁷I have never been
(I)

happier to leave a party.

45 ESL Pointers

This section covers rules that most native speakers of English take for granted but that are useful for speakers of English as a second language (ESL).

Articles with Count and Noncount Nouns

Articles are noun markers—they signal that a noun will follow. (A noun is a word used to name something—a person, place, thing, or idea.) The indefinite articles are *a* and *an*. (Use *a* before a word that begins with a consonant sound: **a c**ar, **a p**iano, **a u**niform—the *u* in *uniform* sounds like the consonant *y* plus *u*. Use *an* before a word beginning with a vowel sound: **an e**gg, **an o**ffice, **an h**onor—the *h* in *honor* is silent.) The definite article is *the*. An article may immediately precede a noun: **a** smile, **the** reason. Or it may be separated from the noun by modifiers: **a** slight smile, **the** very best reason.

To know whether to use an article with a noun and which article to use, you must recognize count and noncount nouns.

Note: There are various other noun markers, including quantity words (*some, several, a lot of*), numerals (*one, ten, 120*), demonstrative adjectives (*this, these*), possessive adjectives (*my, your, our*), and possessive nouns (*Jaime's, the school's*).

Count nouns name people, places, things, or ideas that can be counted and made into plurals, such as *teacher, restroom,* and *joke* (*one teacher, two restrooms, three jokes*).

Noncount nouns refer to things or ideas that cannot be counted, such as *flour, history,* and *truth.* The following box lists and illustrates common types of non-count nouns.

Common Noncount Nouns

Abstractions and emotions: anger, bravery, health, pride, truth

Activities: baseball, jogging, reading, teaching, travel

Foods: bread, broccoli, chocolate, cheese, flour

Gases and vapors: air, helium, oxygen, smoke, steam

Languages and areas of study: Korean, Spanish, algebra, history, physics

Liquids: blood, gasoline, lemonade, tea, water

Materials that come in bulk form: aluminum, cloth, dust, sand, soap

Natural occurrences: magnetism, moonlight, rain, snow, thunder

Other things that cannot be counted: clothing, furniture, homework, machinery, money, news, transportation, vocabulary, work

The quantity of a noncount noun can be expressed with a word or words called a **qualifier**, such as *some, a lot of, a unit of,* and so on. (In the following two examples, the qualifiers are shown in *italic* type, and the noncount nouns are shown in **boldface** type.)

Please have *some* **patience.**

We need to buy *two bags of* **flour** today.

Some words can be either count or noncount nouns, depending on whether they refer to one or more individual items or to something in general.

Certain **cheeses** give some people headaches.
(This sentence refers to individual cheeses; *cheese* in this case is a count noun.)

Cheese is made in almost every country where milk is produced.
(This sentence refers to cheese in general; in this case, *cheese* is a noncount noun.)

Using *a* or *an* with Nonspecific Singular Count Nouns

Use *a* or *an* with singular nouns that are nonspecific. A noun is nonspecific when the reader doesn't know its specific identity.

A left-hander faces special challenges with right-handed tools.
(The sentence refers to any left-hander, not a specific one.)

Today, our cat proudly brought **a** baby bird into the house.
(The reader isn't familiar with the bird. This is the first time it is mentioned.)

Using *the* with Specific Nouns

In general, use *the* with all specific nouns—specific singular, plural, and noncount nouns. Certain conditions make a noun specific and therefore require the article *the*.
A noun is specific in the following cases:

- When it has already been mentioned once

  Today, our cat proudly brought a baby bird into the house. Luckily, **the** bird was still alive.
  (The is used with the second mention of *bird.)*

- When it is identified by a word or phrase in the sentence

  The pockets in the boy's pants are often filled with sand and dirt.
  (Pockets is identified by the words *in the boy's pants.)*

- When its identity is suggested by the general context

  At Willy's Diner last night, **the** service was terrible and **the** food was worse.
  (The reader can conclude that the service and food being discussed were at Willy's Diner.)

- When it is unique

  There will be an eclipse of **the** moon tonight.
  (Earth has only one moon.)

- When it is preceded by a superlative adjective (*best, biggest, wisest*)

  The best way to store broccoli is to refrigerate it in an open plastic bag.

Omitting Articles

Omit articles with nonspecific plurals and noncount nouns. Plurals and noncount nouns are nonspecific when they refer to something in general.

> **Pockets** didn't exist until the end of the 1700s.
>
> **Service** is as important as **food** to a restaurant's success.
>
> Iris serves her children homemade **lemonade**.

Using *the* with Proper Nouns

Proper nouns name particular people, places, things, or ideas and are always capitalized. Most proper nouns do not require articles; those that do, however, require *the*. Following are general guidelines about when and when not to use *the*.

1. Do not use *the* for most singular proper nouns, including names of the following:

   - *People and animals* (Benjamin Franklin, Fido)
   - *Continents, states, cities, streets, and parks* (North America, Illinois, Chicago, First Avenue, Washington Square)
   - *Most countries* (France, Mexico, Russia)
   - *Individual bodies of water, islands, and mountains* (Lake Erie, Long Island, Mount Everest)

2. Use *the* for the following types of proper nouns:

   - *Plural proper nouns* (the Turners, the United States, the Great Lakes, the Rocky Mountains)
   - *Names of large geographic areas, deserts, oceans, seas, and rivers* (the South, the Gobi Desert, the Atlantic Ocean, the Black Sea, the Mississippi River)
   - *Names with the format* the _____ of _____ (the Fourth of July, the People's Republic of China, the University of California)

Activity

Underline the correct form of the noun in parentheses.

1. (A library, Library) is a valuable addition to a town.
2. This morning, the mail carrier brought me (a letter, the letter) from my cousin.
3. As I read (a letter, the letter), I began to laugh at what my cousin wrote.
4. Every night we have to do lots of (homework, homeworks).
5. We are going to visit our friends in (the Oregon, Oregon) next week.
6. Children should treat their parents with (the respect, respect).
7. The soldiers in battle showed a great deal of (courage, courages).
8. A famous sight in Arizona is (Grand Canyon, the Grand Canyon).
9. My son would like to eat (the spaghetti, spaghetti) at every meal.
10. It is dangerous to stare directly at (the sun, sun).

Subjects and Verbs

Avoiding Repeated Subjects

In English, a particular subject can be used only once in a clause. Don't repeat a subject in the same clause by following a noun with a pronoun.

Incorrect: The *manager he* asked Dmitri to lock up tonight.
Correct: The **manager** asked Dmitri to lock up tonight.
Correct: **He** asked Dmitri to lock up tonight.

Even when the subject and verb are separated by a long word group, the subject cannot be repeated in the same clause.

Incorrect: The *girl* who danced with you *she is* my cousin.
Correct: The **girl** who danced with you **is** my cousin.

Including Pronoun Subjects and Linking Verbs

Some languages may omit a pronoun as a subject, but in English, every clause other than a command must have a subject. In a command, the subject *you* is understood: (**You**) Hand in your papers now.

Incorrect: The Grand Canyon is in Arizona. *Is* 217 miles long.
Correct: The Grand Canyon is in Arizona. **It is** 217 miles long.

Every English clause must also have a verb, even when the meaning of the clause is clear without the verb.

Incorrect: Angelita's piano teacher very patient.
Correct: Angelita's piano teacher **is** very patient.

Including *There* and *Here* at the Beginning of Clauses

Some English sentences begin with *there* or *here* plus a linking verb (usually a form of *to be: is, are,* and so on). In such sentences, the verb comes before the subject.

There are masks in every culture on Earth.
The subject is the plural noun *masks*, so the plural verb *are* is used.

Here is your driver's license.
The subject is the singular noun *license*, so the singular verb *is* is used.

In sentences like those above, remember not to omit *there* or *here*.

Incorrect: *Are* several chickens in the Bensons' yard.
Correct: **There are** several chickens in the Bensons' yard.

Not Using the Progressive Tense of Certain Verbs

The progressive tenses are made up of forms of *be* plus the *-ing* form of the main verb. They express actions or conditions still in progress at a particular time.

George **will be taking** classes this summer.

However, verbs for mental states, the senses, possession, and inclusion are normally not used in the progressive tense.

Incorrect: All during the movie they *were hearing* whispers behind them.
Correct: All during the movie they **heard** whispers behind them.
Incorrect: That box *is containing* a surprise for Pedro.
Correct: That box **contains** a surprise for Pedro.

Common verbs not generally used in the progressive tense are listed in the following box.

Common Verbs Not Generally Used in the Progressive

Thoughts, attitudes and desires: agree, believe, imagine, know, like, love, prefer, think, understand, want, wish

Sense perceptions: hear, see, smell, taste

Appearances: appear, seem

Possession: belong, have, own, possess

Inclusion: contain, include

Using Only Transitive Verbs for the Passive Voice

Only transitive verbs—verbs that need direct objects to complete their meaning—can have a passive form (one in which the subject receives the action instead of performing it). Intransitive verbs cannot be used in the passive voice.

> Incorrect: If you don't fix those brakes, an accident *may be happened.*
> (*Happen* is an intransitive verb—no object is needed to complete its meaning.)
> Correct: If you don't fix those brakes, an accident **may happen.**

If you aren't sure whether a verb is transitive or intransitive, check your dictionary. Transitive verbs are indicated with an abbreviation such as *tr. v.* or *v. t.* Intransitive verbs are indicated with an abbreviation such as *intr. v.* or *v. i.*

Using Gerunds and Infinitives After Verbs

A gerund is the *-ing* form of a verb that is used as a noun: For Walter, **eating** is a daylong activity. An infinitive is *to* plus the basic form of the verb (the form in which the verb is listed in the dictionary): **to eat.** The infinitive can function as an adverb, an adjective, or a noun. Some verbs can be followed by only a gerund or only an infinitive; other verbs can be followed by either. Examples are given in the following lists. There are many others; watch for them in your reading.

Verb + gerund (*admit + stealing*)
Verb + preposition + gerund (*apologize + for + yelling*)

Some verbs can be followed by a gerund but not by an infinitive. In many cases, there is a preposition (such as *for, in,* or *of*) between the verb and the gerund. Following are some verbs and verb/preposition combinations that can be followed by gerunds but not by infinitives:

admit	deny	look forward to
apologize for	discuss	postpone
appreciate	dislike	practice
approve of	enjoy	suspect of
avoid	feel like	talk about
be used to	finish	thank for
believe in	insist on	think about

Incorrect: He must *avoid to jog* until his knee heals.
Correct: He must **avoid jogging** until his knee heals.

Incorrect: The instructor *apologized for to be* late to class.
Correct: The instructor **apologized for being** late to class.

Verb + infinitive (*agree + to leave*)

Following are common verbs that can be followed by an infinitive but not by a gerund:

agree	decide	plan
arrange	have	refuse
claim	manage	wait

Incorrect: The children *want going* to the beach.
Correct: The children **want to go** to the beach.

Verb + noun or pronoun + infinitive (*cause + them + to flee*)

Below are common verbs that are first followed by a noun or pronoun and then by an infinitive (not a gerund):

cause	force	remind
command	persuade	warn

Incorrect: The coach *persuaded Mario studying* harder.
Correct: The coach **persuaded Mario to study** harder.

Following are common verbs that can be followed either by an infinitive alone or by a noun or pronoun and an infinitive:

ask	need	want
expect	promise	would like

Dena asked to have a day off next week.
Her boss asked her to work on Saturday.

Verb + gerund or infinitive (*begin + packing* or *begin + to pack*)

Following are verbs that can be followed by either a gerund or an infinitive:

begin	hate	prefer
continue	love	start

The meaning of each of the above verbs remains the same or almost the same whether a gerund or an infinitive is used.

Faith hates **being** late.
Faith hates **to be** late.

With the verbs below, the gerunds and the infinitives have very different meanings.

forget	remember	stop

Esta **stopped to call** home.
(She interrupted something to call home.)

Esta **stopped calling** home.
(She discontinued calling home.)

Activity

Underline the correct form in parentheses.

1. The doctor (asked me, she asked me) if I smoked.
2. The coffee is very fresh. (Is, It is) strong and delicious.
3. (Are mice, There are mice) living in our kitchen.
4. The box (is containing, contains) a beautiful necklace.
5. Unless you take your foot off the brake, the car will not (be gone, go).
6. Most basketball players (very tall, are very tall).
7. Many people (enjoy to spend, enjoy spending) a day in the city.
8. The teacher (plans taking, plans to take) us on a field trip tomorrow.
9. Some old men in my neighborhood (play cards, they play cards) every afternoon.
10. When I am happy, I feel like (to sing, singing).

Adjectives

Following the Order of Adjectives in English

Adjectives modify nouns and pronouns. In English, an adjective usually comes directly before the word it describes or after a linking verb (a form of *be* or a "sense" verb such as *look, seem,* and *taste*), in which case it modifies the subject. In each of the following two sentences, the adjective is **boldfaced** and the noun it describes is *italicized*.

That is a **false** *story*.

The *story* is **false.**

When more than one adjective modifies the same noun, the adjectives are usually stated in a certain order, though there are often exceptions. Following is the typical order of English adjectives:

Typical Order of Adjectives in a Series

1 **Article or other noun marker:** a, an, the, Lee's, this, three, your
2 **Opinion adjective:** dull, handsome, unfair, useful
3 **Size:** big, huge, little, tiny
4 **Shape:** long, short, round, square
5 **Age:** ancient, medieval, old, new, young
6 **Color:** blue, green, scarlet, white
7 **Nationality:** Italian, Korean, Mexican, Vietnamese
8 **Religion:** Buddhist, Catholic, Jewish, Muslim
9 **Material:** cardboard, gold, marble, silk
10 **Noun used as an adjective:** house (as in *house call*), tea (as in *tea bag*), wall (as in *wall hanging*)

Here are some examples of the above order:

a long cotton scarf

the beautiful little silver cup

your new lavender evening gown

Ana's sweet Mexican grandmother

In general, use no more than two or three adjectives after the article or another noun marker. Numerous adjectives in a series can be awkward: **the beautiful big new blue cotton** sweater.

Using the Present and Past Participles as Adjectives

The present participle ends in *-ing*. Past participles of regular verbs end in *-ed* or *-d*; a list of the past participles of many common irregular verbs appears on pages 443–445. Both types of participles may be used as adjectives. A participle used as an adjective may precede the word it describes: That was an **exciting** *ballgame*. It may also follow a linking verb and describe the subject of the sentence: The *ball-game* was **exciting**.

While both present and past participles of a particular verb may be used as adjectives, their meanings differ. Use the present participle to describe whoever or whatever causes a feeling: an **embarrassing** *incident* (the incident is what causes the embarrassment). Use the past participle to describe whoever or whatever experiences the feeling: the **embarrassed** *parents* (the parents are the ones who are embarrassed).

> The long day of holiday shopping was **tiring**.
> The shoppers were **tired**.

Following are pairs of present and past participles with similar distinctions:

annoying / annoyed	exhausting / exhausted
boring / bored	fascinating / fascinated
confusing / confused	frightening / frightened
depressing / depressed	surprising / surprised
exciting / excited	

Activity

Underline the correct form in parentheses.

1. The Johnsons live in a (stone big, <u>big stone</u>) house.
2. Mr. Kim runs a (<u>popular Korean</u>, Korean popular) restaurant.
3. For her party, the little girl asked if her mother would buy her a (<u>beautiful long velvet</u>, beautiful velvet long) dress.
4. When their son didn't come home by bedtime, Mr. and Mrs. Singh became (<u>worried</u>, worrying).
5. In the center of the city is a church with (<u>three enormous colorful stained-glass</u>, three stained-glass colorful enormous) windows.

Prepositions Used for Time and Place

The use of prepositions in English is often idiomatic—a word that means "peculiar to a certain language"—and there are many exceptions to general rules. Therefore, correct preposition use must be learned gradually through experience. Following is a chart showing how three of the most common prepositions are used in some customary references to time and place:

Use of On, In, *and* At *to Refer to Time and Place*

Time

On *a specific day:* on Monday, on January 1, on your anniversary

In *a part of a day:* in the morning, in the daytime (but at night)

In *a month or a year:* in December, in 1776

In *a period of time:* in an hour, in a few days, in a while

At *a specific time:* at 10:00 A.M., at midnight, at sunset, at dinnertime

Place

On *a surface:* on the desk, on the counter, on a ceiling

In *a place that is enclosed:* in my room, in the office, in the box

At *a specific location:* at the mall, at his house, at the ballpark

Activity

Underline the correct preposition in parentheses.

1. Can you baby-sit for my children (<u>on</u>, at) Thursday?
2. Please come to my office (on, <u>at</u>) 3:00.
3. You will find some computer disks (<u>in</u>, on) the desk drawer.
4. Miguel will begin his new job (<u>in</u>, at) two weeks.
5. A fight broke out between two groups of friends (on, <u>at</u>) the park.

■ Review Test

Underline the correct form in parentheses.

1. During the storm, I was startled by the loud (<u>thunder</u>, thunders).
2. (Is, <u>Here is</u>) your new textbook.
3. The ending of the movie was very (surprised, <u>surprising</u>).
4. Many animals that sleep all day are active (<u>at</u>, in) night.
5. (<u>The people</u>, People) in the photograph are my mother's relatives.
6. The city streets were full of (<u>big yellow</u>, yellow big) taxis.
7. My friend and I (are usually agreeing, <u>usually agree</u>) with each other.
8. In the West, New Year's Day is celebrated (in, <u>on</u>) January 1.
9. If the weather is nice tomorrow, let's (think about to go, <u>think about going</u>) to the city ourselves.
10. Most (cheese, <u>cheeses</u>) are made from cow's milk, but others are made from the milk of sheep or goats.

Index

Instructor's Guide

Note: An *Instructor's Manual and Test Bank*, providing thirty supplementary activities and tests along with the materials in this Instructor's Guide and a full answer key, is available separately for instructors who use *College Writing Skills* as a classroom text.

Suggested Approaches and Techniques

On the following pages, I describe briefly some approaches and techniques I have found helpful while using the materials in *College Writing Skills*.

Beginning the Course

Here are three brief activities—"Getting Acquainted," "Prewriting," and Outlining"—that, right at the start of the course, will get students working together, writing, and thinking.

Getting Acquainted

An excellent way to get a class started is to leave it. I tell students that I'm going to go out of the classroom for about ten minutes, and that during that time I want them to learn each other's first names. I explain that on returning, I want to be able to ask any one of them to introduce me to all the people in the room. I don't tell them how to learn each other's first names; I let them work out their own method. A current of nervous energy and excitement is invariably flowing as I walk out the door, and it is still there when I return. I then ask for a volunteer to introduce me to everyone else. I remind the class that they won't be shot on the spot if they miss a name. I say that they're not expected to remember every name (though in fact they usually do). Someone always volunteers, and as the introductions proceed, I shake everyone's hand. It's a little corny, but everyone enjoys it, and providing this personal touch at the start of a semester seems like a good thing to do. I often have about five other volunteers go through the names as well (though I dispense with the handshaking for these subsequent rounds). It's a good way for me and the students to begin to learn everyone's name. I congratulate the class afterward on their impressive performance and say I hope they'll all be around so that I can shake their hands at the end of the course.

Prewriting

Freewriting.   To get students writing from the very beginning of the course, I say something like this:

"Often, people don't like to write because they feel they have nothing to write about. I'm now going to introduce you to a technique that will help you get words and ideas down on paper. It's a technique called *freewriting*. Freewriting means trying to write on a specific subject for ten minutes. You write whatever comes into your head about the subject, and you *don't* worry about making mistakes in spelling, punctuation, or grammar. Mistakes don't matter; all that matters is getting thoughts and information down on paper.

"The subject that I want you to write about is *movies*. Everyone goes to the movies at times; some people go a lot. I want you to write about why you like going to movies or about why you dislike going to movies. See if you can write for ten minutes about why you like or don't like going to the movies. If you run out of things to say, just write *I am looking for something to say* until something comes. Remember not to worry about errors; they don't count. And don't worry about putting things in logical order; that doesn't count either. Try to keep your pen moving. Write all the details you can think of about why you like going to movies or don't like going to movies."

After the ten minutes are up, I say something like this:

"It looks as though you did a good job with the freewriting. You'll find that this can be a good way of getting started whenever you have an assignment to write. Freewriting helps you think about and explore a topic as you get words on paper. It helps you accumulate some raw material that you can then work with and shape in writing the assignment."

List Making: I next introduce list making, or brainstorming:

"Let's suppose that you're going to write about why you dislike going to the movies. I'm going to write on the board the sentence, *There are several reasons why I don't like going to the movies.* Let's *brainstorm* this sentence. Brainstorming, much like freewriting, can help us generate ideas and details. We'll work together and think of as many reasons as possible why people might not like going to the movies. Reasons might include things like the high cost of tickets or the behavior of some moviegoers."

The students and I brainstorm a list of reasons. I write down all their ideas under the topic sentence on the board. After we have a long list, we talk about items that overlap. We also talk a little (in what serves as an informal introduction to organizing details) about how some items fit under other items (that is, how some items are reasons and other items are supporting details for those reasons), and about how we might narrow the list down to three main reasons and supporting details for each of those reasons.

Outlining

I next explain that, even more than freewriting and list making, outlining is a key to effective writing. I pass out copies of pages 4–8 of the text (which students may not have bought as yet). We read and outline the paragraph on moviegoing. I emphasize the basic structure: that a *point* is made and followed by *support* for that point. Then I draw the following diagram across the entire front blackboard to dramatize visually the essential structure of a paragraph:

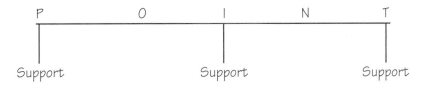

We then read and outline the essay on moviegoing. I talk a bit about the difference between a paragraph and an essay, and about the reasons for writing essays. I then change the diagram on the board so that it becomes:

Students are thus introduced immediately to the fundamentals of sound essay writing. All the essays in *College Writing Skills* go on to reinforce the same relentlessly logical three-part structure. The result is that by the end of the semester, if not before, students have internalized the clear thinking process needed to write an effective paper—whether the paper is a five-hundred-word essay or some more specialized type of writing.

If there is time left in a class after the above introduction to writing essays, I hand out copies of the mastery test titled "General Outlining Activities" (in the *Instructor's Manual and Test Bank*), and the students and I go through the activities together. This early attention to the logic involved in good writing strikes the right note for the unfolding semester.

Teaching with the Text: Using the Activities

College Writing Skills is designed as a core text; a course can easily be built around it by instructors using a traditional classroom approach. For instance, an instructor could begin by explaining step 1 in essay writing on page 51. (Alternatively, the instructor could have a student read this section aloud in class.) Then, after looking at the examples of narrowed subjects, the class could work through the activity on pages 52–53. The book follows this sequence throughout: explanation and illustration of a skill, followed by hands-on experience in learning that skill.

For the sake of variety, I approach the activities in the book in several different ways:

1 Instructor and class work together on an activity. When a student figures out an answer, he or she raises a hand and volunteers the answer to the class.

2 Students work individually in class. The instructor goes around, looks over people's shoulders, offers suggestions, and confirms correct answers.

3 Students work in groups of three or four. The class then comes together, with the instructor calling on a spokesperson for each group to give answers. Often some lively group competition is possible here. The spokesperson for each group goes to the board and records that group's answers. When all the answers for all the groups are on the board, they can be compared and used as a basis for class discussion. For example, each group could decide on supporting points needed to complete the six informal outlines on pages 56–57. After answers are written on the board, the instructor and class can decide whether all the answers logically fit. Or the group can put the answers to the activity on page 59 on the board. The answers—and especially differences in answers—can serve as the basis for a class discussion of what constitutes *specific* evidence.

4 Students work on activities at home. The activities are then discussed in class or collected and graded by the instructor. An effective strategy here is *not* to let students know in advance whether you will or will not collect and grade an assignment.

5 Students work on activities independently, on the basis of their individual needs. They are then given copies of the appropriate answer pages (these appear in the *Instructor's Manual and Test Bank*) so they can evaluate their work. The instructor thus has more time to spend conferring with students about their work.

The activities in *College Writing Skills* lend themselves to all of these approaches.

Evaluating Students' Papers

Students' papers are generally evaluated in terms of both form and content.

I always insist that students present papers in correct manuscript *form*, including wide margins. I cover Chapter 34, "Manuscript Form," in class early in the semester and reinforce it thereafter. A neat paper represents a minimal, initial kind of organization that some students need to learn.

With regard to *content*, papers can be evaluated for their effectiveness in terms of the four bases in Chapter 6. I introduce a grading scale after I have covered the chapters in Part One. As my model syllabus suggests, this may be about the fifth week of the semester, because I have not gone straight through Part One but have included material from Part Two as well. Students know at this point that a paper should achieve all four of the bases summarized on the inside front cover of the book.

I explain that in grading I give a maximum of one point for each base that is fully realized in a paper. Thus, for each base there is a scale of 0 to 1. For example, if a paper is unified—if it has a clear thesis statement and its supporting topic sentences and details are on target in backing up the thesis statement—it receives 1 for *unity*. On the other hand, if the paper lacks, say, one or more clear supporting topic sentences, it might receive 0.7. If a paper is fully supported, it receives 1 for *support*. If more details are needed, it may receive, for example, 0.6. A fully coherent paper receives 1 for *coherence*; a paper without a clear method of organization or without helpful transitions may get 0.2. A paper with no sentence-skills mistakes earns 1 for *sentence skills*; two run-ons, say, may result in 0.8.

The following grading scale results:

3.5–4 points	=	A
2.8–3.4 points	=	B
2–2.7 points	=	C
Less than 2 points	=	R (rewrite)

For example, a given paper might be graded as follows:

Unity	0.7
Support	0.6
Coherence	0.2
Sentence skills	0.8
Total	2.3 = grade of C

Notes on Evaluating Papers

1 I do not always supply a numerical breakdown of the four bases. Often, I simply give a letter grade along with comments on how the paper stands in light of the four bases.

2 I explain to my class that I reserve the right to grade a paper *S* (for *satisfactory*) rather than give a letter grade. *S* seems more appropriate when, say, the writing is especially personal (at no time is a grading system more unnatural).

3 Rather than marking a very ineffective paper *U*, for *unsatisfactory*, I simply indicate with an *R* that it needs to be *rewritten*.

4 Some teachers may want to include a fifth base, "style." This may mean, variously, imagination, originality, flair, or interest level. I prefer to emphasize basic clarity and logic. If students achieve these things, I feel they have done enough to merit a high grade.

5 To show students how the four bases can make grading a more objective process, I periodically have people discuss and grade papers in small groups. (The papers can be either shown with an overhead projector or reproduced on a copying machine.) Students use the "Form for Peer Review" on page IG-12 as a guideline. A spokesperson for each group goes to the board and records the agreed-upon grade for each paper. Class discussion follows, in which the groups support their grading decisions by indicating how the paper specifically does or does not realize each of the four bases. After several such sessions, groups come surprisingly close to agreement on the exact grade any given paper deserves.

Class consideration of individual papers is also an excellent way to teach the art of revision. Students whose papers have been discussed know exactly what areas they must work on to improve an essay.

Individual Conferences and Rewriting

Individual conferences with students and the rewriting that often follows such conferences are two of the most important techniques in teaching students to write effectively. One of the main reasons I have provided so many activities in *College Writing Skills* is that they free me to spend more time in conferences with students. To teach a skill, five minutes of personal discussion about a paper may do more than an entire page of written comments.

Here are some approaches I find helpful in individual conferences.

Comments and Corrections

Positive comments should balance negative comments. Some words of praise are essential—"You have a good specific detail here." "Nicely written topic sentence." "This is a good transition." "This paper shows a definite improvement in your writing." "I like your touch of humor here." "This is real; it's honest, and that's often a hard thing to do." "This paper is going in the right direction." Without some positive feedback, students may lack the incentive (or the belief in their own ability) needed to improve their writing.

Corrections in any single conference should be limited in number. After skimming a paper, an instructor may decide to focus on the central logic of a paragraph; if so, he or she should resist the urge to correct spelling, fix run-ons, cross out an incorrect apostrophe, and so on. (On the other hand, the instructor may enter some corrections without commenting on them in the conference, so that the student won't repeat them when rewriting.) No one, especially a student with unhappy past experiences in writing, can effectively absorb and profit from a great deal of negative feedback at one time. At the end of the conference, the instructor should list specific skills for the student to concentrate on in rewriting. The instructor may also want to list one or more related activities in the text for the student to complete.

"Mini-Outlines"

Very often, the first thing I do in a conference is to ask a student to write a "mini-outline" of a paper. For instance, a mini-outline of the moviegoing essay on pages 7–8 of the text would be:

Moviegoing presents problems.

1. Getting there

2. Theater itself

3. Other moviegoers

The mini-outline enables me to quickly check and discuss the fundamental logic of the student's essay. Such an outline is also an indispensable guide when I'm helping a student plan an essay. A student with a clear mini-outline is ready to start working on the more detailed "Diagram of an Essay" on page 11 of the text.

Self-Evaluation and Peer Review

I sometimes precede a conference with a student by asking the student to evaluate his or her own paper and to have a fellow student evaluate it also. Specifically, I ask the student to fill in the "Form for Self-Evaluation" on page IG-11 and the "peer" to fill in the "Form for Peer Review" on page IG-12.

Note: For a larger version of either evaluation sheet, see the *Instructor's Manual and Test Bank.*

At times, I also ask students to check the logic of each other's paragraphs. Each student prepares a mini-outline of his or her own paragraph. This outline is referred to as the paper is read. The students then decide if the logic is (1) very clear, (2) clear, (3) fair, (4) doubtful, or (5) absent.

I may also ask the two students to proofread each other's essays. To do this, they sit alongside (not facing) each other, so they can both see the paper clearly. One reads his or her paper aloud to the other, and both look and listen for awkwardly written sentences that are difficult to read smoothly and clearly, and for sentence-skills mistakes such as fragments, run-ons, incorrect verbs, incorrect pronouns, and so on. The writer of the paper must correct all such mistakes (rewriting the paper if more than five errors have been found) before conferring with the instructor.

FORM FOR SELF-EVALUATION:
FOUR BASES FOR REVISING ESSAYS

Title of your paper: _____

Your name: _____

Base 1: Unity

- Is there a clear opening statement of the point of the paper?
- Does all the material in the paper support the opening point?

Your comments:

Score (up to 1 point): _____

Base 2: Support

- *Specific* evidence?
- Plenty of it?

Your comments:

Score (up to 1 point): _____

Base 3: Coherence

- Clear method of organization? (List of items or time order?)
- Use of transitions to connect sentences and ideas?

Your comments:

Score (up to 1 point): _____

Base 4: Sentence Skills

- Are there any rough spots where the sentences do not flow smoothly and clearly?

Your comments:

Score (up to 1 point): _____

Total score (up to 4 points): _____

Less than 2 points = rewrite   2 to 2.7 = C   2.8 to 3.4 = B   3.5 to 4 = A

FORM FOR PEER REVIEW:
FOUR BASES FOR REVISING ESSAYS

Title of paper being evaluated: _____

Author of paper: _____

Evaluator of paper: _____

Base 1: Unity

- Is there a clear opening statement of the point of the paper?
- Does all the material in the paper support the opening point?

Your comments:

Score (up to 1 point): _____

Base 2: Support

- *Specific* evidence?
- Plenty of it?

Your comments:

Score (up to 1 point): _____

Base 3: Coherence

- Clear method of organization? (List of items or time order?)
- Use of transitions to connect sentences and ideas?

Your comments:

Score (up to 1 point): _____

Base 4: Sentence Skills

- Are there any rough spots where the sentences do not flow smoothly and clearly?

Your comments:

Score (up to 1 point): _____

Total score (up to 4 points): _____

Less than 2 points = rewrite   2 to 2.7 = C   2.8 to 3.4 = B   3.5 to 4 = A

Conference Record-Keeping

For conferences, I use the kind of record sheet shown below. The student keeps it in a folder with his or her papers.

RECORD OF CONFERENCES

Name _____   Section _____

1 Date _____   Paper or skill discussed: _____
Comments:

2 Date _____   Paper or skill discussed: _____
Comments:

3 Date _____   Paper or skill discussed: _____
Comments:

4 Date _____   Paper or skill discussed: _____
Comments:

5 Date _____   Paper or skill discussed: _____
Comments:

6 Date _____   Paper or skill discussed: _____
Comments:

7 Date _____   Paper or skill discussed: _____
Comments:

8 Date _____   Paper or skill discussed: _____
Comments:

Papers Completed

1. _____   5. _____

2. _____   6. _____

3. _____   7. _____

4. _____   8. _____

Improving Spelling

Instead of spending all-too-limited class time on spelling rules (which, in any case, work for some students but not for others), I emphasize the techniques in Chapter 41 of the text. Also, I ask students to keep track of their spelling mistakes in a personal spelling list, as shown on pages 529–530. As spelling mistakes accumulate on the list, patterns of errors or repeated errors can be discovered and pointed out to the student.

Developing Vocabulary

I work on vocabulary development in the following way. I ask students to collect unfamiliar words from their leisure reading (no matter what the source), television, other students' papers, and other courses. I also periodically write five or so words on the board and hold students responsible for those words, as well as for the words in their personal collections. Students must collect and master five words a week, so that by the end of the semester they have added about seventy-five words (more when derivations are included) to their vocabulary.

The number of words involved is modest. The intention is to get students into the habit of following through on puzzling words, and to make them believe that unknown words need not be ignored: these words can be looked up and mastered.

Aids for Teaching and Learning

Several aids for teaching and learning are part of *College Writing Skills* or accompany it.

1 Two visual aids will help students in the process of writing a paragraph. Students stand an excellent chance of writing solid papers if they refer to the "Checklist of the Four Steps in Writing an Essay" (on the inside front cover) and complete the "Diagram of an Essay" (on page 11 and also provided in the *Instructor's Manual*).

2 The separate *Instructor's Manual and Test Bank* contains a detailed answer key and also contains thirty additional activities and tests that can serve as supplemental learning aids. These activities and tests can be easily duplicated on a photocopying machine.

A Model Syllabus

The following syllabus serves as a general guide for *College Writing Skills*. It is based on a three-hour class meeting once a week for fifteen weeks. (For classes that meet in shorter time blocks, the syllabus can, of course, be adjusted accordingly.) It also assumes that time is allowed in class for discussion of papers and for review of homework activities or matters covered in previous class sessions. Rarely do I cover everything that is on the syllabus; instead, I select whatever is most appropriate for the individual needs of the students.

Instructors will note that I do *not* suggest teaching the textbook straight through. Because parts and chapters are self-contained, they can be taught easily in any order, depending on the preferences of the instructor and the needs of the class. I suggest that at the same time Part One is being covered, instructors start assigning essays from Part Two. And the skills in Parts Three and Four may be taken up as needed as the class proceeds through the semester. Varying the mix of writing activities in the four parts of the book will sustain students' interest more effectively.

Class I

- Business matters.
- Introduction to each other (see page IG-3).
- Introduction to the instructor (personal anecdotes) and to the course. This includes the material in Chapter 1, "An Introduction to Writing."
- In-class prewriting and outlining activities (see pages IG-3 to IG-5).
- Homework assignment: Get the book, read "An Introduction to Writing" (Chapter 1), and prepare for an objective test on the chapter.

Class 2

- Mastery test on Chapter 1, "An Introduction to Writing." (*Note*: Mastery tests are provided in the separate *Instructor's Manual and Test Bank*.)
- Read and work through Chapter 2, "The Writing Process."
- Read and work through selected parts of Chapter 3, "The First and Second Steps in Essay Writing."
- Homework assignment: Continue work on "The First and Second Steps in Essay Writing" and prepare for an objective test on "The Writing Process."

Class 3

- Mastery test on "The Writing Process."
- Do selected activities in "The First and Second Steps in Writing" on pages 61–75.
- Work through "Use Parallelism" in Chapter 5. (This is a skill needed to write a balanced thesis statement). See page 103.
- Read Chapter 7, "Introduction to Essay Development." Go over Chapter 34, "Manuscript Form."
- Cover the "Examples" essays in Chapter 10, reading the student essays and the professional essay in class and then discussing the ten questions that follow the essays. If there is time, do the prewriting activity on page 224.
- Homework assignment: Prepare for a mastery test on "The First and Second Steps in Writing."

Class 4

- Mastery test on "The First and Second Steps in Writing."
- Read and work through selected parts of Chapters 4 and 5, on the third and fourth steps in essay writing.
- Homework assignment 1: Do selected activities on pages 94–102 and prepare for an objective test on these chapters.
- Homework assignment 2: Write the examples essay on pages 224–225. For more advanced students, the instructor may want to substitute one of the less structured assignments on pages 227–230.

Class 5

- Mastery test on Chapters 4 and 5.
- Read and discuss selected examples essays turned in by students. I suggest that you refuse to accept any papers that appear to have been written carelessly at the last minute. Instead, return such papers, telling students that they are not being fair to themselves or to you, and ask them to rewrite the paper and resubmit it in the following class.
- Review the activities on pages 94–102 done at home and work through other activities on these pages.
- Do in class the outlining exercises on pages 44–48.
- Homework assignment: Continue work on outlining with the two activities on pages 44–48.

Class 6

- Mastery test on "Outlining an Essay I."
- Read and work through Chapter 6, "Four Bases for Revising Essays."
- Review Chapter 24, "Fragments."
- Homework assignment: Do selected activities on pages 152–164 and prepare for a mastery test on fragments.

Class 7

- Mastery test on "Fragments."

  Note: Here and in later classes, other mastery tests can be used for in-class exercises, extra-credit work, and homework assignments. For example, "Outlining an Essay II," "Writing a Thesis Statement," and "Evaluating an Essay for Coherence" all serve to review important skills in essay writing.

- Review the activities on pages 152–164 done at home and work through other activities on these pages.
- Review Chapter 25, "Run-Ons."
- Cover the "Cause and Effect" essays in Chapter 12, reading the student essays and the professional essay in class and then discussing the ten questions that follow the essays. Do the activities on pages 259–264.
- Homework assignment: Write the cause-effect essay on pages 259–260. For more advanced students, the instructor may want to substitute one of the less structured assignments on pages 261–264. Students should also prepare for a mastery test on run–ons.

Class 8

- Mastery test on "Run-Ons."
- Discuss students' cause-effect essays in class.
- Review the skills sections on verbs in Chapters 26, 27, and 28.
- Cover one or more "Special Skills" appropriate for students in the class (such as Chapter 17, "Taking Essay Exams"; Chapter 19, "Writing a Report"; and Chapter 21, "Using the Library and the Internet").
- Homework assignment: Review Chapter 35, "Capital Letters"; and Chapters 37 to 40, on punctuation marks.

Class 9

- Mastery test on "Punctuation Marks."
- Cover the "Process" essays in Chapter 11, reading the student essays and the professional essay in class and then discussing the ten questions that follow the essays. If there is time, do the prewriting activities on pages 243–245.
- Homework assignment: Write the process essay on pages 243–245. For more advanced students, the instructor may want to substitute one of the less structured assignments on pages 245–247.

Class 10

- Discuss students' process essays in class.
- Review any final sentence skills that seem appropriate for students in the class. Do "Editing Test I" on page 551.
- Cover one or more of the remaining "Special Skills" in Part Three.
- Have students rewrite an earlier essay in class, in light of the four standards of effective writing.
- Homework assignment: Do "Editing Test 2," "Editing Test 3," and "Editing Test 4" on pages 552–554.

Class 11

- Mastery test on "Editing for Sentence-Skills Mistakes."
- Cover the "Comparison and Contrast" essays in Chapter 13, reading the student essays and the professional essay in class and then discussing the ten questions that follow the essays.
- Homework assignment: Write the comparison-contrast essay on pages 278–282. For more advanced students, the instructor may want to substitute one of the less structured assignments on pages 282–284.

Class 12

- Discuss students' comparison-contrast essays in class.
- Have students rewrite an earlier essay in class, in light of the four standards of effective writing.
- Homework assignment: Read the introduction to Chapter 16, "Argumentation," and the student and professional argumentation essays on pages 322–331, and answer the questions that follow.

Class 13

- Discuss answers to the questions about the argumentation essays. Do the argumentation prewriting activity on page 334.
- Have students work on the argumentation essay in class, conferring with the instructor or with other students along the way.
- Homework assignment: Write the final draft of the argumentation essay worked on in class.

Class 14

- Cover one of the following: "Description" essays in Chapter 8; "Narration" essays in Chapter 9; "Definition" essays in Chapter 14; or "Division and Classification" essays in Chapter 15. Then have students write and complete in class one of these four types of essays.

  Note: This essay can serve either for extra credit or as a backup essay for students who have an "off day" while writing the final exam essay in the last class of the semester.

Class 15

- Final exam: Write in class one of the "Essay Writing Assignments I" included in the *Instructor's Manual.*
- Hand in to the instructor a "Collected Works" folder of completed essays.